International Marketing
third edition

Pervez Ghauri and Philip Cateora

International Marketing
third edition

The **McGraw·Hill** Companies

London	Boston	Burr Ridge, IL	Dubuque, IA	Madison, WI	New York
San Francisco	St. Louis	Bangkok	Bogotá	Caracas	Kuala Lumpur
Lisbon	Madrid	Mexico City	Milan	Montreal	New Delhi
Santiago	Seoul	Singapore	Sydney	Taipei	Toronto

International Marketing, third edition
Pervez Ghauri and Philip Cateora
ISBN-13 978-0-07-712285-0
ISBN-10 0-07-712285-2

McGraw-Hill
Higher Education

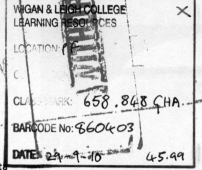

Published by McGraw-Hill Education
Shoppenhangers Road
Maidenhead
Berkshire
SL6 2QL
Telephone: 44 (0) 1628 502 500
Fax: 44 (0) 1628 770 224
Website: www.mcgraw-hill.co.uk

British Library Cataloguing in Publication Data
A catalogue record for this book is available from the British Library

Library of Congress Cataloguing in Publication Data
The Library of Congress data for this book has been applied for from the Library of Congress

Senior Commissioning Editor: Rachel Gear
Development Editor: Karen Harlow
Marketing Director: Alice Duijser
Senior Production Editor: James Bishop

Cover design by Adam Renvoize
Printed and bound in Great Britain by Ashford Colour Press

ISBN-13 978-0-07-712285-0
ISBN-10 0-07-712285-2

The **McGraw·Hill** Companies

Dedication

For Saad Ghauri

Brief Table of Contents

Part 5: Developing International Marketing Strategies

Part 6: Supplementary Resources

Detailed Table of Contents

Contents

Part 1: An Overview

Part 2: The Impact of Culture on International Marketing

Part 3: Assessing International Market Opportunities

Part 4: Developing International Marketing Strategies

Part 5: Developing International Marketing Strategies

Part 6: Supplementary Resources

Preface

During the last five years the international marketing field has developed enormously and the marketing function has now taken the central position in most companies. Increasing interdependence of the world economies has created new markets but also has led to an increased competition in the market place. The globalisation of the marketplace is now a reality, but it led us to some misunderstandings. The concept of the global market, or global marketing, thus needs some clarification. Generally, the concept views the world as one market and is based on identifying and targeting cross-cultural similarities. In our opinion, the global marketing concept is based on the premise of cultural differences and is guided by the belief that each foreign market requires its own culturally adapted marketing strategies. Although consumers dining at McDonald's in New Delhi, Moscow and Beijing is a reality, the idea of marketing a standardised product with a uniform marketing plan remains 'purely theoretical'.

The global marketing strategy is thus different from the globalisation of the market. One has to do with efficiency of operations, competitiveness and orientation, the other with homogeneity of demand across cultures. In this book we consider it important to make this distinction and to see how it affects international marketing strategies.

In Europe, where home markets are smaller, companies like Philips, Unilever, Ericsson, Nokia, HSBC, Akzo Nobel and Nestle are deriving up to 80 per cent of their revenues from abroad. The companies that succeed in the twenty-first century will be those capable of adapting to constant change and adjusting to new challenges.

The economic, political and social changes that have occurred over the last decade have dramatically altered the landscape of global business. Consider the present and future impact of:

- the emergence of China as a full player in the international market
- the economic crisis
- the European Union as the biggest single market, with 500 million affluent consumers
- emerging markets in Eastern Europe, Asia and Latin America where, in spite of economic and political crises, more than 75 per cent of the growth in world trade over the next 20 years is expected to occur
- the job shift in services from Western to emerging markets
- the rapid move away from traditional distribution structures in Europe, the USA and many emerging markets
- the growth of middle-income households the world over
- an increasingly effective World Trade Organization (WTO) and decreasing restrictions on trade
- the transformation of the Internet from a toy for 'cybernerds' to a major international business tool for research, advertising, communications, exporting and marketing
- the increased awareness of ethical issues and social responsibility.

As global economic growth occurs, understanding marketing in all cultures is increasingly important. Whether a company wants to involve itself directly in international marketing or not, it cannot escape increasing competition from international firms. This book addresses global issues and describes concepts relevant to all international marketers, regardless of the extent of their international involvement. Emphasis is on the strategic implications of competition in the markets of different countries. An environmental/cultural approach to international marketing permits a truly global orientation. The reader's horizons are not limited to any specific nation or to the particular ways of doing business in a single country. Instead, we provide an approach and framework for identifying and

analysing the important cultural and environmental uniqueness of any country or global region.

The text is designed to stimulate curiosity about the management practices of companies, large and small, seeking market opportunities outside their home country and to raise the reader's consciousness about the importance of viewing international marketing management strategies from a global perspective.

Although this revised edition is infused throughout with a global orientation, export marketing and operations of smaller companies are not overlooked. Issues specific to exporting are discussed where strategies applicable to exporting arise and examples of marketing practices of smaller companies are examined.

New and Expanded Features in this Edition

As a result of extensive review work with the publishers and comments from many reviewers, we evaluated the table of contents and for this new edition have reorganised it so that it better reflects the way topics are taught on most international marketing courses, in particular the chapter on ethics and social responsibility has been brought forward in section four, emphasizing its importance for international marketing strategies.

New Content

As brands have become the most important assets companies can have, a **brand new chapter** has been added **on international branding strategies**. This examines the development of branding, brand elements and characteristics, brand management, brand strategy and corporate branding.

The new and expanded topics in this edition reflect issues in competition, changing marketing structures, the importance of cultural issues, ethics and social responsibility, and negotiations. The global market is swiftly changing from a seller's market to a buyer's market. This is a period of profound social, economic and political change. To remain competitive globally, companies must be aware of all aspects of the emerging global economic order.

Additionally, the evolution of global communications and its known and unknown impact on how international business is conducted cannot be minimised. In the third millennium, people in the 'global village' will grow closer than ever, and will hear and see each other as a matter of course. An executive in the United Kingdom will be able to routinely pick up his or her video-phone to hear and see his or her counterpart in an Australian company or anywhere else in the world. In many respects, distance is becoming irrelevant. Tele-communications, video-phones, the Internet, nanotechnology and satellites are helping companies optimise their planning, production and procurement processes. Information – and, in its wake, the flow of goods – is moving around the globe at lightning speed. Increasingly powerful networks spanning the globe enable the delivery of services that reach far beyond national and continental boundaries, fuelling and fostering international trade. The connections of global communications bring people all around the world together in new and better forms of dialogue and understanding.

This dynamic nature of the international marketplace is reflected in the number of new and expanded topics in this edition, including:

- brand new dedicated chapter on international branding strategies
- the importance of ethics and social responsibility in marketing
- the impact of the economic crisis
- the European Union of 27 countries and the impact of the euro
- the Internet and its expanding role in international marketing
- big emerging markets (BEMs), particularly China and India
- evolving global middle-income households

- the importance of marketing research for marketing decision making
- enhanced emphasis on cultural issues relevant for international marketing
- an expanded chapter on ethical issues in marketing

New Features

More than fifty of the boxed **Going International** examples are brand new to this edition. These examples are carefully chosen to illustrate the points made in the text. For the third edition, most of these examples now act as provocative mini-cases that can be used as discussion points – featuring questions aimed to initiate exercises and discussion in the classroom. Exhibits and the discussions around them have been updated and a number of new ones added.

The **key terms feature**, which we introduced in the last edition, has been kept and expanded following the reviewers' comments. All key terms are emboldened in the text the first time they are used, and definitions provided in the margin for quick reference. A full **glossary** of key terms is provided at the back of the book and on the Online Learning Centre (OLC).

At the end of each chapter, you'll find an improved **Further Reading** feature, where we present a selection of readings that reflect the most classical, most influential and most recent studies in the area covered by the chapter. This feature has been updated throughout to include most interesting and provocative new research that will not only encourage students to go deeper into different topics, but will also help teachers in preparing interesting and enriched lectures.

Structure of the Text

The text is divided into six parts. In **Part 1**, 'An Overview', the two chapters introduce the reader to international marketing and to three international marketing management concepts: the domestic market expansion concept, the multidomestic market concept and the global marketing concept. As companies restructure for the global competitive rigours of the twenty-first century, so too must tomorrow's managers. The successful manager must be globally aware and have a frame of reference that goes beyond a country, or even a region, and encompasses the world. What global awareness means and how it is acquired is discussed early in the text; it is the foundation of global marketing.

Chapter 2 focuses on the dynamic environment of international trade and the competitive challenges and opportunities confronting today's international marketer. The importance of the creation of the World Trade Organization (WTO), as the successor to GATT, is fully explored.

The first three chapters in **Part 2** deal with the impact of culture on international marketing. A global orientation requires the recognition of cultural differences and the critical decision of whether or not it is necessary to accommodate them.

Geography and history (**Chapter 3**) are included as important dimensions in understanding cultural and market differences between countries. Not to be overlooked is concern for the deterioration of the global ecological environment and the multinational company's critical responsibility to protect it.

Chapter 4 presents a broad review of culture and its impact on human behaviour as it relates to international marketing. Specific attention is paid to Geert Hofstede's study of cultural value and behaviour.

Chapter 5 focuses on business customs and practices. Knowledge of the business culture, management attitudes and business methods existing in a country and a willingness to accommodate the differences are important to success in an international market. The chapter provides several examples to deal with these different business practices and customers.

The political climate in a country is a critical concern for the international marketer. In **Chapter 6**, we take a closer look at the political environment. We discuss the stability of government policies, the political risks confronting a company, and the assessment and reduction of political vulnerability of products. Legal problems common to most international marketing transactions, which must be given special attention when operating abroad, are also discussed in this chapter.

In **Part 3, Chapters 7, 8** and **9** are concerned with assessing global market opportunities. As markets expand, segments grow within markets, and as market segments across country markets evolve, marketers are forced to understand market behaviour within and across different cultural contexts. Multicultural research and qualitative and quantitative research are discussed in **Chapter 7**.

Chapters 8 and **9** explore the impact of the three important trends in global marketing: (1) the growth and expansion of the world's big emerging markets; (2) the rapid growth of middle-income market segments; (3) the steady creation of regional market groups that include the European Union (EU), the North American Free Trade Agreement (NAFTA), the Southern Cone Free Trade Area (Mercosur), the ASEAN Free Trade Area (AFTA) and the Asian–Pacific Economic Cooperation (APEC).

The strategic implications of the shift from socialist-based to market-based economies in Eastern Europe and the returning impact of China on international commerce are examined. Attention is also given to the efforts of the governments of India and many Latin American countries to reduce or eliminate barriers to trade, open their countries to foreign investment and privatise state-owned enterprises.

In **Part 4**, 'Strategies in International Markets', planning and organising for international marketing are discussed in **Chapter 10**. Many multinational companies realise that to fully capitalise on the opportunities offered by global markets, they must have strengths that often exceed their capabilities. **Chapter 11** has been dedicated to entry strategies. Here we provide a model that can be followed to analyse different markets while making decisions on market selection.

Chapter 12 is a brand new chapter on international branding strategies which examines the different issues surrounding branding, in recognition of its growing importance to international marketing. In **chapter 13,** the special issues involved in moving a product from one country market to another, and the accompanying mechanics of exporting, are addressed. The exporting mechanisms and documentation are explained.

Chapters 14 now deals with an expanded discussion on ethical issues in marketing, this chapter has been brought forward to emphasize the strategic nature of these issues.

Part 5 looks at developing international marketing strategies and **Chapters 15 and 16** focus on product management, reflecting the differences in strategies between consumer and industrial products and the growing importance in world markets for business services. Additionally, the discussion on the development of global products stresses the importance of approaching the adaptation issue from the viewpoint of building a standardised product platform that can be adapted to reflect cultural differences. The competitive importance in today's global market of quality, innovation and technology as the keys to marketing success is explored.

Chapter 17 takes the reader through the distribution process, from home country to the consumer, in the target country market. The structural impediments to market entry imposed by a country's distribution system are examined in the framework of a detailed presentation of the American and European distribution structure. In addition, the rapid changes in channel structure that are occurring in Japan and in other countries, and the emergence of the World Wide Web as a distribution channel, are presented.

Price escalations and ways in which these can be lessened, countertrade practices and price strategies under varying currency conditions are concepts presented in **Chapter 18**. The factors influencing pricing decisions are thoroughly discussed.

Chapter 19 covers advertising and addresses the promotional element of the international marketing mix. Included in the discussion of global market segmentation are recognition of the rapid growth of market segments across country markets and the importance of market segmentation as a strategic competitive tool in creating an effective promotional message.

Chapter 20 discusses personal selling and sales management, and the critical nature of training, evaluating and controlling sales representatives. Here we also pay attention to negotiating with customers, partners and other actors in our networks. We discuss the factors influencing business negotiations, and varying negotiation styles.

Finally, in **Part 6**, the **country note book,** presents an excellent framework for assignments and for marketing research exercises. This focuses on the new realities of international marketing.

Pedagogical Features of the Text

The text portion of the book provides a thorough coverage of its subject, with specific emphasis on the planning and strategic problems confronting companies that market across cultural boundaries. The pedagogy we have developed for this textbook is designed to perfectly complement the rest of the book, and has been constructed with the very real needs of students and lecturers in mind.

Current, pithy, sometimes humorous and always relevant examples are used throughout each chapter to stimulate interest and increase understanding of the ideas, concepts and strategies presented, emphasising the importance of understanding the cultural uniqueness and relevant business practices and strategies.

The **Going International** boxes, an innovative feature since the first edition of *International Marketing*, have always been popular with students. This edition includes over 50 new boxes such as these, many now with questions and all providing up-to-date and insightful examples of cultural differences and international marketing at work, as well as illustrating concepts presented in the text. They reflect contemporary issues in international marketing and real-life marketing scenarios, and can be used as a basis for solo study and as mini-case studies for lectures, as well as to stimulate class discussion. They are unique to this text, lively to read, and will stimulate all who use this book.

'**The Country Notebook: a Guide for Developing a Marketing Plan'**, found in **part 6**, is a detailed outline that provides both a format for a complete cultural and economic analysis of a country and guidelines for a marketing plan. This can be readily used by students and teachers for extended assignments.

Cases

Building on the success of the case section from the previous edition, we have included a substantial section of excellent case-study material that can be used by students and lecturers to aid learning. You'll find 20 cases in total, half of which are brand new to this edition. The cases reflect all regions and by working through them you will encounter all kinds of marketing scenarios in all kinds of companies in all geographical territories. From supermarket chains in Germany to footballers in China; from iPhone to UGG boots' global success as a brand – each case study is lively, contemporary, thought-provoking and expertly designed to bring out the real issues in international marketing. The shorter cases focus on a single problem, serving as the basis for discussion of a specific concept or issue. The longer, more integrated cases are broader in scope and focus on more than one marketing management problem. Information is provided in a way that enables the cases to be studied as complete works in themselves but, importantly, they also lend themselves to more in-depth analysis that requires students to engage in additional research and data collection.

Online supplements

In addition to the resources in this textbook, you'll find more supplements in the **Online Learning Centre (OLC)**, which can be found at: **www.mcgraw-hill.co.uk/textbooks/ghauri**. A full list of features can be found on page xxxii.

Acknowledgements

Publisher's Acknowledgements

Our thanks go to the following reviewers for their comments at various stages in the text's development:

Xuemei Bian, University of Hull

Caroline Burr, Bournemouth University

Antje Cockill, Swansea University

Ying Fan, Brunel University

Kyoko Fukukawa, University of Bradford

Al Holborg, Coventry University

Geraldine McGing, Griffith College, Dublin

Mary McKinley, ESCEM, France

Nana Owusu-Frimpong, London Metropolitan University

Christine Sorensen, Northumbria University

Anne Souchon, Loughborough University

Lynn Sudbury, Liverpool John Moores University

Lynn Vox, Coventry University

Jonathan Wilson, Anglia Ruskin University

We would also like to thank the following who have contributed case studies to the new edition:

Tobias Dauth, ESCP Europe

Ulf Elg, Lund University

Sylvie Hertrich, Ecole de Management, Strasbourg

Anna Jonsson, Lund University

Claudia Klauegger, Wirtschaftsuniversität, Wien

Summary
These summaries briefly review and reinforce the main topics covered in each chapter to ensure you have acquired a solid understanding of the topics.

Summary
The first section of *International Marketing* offers an overview of international marketing, and a discussion of the global business, political and legal environments confronting the marketer. International marketing is defined as the performance of business activities beyond national borders. The task of the international marketer is explained. Key obstacles to international marketing are not just foreign environments but also our own self-reference criteria (SRC) and ethnocentrism. This section deals exclusively with the uncontrollable elements of the environment and their assessment. The next section offers chapters on assessing international market opportunities. Then, management issues in developing global marketing strategies are discussed. In each chapter the impact of the environment and culture on the marketing process is illustrated. Space prohibits an encyclopaedic approach to all the issues; nevertheless, the authors have tried to present sufficient detail so readers appreciate the real need to make a thorough analysis whenever the challenge arises. The next chapter provides a framework for this task.

Questions
1 'The marketer's task is the same whether applied in Amsterdam, London or Kuala Lumpur.' Discuss.
2 How can the increased interest in international marketing on the part of European firms be explained?
3 Discuss the four phases of international marketing involvement.
4 Discuss the conditions that have led to the development of global markets.
5 Differentiate between a global company and a multinational company.
6 Differentiate among the three international marketing orientations.
7 Relate the three international marketing orientations to the EPRG schema.
8 Discuss the factors necessary to achieve global awareness.
9 What is meant by global markets? How does this influence the adaptation of products and marketing strategies?
10 Define and explain the following:
 – controllable elements in the international marketer's task
 – uncontrollable elements in the international marketer's task
 – self-reference criterion (SRC)
 – international marketing orientation
 – global awareness.

Questions
These questions help you test the knowledge you have acquired from the chapter.

Further Reading
Theodore Levitt, 'The Globalization of Markets', *Harvard Business Review*, 1983, May–June, pp. 92–102.
Peter Buckley and Pervez Ghauri, 'Globalization, Economic Geography and Multinational Enterprises', *Journal of International Business Studies*, 2004, 35(2), pp. 81–98.
Firat Fuat, 'Educator Insights: Globalization of Fragmentation – A Framework for Understanding Contemporary Global Markets', *Journal of International Marketing*, 5(2), pp. 77–86.

Further Reading
The further reading for each chapter guides you towards the best secondary sources available.

Country notebook
This feature provides a format for undertaking both a complete cultural and economic analysis of a country, as well as guidelines for a marketing plan.

Case 1.1 Strategy Formulation at Zanzibar

At high tide, waves submerge the mangrove and beat the balustrade of hotelier resorts along the seafront. These sumptuous tourist havens for the privileged pearl the coast of Zanzibar, the famous Spice Island, leaving only a narrow strip of white sand. The bungalows are cleverly scattered, facing the Indian Ocean, immersed in a generous and lush flora,

composed of exotic shrubs of tropical flowers – bougainvillea, saintpaulias – coconut palms casually swinging in the wind, permanently populated by an army of attentive gardeners who circulate on the small interlacing alleys that link them to the reception, restaurants and meeting rooms. Here you can find the congressmen whose attention easily escapes to the distracting surrounding scenery.

Everything here recalls a colonial past, with numerous staff, attentive and omnipresent, now working to make a reappearance: as a sign, fruit cocktails or alcohol or the excellent local beers with names evoking the African magic – like the suave Kilimanjaro – are offered to American, African, European and Asian visitors, already under the spell, before lingering in front of the buffets prepared outdoors where the specialities are available from all continents, fruits of the fishing and local farming, combining the culinary traditions to accommodate unexpected associations with local dishes – kebabs made from marinated meat, seafood cooked in coconut milk, all kinds of grilled meat or fish, accompanied by succulent rice cakes that they will enjoy under the shade, at small tables with immaculate tablecloths reaching to the ground. Crews of dhows with pointed bows, almost aggressive, with their matte look, suggesting speed, bearing a large triangular sail, the shade of a large canvas, arranged for diving or walking, or even with powerful outboard engines with high infrastructure equipped for fishing await to discover

Case studies

The book includes an extensive case study section, featuring in-depth studies of a variety of companies from around the world.

Glossary

accounts-receivable – A comprehensive billing and customer information system that helps you manage your receivables, streamline the collection and control of cash, and separately track individual clients, organisations and funding sources.

act of God – An extraordinary happening of nature not reasonably anticipated by either party to a contract, i.e. earthquakes, floods, etc.

activist groups – See Green activist. Refers to these groups, e.g. Greenpeace.

adaptation – Making changes to fit a particular culture/environment/conditions; when we produce special/modified products for different markets.

administered pricing – Relates to attempts to establish prices for an entire market.

advertising campaign – Designing and implementing particular advertising for a particular product/purpose over a fixed period.

advertising media – Different alternatives available to a company for its advertising (e.g. TV, magazine).

after-sales service – Services that are available after the product has been sold (e.g. repairs).

air freight – Sending a product by air.

analogy – Reasoning from parallel cases/examples.

Andean Common Market (ANCOM) – A sub-regional economic integration organisation existing out of Bolivia, Colombia, Ecuador, Peru and Venezuela.

anti-trust laws – Laws to prevent businesses from creating unjust monopolies or competing unfairly in the marketplace.

APEC – Asia Pacific cooperation among 21 member states. APEC promotes free trade and economic cooperation between members.

arbitration – Mediation done by a third party in case of a commercial dispute.

ASEAN – The fourth biggest trade area of the world comprising 10 Southeast Asian countries.

Asian crisis – In 1996/1997, stock exchanges and currency values in a number of Asian countries lost a major part of their value.

back translation – When a questionnaire/slogan/theme is translated into another language, then translated back to the original language by another party. Helps to pinpoint misinterpretation and misunderstandings.

balance of payments – System of accounts that records a nation's international financial transactions.

barriers to exporting – Obstacles/hindrances to export.

barter – Direct exchange of goods between two parties in a transaction.

barter house – International trading company that is able to introduce merchandise to outlets and geographic areas previously untapped.

billboards – Large stands that comprise advertising space, usually found on the sides of roads.

blocked currency – Blockage cuts off all importing or all importing above a certain level. Blockage is accomplished by refusing to allow importers to exchange national currency for the seller's currency.

Boston Consulting Group (BCG) – An international strategy and general management consulting firm, it uses specific models to tackle management problems.

boycott – A coordinated refusal to buy or use products or services of a certain company/country.

brand loyalty – When customers always buy the same brand.

branding – Developing and building a reputation for a brand name.

Bretton Woods Agreement – An agreement made in 1944. It set fixed exchange rates for major currencies and subsequently established the IMF.

bribery – Voluntarily offered payments by someone seeking unlawful advantage.

broker – A catchall term for a variety of middlemen performing low-cost agent services.

business culture – Values and norms followed in business activities.

business services – Services that are sold to other companies (e.g. advertising).

capital account – A record of direct investment portfolio activities, and short-term capital movements to and from countries.

cartel – A cartel exists when various companies producing similar products work together to control markets for the types of goods they produce.

census data – A record of population and its breakdown.

centralisation – When most decisions are made at the top or head office.

Glossary

The comprehensive glossary at the end of the text provides a quick reference tool for learning.

Technology to Enhance Learning and Teaching

 **Online LearningCentre**

Visit www.mcgraw-hill.co.uk/textbooks/ghauri today

Online Learning Centre (OLC)

After completing each chapter, log on to the supporting Online Learning Centre website. Take advantage of the study tools offered to reinforce the material you have read in the text, and to develop your knowledge of international marketing in a fun and effective way.

Resources for students include:

- Self-test questions
- Videos
- Weblinks
- Glossary

Also available for lecturers:

- PowerPoint presentations
- Lecture Outlines
- Answers to end of chapter questions
- Teaching suggestions
- Case study teaching notes
- Cases from previous editions
- Additional essay questions
- EZTest Test Bank

Test Bank available in McGraw-Hill EZ Test Online

A test bank of hundreds of questions is available to lecturers adopting this book for their module. A range of questions is provided for each chapter including multiple choice, true or false, and short answer or essay questions. The questions are identified by type, difficulty, and topic to help you to select questions that best suit your needs and are accessible through an easy-to-use online testing tool, **McGraw-Hill EZ Test Online**.

McGraw-Hill EZ Test Online is accessible to busy academics virtually anywhere – in their office, at home or while travelling – and eliminates the need for software installation. Lecturers can chose from question banks associated with their adopted textbook or easily create their own questions. They also have access to hundreds of banks and thousands of questions created for other McGraw-Hill titles. Multiple versions of tests can be saved for delivery on paper or online through WebCT, Blackboard and other course management systems. When created and delivered though EZ Test Online, students' tests can be immediately marked, saving lecturers time and providing prompt results to students.

To register for this FREE resource, visit www.eztestonline.com

Maps

1 **World**

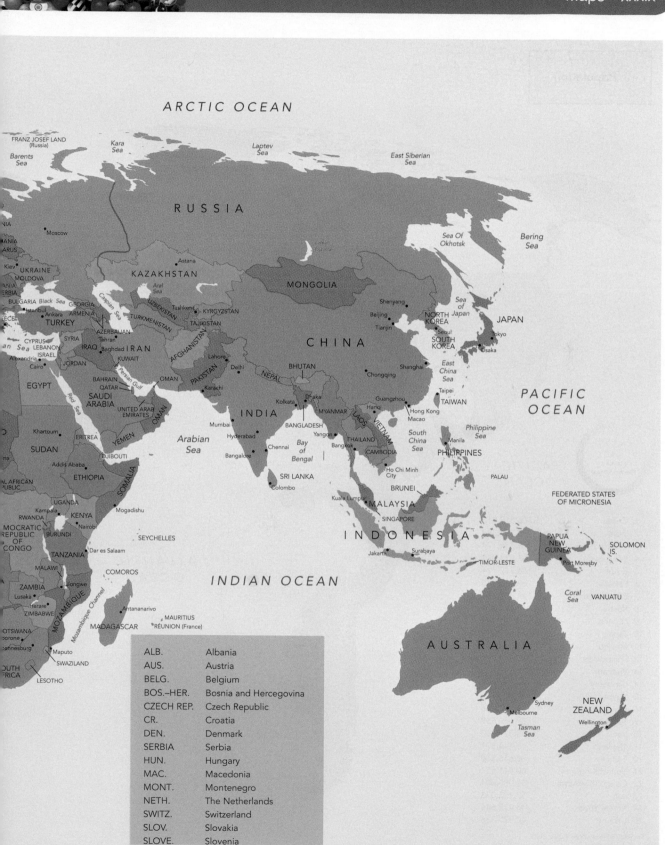

ARCTIC OCEAN

FRANZ JOSEF LAND
(Russia)

Barents
Sea

Kara
Sea

Laptev
Sea

East Siberian
Sea

RUSSIA

Moscow

NIA

ANIA

ARUS

UKRAINE

Kiev

MOLDOVA

Astana

KAZAKHSTAN

MONGOLIA

Sea Of
Okhotsk

Bering
Sea

ERBIA

BULGARIA Black Sea

GEORGIA

Caspian Sea

Aral
Sea

Tashkent

UZBEKISTAN

KYRGYZSTAN

Shenyang

Sea
of
Japan

Seoul

NORTH
KOREA

JAPAN

Tokyo

ECE

Istanbul

Ankara ARMENIA

TURKEY

TURKMENISTAN

TAJIKISTAN

Beijing

Tianjin

CHINA

SOUTH
KOREA

Osaka

CYPRUS

SYRIA

AZERBAIJAN

an Sea LEBANON

ISRAEL

Tehran

IRAQ Baghdad

IRAN

AFGHANISTAN

Lahore

Shanghai

Chongqing

East
China
Sea

Alexandria

JORDAN

KUWAIT

Delhi

NEPAL

BHUTAN

Cairo

BAHRAIN

Persian Gulf

QATAR

OMAN

PAKISTAN

Karachi

Taipei

TAIWAN

Guangzhou

Hong Kong
Macao

EGYPT

SAUDI
ARABIA

UNITED ARAB
EMIRATES

OMAN

INDIA

Kolkata

Dhaka

MYANMAR

LAOS

VIETNAM

Hanoi

PACIFIC
OCEAN

Khartoum

ERITREA

YEMEN

Arabian
Sea

Mumbai

BANGLADESH

Yangon

South
China
Sea

Philippine
Sea

Manila

SUDAN

DJIBOUTI

Hyderabad

Chennai

Bay
of
Bengal

Bangkok

THAILAND

CAMBODIA

PHILIPPINES

ma

Addis Ababa

ETHIOPIA

SOMALIA

Bangalore

SRI LANKA

Ho Chi Minh
City

PALAU

AL AFRICAN
PUBLIC

UGANDA

Colombo

BRUNEI

FEDERATED STATES
OF MICRONESIA

MOCRATIC
REPUBLIC
OF
CONGO

Kampala

RWANDA

BURUNDI

KENYA

Nairobi

Mogadishu

SEYCHELLES

Kuala Lumpur

MALAYSIA

SINGAPORE

INDONESIA

PAPUA
NEW
GUINEA

SOLOMON
IS.

TANZANIA

Dar es Salaam

Jakarta

Surabaya

TIMOR-LESTE

Port Moresby

MALAWI

COMOROS

ZAMBIA

Lilongwe

Lusaka

Harare

ZIMBABWE

Antananarivo

MADAGASCAR

MAURITIUS

RÉUNION (France)

INDIAN OCEAN

Coral
Sea

VANUATU

OTSWANA

orone

Maputo

SWAZILAND

AUSTRALIA

OUTH
FRICA

LESOTHO

ALB.   Albania
AUS.   Austria
BELG.   Belgium
BOS.–HER.   Bosnia and Hercegovina
CZECH REP. Czech Republic
CR.   Croatia
DEN.   Denmark
SERBIA   Serbia
HUN.   Hungary
MAC.   Macedonia
MONT.   Montenegro
NETH.   The Netherlands
SWITZ.   Switzerland
SLOV.   Slovakia
SLOVE.   Slovenia

Sydney

Melbourne

NEW
ZEALAND

Wellington

Tasman
Sea

2 Population

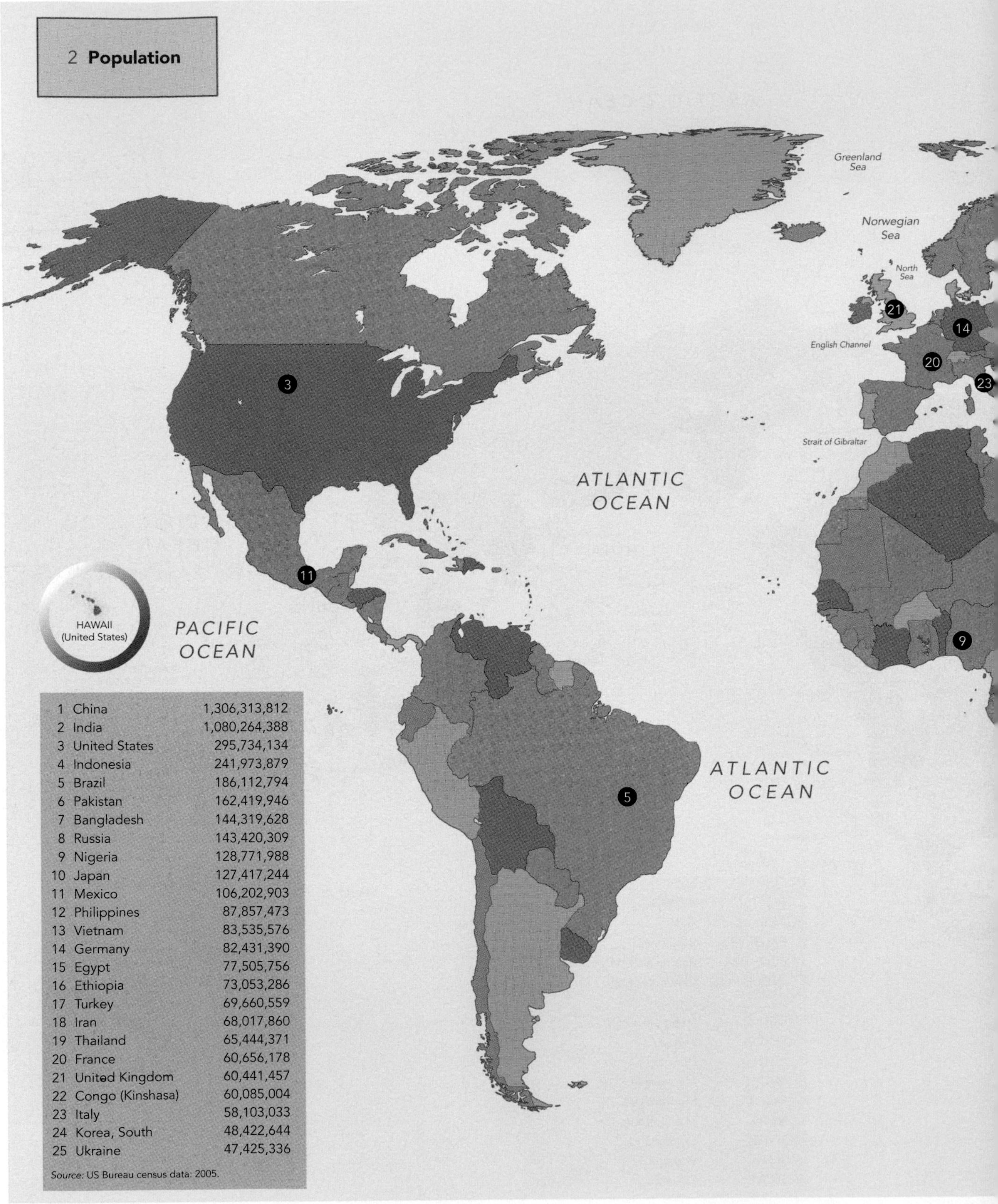

Greenland Sea

Norwegian Sea

North Sea

21

14

English Channel

20

23

Strait of Gibraltar

3

ATLANTIC
OCEAN

11

9

HAWAII
(United States)

PACIFIC
OCEAN

5

ATLANTIC
OCEAN

#	Country	Population
1	China	1,306,313,812
2	India	1,080,264,388
3	United States	295,734,134
4	Indonesia	241,973,879
5	Brazil	186,112,794
6	Pakistan	162,419,946
7	Bangladesh	144,319,628
8	Russia	143,420,309
9	Nigeria	128,771,988
10	Japan	127,417,244
11	Mexico	106,202,903
12	Philippines	87,857,473
13	Vietnam	83,535,576
14	Germany	82,431,390
15	Egypt	77,505,756
16	Ethiopia	73,053,286
17	Turkey	69,660,559
18	Iran	68,017,860
19	Thailand	65,444,371
20	France	60,656,178
21	United Kingdom	60,441,457
22	Congo (Kinshasa)	60,085,004
23	Italy	58,103,033
24	Korea, South	48,422,644
25	Ukraine	47,425,336

Source: US Bureau census data: 2005.

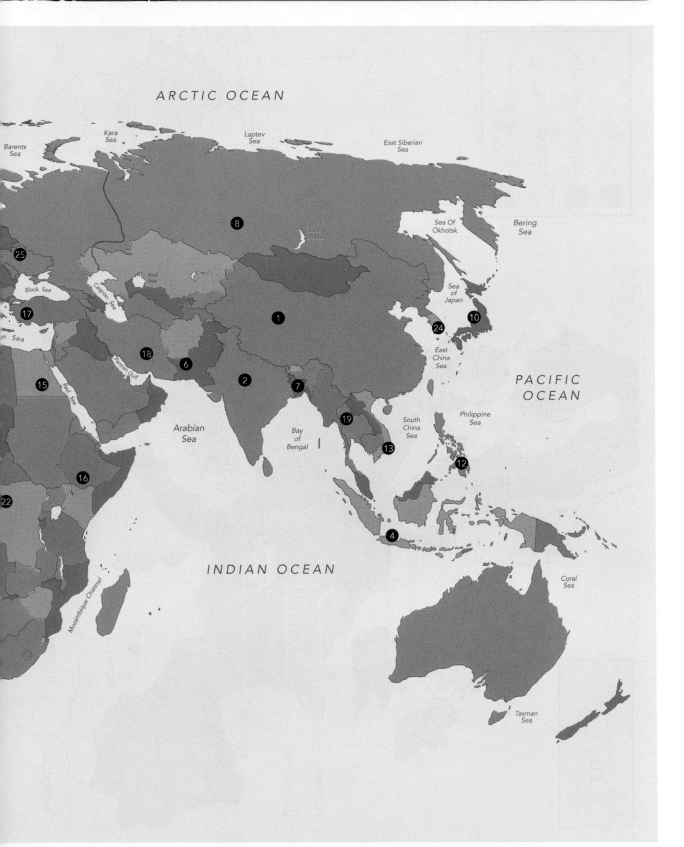

ARCTIC OCEAN

Barents
Sea

Kara
Sea

Laptev
Sea

East Siberian
Sea

Sea Of
Okhotsk

Bering
Sea

Lake
Baikal

Sea
of
Japan

Black Sea

Aral
Sea

Caspian Sea

Persian Gulf

East
China
Sea

PACIFIC
OCEAN

Red Sea

Arabian
Sea

Bay
of
Bengal

South
China
Sea

Philippine
Sea

INDIAN OCEAN

Mozambique Channel

Coral
Sea

Tasman
Sea

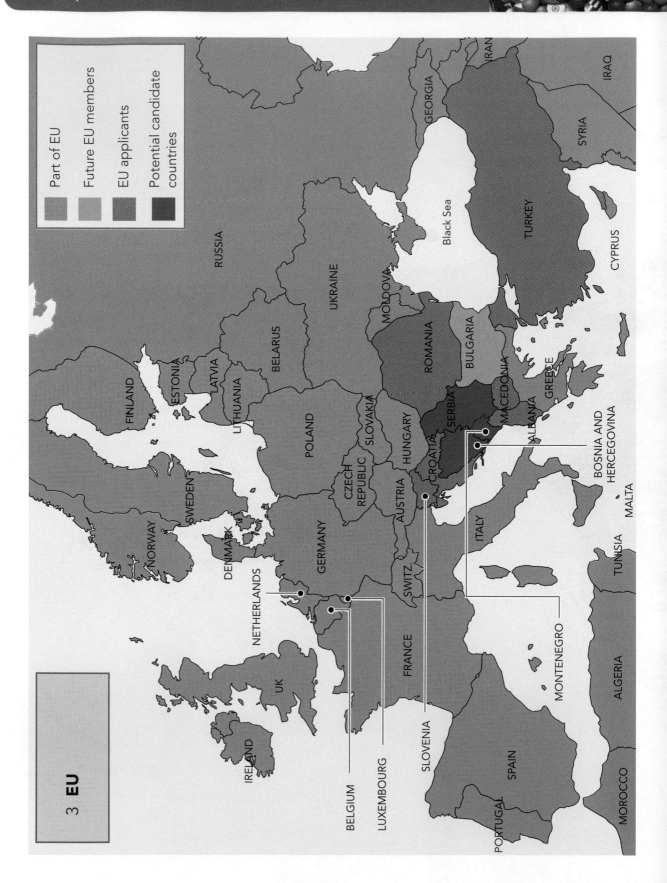

3 EU

Part of EU
Future EU members
EU applicants
Potential candidate countries

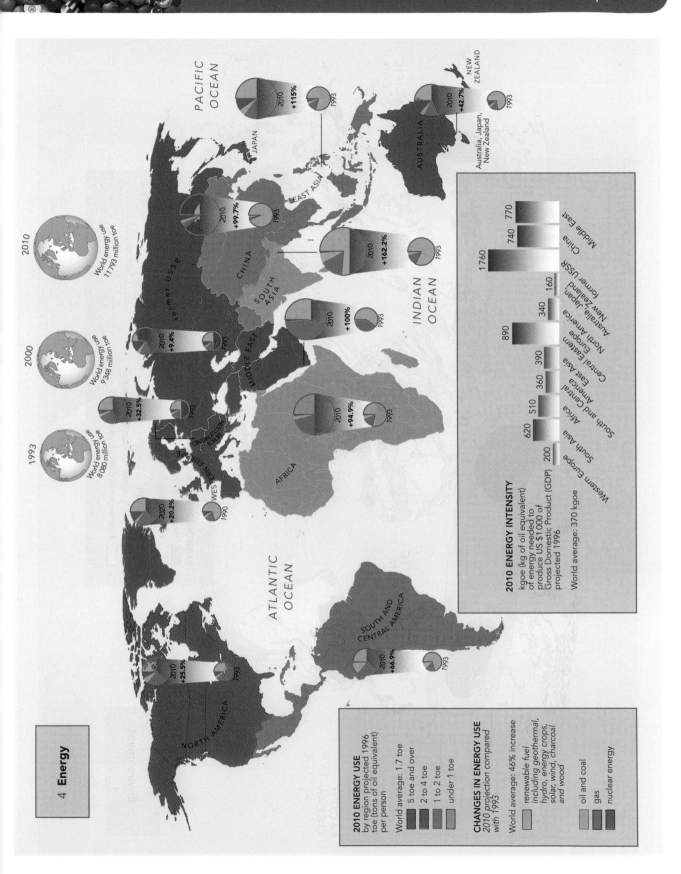

4 Energy

PACIFIC OCEAN

JAPAN

2010 +115%
1993

AUSTRALIA

NEW ZEALAND

2010 +42.7%
1993

Australia, Japan, New Zealand

2010
World energy use 11793 million toe

2000
World energy use 9348 million toe

1993
World energy use 8080 million toe

former U.S.S.R

2010 +9.4%
1993

CHINA

2010 +99.7%
1993

SOUTH ASIA

2010 +162.2%
1993

EAST ASIA

MIDDLE EAST

2010 +100%
1993

CENTRAL/EASTERN EUROPE

2010 +32.5%
1993

WESTERN EUROPE

2020 +20.2%
1990

AFRICA

2010 +94.9%
1993

INDIAN OCEAN

ATLANTIC OCEAN

NORTH AMERICA

2010 +25.5%
1993

SOUTH AND CENTRAL AMERICA

2010 +66.9%
1993

2010 ENERGY INTENSITY
kgoe (kg of oil equivalent)
of energy needed to
produce US $1000 of
Gross Domestic Product (GDP)
projected 1996

World average: 370 kgoe

Middle East 770

China 740

former USSR 1760

East Asia 340

North America 160

Central/ Eastern Europe 890

Africa 390

South and Central America 360

South Asia 510

Western Europe 620

Australia, Japan, New Zealand 200

2010 ENERGY USE
by region projected 1996
toe (tons of oil equivalent)
per person

World average: 1.7 toe

- 5 toe and over
- 2 to 4 toe
- 1 to 2 toe
- under 1 toe

CHANGES IN ENERGY USE
2010 projection compared
with 1993

World average: 46% increase

- renewable fuel
  including geothermal,
  hydro, energy crops,
  solar, wind, charcoal
  and wood
- oil and coal
- gas
- nuclear energy

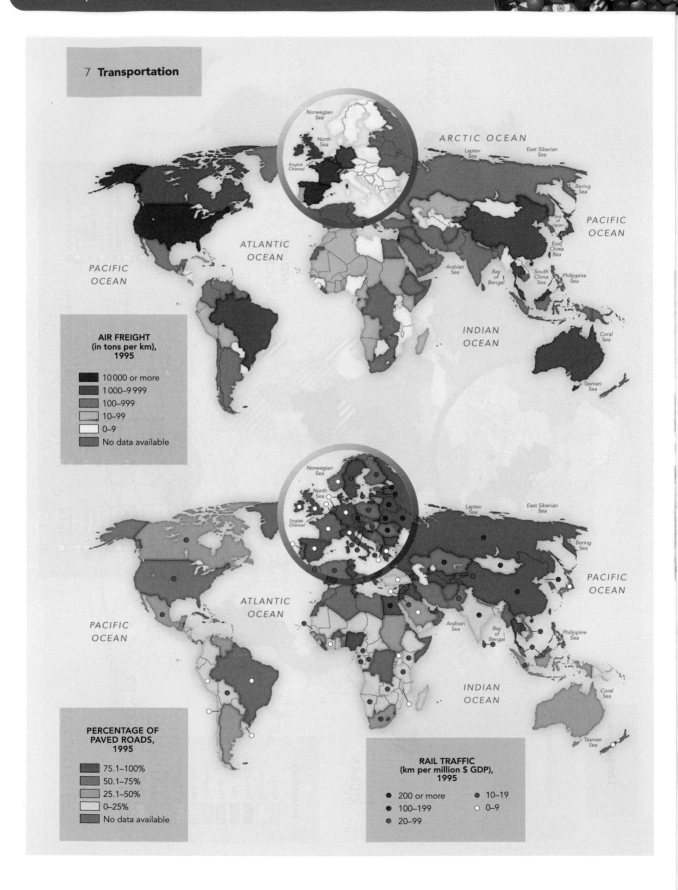

7 Transportation

AIR FREIGHT
(in tons per km),
1995

- 10 000 or more
- 1 000–9 999
- 100–999
- 10–99
- 0–9
- No data available

**PERCENTAGE OF
PAVED ROADS,**
1995

- 75.1–100%
- 50.1–75%
- 25.1–50%
- 0–25%
- No data available

RAIL TRAFFIC
(km per million $ GDP),
1995

- 200 or more
- 100–199
- 20–99
- 10–19
- 0–9

Part 1
An Overview

Chapter 1
The Scope and Challenge of International Marketing

Exhibit 1.1 Top 30 countries for trade and expansion

Rank 2007	Country	GDP (millions of USD)	Trade blocs/agreements	Population (millions)	Imports (billion $)	Export (billion $)
1	United States	13 807 550	NAFTA, WIPO, WTO, APEC, ISRAEL	303	1968	1148
2	Japan	4 381 576	WIPO, WTO, APEC	127	573.3	678.1
3	Germany	3 320 913	EU, EMU, WIPO, WTO, SCH, ISRAEL, MEXICO	82	1075	1354
4	China (PRC)	3 280 224	WIPO, WTO, APEC, EA, ARF	1330	904.6	1220
5	United Kingdom	2 804 437	EU, WIPO, WTO, ISRAEL, MEXICO	60	621.4	442.2
6	France	2 593 779	EU, EMU, WIPO, WTO, SCH, ISRAEL, MEXICO	64	600.9	546
7	Italy	2 104 666	EU, EMU, WIPO, SCH, ISRAEL, MEXICO	58	498.1	502
8	Spain	1 439 983	EU, EMU, WIPO, WTO, SCH, ISRAEL, MEXICO	40	380.2	256.7
9	Canada	1 436 086	NAFTA, WIPO, WTO, APEC, CHILE, ISRAEL	33	386.4	431.1
10	Brazil	1 313 590	WTO, Unasur, Mecosur	196	120.6	160.6
11	Russia	1 289 535	WTO, EAEC	140	223.4	355.5
12	India	1 100 695	WIPO, WTO, APEC, ARF	1147	230.5	151.3
13	Mexico	1 022 816	NAFTA, WTO	109	281.9	271.9
14	South Korea	969 871	WIPO, WTO, APEC	48	349.6	379
15	Australia	908 990	APAC, WTO, ARF	21	160	142.1
16	Netherlands	777 241	EU, EMU, WIPO, WTO, SCH, ISRAEL, MEXICO	16	406.3	456.8
17	Turkey	659 276	WTO	71	162	115.3
18	Sweden	454 839	EU, WIPO, WTO, SCH, ISRAEL, MEXICO	9	151.4	170.1
19	Belgium	453 283	EU, EMU, WIPO, WTO, SCH, ISRAEL, MEXICO	10	323.2	322.2
20	Indonesia	432 944	ASEAN, WTO	237	84.9	118
21	Switzerland	427 074	WIPO, WTO, SCH, ISRAEL, MEXICO	7	187.1	200.1
22	Poland	422 090	EU, EMU, WIPO, WTO, SCH, ISRAEL, MEXICO	35	160.2	144.6

Exhibit 1.1 (Top 30 countries for trade and expansion, continued)

Rank 2007	Country	GDP (millions of USD)	Trade blocs/agreements	Population (millions)	Imports (billion $)	Export (billion $)
23	Norway	389 457	EFTA, WIPO, WTO	8	77.2	140.3
24	Republic of China (Taiwan)	383 347	WTO, APEC	22	215.1	246.5
25	Saudi Arabia	381 938	GAFTA, OPEC	28	82.6	226.7
26	Austria	371 219	EU, EMU, WIPO, WTO, SCH, EFTA, ISRAEL, MEXICO		160.3	162.1
27	Greece	313 806	EU, EMU, WIPO, WTO, ISRAEL, MEXICO	10	80.7	23.9
28	Denmark	312 046	EU, EMU, WIPO, WTO, ISRAEL, MEXICO	5	102	101.2
29	Iran	285 304	OPEC, SAARC	65	53.8	88.2
30	South Africa	283 071	AEC, WTO	48	81.8	76.1

Sources: IMF, CIA factbook, WTO, 2008.

Exhibit 1.2 Direct investment flows around Europe, the United States and Japan, 2007

Countries	Inflow (billion $)	Outflow (million $)	Net outflow (million $)
United States	232.8	314	−81.2
Canada	108.7	53.8	−54.9
Belgium	40.6	49.6	9
United Kingdom	240	266	26
France	157.9	225	67.1
Italy	40.1	90.7	50.6
Poland	17.6	3.3	−14.3
Switzerland	40.3	50.9	10.6
Spain	53.3	119.6	66.3
Sweden	20.9	37.7	16.8
The Netherlands	99.4	31.1	−68.3
Germany	51	167	116
Japan	22.5	73.5	51

Source: World Investment Report 2008.

Furthermore, if internal economic conditions deteriorate, restrictions against foreign investment and purchasing may be imposed to strengthen the domestic economy.

Inextricably entwined with the effects of the domestic environment are the constraints imposed by the environment of each foreign country.

Foreign Uncontrollables

In addition to uncontrollable domestic elements, a significant source of uncertainty is the number of uncontrollable foreign business environments (depicted in Exhibit 1.3 by the outer circles). A business operating in its home country undoubtedly feels comfortable in forecasting the business climate and adjusting business decisions to these elements. The process of evaluating the uncontrollable elements in an international marketing programme, however, often involves substantial doses of cultural, political and economic shock.

GOING INTERNATIONAL 1.2

McDonald's revolutions

Interior of a McDonald's Restaurant in Egypt
© P. Ghauri

In 2002 McDonald's, the biggest global brand after Coca-Cola, was about to announce its first quarterly loss since going public in 1965. Sales were falling and hundreds of underperforming restaurants were closed; earnings per share had fallen in six out of eight previous quarters. Market share was contested by a new breed of 'quick casual' restaurants such as Panera Bread and Prêt À Manger. The chain ranked at the bottom of the University of Michigan's American Customer Satisfaction Index. To cap it all, it was targeted by a number of lawsuits brought against fast-food companies in the US, and shirts and mugs emblazoned with the words 'Stop super-sizing us' started multiplying across the country. However, as the company responded to the crisis, sales in the US were boosted by new main-course salads and breakfast sandwiches in the first half of 2003, bringing the share prices up by 80 per cent. Nevertheless, it is still for the future to show whether the recovery will be sustainable. Meanwhile, the company is attempting to turn McDonald's into a 'lifestyle' brand, comparable with Apple or Nike, through better products, better marketing and better restaurants.

The company revised its growth targets. Previous targets of 10–15 per cent a year resulted in a focus on opening new restaurants, and service in the existing ones was neglected. Now McDonald's is aiming for annual sales growth of 3–5 per cent from 2005 onwards, with only 2 percentage points coming from new restaurants. The partially lapsed system of sending inspectors round to grade restaurants on quality, service and cleanliness was standardised and toughened up, making it easier to weed out underperforming franchises. Premium salads were added to the menu in March 2003. A 'Salad Plus' menu, offering a variety of low-fat foods, is being tested in Australia. Apple slices are being tested in children's Happy Meals. A new global advertising campaign, featuring the new slogan 'I'm Lovin' It', is the first time McDonald's advertisements in 118 operating countries have used the same slogan. In 2008 McDonald's announced that 11 of its restaurants in north England have been using a biomass trial that had cut its waste

and carbon footprint by half in the area. In addition, in Europe McDonald's has been recycling vegetable grease by converting it to fuel for their diesel trucks.

Other changeover ideas came from one of the most unlikely places – France. Despite the somewhat sour Franco-US relations, France is McDonald's best performing European subsidiary in terms of operating income per outlet and is in the global vanguard of redesigning restaurants and launching products. French management attributes its success to the adaptation to local tastes and habits. In particular, McDonald's France has an important focus on the 'modernity' of the restaurant image. The company transformed many outlets into so-called 'casual restaurants' by using softer interior materials, and making the seating space more comfortable and attractive. There are lounge chairs in place of hard, fixed plastic seats, and some restaurants have Apple iPod digital music players installed around the walls, so diners can don headphones and listen to music of their choice. In 2006, McDonald's introduced its 'Forever Young' brand by redesigning all of their restaurants – the first major redesign since the 1970s.

● Has McDonalds been successful in this new strategy? Discuss.

Source: adapted from N. Buckley, 'Eyes on the Fries: Will New Products, Restaurant Refits and a Marketing Overhaul Sustain the Golden Arches?', *Financial Times*, 29 August 2008, p. 15'; R. Minder, 'Croques, Leather and Headphones put France in the Vanguard', *Financial Times*, 29 August 2003, p. 15; and 'Battling against Big Food', *The Economist*, 21 December 2002, p. 116.

A business operating in a number of foreign countries might find polar extremes in political stability, class structure and economic climate – critical elements in business decisions. The dynamic upheavals in some countries further illustrate the problems of dramatic change in cultural, political and economic climates over relatively short periods of time.

GOING INTERNATIONAL 1.3

Evolution of a multinational company

1964 Phil Knight, an accountant at Price Waterhouse, and college track coach Bill Bowerman put in $500 each to start Blue Ribbon Sports.

1970 Bowerman, inspired by the waffle iron, dreams up new shoe treads, which evolve to become the best-selling US training shoe.

1971 Blue Ribbon changes its name to Nike and adopts the swoosh as its logo, designed by a college student for $35. She later gets an undisclosed number of stocks.

1973 Steve Prefontaine, the long-distance runner, becomes the first major athlete to wear Nike in competitions.

© P. Ghauri

1980 Nike goes public with 2.4 million shares at $11. After several splits, stock is worth $78 per share in September 2004.

to our society without thinking about it because we are culturally responsive to our environment. The experiences we have gained throughout life have become second nature and serve as the basis for our behaviour.

The task of cultural adjustment is perhaps the most challenging and important one confronting international marketers; they must adjust their marketing efforts to cultures to which they are not attuned.

When a marketer operates in other cultures, marketing attempts may fail because of unconscious responses based on frames of reference acceptable in one's own culture but unacceptable in different surroundings. Unless special efforts are made to determine local cultural meanings for every market, the marketer is likely to overlook the significance of certain behaviours or activities and proceed with plans that result in a negative or unwanted response.

For example, a Westerner must learn that white is a symbol of mourning in parts of Asia, quite different from Western culture's white for bridal gowns. Also, time-conscious Westerners are not culturally prepared to understand the meaning of time to Latin Americans or Arabs. These differences must be learned in order to avoid misunderstandings that can lead to marketing failures.

To avoid such errors, the foreign marketer should be aware of the principle of *marketing relativism*: that is, marketing strategies and judgements are based on experience, and experience is interpreted by each marketer in terms of his or her own culture and experience. We take into the marketplace, at home or in a foreign country, frames of reference developed from past experiences that determine or modify our reactions to the situations we face.

Cultural conditioning is like an iceberg – we are not aware of nine-tenths of it. In any study of the market systems of different people, their political and economic structures, religions and other elements of culture, foreign marketers must constantly guard against measuring and assessing the markets against the fixed values and assumptions of their own cultures. They must take specific steps to make themselves aware of the home cultural reference in their analyses and decision making.

Self-Reference Criterion: an Obstacle

The key to successful international marketing is adaptation to the environmental differences from one market to another. Adaptation is a conscious effort on the part of the international marketer to anticipate the influences of both the foreign and domestic uncontrollable environments on a marketing mix, and then to adjust the marketing mix to minimise the effects.

The primary obstacle to success in international marketing is a person's **self-reference criterion (SRC)** in making decisions, that is, an unconscious reference to one's own cultural values, experiences and knowledge as a basis for decisions. The SRC impedes the ability to assess a foreign market in its true light.

When confronted with a set of facts, we react spontaneously on the basis of knowledge assimilated over a lifetime – knowledge that is a product of the history of our culture. Quite often we do not know ourselves why we behave in a certain way in a certain situation, as we do that unconsciously. We seldom stop to think about a reaction; we react. Thus, when faced with a problem in another culture, the tendency is to react instinctively, referring only to our SRC for a solution.

To illustrate the impact of the SRC, consider misunderstandings that can occur about personal space between people of different cultures. In the West unrelated individuals keep a certain physical distance between themselves and others when talking to each other or in groups. We do not consciously think about that distance; we just know what feels right without thinking. When someone is too close or too far away, we feel uncomfortable and either move further away or get closer to correct the distance – we are relying on our SRC (see Exhibit 1.4). In some cultures the acceptable distance between

SELF-REFERENCE CRITERION (SRC) considering our own conditions, values and norms while evaluating others

Exhibit 1.4 Four circles of intimacy

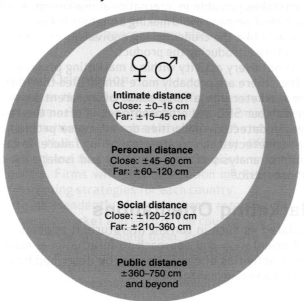

Intimate distance
Close: ±0–15 cm
Far: ±15–45 cm

Personal distance
Close: ±45–60 cm
Far: ±60–120 cm

Social distance
Close: ±120–210 cm
Far: ±210–360 cm

Public distance
±360–750 cm
and beyond

Source: based on Raymond Lesikar and John Pettit, *Business Communication: Theory and Practice* (Homewood, IL: Irwin, 1989).

individuals is substantially less than that comfortable to Westerners. When Westerners, unaware of another culture's acceptable distance, are approached too closely by someone from another culture, they unconsciously react by backing away to restore the proper distance (i.e. proper by their own standards) and confusion results for both parties. Westerners assume 'foreigners' are pushy, while foreigners assume Westerners are unfriendly and standoffish. Both react to the values of their own SRCs, making them all victims of a cultural misunderstanding.

Your SRC can prevent you from being aware that there are cultural differences, or from recognising the importance of those differences. Thus, you fail to recognise the need to take action, discount the cultural differences that exist among countries or react to a situation in a way that is offensive to your hosts. A common mistake made by Westerners is to refuse food or drink when offered. In Europe, a polite refusal is certainly acceptable, but in many countries in Asia and the Middle East, a host is offended if you refuse hospitality.

If we evaluate every situation through our SRC, then we are ethnocentric. The ethnocentrism and the SRC can influence an evaluation of the appropriateness of a domestically designed marketing mix for a foreign market. If Western marketers are not aware, they may evaluate a marketing mix on Western experiences (i.e. their SRC) without fully appreciating the cultural differences requiring adaptation. ESSO, a brand name for petrol, was a successful name in the United States and would seem harmless enough for foreign countries; however, in Japan, the name phonetically means 'stalled car', an undesirable image for petrol. Another example is 'Pet' in Pet Milk. The name has been used for decades; yet in France, the word *pet* means, among other things, flatulence – again, not the desired image for canned milk. Both of these examples of real mistakes made by major companies stem from relying on SRC in making a decision. In international marketing, relying on one's SRC can produce an inadequately adapted marketing programme that ends in failure.

The most effective way to control the influence of the SRC is to recognise its existence in our behaviour. Although it is almost impossible for someone to learn every culture in depth and to be aware of every important difference, an awareness of the need to be

Flexible and open These people demonstrate a good ability to adapt to changes and unexpected circumstances. They may even seek these situations for gaining novel experiences or new adventures.

Begin from a position of trust These people are able to maintain relationships as they often begin from a position of trust when starting new relationships. This makes them tolerant and more approving of others.

Orientation of International Marketing

Most problems encountered by the foreign marketer result from the unfamiliar environment within which marketing programmes must be implemented. Success hinges, in part, on the ability to assess and adjust properly to the impact of a strange environment. In light of all the variables involved, with what should a text in international marketing be concerned? In our opinion, a study of foreign marketing environments and cultures, and their influences on the total marketing process is of primary concern and is the most effective approach to a meaningful presentation.

Consequently, the orientation of this text can best be described as an environmental and cultural approach to international strategic marketing. By no means is it intended to present principles of marketing; rather it is intended to demonstrate the unique problems of international marketing. It attempts to relate the foreign environment to the marketing process and to illustrate the many ways in which the environment can influence the marketing task. Although marketing principles are universally applicable, the environment and culture within which the marketer must implement marketing plans can change dramatically from country to country. It is with the difficulties created by different environments and cultural differences that this text is primarily concerned.

Further, the text is concerned with any company marketing in or into any other country or groups of countries, however slight the involvement or the method of involvement. Hence, this discussion of international marketing ranges from the marketing and business practices of small exporters, such as a Groningen-based company that generates more than 50 per cent of its $40 000 (€36 000) annual sales of fish-egg sorters in Canada, Germany and Australia, to the practices of global companies, such as Philips, British Airways, Nokia, ABB and Sony, which generate more than 70 per cent of their annual profits from the sales of multiple products to multiple country-market segments all over the world.[16]

Summary

The first section of *International Marketing* offers an overview of international marketing, and a discussion of the global business, political and legal environments confronting the marketer. International marketing is defined as the performance of business activities beyond national borders. The task of the international marketer is explained. Key obstacles to international marketing are not just foreign environments but also our own self-reference criteria (SRC) and ethnocentrism. This section deals exclusively with the uncontrollable elements of the environment and their assessment. The next section offers chapters on assessing international market opportunities. Then, management issues in developing global marketing strategies are discussed. In each chapter the impact of the environment and culture on the marketing process is illustrated. Space prohibits an encyclopaedic approach to all the issues; nevertheless, the authors have tried to present sufficient detail so readers appreciate the real need to make a thorough analysis whenever the challenge arises. The next chapter provides a framework for this task.

Questions

1 'The marketer's task is the same whether applied in Amsterdam, London or Kuala Lumpur'. Discuss.
2 How can the increased interest in international marketing on the part of European firms be explained?
3 Discuss the four phases of international marketing involvement.
4 Discuss the conditions that have led to the development of global markets.
5 Differentiate between a global company and a multinational company.
6 Differentiate among the three international marketing orientations.
7 Relate the three international marketing orientations to the EPRG schema.
8 Discuss the factors necessary to achieve global awareness.
9 What is meant by global markets? How does this influence the adaptation of products and marketing strategies?
10 Define and explain the following:
 – controllable elements in the international marketer's task
 – uncontrollable elements in the international marketer's task
 – self-reference criterion (SRC)
 – international marketing orientation
 – global awareness.

Further Reading

Theodore Levitt, 'The Globalization of Markets', *Harvard Business Review*, 1983, May–June, pp. 92–102.

Peter Buckley and Pervez Ghauri, 'Globalization, Economic Geography and Multinational Enterprises', *Journal of International Business Studies*, 2004, 35(2), pp. 81–98.

Firat Fuat, 'Educator Insights: Globalization of Fragmentation – A Framework for Understanding Contemporary Global Markets', *Journal of International Marketing*, 5(2), pp. 77–86.

References

1 S. Tamer Cavusgil, Pervez Ghauri and Milind Agarwal, *Doing Business in Emerging Markets: Entry and Negotiation Strategies* (Thousand Oaks: Sage, 2002).
2 Peter Buckley and Pervez Ghauri, 'Globalization, Economic Geography and International Business', *Journal of International Business Studies*, 2004, 35(2), pp. 81–98.
3 Allan Bird and Michael Stevens, 'Towards an Emerging Global Culture and the Effects of Globalisation on Obsolescing National Cultures', *Journal of International Management*, 2003, 6, pp. 395–407, and T. Clark and L.L. Mathur, 'Global Myopia: Globalisation Theory in International Business', *Journal of International Management*, 2003, 9, pp. 361–72.
4 Nestlé: http://www.nestle.com, 2004.
5 Toyota: http://www.toyota.co.jp, 2004.
6 'Borderless Management: Companies Strive to Become Truly Stateless', *Business Week*, 23 May 1994, pp. 24–6.
7 David A. Ricks, *Blunders in International Business* (Cambridge, Mass.: Blackwell Publishers, 1993), p. 43.

8   For a report on research that examines the internationalisation of a firm, see Peter Buckley and Pervez Ghauri (eds), *The Internationalization of the Firm: A Reader*, second edition (London: Dryden Press, 1999).

9   Yoram Wind, Susan P. Douglas and Howard V. Perlmutter, 'Guidelines for Developing International Marketing Strategy', *Journal of Marketing*, April 1973, pp. 14–23.

10 Theodore Levitt, 'The Globalization of Markets', *Harvard Business Review*, May–June 1983, pp. 92–102.

11 Levitt, 'Globalization', p. 92.

12 For an opposing view, see Richard A. Kustin, 'Marketing Globalization: A Didactic Examination of Corporate Strategy', *International Executive*, January–February 1994, pp. 79–93.

13 Punkaj Ghemawat, 'Semiglobalisation and International Business Strategy', *Journal of International Business Studies*, 2003, 34(1), pp. 139–52.

14 Webster's unabridged dictionary defines tolerance as a fair and objective attitude towards those whose opinions, practices, race, religion, nationality, etc. differ from one's own: freedom from bigotry. It is with this meaning that the authors are using tolerance.

15 Louis Amato and Ronald Wilder, 'Global Competition and Global Markets: Some Empirical Results', *International Business Review*, 2004, 13(3), pp. 401–16.

16 Here, and in the rest of the book, the euro (€) to dollar ($) exchange rate is that of € = US$0.71 and US$ = €1.40.

Chapter 2
The Dynamics of International Markets

Exhibit 2.4 The top 10 economies, GDP at PPP*, 2007, $ trillion

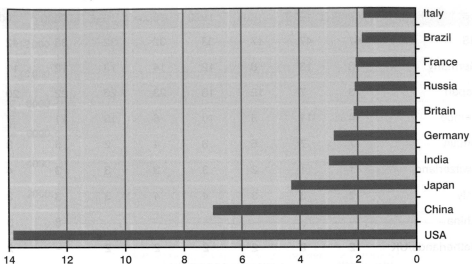

*Purchasing-power parity.
Source: International Monetary Fund, 2008.

happening in Asia that will make such a prediction reality. The Chinese government has announced a consolidation of its motor vehicle production into a few large manufacturing plants to produce an affordable compact sedan for the masses.[5] Production is expected to double to 3 million units over the next five years.[6] Tata, the Indian conglomerate, has introduced a people's car that will cost less than £2000 in emerging markets.[7] Such increases in consumer demand are not limited to motor vehicles; the shopping lists of the hundreds of millions of households that will enter or approach the middle class over the next decade will include washing machines, televisions and all the other trappings of affluence.

This does not mean that markets in Europe, Japan and the United States will cease to be important; those economies will continue to produce large, lucrative markets and the companies established in those markets will benefit. It does mean that for a company to be a major player in the next century, now is the time to begin laying the groundwork.

How will these changes that are taking place in the global marketplace impact on international marketing? For one thing, the level and intensity of competition will change as companies focus on gaining entry into or maintaining their position in emerging markets,

GOING INTERNATIONAL 2.1

A rise in protection would worsen the already grim outlook for world trade

Remember 1982, when the Soviet threat haunted America and China was still a giant backwater that had only just started reforming its economy? Few will recall that it was also the last year in which the volume of world trade shrank. Twenty-seven years later, it is likely to fall once again – by 2 per cent, the World Bank predicts.

It is not just that China's export juggernaut has stalled. Caroline Freund, an economist at the Bank, says that most countries for which data are available have

reported double-digit declines in exports in the year to November. Exports from Chile, South Korea and Taiwan dropped by about 20 per cent. November's figures may have exaggerated the gloom because of a precautionary run-down of inventories and a shortage of trade finance. Both of which may be short lived. But there is little dispute that a serious slowdown in trade is under way.

Overlaying the worsening economic outlook is the lingering threat of protectionism, which could drive trade volumes even lower next year. It is always tempting for politicians to throw up new trade barriers when jobs and wages are at risk, even if such a response, though individually appealing, is collectively futile.

Tariff increases may be the protectionist's barrier of choice, despite limits agreed by members of the World Trade Organization (WTO). This is because in the past decade many countries have unilaterally cut tariffs to well below those limits. They have plenty of room to raise them without breaking any rules.

If all countries were to raise tariffs to the maximum allowed, the average global rate of duty would be doubled, according to Antoine Bouet and David Laborde of the International Food Policy Research Institute in Washington, DC. The effect could shrink global trade by 7.7 per cent.

There are other, more subtle, means of protection available. Marc Busch, a professor of trade policy at Georgetown University in Washington, DC, worries that health and safety standards and technical barriers to trade, such as licensing and certification requirements, will be used aggressively to shield domestic industries as the global downturn drags on.

- Is protectionism on the rise? Is it good for national economies? Is it good for global economies?

Source: The Economist; Finance and economics, 20 December 2008.

Golden years

Indices, 1990 = 100:

- - - - World trade volume
— — World GDP
——— Average tariff applied, %

*Forecast
Sources: World Bank; IMF.

regional trade areas, and the established markets in Europe, Japan and the United States.

Companies are looking for ways to become more efficient, improve productivity and expand their global reach while maintaining an ability to respond quickly to deliver a product the market demands. For example, large multinational companies, such as Matsushita of Japan and Samsung of Korea, continue to expand their global reach.[8] Nestlé is consolidating its dominance in global consumer markets by acquiring and vigorously marketing local-country major brands;[9] and Whirlpool, the US appliance manufacturer, which secured first place in the global appliance business by acquiring the European appliance maker Philips NV, immediately began restructuring itself into its version of a global company.[10] These are a few examples of changes that are sweeping multinational companies as they gear up for the future. Exhibit 2.5 shows the state of the world during the last millennium.

Most protectionists argue the need for tariffs on one of the three premises recognised by economists whether or not they are relevant to their products. Proponents are also likely to call on the maintenance of employment argument because it has substantial political appeal. When arguing for protection, the basic economic advantages of international trade are ignored. The fact that the consumer ultimately bears the cost of tariffs and other protective measures is conveniently overlooked. Agriculture and textiles are good examples of protected industries in the United States and European countries, where not only are high tariffs imposed on imports out also the sectors are heavily subsidised, which cannot be justified by any of the three arguments. In 2008 these subsidies represented about 45 per cent of the European Commission's budget. Local prices are artificially held higher than world prices for no sound economic reason (see Exhibit 2.6)

Exhibit 2.6 The price of protectionism

Protected industry	Jobs saved	Total cost (in millions $)	Annual cost per job saved ($)
Benzenoid chemicals	216	297	1 376 435
Luggage	226	290	1 285 078
Softwood lumber	605	632	1 044 271
Sugar	2261	1868	826 104
Polyethylene resins	298	242	812 928
Dairy products	2378	1630	685 323
Frozen concentrated orange juice	609	387	635 103
Ball bearings	146	88	603 368
Maritime services	4411	2522	571 668
Ceramic tiles	347	191	551 367
Machine tools	1556	746	479 452
Ceramic articles	418	140	335 876
Women's handbags	773	204	263 535
Canned tuna	390	100	257 640
Glassware	1477	366	247 889
Apparel and textiles	168 786	33 629	199 241
Peanuts	397	74	187 223
Rubber footwear	1701	286	168 312
Women's non-athletic footwear	3702	518	139 800
Costume jewellery	1067	142	132 870
Total	191 764	44 352	

Source: 2002 Annual Report—Federal Reserve Bank of Dallas and Oxelhiem and Ghauri, 2003.

GOING INTERNATIONAL 2.2

Protectionism will prolong the economic crisis

Are we already seeing the beginning of the kind of downward spiral in trade and cross-border investment that turned the 1930s into an economic and political catastrophe?

The threat is also imminent. The extent of the integration of most of the world's economies means twenty-first-century protectionism takes many forms, and we are starting to see a number of them. The US House of Representatives attached 'Buy America' provisions to the government stimulus package. The British government has persuaded oil company Total to give jobs to British workers in order to end wildcat strikes over the employment of Italians. Malaysia's government

© P. Ghauri

has instructed its firms to lay off foreign nationals first. Brazil's government has edged up tariffs on manufactured goods. Some commentators in the UK have welcomed devaluation as a useful tool in the policy armoury. As Professor Simon Evenett of the University of St Gallen points out, there has been a dramatic increase in the discussion of protectionism in the world's media. This development reflects the trend in the policy debate.

It is all too easy to disguise protectionist measures and all too tempting to engage in them, given the political pressures from voters to safeguard their jobs and living standards. Many politicians continue to pay lip service to the importance of trade and open economies while advocating measures that will actually undermine the openness which is the only possible engine for restoring growth in the future.

I am not sure that the lessons of the 1930s have been absorbed by our political leaders. They have poured taxpayers' money into bank bail-outs, increased spending programmes and encouraged central banks to slash interest rates and 'print money'. But there is no sign that they understand that all the nations of the world economy sink or swim together, and that history's verdict on their management of this crisis will depend on looking outward for our lifeboats.

● Is the present economic crisis leading towards protectionism? Are countries justified in protecting their economies? Argue.

Sources: Wall Street Journal; Editorials & Opinion, Tuesday, 10 February 2009, p. 13; *Europe and Recovery* by Peter D. Sutherland.

MONETARY BARRIERS
putting monetary restrictions on trade, e.g. availability of foreign exchange for imports

MARKET BARRIERS
barriers to trade imposed in an attempt to promote domestic industry

Trade Barriers

To encourage the development of domestic industry and protect existing industry, governments may establish such barriers to trade as tariffs, quotas, boycotts, **monetary barriers**, non-tariff barriers and **market barriers**. Barriers are imposed against imports and against foreign businesses. While the inspiration for such barriers may be economic or political, they are encouraged by local industry. Whether or not the barriers are economically logical, the fact is that they exist.

Exhibit 2.7 Types of non-tariff barrier

Specific Limitations on Trade
  Quotas
  Import licensing requirements
  Proportion restrictions of foreign to domestic goods (local content requirements)
  Minimum import price limits
  Embargoes

Customs and Administrative Entry Procedures
  Valuation systems
  Anti-dumping practices
  Tariff classifications
  Documentation requirements
  Fees

Standards
  Standards disparities
  Intergovernmental acceptances of testing methods and standards
  Packaging, labelling, marking standards

Governmental Participation in Trade
  Government procurement policies
  Export subsidies
  Countervailing duties
  Domestic assistance programmes

Charges on Imports
  Prior import deposit requirements
  Administrative fees
  Special supplementary duties
  Import credit discriminations
  Variable levies
  Border taxes

Others
  Voluntary export restraints
  Orderly marketing agreements

Source: A.D. Cao, 'Non Tariff Barriers to US Manufactured Exports', *Columbia Journal of World Business,* Summer 1980, p. 94.

'voluntary' in that the exporting country sets the limits; however, it is generally imposed under the threat of stiffer quotas and tariffs being set by the importing country if a VER is not established.

Boycott   A government boycott is an absolute restriction against the purchase and importation of certain goods from other countries. A public boycott can be either formal or informal and may be government sponsored or sponsored by an industry. It is not unusual for the citizens of a country to boycott goods of other countries at the urging of their government or civic groups. Nestlé products were boycotted by a citizens' group

GOING INTERNATIONAL 2.4

Are higher tariffs justified?

According to the development group Oxfam, US tariffs on imports from developing countries are as much as 20 times higher than those charged on imports from other rich nations. The average rate of tariffs on imports from Bangladesh in 2002 was 14 per cent, and duties amounted to $301 million, although the country supplied only 0.1 per cent of total US imports. That value was only slightly smaller than the duties paid on imports from France, which bore an average tariff of 1 per cent and accounted for 2.4 per cent of US imports. Tariffs on imports from India were four times higher than on those from the UK.

The European Union was also said to be discriminating heavily against developing countries. Its duties on imports from India were about four times higher than on those from the US, and more than eight times higher in the case of Sri Lanka and Uruguay. In 2008 Vietnam's footwear makers claimed that an EU plan to increase tariffs would cost them over 100 million dollars and harm their workers.

Oxfam said, 'The overall effect of discriminatory tariff systems is to lower demand for goods produced by the poor, and to exclude them from a stake in global prosperity … northern tariff structures are designed to undermine developing country exports in precisely those areas where they have a comparative advantage', such as textiles and clothing. Rich countries also charge escalating tariffs on products at each stage of processing: the EU tariff on yarn imports was less than 4 per cent, but 14 per cent on garments. The US and EU charged no tariffs on imports of raw cocoa beans, but as much as 14 per cent on items such as paste and chocolate. As a result, developing countries produced more than 90 per cent of all cocoa beans, but less than 5 per cent of world chocolate output. Also developing countries are competing with each other. For example, Chinese manufactures are competing hard against Brazilian clothing and footwear products. Chinese products are usually a lot cheaper and sometimes enter the country illegally. Because of this trend, Brazilian manufacturers suffered from the Chinese ability to enter foreign markets, both in terms of their competitiveness in export markets as well as their position in Brazil. Brazilian associations and unions pressured the government to take action to protect their products and some legal measures were achieved.

● Do you think developed countries are justified in putting high tariffs on products?

Sources: adapted from Guy de Janquières, 'Oxfam Report: US and EU Tariffs Higher for Third World', *Financial Times,* 2 September 2003, p. 13; *EU Business,* 17 June 2008.

that considered that the way Nestlé promoted baby milk formula to Third World mothers was misleading and harmful to their babies.[11]

Monetary Barriers A government can effectively regulate its international trade position by various forms of **exchange-control** restrictions. A government may enact such restrictions to preserve its balance-of-payments position or specifically for the advantage or encouragement of particular industries. There are three barriers to consider: blocked currency, differential exchange rates and government approval requirements for securing foreign exchange.

EXCHANGE CONTROL
when rate of exchange (e.g. for money) is controlled or fixed by the authority

restrictions can be major trade barriers and are therefore included, for the first time, under GATT procedures.[17] An initial set of prohibited practices included local content requirements specifying that some amount of the value of the investor's production must be purchased from local sources or produced locally; trade balancing requirements specifying that an investor must export an amount equivalent to some proportion of imports or condition the amount of imports permitted on export levels; and foreign exchange balancing requirements limiting the importation of products used in local production by restricting its access to foreign exchange to an amount related to its exchange inflow.

GOING INTERNATIONAL 2.6

Round and round: a GATT/WTO chronology

1947	Birth of GATT, signed by 23 countries on 30 October at the Palais des Nations in Geneva.
1948	GATT comes into force. First meeting of its members in Havana, Cuba.
1949	Second round of talks in Annecy, France. Some 5000 tariff cuts agreed; 10 new countries admitted.
1950–51	Third round in Torquay, England. Members exchange 8700 trade concessions and welcome four new countries.
1956	Fourth round in Geneva. Tariff cuts worth $1.3 trillion (€1.17 trillion) at todays prices.
1960–62	The Dillon round, named after US Under-Secretary of State Douglas Dillon, who proposed the talks. A further 4400 tariff cuts.
1964–67	The Kennedy round. Many industrial tariffs halved. Signed by 50 countries. Code on dumping agreed to separately.
1973–79	The Tokyo round, involving 99 countries. First serious discussion of non-tariff trade barriers, such as subsidies and licensing requirements. Average tariff on manufactured goods in the nine biggest markets cut from 7 to 4.7 per cent.
1986–93	The Uruguay round. Further cuts in industrial tariffs, export subsidies, licensing and customs valuation. First agreements on trade in services and intellectual property.
1995	Formation of World Trade Organization with power to settle disputes between members.
1997	Agreements concluded on telecommunication services, information technology and financial services.
1998	The WTO has 132 members. More than 30 others are waiting to join.
2001	The Doha agenda. A new round of negotiations, which includes tariffs, agriculture, services and anti-dumping. China becomes the 143rd member of the WTO.
2004	The WTO has 148 members.
2007	A deadlock in Doha found, as developing countries demand that the US and EU should cut their state subsidies to agricultural sector.
2008	After eight years of negotiating an agreement on the Doha Development Agenda is expected in 2009. The 153 members have to make a decision by consensus.

Source: WTO, www.wto.org.

INTELLECTUAL PROPERTY
a non-material asset that can be bought, sold, licensed, exchanged or gradually given away like any other form of property

Another objective of the EU for the Uruguay round was achieved by an agreement on **Trade-Related Aspects of Intellectual Property Rights (TRIPs)**. The TRIPs agreement establishes substantially higher standards of protection for a full range of intellectual property rights (patents, copyrights, trademarks, trade secrets, industrial designs and semiconductor chip mask works) than are embodied in current international agreements, and it provides for the effective enforcement of those standards both internally and at the border.[18]

World Trade Organization (WTO)

The WTO is an institution, not an agreement as was GATT. It sets the rules governing trade between its members, provides a panel of experts to hear and rule on trade disputes between members, and, unlike GATT, issues binding decisions. It requires, for the first time, the full participation of all members in all aspects of the current GATT and the Uruguay round agreements, and, through its enhanced stature and scope, provides a permanent, comprehensive forum to address the trade issues of the twenty-first-century global market.

Former American president Bush and his trade representative have brought a complaint about Airbus's subsidies to the WTO. The European trade commissioner is bent on confrontation, his office announced. It is high time to put an end to massive illegal US subsidies to Boeing. Boeing claims Airbus received launch aid to market its new plane, the A380. Airbus claims that Boeing gets tax breaks from the US Government and support in the shape of government orders. Moreover, Washington State gave it billions of dollars to develop its new plane, the 7E7, in the state. There are allegations and counter-allegations.

> **TRADE-RELATED ASPECTS OF INTELLECTUAL PROPERTY RIGHTS (TRIPs)** establishes substantially higher standards of protection for a full range of intellectual property rights than are embodied in current international agreements, and provides for the effective enforcement of those standards

---

GOING INTERNATIONAL 2.7

The Doha dilemma – does freer farm trade help poor people?

For years reformers have advocated freer trade on the grounds that market distortions, particularly the rich world's subsidies, depress prices, and hurt rural areas in poor countries, where three-quarters of the world's indigents live. The Doha round of trade talks is dubbed the 'development round' in large part because of its focus on farms. But now high food prices are being blamed for hurting the poor (the topic of a big United Nations summit in Rome starting on 3 June).

The links between trade, food prices and poverty reduction are more subtle. Different types of reform have diverse effects on prices. When countries cut their tariffs on farm goods, their consumers pay lower prices. In contrast, when farm subsidies are slashed, world food prices rise. The lavishness of farm subsidies means that the net effect of fully freeing trade would be to raise prices, by an average of 5.5 per cent for primary farm products and 1.3 per cent for processed goods, according to the World Bank.

The World Bank has often argued that the balance of all these factors is likely to be positive. Although freer farm trade – and higher prices – may raise poverty rates in some countries, it will reduce them in more. One much-cited piece of evidence is a study by Thomas Hertel, Roman Keeney, Maros Ivanic and Alan Winters. This analysis simulated the effect of getting rid of all subsidies and barriers on global prices and trade volumes. It then mapped these results on to detailed household statistics in 15 countries, which between them covered 1 billion people. Fully free trade in farm goods would reduce poverty in 13 countries while raising it in two.

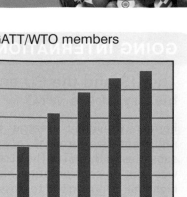

Exhibit 2.8 Joining the club: increasing number of GATT/WTO members

Source: WTO, www.wto.org, 2008.

base of value derived from the value of a group of major currencies. Rather than being denominated in the currency of any given country, trade contracts are frequently written in SDRs because they are much less susceptible to exchange rate fluctuations. Even floating rates do not necessarily accurately reflect exchange relationships. Some countries permit their currencies to float cleanly without manipulation (clean float) while other nations systematically manipulate the value of their currency (dirty float), thus modifying the accuracy of the monetary marketplace. Although much has changed in the world's monetary system since the IMF was first established, it still plays an important role in providing short-term financing to governments struggling to pay current-account debts, and it will be instrumental in helping to establish free markets in emerging markets.

Summary

Regardless of the theoretical approach used in defence of international trade, it is clear that the benefits from absolute or comparative advantage can accrue to any country. Heightened competition around the world has created increased pressure for protectionism from every region of the globe at a time when open markets are needed if world resources are to be developed and utilised in the most beneficial manner for all. It is true that there are circumstances when market protection may be needed and may be beneficial to national defence or the encouragement of infant industries in developing countries, but the consumer seldom benefits from such protection.

Free international markets help participating countries to become full members of world markets and, because open markets provide new customers, most industrialised nations have, since the Second World War, cooperated in working towards freer trade. Such trade will always be partially threatened by various governmental and market barriers that exist or are created for the protection of local businesses. However, the trend has been towards freer trade. The changing economic and political realities are producing unique business structures that continue to protect certain major industries. The emergence of the WTO has played a positive role in easing international trade among different countries and regions. The WTO works on open global markets with controlled and equitable reduction of trade barriers.

Questions

1 Discuss the globalisation of the European economy.
2 Differentiate among the current account, balance of trade and balance of payments.
3 'Theoretically, the market is an automatic, competitive, self-regulating mechanism that provides for the maximum consumer welfare and that best regulates the use of the factors of production.' Explain.
4 Why does the balance of payments always balance even though the balance of trade does not?
5 Enumerate the ways in which a country can overcome an unfavourable balance of trade.
6 France exports about 18 per cent of its gross domestic product, while neighbouring Belgium exports 46 per cent. What areas of economic policy are likely to be affected by such variations in exports?
7 Does widespread unemployment change the economic logic of protectionism?
8 Discuss the evolution of world trade that has led to the formation of the WTO.
9 What are the major differences between GATT and the WTO?
10 Why do countries use trade barriers? What types of trade barrier are used in what countries?

Further Reading

Gary Hamel and C.K. Prahalad, 'Do you Really Have a Global Strategy?', *Harvard Business Review*, 1985, 63(4), pp. 139–48.

Regina Fazio Maruca, 'The Right Way to Go Global: An Interview with Whirlpool CEO David Whitewam', *Harvard Business Review*, 1994, 72(2), pp. 134–45.

Alfredo Mauri and Rakesh Sambharya, 'The Impact of Global Integration on MNC Performance: Evidence from Global Industries', *International Business Review*, 2001, 10(4), pp. 421–40.

Brigitte Lévy, 'The interface between globalization, trade and development: Theoretical issues for international business studies', *International Business Review*, 2007, 16(5), pp. 594–612.

Chapter 3
Geography and History: the Foundations of Cultural Understanding

GOING INTERNATIONAL 3.6

Where have all the women gone?

© iStockphoto.com/ bo1982

Three converging issues in China have the potential to cause a serious gender imbalance: issue 1 – China, the world's most populous country, has a strict one-child policy to curb population growth; issue 2 – traditional values dictate male superiority and a definite parental preference for boys; and issue 3 – prenatal scanning allows women to discover the sex of their foetuses and thereby abort unwanted female children.

As a consequence, Chinese statisticians have begun to forecast a big marriage gap for the generation born in the late 1980s and early 1990s. In 1990 China recorded 113.8 male births for every 100 female births, far higher than the natural ratio of 106 to 100. In rural areas, where parental preference for boys is especially strong, newborn boys outnumber girls by an average of 144.6 to 100. In one rural township, the ratio was reported to be 163.8 to 100.

Not only is there a gender mismatch on the horizon, but there may also be a social mismatch because most of the men will be peasants with little education, while most of the women will live in cities and more likely have high-school or college degrees. In China, men who do physical labour are least attractive as mates, while women who labour with their minds are least popular.

Thanks to technological advancements (prenatal scanning), India is facing the same problem. Families that are able to pay Rs10 000 ($217, €177, £121) can have the scanning done and abort female foetuses. Traditionally, boys are preferred in Indian culture. According to the latest census report, proportions of Indian girls to boys among children up to six years fell from 945 girls to 1000 boys (1991) to 927 girls in 2001. The trend is most pronounced in richer states (as people can pay for the test). For example, Punjab has 798 girls and Gujarat 883 to every 1000 boys. This disparity can have worrying implications especially when, unlike China, India has not been able to impose any family planning.

● Is a one-child policy a good one for China?

Source: adapted from 'Sex Determination before Birth', Reuters News Service, 3 May 1994; 'Seven Times as Many Men', AP News Service, 31 March 1994; Edward Luc, 'Indian Fears Over Falling Female Birth Ratio', Financial Times, 15 September 2004, p. 12.

self-sufficient, and the physical ability to distribute food when the need arises. The world produces enough food to provide adequate diets for all its estimated 6.2 billion people, yet famine exists, most notably in Africa. Long-term drought, economic weakness, inefficient distribution and civil unrest have created conditions that have led to tens of thousands of people starving.

Controlling Population Growth Faced with the ominous consequences of the population explosion, it would seem logical for countries to take appropriate steps to reduce growth to manageable rates, but procreation is one of the most culturally sensitive uncontrollables.

The prerequisites for population control are adequate incomes, higher literacy levels, education for women, better hygiene, universal access to healthcare, improved nutrition and, perhaps most important, a change in basic cultural beliefs about the importance of large families. Unfortunately, progress in providing improved conditions and changing beliefs is hampered by the increasingly heavy demand placed on institutions responsible for change and improvement.

In many cultures, the prestige of a man, whether alive or dead, depends on the number of his progeny, and a family's only wealth is its children. Many religions discourage or ban family planning and thus serve as a deterrent to control. Nigeria has a strong Muslim tradition in the north and a strong Roman Catholic tradition in the east; both faiths discourage family planning. Most traditional religions in Africa encourage large families; in fact, the principal deity for many is the goddess of land and fertility.

Developed World Population Decline   While the developing world faces a rapidly growing population, it is estimated that the industrialised world's population will decline. Birth rates in Western Europe and Japan have been decreasing since the early or mid-1960s; more women are choosing careers instead of children, and many working couples are electing to remain childless. As a result of these and other contemporary factors, population growth in many countries has dropped below the rate necessary to maintain present levels. The populations of France, Sweden, Italy, Switzerland and Belgium are all expected to drop within a few years. Austria, Denmark, Germany, Japan and several other nations are now at about zero population growth and will probably slip to the minus side in another decade. Exhibit 3.6 reveals the old-age dependency in the Europe of the future.

The economic fallout of a declining population has many ramifications. Businesses find their domestic market shrinking for items such as maternity and infant goods, school equipment and selected durables. This leads to reduced production and worker layoffs that affect living standards. Europe, Japan and the United States have special problems because of the increasing percentage of elderly people who must be supported by shrinking numbers of active workers. The elderly require higher government outlays for healthcare and hospitals, special housing and nursing homes, and pension and welfare assistance,

Exhibit 3.6 Europe's old-age dependency

Country	Population		Dependency ratio†	
	2005	2050	2005	2050
	Millions		Millions	
Spain	41.2	37.3	28	72
Italy	57.5	48.1	31	66
Poland	38.5	33.0	20	55
EU	445.2*	431.2*	29**	52**
Germany	83.0	76.0	30	52
France	60.3	62.2	28	50
United States	295.5	419.9	21	39

Notes: † Age 65+ as % of those 20–65; * EU 25; ** EU 15.

Source: Eurostat, UN population Division, US Census Bureau and *The Economist*, 2 October 2004, p. 36.

GOING INTERNATIONAL 3.7

Victorian values

Christmas as a festival of consumerism? It all began in the shop-till-you-drop 1800s, says Judith Flanders.

What we are dreaming about is a traditional Victorian Christmas, as seen on Christmas cards. But the mythical Christmas turns out to be just that: a myth. The Victorians invented Christmas as we know it, and it was a consumer bonanza from the beginning. Materialism is nothing new, and the nineteenth-century merchants knew that bigger festivals meant bigger sales. The advent of the railways, and with them a more mobile population, created the perfect audience for newly minted 'traditions'.

When Charles Dickens first described a typical Christmas – in 1837, the year Queen Victoria came to the throne – some of the trappings of the modern festival were in place: family parties, mistletoe and holly, church-going, charity, turkey, plum pudding and mince pies. But there were no trees, no carols, no cards, no Father Christmas and, perhaps most surprising of all, no presents.

The holiday had been in hibernation since the seventeenth century, when the Puritans condemned it as a 'pagan' festival. It swiftly died in popular memory, replaced by the riot of Twelfth Night, which was a continuation of the old, rowdy winter-solstice celebrations.

When Christmas returned to the calendar, it rapidly became associated with family 'togetherness'.

The railways also brought turkeys to the mass-market. Traditionally, families had eaten goose for the celebration meal, although in the early nineteenth century turkey was also gaining popularity as a larger alternative, better suited to the extended Victorian family. But getting turkeys to the table involved a huge amount of effort.

The ritual of gift-giving to family and the needy started to be associated with Father Christmas towards the end of the century. After the Reformation, St Nicholas, whose Saint's Day was on December 6, vanished, and was replaced by Old Christmas, or Sir Christmas, representing the spirit of the season. Illustrations in the late 1840s show a thin old man, bearded and a bit droopy, rather like Old Father Time. In the 1840s Christmas presents were still mainly given to children, not adults.

By the end of the century, shopping and Christmas were so firmly linked that companies that produced non-Christmas items refused to be left behind. Many ran seasonal advertisements for the most non-seasonal of goods: Pears' Soap advertisements showed a small child hiding under an overturned bathtub, with the caption, 'Oh! Here's a Merry Christmas'.

Source: FT magazine, 9 December 2006, pp. 22–3.

History is Subjective

History is important in understanding why a country behaves as it does, but history from whose viewpoint? Historical events are always viewed from one's own biases, and thus what is recorded by one historian may not be what another records, especially if the historians are from different cultures. Historians are traditionally objective, but few can help filtering events through their own cultural biases. Not only is history sometimes subjective, but there are other subtle influences on our perspective. Maps of the world sold in the United States generally show the United States as the centre, as maps in Britain show Britain at the centre, while maps in Australia look totally different, with Australia being the centre of the world and the rest lying east, west or north of the centre.

Summary

One British authority admonishes foreign marketers to study the world until 'the mere mention of a town, country or river enables it to be picked out immediately on the map'. Although it may not be necessary for the student of international marketing to memorise the world map to that extent, a prospective international marketer should be reasonably familiar with the world, its climate and topographic differences. Otherwise, the important marketing characteristics of geography could be completely overlooked when marketing in another country. The need for geographical and historical knowledge goes deeper than being able to locate continents and their countries. For someone who has never been in a tropical rainforest with an annual rainfall of at least 1.5 metres and sometimes more than 5 metres, it is difficult to anticipate the need for protection against high humidity, or to anticipate the difficult problems caused by dehydration in constant 38°C or more heat in the Sahara region. Without a historical understanding of a culture, the attitudes within the marketplace may not be understood. An understanding of world population and its expected growth in regions and countries can have a profound impact on a company's international marketing strategies. The same goes for the geographic locations of resources and other raw materials.

Aside from the simpler and more obvious ramifications of climate and topography, there are complex geographical and historical influences on the development of the general economy and society of a country. In this case, the need for studying geography and history is to provide the marketer with an understanding of why a country has developed as it has rather than as a guide for adapting marketing plans. Geography and history are two of the environments of foreign marketing that should be understood and that must be included in foreign marketing plans to a degree commensurate with their influence on marketing effort.

Questions

1 Study the data in Exhibit 3.1 and briefly discuss the long-term prospects for industrialisation of an underdeveloped country with a high population growth and minimum resources.
2 Why study geography in international marketing? Discuss.
3 Pick a country and show how employment and topography affect marketing within that country.
4 Discuss the bases of world trade. Give examples illustrating the different bases.
5 The marketer 'should also examine the more complex effect of geography on general market characteristics, distribution systems, and the state of the economy'. Comment.
6 The world population pattern is shifting from rural to urban areas. Discuss the marketing ramifications.
7 Select a country with a stable population and one with a rapidly growing population. Contrast the marketing implications of these two situations.

8 'The basis of world trade can be simply stated as the result of equalising an imbalance in the needs and wants of society on one hand and its supply of goods on the other.' Explain.

9 How do differences in people constitute a basis for trade?

10 'World trade routes bind the world together.' Discuss.

11 Why are the 1990s called the 'Decade of the Environment'? Explain.

12 Some say the global environment is a global issue rather than a national one. What does this mean? Discuss.

Further Reading

Peter J. Buckley and Pervez N. Ghauri, Globalisation, Economic Geography and the Strategy of Multinational Enterprises, *Journal of International Business Studies*, JIBS, 2004, 35(2), 81–98.

A.J. Scott, 'Economic Geography: The Great Half Century', in G.L. Clark, M.P. Feldman and M.S. Gertler (eds), *The Oxford Handbook of Economic Geography* (Oxford: Oxford University Press, 2000) pp. 483–504.

The Economist, *Globalisation – Making Sense of an Integrating World* (London: Profile Books, 2001).

References

1 For an interesting book on the effects of geography, technology and capitalism on an economy, see Dean M. Hanik, *The International Economy: A Geographical Perspective* (New York: Wiley, 1994).

2 'Chunnel Vision', *Europe*, May 1994, p. 43.

3 'Assessing the Channel Tunnel's Benefits', *Business Europe*, 10–16 January 1994, p. 2.

4 World Bank, *World Development Indicators*, CD-ROM, 2003.

5 'A Survey on Development and the Environment', *The Economist*, 21 March 1998.

6 Yoshihide Soeya, 'Balance and Growth', *Look Japan*, January 1994, p. 19.

7 Visit the OECD's website to find out more about sustainable development: www.oecd.org.

8 United Nations, *World Population Projections to 2150*, Department of Economic and Social Affairs, Population Division (New York: United Nations, 1998).

9 'Our World in 2020', Special Survey, *Guardian*, 11 September 2004.

10 This figure represents Tokyo's core suburbs and exurbs.

11 United Nations, *World Urbanization Prospects*, 2003, New York: United Nations.

12 United Nations, *World Population Projections to 2150*, Department of Economic and Social Affairs, Population Division (New York: United Nations, 1998).

13 For insights into some of these questions, see Boye Lafayette DeMente, *Japanese Etiquette and Ethics in Business*, 6th edn (Lincolnwood, IL: NTC Business Books, 1994).

Chapter 4
Cultural Dynamics in International Marketing

Chapter Outline

GOING INTERNATIONAL 4.1

Wal-Mart finds German failures hard to swallow

Nie mehr suchen: Niedrigpreise das ganze Jahr!

www.walmartgermany.de

WAL★MART®

'Don't look now: low prices all year round!'

When German shoppers gathered in Mannheim for the opening of the renovated Wal-Mart Super-center, they were treated to a novel experience. There was space to walk around, freshly baked bagels, free carrier bags and, according to Alfred Brandstetter, the store manager, 'probably the biggest fish counter in Baden-Wurttemberg'.

Yet behind the smiles of its uniformed atten-dants, the world's largest retailer is increasingly worried about the challenges faced by its nearly eight-year-old German venture in Europe's biggest economy. Germany is the only country in the world where Wal-Mart was making a loss.

Bolted together from two acquisitions in 1997 and 1998, Wal-Mart Germany was the country's fourth largest hypermarket chain with 10 per cent of the market. Although a drop in the ocean for the worldwide group – it generated less than 2 per cent of Wal-Mart's sales – its poor performance was a stain on the group's record. Wal-Mart did not publish regional profit figures but the operation was said to be losing $200–300 million (€166–249 million) a year.

'We made mistakes,' says Volker Barth, head of Wal-Mart Germany, 'but one mistake we never made was to underestimate the German market.' Making a mark on Europe's largest and most competitive food retail markets was never going to be easy. But some of Wal-Mart's early mistakes may be impossible to redress. The most glaring one, says an insider, was to disregard the structure of distribution in German food retailing. Drawing on the US model, Wal-Mart decided it wanted to control distribution to stores rather than leave it to suppliers. The result was chaos because suppliers could not adapt to Wal-Mart's centralised demands. With many deliveries failing to arrive in time, out-of-stock rates were sometimes up to 20 per cent, compared to a 7 per cent average for the industry.

Jurgen Elfers, analyst at Commerzbank, blamed the failures on the poor quality of the Interspar chain, Wal-Mart's second and largest acquisition. In a Machiavellian twist, Spar-Handels, the seller, extracted a commitment from Wal-Mart to retain 200 hand-picked employees, a large number of whom were later found to be poorly trained, prompting even long-suffering German shoppers to complain of sloppy service. Facing renovation costs up to five times those in the US, and struggling to navigate Germany's Byzantine planning and social regulations, the group has refurbished only a quarter of its 95 stores and many sites remain unattractive, too small, cramped or poorly located. The Kundenmonitor, a yearly survey of customer satisfaction, gave Wal-Mart the poorest mark of all retailers for general customer sentiment in its latest issue – it ranked higher on value for money. 'The problem is that Germany was beginning to raise questions about the group's entire international strategy,' says Andrew Fowler, food retail analyst at Morgan Stanley Dean Witter (see Case Study 4.1 for a more in-depth analysis).

The German supermarket chain Metro, which is part of one of Germany's largest retail groups, acquired all 85 hypermarkets of Wal-Mart in Germany in the summer of 2006. Wal-Mart could not repeat the US success in Europe's biggest economy. After eight years Wal-Mart had to say Auf Wiedersehen to Germany. It was estimated that the Wal-Mart retreat from Germany cost about $1 billion (794 million Euros).

● What do you think were the main problems Wal-Mart faced in Germany? How could Wal-Mart have prevented failure in Germany?

Source: Bertrand Benoit, 'Wal-Mart finds German Failures Hard to Swallow', *Financial Times*, 12 October 2000; Erich Culp, 'Juggernaut Wal-Mart Goes Slow in Germany', *The Business*, 26/27 September 2004, p. 4.

The marketer's **frame of reference** must be that markets do not occur or exist naturally – they become, they evolve; they are not static but change, expand and contract in response to marketing effort, economic conditions and other cultural influences. Markets and market behaviour are part of a country's culture. One cannot truly understand how markets evolve or how they react to a marketer's effort without appreciating that markets are a result of culture. Markets are dynamic living phenomena, expanding and contracting not only in response to economic change, but also in response to changes in other aspects of the culture. Marketers are constantly adjusting their efforts to the cultural demands of the market, but they are also acting as agents of change whenever the product or idea being marketed is innovative. Whatever the degree of acceptance in whatever level of culture, the use of something new is the beginning of **cultural change** and the marketer becomes a change agent.

FRAME OF REFERENCE
see SELF-REFERENCE CRITERION (on p. 85)

CULTURAL CHANGE
change in cultural conditions, e.g. Americanisation

Cultural Knowledge

There are two kinds of knowledge about cultures. One is **factual knowledge** about a culture; it is usually obvious and must be learned. Different meanings of colour, different tastes and other traits indigenous to a culture are facts that a marketer can anticipate, study and absorb. The other is **interpretive knowledge** – an ability to understand and to appreciate fully the nuances of different cultural traits and patterns. For example, the meaning of time, attitudes towards other people and certain objects, the understanding of one's role in society, and the meanings of life can differ considerably from one culture to another and may require more than factual knowledge to be fully appreciated.

FACTUAL KNOWLEDGE
something that is usually obvious but that must be learnt, i.e. different meaning of colours

Factual Knowledge

Frequently, factual knowledge has meaning as a straightforward fact about a culture, but assumes additional significance when interpreted within the context of the culture. For example, that Mexico is 98 per cent Roman Catholic is an important bit of factual knowledge. But equally important is what it means to be Catholic within Mexican culture versus being Catholic in Spain or Italy. Each culture practises Catholicism in slightly different ways. For example, All Souls' Day is an important celebration among some Catholic countries; in Mexico, however, the celebration receives special emphasis. The Mexican observance is a unique combination of pagan (mostly Indian influence) and Catholic tradition. On the Day of the Dead, as All Souls' Day is called by many in Mexico, it is believed that the dead return to feast. Hence, many Mexicans visit the graves of their departed, taking the dead's favourite foods to place on the graves for them to enjoy. Prior to All Souls' Day, bakeries pile their shelves with bread shaped like bones and coffins, and candy stores sell sugar skulls and other special treats to commemorate the day. As the souls feast on the food, so do the living celebrants. Although the prayers, candles and the idea of the soul are Catholic, the idea of the dead feasting is very pre-Christian Mexican. Thus, a Catholic in

INTERPRETIVE KNOWLEDGE
ability to understand and appreciate fully the nuances of different cultural traits and patterns

step is the recognition that cultures are not right or wrong, better or worse; they are simply different. For every amusing, annoying, peculiar or repulsive cultural trait we find in a country, there is a similarly amusing, annoying or repulsive trait others see in our culture. We find it peculiar that the Chinese eat dogs, while they find it peculiar that we eat lambs and most other animals but not dogs and cats.

Just because a culture is different does not make it wrong. Marketers must understand how their own culture influences their assumptions about another culture. The more exotic the situation, the more sensitive, tolerant and flexible one needs to be. Being more culturally sensitive will reduce conflict, improve communications and thereby increase success in collaborative relationships.

It is necessary for a marketer to investigate the assumptions on which judgements are based, especially when the frames of reference are strictly from his or her own culture.

Culture and its Elements

The student of international marketing should approach an understanding of culture from the viewpoint of the anthropologist. Every group of people or society has a culture because culture is the entire social heritage of the human race: 'the totality of the knowledge and practices, both intellectual and material of society … [it] embraces everything from food to dress, from household techniques to industrial techniques, from forms of politeness to mass media, from work rhythms to the learning of familiar rules'.[7] Culture exists in New York, London and Moscow just as it does among the Gypsies, the South Sea Islanders or the Aborigines of Australia.

Elements of Culture

The anthropologist studying culture as a science must investigate every aspect of a culture if an accurate, total picture is to emerge. To implement this goal, there has evolved a cultural scheme that defines the parts of culture. For the marketer, the same thoroughness is necessary if the marketing consequences of cultural differences within a foreign market are to be accurately assessed.

Culture includes every part of life. The scope of the term 'culture' to the anthropologist is illustrated by the elements included within the meaning of the term. These are:

1. material culture
   technology
   economics
2. social institutions
   social organisation
   political structures
3. education
   literacy rate
   role and levels
4. belief systems
   religion
   superstitions
   power structure
5. aesthetics
   graphic and plastic arts
   folklore
   music, drama and dance
6. language[8]
   usage of foreign languages
   spoken versus written language.

Exhibit 4.3 Elements of culture

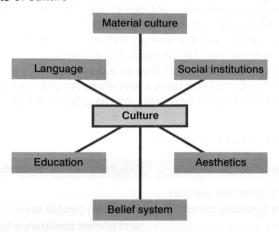

In the study of humanity's way of life, the anthropologist finds these six dimensions useful because they encompass all the activities of social heritage that constitute culture (Exhibit 4.3). Foreign marketers may find such a cultural scheme a useful framework in evaluating a marketing plan or in studying the potential of foreign markets. All the elements are instrumental to some extent in the success or failure of a marketing effort because they constitute the environment within which the marketer operates. Furthermore, because we automatically react to many of these factors in our native culture, we must purposely learn them in another. Finally, these are the elements with which marketing efforts interact and so are critical to understanding the character of the marketing system of any society.

Material Culture   Material culture is divided into two parts: technology and economics. Technology includes the techniques used in the creation of material goods; it is the technical know-how possessed by the people of a society. A culture's level of technology is manifest in many ways. Such concepts as preventive maintenance are foreign in many low-technology cultures. In Germany, the United States, Japan or other countries with high levels of technology, the general population has a broad level of technical understanding that allows them to adapt and learn new technology more easily than populations with lower levels of technology. Simple repairs, preventive maintenance and a general understanding of how things work all constitute a high level of technology. In China, one of the burdens of that country's economic growth is providing the general working population with a modest level of mechanical skill, that is, a level of technology.

Economics is the manner in which people employ their capabilities and the resulting benefits. Included in the subject of economics are the production of goods and services, their distribution, consumption, means of exchange and the income derived from the creation of utilities.

Material culture affects the level of demand, the quality and types of products demanded and their functional features, as well as the means of production of these goods and their distribution. The marketing implications of the material culture of a country are many: electric can openers and electric juicers are acceptable in the United States, but, in less affluent countries and even some European countries, not only are they unattainable and probably unwanted, they would be a spectacular waste because **disposable income** could be spent more meaningfully on better houses, clothing or food.

Social Institutions   Social organisation and political structures are concerned with the ways in which people relate to one another, organise their activities to live in harmony

DISPOSABLE INCOME
that proportion of your income that is not already accounted for – for example, by mortgages, loans, bills, and so on

GOING INTERNATIONAL 4.5

Struggling McDonald's Japan is trying a new recipe

Passers-by consider the McDonald's halfprice sale
AP/Wide World Photos

McDonald's Japan has suffered two consecutive disastrous years, losing a total of $87.5 million, with overall sales falling 4.4 per cent in 2003. When BSE broke out in the US, and Japan imposed a ban on imports of American beef, hamburgers suddenly became unpopular. Given that the Japanese operation generates nearly $2.7 billion in sales and is the biggest franchise of McDonald's Corp. outside the US, the troubles here made headquarters a bit worried, so it ended a 30-year contract with its Japanese partner, taking a one-time charge that contributed to 2003's year's losses. McDonald's US then installed Pat Donahue as chairman, who ran McDonald's Canadian operation, to replace McDonald's Japan's Fujita. (Fujita and his family still own 26 per cent, while McDonald's has a controlling 50 per cent stake.)

Now Makudonarudo, as the Japanese call McDonald's, is on a crash diet. It has cut costs by closing unprofitable franchises and laying off 15 per cent of the staff at the Tokyo headquarters. Three years ago, Fujita boasted that he would have 10 000 McDonald's restaurants by 2010. In 2004 there were 3752, down from 3891 in 2002. The company took a $23.4 million loss in 2003 to pull out of a failed high-end sandwich venture with British company Prêt À Manger.

However, the outlook is beginning to improve. Same-store sales in local currency terms increased in 2004. In addition to existing Japanese-style entrees such as the Teriyaki Burger, the company is rolling out spicy Korean-style burgers, a low-calorie tofu sandwich that's being marketed to women, and a bigger Premium Mac aimed at hungry men. The challenge now is getting back the magic that made McDonald's one of the most successful US investments in Japan.

● Do you think McDonald's can turn things around in Japan? Can you advise it on what to do?

Source: adapted from 'Can Makudonarudo Turn up the Heat?', *Business Week*, 15 March 2004, p. 32.

Religion is one of the most sensitive elements of a culture. When the marketer has little or no understanding of a religion, it is easy to offend, albeit unintentionally. Like all cultural elements, one's own religion is often not a reliable guide of another's beliefs. Many do not understand religions other than their own, and what is 'known' about other religions is often incorrect. The Islamic religion is a good example of the need for a basic understanding. There are more than 1 billion in the world who embrace Islam.

Superstition plays a much larger role in a society's belief system in some parts of the world than it does in Western culture. What Westerners might consider as mere superstition can be a critical aspect of a belief system in another culture. For example, in some countries, ghosts, fortune-telling, palmistry, head-bump reading, phases of the moon, demons and soothsayers are all integral parts of certain cultures. Astrologers are routinely called on in India and Thailand to determine the best location for a structure. The Thais insist that all wood in a new building must come from the same forest to prevent the boards from quarrelling with each other. Houses should have an odd number of rooms for luck, and they should be one storey because it is unlucky to have another's foot over your head.

It can be an expensive mistake to make light of superstitions in other cultures when doing business there. To make a fuss about being born in the right year under the right phase of the moon and to rely heavily on handwriting and palm-reading experts, as in Japan, can be worrisome to a Westerner who seldom sees a 13th floor in a building, refuses to walk under a ladder or worries about the next seven years after breaking a mirror.[9]

Aesthetics   Closely interwoven with the effect of people and the universe on a culture are its aesthetics; that is, the arts, folklore, music, drama and dance. Aesthetics are of particular interest to the marketer because of their role in interpreting the symbolic meanings of various methods of artistic expression, colour and standards of beauty in each culture. The uniqueness of a culture can be spotted quickly in symbols having distinct meanings.

Without a culturally correct interpretation of a country's aesthetic values, a whole host of marketing problems can arise. Product styling must be aesthetically pleasing to be successful, as must advertisements and package designs. Insensitivity to aesthetic values can offend, create a negative impression and, in general, render marketing efforts ineffective. Strong symbolic meanings may be overlooked if one is not familiar with a culture's aesthetic values.

Language   The importance of understanding the language of a country cannot be overestimated. The successful marketer must achieve expert communication; this requires a thorough understanding of the language as well as the ability to speak it. Advertising copywriters should be concerned less with obvious differences between languages and more with the idiomatic meanings expressed.

A dictionary translation is not the same as an **idiomatic interpretation**, and seldom will the dictionary translation suffice. Quite often there is a difference between spoken and written language. One national food processor's familiar 'Jolly Green Giant' translated into Arabic as 'Intimidating Green Ogre'. One airline's advertising campaign designed to promote its plush leather seats urged customers to 'fly on leather'; when translated for its Hispanic and Latin American customers, it told passengers to 'fly naked'. Pepsi's familiar 'Come Alive with Pepsi', when translated into German, conveyed the idea of coming alive from the grave. Schweppes was not pleased with its tonic water translation into Italian: 'Il Water' idiomatically means the bathroom. Electrolux's advertisement for its vacuum cleaner with the slogan 'Nothing Sucks Better than Electrolux' was not particularly appreciated in Ireland. Carelessly translated advertising statements not only lose their intended meaning, but can suggest something very different, obscene, offensive or just plain ridiculous. One authority suggests, as a cultural translator, a person who translates not only among languages, but also among different ways of thinking and among different cultures.[10]

Many believe that to appreciate the true meaning of a language it is necessary to live with that language for years. Whether or not this is the case, foreign marketers should never take it for granted that they are communicating effectively in another language. Until a marketer can master the vernacular, the aid of a national within the foreign country should be enlisted; even then, the problem of effective communications may still exist. For example, in French-speaking countries, the trademark toothpaste brand name 'Cue' was a crude slang expression for derrière. The intent of a major fountain pen company advertising in Latin America suffered in translation when the new pen was promoted to 'help prevent unwanted pregnancies'. The poster of an engineering company at a Russian trade show did not mean to promise that its oilwell completion equipment was dandy for 'improving a person's sex life'.[11]

IDIOMATIC INTERPRETATION interpretation according to the characteristics of a particular language

Analysis of Elements

Each cultural element must be evaluated in light of how it could affect a proposed marketing programme; some may have only indirect impact, others may be totally involved. Generally, conservative and resists change. The dynamic character of culture is significant in assessing new markets even though changes occur in the face of resistance. In fact, any change in the currently accepted way of life meets with more initial resistance than acceptance.[12]

There are a variety of ways a society solves the problems created by its existence. Accident has provided solutions to some of them; invention has solved many others. More commonly, however, societies have found answers by looking to other cultures from which they can borrow ideas. Cultural borrowing is common to all cultures. Although each society has a few truly unique situations facing it, most problems confronting all societies are similar in nature, with alterations for each particular environment and culture.[13]

Cultural Borrowing

Cultural borrowing is a responsible effort to borrow those cultural ways seen as helpful in the quest for better solutions to a society's particular problems. If what it does adopt is adapted to local needs, once the adaptation becomes commonplace, it is passed on as cultural heritage. Thus, cultures unique in their own right are the result, in part, of borrowing from others. Consider, for example, American culture (United States) and the typical US citizen who:

> ... begins breakfast with an orange from the eastern Mediterranean, a cantaloupe from Egypt, or perhaps a piece of African watermelon ... After his fruit and Colombian coffee he goes on to waffles, cakes made by a Scandinavian technique from wheat domesticated in Asia Minor. Over these he pours maple syrup, invented by the Indians of the Eastern US woodlands. As a side dish he may have the eggs of a species of bird domesticated in Indo-China, or thin strips of the flesh of an animal domesticated in Eastern Asia, which have been salted and smoked by a process developed in northern Europe ...
>
> While smoking, he reads the news of the day, imprinted in characters invented by the ancient Semites upon a material invented in China by a process invented in Germany. As he absorbs the accounts of foreign troubles he will, if he is a good conservative citizen, thank a Hebrew deity in an Indo-European language that he is 100 per cent American.[14]

Actually, this citizen is correct to assume that he or she is 100 per cent American, because each of the borrowed cultural facets has been adapted to fit his or her needs, moulded into uniquely American habits, foods and customs. Americans behave as they do because of the dictates of their culture. Regardless of how or where solutions are found, once a particular pattern of action is judged acceptable by society, it becomes the approved way and is passed on and taught as part of the group's cultural heritage. Cultural heritage is one of the fundamental differences between humans and other animals. Culture is learned; societies pass on to succeeding generations solutions to problems, constantly building on and expanding the culture so that a wide range of behaviour is possible. The point is, of course, that although much behaviour is borrowed from other cultures, it is combined in a unique manner, which becomes typical for a particular society. To the foreign marketer, this similar-but-different feature of cultures has important meaning in gaining cultural empathy.

Similarities: an Illusion

For the inexperienced marketer, the similar-but-different aspect of culture creates illusions of similarity that usually do not exist. Several nationalities can speak the same language or have similar race and heritage, but it does not follow that similarities exist in other respects – that a product acceptable to one culture will be readily acceptable to the other, or that promotional message that succeeds in one country will succeed in the other. Even though people start with a common idea or approach, as is the case among English-speaking Australians, Americans and the British, cultural borrowing and assimilation to meet individual needs translate over time into quite distinct cultures. A common language does not guarantee a similar interpretation of even a word or phrase. Both the British and the Americans speak English, but their cultures are sufficiently different that a single phrase has different meanings to each and can even be completely misunderstood. In England, one asks to be directed to a lift instead of an elevator, and an American, when speaking of a bathroom, generally refers to a toilet, while in England a bathroom is a place to take a tub bath. Also, the English 'hoover' a carpet whereas Americans vacuum clean it.

Differences run much deeper than language differences, however. The approach to life, values and concepts of acceptable and unacceptable behaviour may all have a common heritage and may appear superficially to be the same. In reality, profound differences do exist. Among the Spanish-speaking Latin American countries, the problem becomes even more difficult because the idiom is unique to each country, and national pride tends to cause a mute rejection of any 'foreign-Spanish' language. In some cases, an acceptable phrase or word in one country is not only unacceptable in another, it can very well be indecent or vulgar. In Spanish, *coger* is the verb 'to catch', but in some countries it is used as a euphemism with a baser meaning.

Asians are frequently grouped together as if there were no cultural distinctions among Japanese, Koreans and Chinese, to name but a few of the many ethnic groups in the Pacific region. Asia cannot be viewed as a homogeneous entity and the marketer must understand the subtle and not-so-subtle differences among Asian cultures. Each country (culture) has its own unique national character.

There is also the tendency to speak of the 'European consumer' as a result of growing integration in Europe. Many of the obstacles to doing business in Europe have been or will be eliminated as the EU takes shape, but marketers anxious to enter the market must not jump to the conclusion that a unified Europe means a common set of consumer wants and needs. Cultural differences among the members of the EU are the products of centuries of history that will take further centuries to erase.

Even the United States has many subcultures that today, with mass communications and rapid travel, defy complete homogenisation. It would be folly to suggest that the South is in all respects culturally the same as the Northeastern or Midwestern parts of the United States. It also would be folly to assume that the unification of Germany has erased cultural differences that have arisen from over 40 years of political and social separation.[15]

A single geopolitical boundary does not necessarily mean a single culture: Canada is divided culturally between its French and English heritages although it is politically one country. A successful marketing strategy among the French Canadians may be a certain failure among remaining Canadians. Within most cultures there are many subcultures that can have marketing significance.

India is another example: people from the south speak different languages and do not even understand Hindi or other languages of the north, west or east. There are more than 100 languages spoken in India, 25 of which are official languages. In fact, the only language that unites India is English.

Resistance to Change

A characteristic of human culture is that change occurs. That people's habits, tastes, styles, behaviour and values are not constant but are continually changing can be verified by reading 20-year-old magazines. This gradual cultural growth does not occur without some resistance. New methods, ideas and products are held to be suspect before they are accepted, if ever, as right.

The degree of resistance to new patterns varies; in some situations new elements are accepted completely and rapidly, and in others, resistance is so strong that acceptance is never forthcoming. Studies show that the most important factor in determining what kind and how much of an innovation will be accepted is the degree of interest in the particular subject, as well as how drastically the new will change the old, that is, how disruptive the innovation will be to presently acceptable values and patterns of behaviour. Observations indicate that those innovations most readily accepted are those holding the greatest interest within the society and those least disruptive. For example, rapid industrialisation

On the surface, it would appear that the introduction of a processed feeding formula into the diet of babies in developing countries where protein deficiency was a health problem would have all the functional consequences of better nutrition and health, stronger and faster growth, and so forth.[17] There is evidence, however, that in at least one situation the dysfunctional consequences far exceeded the benefits. In India, as the result of the introduction of the formula, a significant number of babies annually were changed from breastfeeding to bottle-feeding before the age of six months. In Western countries, with appropriate refrigeration and sanitation standards, a similar pattern exists with no apparent negative consequences. In India, however, where sanitation methods are inadequate, a substantial increase in dysentery and diarrhoea, and a higher infant mortality rate resulted. This was the result of two factors: the impurity of the water used with the milk and the loss of the natural immunity to childhood disease that a mother's milk provides.[18]

Summary

A complete and thorough appreciation of the dimensions of culture may well be the single most important gain to a foreign marketer in the preparation of marketing plans and strategies. Marketers can control the product offered to a market – its promotion, price and eventual distribution methods – but they have only limited control over the cultural environment within which these plans must be implemented. Because they cannot control all the influences on their marketing plans, they must attempt to anticipate the eventual effect of the uncontrollable elements and plan in such a way that these elements do not preclude the achievement of marketing objectives. They can also set about to effect changes that lead to faster acceptance of their products or marketing programmes. Planning marketing strategy in terms of the uncontrollable elements of a market is necessary in a domestic market as well, but when a company is operating internationally, each new environment influenced by elements unfamiliar and sometimes unrecognisable to the marketer complicates the task. For these reasons, special effort and study are needed to absorb enough understanding of the foreign culture to cope with the uncontrollable features. Perhaps it is safe to generalise that of all the tools the foreign marketer must have, those that help generate empathy for another culture are the most valuable. Each of the cultural elements is explored in depth in subsequent chapters. Specific attention is given to business customs, political culture and legal culture in the following chapters.

Questions

1 Which role does the marketer play as a change agent?
2 Discuss the three cultural change strategies a foreign marketer can pursue.
3 'Culture is pervasive in all marketing activities.' Discuss.
4 What is the importance of cultural empathy to foreign marketers? How do they acquire cultural empathy?
5 Why should a foreign marketer be concerned with the study of culture?
6 What is the popular definition of culture? What is the viewpoint of cultural anthropologists? What is the importance of the difference?

7 It is stated that members of a society borrow from other cultures to solve problems, which they face in common. What does this mean? What is the significance to marketing?

8 'For the inexperienced marketer, the "similar-but-different" aspect of culture creates an illusion of similarity that usually does not exist'. Discuss and give examples.

9 Outline the elements of culture as seen by an anthropologist. How can a marketer use this 'cultural scheme'?

10 What is material culture? What are its implications for marketing? Give examples.

11 What are some particularly troublesome problems caused by language in foreign marketing? Discuss.

12 Suppose you were requested to prepare a cultural analysis for a potential market. What would you do? Outline the steps and comment briefly on each.

13 Cultures are dynamic. How do they change? Are there cases where changes are not resisted but actually preferred? Explain. What is the relevance to marketing?

14 How can resistance to cultural change influence product introduction? Are there any similarities in domestic marketing? Explain, giving examples.

15 Defend the proposition that a multinational corporation has no responsibility for the consequences of an innovation beyond the direct effects of the innovation such as the product's safety, performance and so forth.

16 Find a product whose introduction into a foreign culture may cause dysfunctional consequences. Describe how the consequences might be eliminated and the product still profitably introduced.

Further Reading

P. Magnusson, D.W. Baack, S. Zdravkovic, K.M. Staub and L.S. Amine, 'Meta-analysis of cultural differences: Another slice at the apple', *International Business Review*, 2008, 17(5), pp. 520–32.

C. Barmeyer and U. Mayrhofer, 'The contribution of intercultural management to the success of international mergers and acquisitions: An analysis of the EADS group', *International Business Review*, 2008, 17(1), pp. 28–38.

Allan Bird and Michael Steven, 'Toward an Emerging Global Culture and the Effects of Globalization on Obsolescing National Cultures', *Journal of International Management*, 2003 (9), pp. 395–407.

Leonidas Leonidou, 'Product Standardization or Adaptation: The Japanese Approach', *Journal of Marketing Practice: Applied Marketing Science*, 1996, 2(4), pp. 53–71.

References

1 Gary P. Ferraro, *The Culture Dimension of International Business*, 2nd edn (Englewood Cliffs, NJ: Prentice-Hall, 1994), p. 17.

2 Francis Fukuyama, *Trust: The Social Virtues and the Creation of Prosperity* (London: Penguin, 1996).

3 Geert Hofstede, *Cultures and Organizations: Software of the Mind* (London: McGraw-Hill, 1991), p. 5; see also other publications by Hofstede, e.g. *Culture's Consequences: Comparing Values, Behaviours, Institutions and Organisations Across Nations* (Thousand Oaks: Sage, 2001).

4 Nigel Holden, *Cross-Cultural Management* (Harlow: FT Prentice Hall, 2002), pp. 21–2.

5 Cited in Jean-Claude Usunier, *Marketing Across Cultures*, 2nd edn (Hemel Hempstead: Prentice Hall, 1996), pp. 78–9.

6 Lawrence Rout, 'To Understand Life in Mexico, Consider the Day of the Dead', *The Wall Street Journal*, 4 November 1981, p. 1; and John Rice, 'In Mexico, Death Takes a Holiday', Associated Press, 20 October 1994.

7 Colette Guillaumin, 'Culture and Cultures', *Cultures*, vol. 6, no. 1, 1979, p. 1.

8 Melvin Herskovits, *Man and His Works* (New York: Knopf, 1952), p. 634.

9 See, for example, R.W. Scribner, 'Magic, Witchcraft and Superstition', *The Historical Journal*, March 1994, p. 219.

10 For a comprehensive business guide to cultures and customs in Europe, see John Mole, *When in Rome* (New York: Amacom, 1991).

11 For other examples of mistakes, see David A. Ricks, *Blunders in International Business* (Cambridge, MA: Blackwell, 1994).

12 Elizabeth K. Briody, 'On Trade and Cultures', *Trade and Culture*, March–April 1995, pp. 5–6.

13 For an interesting article on cultural change, see Norihiko Shimizu, 'Today's Taboos May Be Gone Tomorrow', *Tokyo Business Today*, January 1995, pp. 29–51.

14 R. Linton, *The Study of Man* (New York: Appleton-Century-Crofts, 1936), p. 327.

15 See, for example, Denise M. Johnson and Scott D. Johnson, 'One Germany … But is There a Common German Consumer? East–West Differences for Marketers to Consider', *The International Executive*, May–June 1993, pp. 221–8.

16 Chris Halliburton and Reinhard Hünerberg, 'Executive Insights: Pan-European Marketing – Myth or Reality?', *Journal of International Marketing*, 1993, 1(3), pp. 77–92.

17 For an interesting text on change agents, see Gerald Zaltman and Robert Duncan, *Strategies for Planned Change* (New York: Wiley, 1979).

18 For a comprehensive look at this issue, see S. Prakash Sethi, *Multinational Corporations and the Impact of Public Advocacy on Corporate Strategy: Nestlé and the Infant Formula Controversy* (Boston, MA: Kluwer Academic, 1994).

Chapter 5
Business Customs and Practices in International Marketing

Chapter Outline

misunderstanding. The self-reference criterion (SRC) is especially operative in business customs. If we do not understand our foreign counterpart's customs, we are more likely to evaluate that person's behaviour in terms of what is acceptable to us.

The key to adaptation is to remain yourself but to develop an understanding and willingness to accommodate differences that exist. A successful marketer knows that in Asia it is important to make points without winning arguments; criticism, even if asked for, can cause a host to 'lose face'. In Germany and the Netherlands it is considered discourteous to use first names unless specifically invited to do so; always address a person as Herr, Frau or Fräulein, and Meneer or Mevrouw with the last name. In Brazil and in Indonesia do not be offended by the Brazilian or Indonesian inclination towards touching during conversation. Such a custom is not a violation of your personal space but the way of greeting, emphasising a point or as a gesture of goodwill and friendship.

A Chinese, Indian or Brazilian does not expect you to act like one of them. After all, you are not Chinese, Indian or Brazilian but a Westerner, and it would be foolish for a Westerner to give up the ways that have contributed so notably to Western success. It would be equally foolish for others to give up their ways. When different cultures meet, open tolerance and a willingness to accommodate each other's differences are necessary. Once a marketer is aware of the possibility of cultural differences and the probable consequences of failure to adapt or accommodate, the seemingly endless variety of customs must be assessed. Where does one begin? Which customs should be adhered to absolutely, which others can be ignored? Fortunately, among the many obvious differences that exist between cultures, only a few are troubling.

GOING INTERNATIONAL 5.1

Success through cultural customisation

Source: courtesy of Dell Inc.

The secret of success in emerging markets is to develop products that are especially designed to meet the needs of the customers in these markets. In 2000 Dell introduced a new consumer PC for the Chinese market called 'Smart PC', different from those it sells anywhere else. It was built by a Taiwanese company, which allowed Dell to sell it at a very low price. It helped Dell to become the number one foreign supplier in China. New markets need new strategies and new products. To develop new products to tap these markets, companies are doing a lot of market research. Intel appointed 10 ethnographers to travel around the world to find out how to redesign its existing or develop new products to fit different cultures and segments in these markets. One of the ethnographers visited hundreds of families in China and reported that Chinese families were reluctant to buy PCs. Parents were concerned that their children would listen to pop music and surf the web, distracting them from their school work.

Learning from this research, Intel developed a 'Home Learning PC'. It comes with four educational applications and a proper lock and key to allow parents to control computer usage by their children.

The new products developed for new markets need to be simple and capable of operating in harsh environments. For example, India's TVS Electronics has developed an all-inclusive machine for 1.2 million smaller shopkeepers. It is a cash register-cum-computer, it tolerates heat, dust and voltage variations, and costs only $180. Price is often a major factor if a company needs to tap mass markets. HP has set up a pilot programme in rural Africa, where the average person makes less than $1 a day. As many of these people cannot buy computers, HP introduced a solution: 441 (four users for one computer). It is a computer set up in a school or a library but is connected to four keyboards and screens. All four can use the net and send e-mails simultaneously.

When companies modify their products for emerging markets, it can lead to broader improvements. Nokia, for example, developed Smart Radio Technology to cut the number of transmission operators by half in Thailand. This means that operators can build networks with up to 50 per cent less costs. This technology is now exported all over the place by Nokia, from Thailand to Peru.

Source: compiled from Steve Hamm, 'Tech's Future', cover story, *Business Week*, 27 September 2004, pp. 52–9.

Imperatives, Adiaphora and Exclusives

Although you are not obliged to adhere to the maxim 'while in Rome, do as Romans do', you need to be aware of the culture of the market in which you are or are planning to enter. This will allow you to be culturally sensitive so that you will not, at least, annoy people/locals with your behaviour. There are certain characteristics of a culture you must know and certain that you need to follow. Business customs can be grouped into imperatives (customs that must be recognised and accommodated), adiaphora (customs to which adaptation is optional) and exclusives (customs in which an outsider must not participate). An international marketer must appreciate the nuances of cultural imperative, cultural adiaphora and cultural exclusives.

Cultural imperative refers to the business customs and expectations that must be met and conformed to if relationships are to be successful. Successful business people know the Chinese word *guan-xi*, the Japanese *ningen kankei*, or the Latin American *compadre*. All refer to friendship, human relations or attaining a level of trust. They also know there is no substitute for establishing friendship in some cultures before effective business relationships can begin.

Informal discussions, entertaining, mutual friends, contacts and just spending time with others are ways *guan-xi*, *ningen kankei*, *compadre* and other trusting relationships are developed. In those cultures where friendships are a key to success, the business person should not skimp on the time required for their development. Friendship motivates local agents to make more sales and friendship helps establish the right relationship with end users, leading to more sales over a longer period.[4] Naturally, after-sales service, price and the product must be competitive, but the marketer who has established *guan-xi*, *ningen kankei* or *compadre* has the edge. Establishing friendship is an important Asian and Latin American custom. It is imperative that establishing friendship be observed or one risks not earning trust and acceptance, the basic cultural prerequisites for developing and retaining effective business relationships.

Cultural adiaphora relates to areas of behaviour or to customs that cultural aliens may wish to conform to or participate in but that are not required. It is not particularly important, but it is permissible to follow the custom in question; the majority of customs fit into this category. One need not adhere to local dress, greet another man with a kiss (a custom in some countries) or eat foods that disagree with the digestive system (so long

CULTURAL IMPERATIVE
business customs and expectations that must be met and conformed to if relationships are to be successful

GUAN-XI
relationship building/friendship according to Chinese culture

NINGEN KANKEI
human relationships according to Japanese culture

COMPADRE
friendship according to Latin American culture

CULTURAL ADIAPHORA
areas of behaviour or customs that cultural aliens may wish to conform to or participate in

control. In many developing countries with a semifeudal, land-equals-power heritage, decision-making participation by middle management tends to be de-emphasised; decisions are made by dominant family members.

In Middle Eastern countries, the top man makes all decisions and prefers to deal only with other executives with decision-making powers. There, one always does business with an individual per se rather than an office or title.

As businesses grow and professional management develops, there is a shift towards decentralised management decision making. **Decentralised decision making** allows executives, at various levels of management, authority over their own functions. This mode is typical of large-scale businesses with highly developed management systems such as those found in the United States. A trader in the United States is likely to be dealing with middle management, and title or position generally takes precedence over the individual holding the job.

Committee decision making is by group or consensus. Committees may operate on a centralised or decentralised basis, but the concept of committee management implies something quite different from the individualised functioning of top management and decentralised decision-making arrangements just discussed. Because Asian cultures and religions tend to emphasise harmony, it is not surprising that **group decision making** predominates there. Despite the emphasis on rank and hierarchy in Japanese social structure, business emphasises group participation, group harmony and group decision making – but at top management level.

The demands these three types of authority system place on a marketer's ingenuity and adaptability are evident. In the case of the authoritative and delegated societies, the chief problem would be to identify the individual with authority. In the committee decision set-up, it is necessary that every committee member be convinced of the merits of the proposition or product in question. The marketing approach to each of these situations differs.

DECENTRALISED DECISION MAKING
when every level of the organisation can make its own decisions

COMMITTEE DECISION MAKING
decision making by group or consensus

GROUP DECISION MAKING
when a group makes a decision together

Management Objectives and Aspirations

The training and background (i.e. cultural environment) of managers significantly affect their personal and business outlooks. Society as a whole establishes the social rank or status of management, and cultural background dictates patterns of aspirations and objectives among business people. These cultural influences affect the attitude of managers towards innovation, new products and conducting business with foreigners. To fully understand another's management style, one must appreciate an individual's objectives and aspirations, which are usually reflected in the goals of the business organisation and in the practices that prevail within the company. In dealing with foreign business, a marketer must be particularly aware of the varying objectives and aspirations of management.

Personal Goals   Some cultures emphasise profit or high wages while in other countries security, good personal life, acceptance, status, advancement or power may be emphasised. Individual goals are highly personal in any country, so one cannot generalise to the extent of saying that managers in any one country always have a specific orientation.

Security and Mobility   Personal security and job mobility relate directly to basic human motivation and therefore have widespread economic and social implications. The word 'security' is somewhat ambiguous and this very ambiguity provides some clues to managerial variation. To some, security means good wages and the training and ability required for moving from company to company within the business hierarchy; for others, it means the security of lifetime positions with their companies; to still others, it means adequate retirement plans and other welfare benefits.

Personal Life   For many individuals, a good personal life takes priority over profit, security or any other goal. In his worldwide study of individual aspirations, David McClelland discovered that the culture of some countries stressed the virtue of a good personal life as being far more important than profit or achievement. The **hedonistic** outlook of Ancient Greece explicitly included work as an undesirable factor that got in the way of the search for pleasure or a good personal life. Perhaps at least part of the standard of living that we enjoy in the Western world today can be attributed to the hard-working ethic from which we derive much of our business heritage.[6]

HEDONISTIC
carefree and pleasurable

Social Acceptance In some countries, acceptance by neighbours and fellow workers appears to be a predominant goal within business. The Asian outlook is reflected in the group decision making so important in Japan, and the Japanese place great importance on fitting in with their group. Group identification is so strong in Japan and some other Asian countries that when a worker is asked what he does for a living, he generally answers by

GOING INTERNATIONAL 5.3

Business protocol in a unified Europe

Now that 1992 has come and gone and the European Union is a single market, does it mean that all differences have been wiped away? For some of the legal differences, yes. For cultural differences, no.

There is always the issue of language and meaning even when both parties speak English. Then there is the matter of humour. The anecdote you open a meeting with may fly well with your own audience. However, the French will smile, the Belgians laugh, the Dutch will be puzzled and the Germans will take you literally. Humour is strongly influenced by culture and thus doesn't travel well.

And then there are the French, who are very attentive to hierarchy and ceremony. When first meet-

© iStockphoto.com/
sage78

ing with a French-speaking business person, stick with *monsieur, madame* or *mademoiselle*: the use of first names is disrespectful to the French. If you don't speak French fluently, apologise. Such apology shows general respect for the language and dismisses any stigma of arrogance.

The formality of dress can vary with each country also. The Brit, the Swede and the Dutchman will take off their jackets and roll up their sleeves; they mean to get down to business. The Spaniard will loosen his tie, while the German disapproves. He thinks they look sloppy and unbusinesslike. He keeps his coat on throughout the meeting. So does the Italian, but that was because he dressed especially for the look of the meeting.

With all that, did the meeting decide anything? It was, after all, a first meeting. The Brits were just exploring the terrain, checking out the broad perimeters and all that. The French were assessing the other players' strengths and weaknesses, and deciding what position to take at the next meeting. The Italians also won't have taken it too seriously. For them it was a meeting to arrange the meeting agenda for the real meeting. Only the Germans will have assumed it was what it seemed and be surprised when the next meeting starts open-ended.

Source: adapted from Barry Day, 'The Art of Conducting International Business', *Advertising Age*, 8 October 1990, p. 46; and Brad Ketchum Jr, 'Faux Pas Go with the Territory', *Inc.*, May 1994, pp. 4–5.

GOING INTERNATIONAL 5.6

Time: a many cultured thing

Time is cultural, subjective and variable. One of the most serious causes of frustration and friction in cross-cultural business dealings occurs when counterparts are out of sync with each other.

Differences often appear with respect to the pace of time, its perceived nature and its function. Insights into a culture's view of time may be found in their sayings and proverbs. For example:

'Time is money' (United States).

'Those who rush arrive first at the grave' (Spain).

'The clock did not invent man' (Nigeria).

'If you wait long enough, even an egg will walk' (Ethiopia).

'Before the time, it is not yet the time; after the time, it's too late' (France).

Source: adapted from Edward T. Hall and Mildred Reed Hall, *Understanding Cultural Differences* (Yarmouth, ME: Intercultural Press, 1990), p. 196; and Gart M. Wederspahn, 'On Trade and Cultures', *Trade and Culture*, Winter 1993–94, pp. 4–6.

The Westerner's desire to get straight to the point, to get down to business and other indications of directness are all manifestations of M-time cultures. The P-time system gives rise to looser time schedules, deeper involvement with individuals and a wait-and-see-what-develops attitude. For example, two Latins conversing would probably opt to be late for their next appointments rather than abruptly terminate the conversation before it came to a natural conclusion.

P-time is characterised by a much looser notion of on time or late. Interruptions are routine; delays to be expected. It is not so much putting things off until *mañana*, but the concept that human activities are not expected to proceed like clockwork (see Exhibit 5.4).

Most cultures offer a mix of P-time and M-time behaviour, but have a tendency to be either more P-time or M-time in regard to the role time plays. Some are similar to Japan where appointments are adhered to with the greatest M-time precision, but P-time is followed once a meeting begins. The Japanese see Western business people as too time-bound, and driven by schedules and deadlines that thwart the easy development of friendships. The differences between M-time and P-time are reflected in a variety of ways throughout a culture.

When business people from M-time and P-time meet, adjustments need to be made for a harmonious relationship. Often clarity can be gained by specifying tactfully, for example, whether a meeting is to be on Middle Eastern time or Western time. A Westerner who has been working successfully with the Saudis for many years says he has learned to take plenty of things to do when he travels. Others schedule appointments in their offices so they can work until their P-time friend arrives. The important thing for the Western manager to learn is adjustment to P-time in order to avoid the anxiety and frustration that comes from being out of sync with local time. As global markets expand, more business people from P-time cultures are adapting to M-time.

Negotiations Emphasis

All the above differences in business customs and culture come into play more frequently and are more obvious in the negotiating process than in any other aspect of business. The

Exhibit 5.4 Monochronic (M-time) and polychronic (P-time) behaviour

Monochronic	Polychronic
Do one thing at a time	Do many things at a time
Task oriented	People oriented
Focused and concentrated	Easily distracted and subject to interceptions
Take deadlines seriously	Deadlines are flexible and are followed if possible
Follow schedules and procedures	Schedules and procedures are considered flexible
Make and follow plans	Make plans that can easily be changed and updated
Individualist	Collectivist
Seldom borrow or lend	Borrow and lend often
Exercise promptness	Base promptness on the matter and relationship
Accustomed to short-term relationships	Accustomed to lifelong relationships
Treat time as tangible	Treat time as intangible
Value privacy	Like to be surrounded by people (family and friends)

Source: compiled from Edward Hall, 'Monochronic and Polychronic Time', in Larry Samovar and Richard Porter, *International Communication: A Reader* (Belmont, CA: Thompson, 2003), pp. 262–8.

basic elements of business negotiations are the same in any country: they relate to the product, its price and terms, services associated with the product and, finally, friendship between vendors and customers. But it is important to remember that the negotiating process is complicated and the risk of misunderstanding increases when negotiating with someone from another culture.[13]

Attitudes brought to the negotiating table by each individual are affected by many cultural factors and customs often unknown to the other individuals and perhaps unrecognised by the individuals themselves. Each negotiator's understanding and interpretation of what transpires in negotiating sessions is conditioned by his or her cultural background.[14] The possibility of offending one another or misinterpreting each other's motives is especially high when one's SRC is the basis for assessing a situation. One standard rule in negotiating is 'know thyself' first and, second, 'know your opponent'. The SRCs of both parties can come into play here if care is not taken.[15]

Gender Bias in International Business

The gender bias against women managers that exists in many countries creates hesitancy among Western multinational companies to offer women international assignments. Questions such as 'Are there opportunities for women in international business?' and 'Should women represent Western firms abroad?' frequently arise as Western companies become more international. As women move up in domestic management ranks and seek career-related international assignments, companies need to examine their positions on women managers in international business.[16]

In many cultures – Asian, Arab, Latin American and even some European ones – women are not typically found in upper levels of management. Traditional roles in male-dominated societies are often translated into minimal business opportunities for women. This cul-

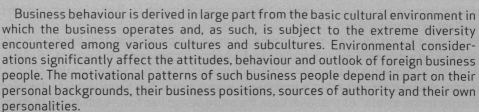

Business behaviour is derived in large part from the basic cultural environment in which the business operates and, as such, is subject to the extreme diversity encountered among various cultures and subcultures. Environmental considerations significantly affect the attitudes, behaviour and outlook of foreign business people. The motivational patterns of such business people depend in part on their personal backgrounds, their business positions, sources of authority and their own personalities.

Varying motivational patterns inevitably affect methods of doing business in different countries. Marketers in some countries thrive on competition, while in others they do everything possible to eliminate it. The authoritarian, centralised decision-making orientation in some countries contrasts sharply with democratic decentralisation in others. International variation characterises contact level, ethical orientation, negotiation outlook, and nearly every part of doing business. The foreign marketer can take no phase of business behaviour for granted.

The new breed of international business person that has emerged in recent years appears to have a heightened sensitivity to cultural variations. Sensitivity, however, is not enough; the international trader must constantly be alert and prepared to adapt when necessary. One must always realise that, no matter how long the outsider is in a country, that person is not a native; in many countries he or she may always be treated as an outsider. Finally, one must avoid the critical mistake of assuming that knowledge of one culture will provide acceptability in another.

Questions

1 'More than tolerance of an alien culture is required; there is a need for affirmative acceptance of the concept "different but equal"'. Elaborate.

2 'We should also bear in mind that in today's business-oriented world economy, the cultures themselves are being significantly affected by business activities and business practices'. Comment.

3 'In dealing with foreign businesses, the marketer must be particularly aware of the varying objectives and aspirations of management.' Explain.

4 Suggest ways in which people might prepare themselves to handle unique business customs that may be encountered during a trip abroad.

5 Business customs and national customs are closely interrelated. In which ways would one expect the two areas to coincide and in which ways would they show differences? How could such areas of similarity and difference be identified?

6 Identify both local and foreign examples of cultural imperatives, adiaphora and exclusives. Be prepared to explain why each example fits into the category you have selected.

7 Contrast the authority roles of top management in different societies. How do the different views of authority affect marketing activities?

8 What effects on business customs might be anticipated from the recent rapid integration of Europe?

9 Interview some foreign students to determine the types of cultural shock they encountered when they first came to your country.

10 Compare three decision-making authority patterns in international business.

11 Explore the various ways in which business customs can affect the structure of competition.

12 Why is it important that the business executive be alert to the significance of business customs?

13 Suggest some cautions that an individual from a high-context culture should bear in mind when dealing with someone from a low-context culture. Do the same for facing low- to high-context situations.

14 Distinguish between P-time and M-time; how can these influence international marketing?

15 Discuss how a P-time person reacts differently from an M-time person in keeping an appointment.

Further Reading

S. Harris, and C. Carr, 'National Culture Values and the Purpose of Business', *International Business Review*, 2008, 17(1), pp. 103–17.

P. Magnusson, D.W. Baack, S. Zdravkovic, K.M. Staub and L.S. Amine, 'Meta-analysis of cultural differences: Another slice at the apple', *International Business Review*, 2008, 17(5), pp. 520–32.

G. Darlington, 'Culture – A Theoretical Review', in P. Joynt and M. Warner, *Managing Across Cultures: Issues and Perspective* (London: Thompson, 1996), pp. 33–55.

Sudhir Kale, 'How National Cultures, Organisational Culture and Personality Impact Buyer–Seller Interaction', in P. Ghauri and J.-C. Usunier, *International Business Negotiations*, 2nd edn (Oxford: Elsevier/Pergamon, 2004), pp. 75–96.

References

1 Yim Yu Wong, 'The Impact of Cultural Differences on the Growing Tensions between Japan and the United States', *SAM Advanced Management Journal*, Winter 1994, pp. 40–8.

2 Edward T. Hall and Mildred Reed Hall, *Understanding Cultural Differences* (Yarmouth, ME: Intercultural Press, 1990), p. 196.

3 Geert Hofstede, 'The Business of International Business is Culture', in Peter J. Buckley and Pervez N. Ghauri (eds), *The Internationalization of the Firm* (London: International Thompson Business Press, 1999), pp. 381–93.

4 Farid Elashmawi, 'China: The Many Faces of Chinese Business Culture', *Trade & Culture*, March–April 1995, pp. 30–2.

5 Haruyasu Ohsumi, 'Cultural Differences and Japan–US Economic Frictions', *Tokyo Business Today*, February 1995, pp. 49–52.

6 *Business Week*, 'Special Report: Mega Europe', 18 November 2002, pp. 24–30.

7 For a discussion of the problems of interpretation of Japanese to English, see Osamu Katayama, 'Speaking in Tongues', *Look Japan*, March 1993, pp. 18–19.

8 Pervez Ghauri and Jean-Claude Usunier, *International Business Negotiations*, 2nd edn (Oxford: Elsevier/Pergamon, 2004).

9   Edward T. Hall, 'Learning the Arabs' Silent Language', *Psychology Today*, August 1979, pp. 45–53. Hall has several books that should be read by everyone involved in international business: *Beyond Culture* (New York: Anchor Press-Doubleday, 1976); *The Hidden Dimension* (New York: Doubleday, 1966); and *The Silent Language* (New York: Doubleday, 1959).

10 For a detailed presentation of the differences in high- and low-context cultures, see Edward T. Hall and Mildred Reed Hall, *Hidden Differences: Doing Business with the Japanese* (New York: Doubleday Anchor Books, 1990), p. 172.

11 Mo Yamin and R. Altunisik, 'A Comparison of Satisfaction Outcomes with Adapted and Non-adapted Products', *International Marketing Review*, 2003, 20(6), pp. 604–21.

12 'Tradition Plays an Important Role in the Business Culture of France', *Business America*, 6 May 1991, pp. 22–3.

13 Stephen Weiss, 'The IBM-Mexico Micro Computer Investment Negotiations', in P. Ghauri and J.-C. Usunier, *International Business Negotiations*, 2nd edn (Oxford: Elsevier/Pergamon, 2004), pp. 327–62.

14 Pervez Ghauri and Tony Fang, 'Negotiations with the Chinese: A Socio-Cultural Analysis', *Journal of World Business*, 2001, 36(3), pp. 303–25.

15 Min Chen, 'Understanding Chinese and Japanese Negotiating Styles', *The International Executive*, March–April 1993, pp. 147–59.

16 Nancy J. Adler, 'Women Managers in a Global Economy', *Training and Development*, April 1994, pp. 31–6.

17 M.T. Claes, 'Women, Men and Management Styles', *International Labor Review*, 1999, 138(4), pp. 431–46.

18 Dafna Izraeli and Yoram Zeira, 'Women Managers in International Business: A Research Review and Appraisal', *Business and the Contemporary World*, Summer 1993, p. 35.

Chapter 6
The International Political and Legal Environment

Exchange Controls   Exchange controls stem from shortages of foreign exchange held by a country. When a nation faces shortages of foreign exchange, controls may be levied over all movements of capital or, selectively, against the most politically vulnerable companies to conserve the supply of foreign exchange for the most essential uses.

Local Content Laws   In addition to restricting imports of essential supplies to force local purchase, a country often requires a portion of any product sold within that country to have local content, that is, to contain locally made parts. This is often imposed on foreign companies that assemble products from foreign-made components. The European Union and NAFTA has had a local-content requirement as high as 65 per cent for 'screwdriver operations', a name often given to foreign-owned assemblers such as Japanese motor vehicle assembly plants in the United Kingdom or in the United States of America.

Import Restrictions   Selective restrictions on the import of raw materials, machines and spare parts are fairly common strategies to force foreign industry to purchase more supplies within the host country and thereby create markets for local industry. Although this is done in an attempt to support the development of domestic industry, the result is often to hamstring and sometimes interrupt the operations of established industries. The problem then becomes critical when there are no adequately developed sources of supply within the country.

Tax Controls   Taxes must be classified as a political risk when used as a means of controlling foreign investments. In such cases they are raised without warning and in violation of formal agreements. A squeeze on profits results from taxes being raised significantly as a business becomes established. In those countries where the economy is constantly threatened with a shortage of funds, unreasonable taxation of successful foreign investments appeals to some governments as the handiest and quickest means of finding operating funds.

Price Controls   Essential products that command considerable public interest, such as pharmaceuticals, food, petrol and cars, are often subjected to price controls. Such controls applied during inflationary periods can be used by a government to control the cost of living. They may also be used to force foreign companies to sell equity to local interests. A side-effect for the local economy can be to slow or even stop capital investment.

Labour Problems   In many countries, labour unions have strong government support that they use effectively in obtaining special concessions from business. Layoffs may be forbidden, profits may have to be shared and an extraordinary number of services may have to be provided. In fact, in many countries, foreign firms are considered fair game for the demands of the domestic labour supply. Labour issues are not only a problem in developing countries; they are equally crucial in developed countries (see Exhibit 6.2).

Encouraging Foreign Investment

Governments also encourage foreign investment. In fact, within the same country, some foreign businesses fall prey to politically induced harassment while others may be placed under a government umbrella of protection and preferential treatment. The difference lies in the evaluation of a company's contribution to the national interest.

The most important reason to encourage foreign investment is to accelerate the development of an economy. An increasing number of countries are encouraging foreign investment with specific guidelines aimed towards economic goals. Multinational corporations may be expected to create local employment, transfer technology, generate export sales, stimulate growth and development of local industry, and/or conserve foreign exchange as a requirement for market concessions.[10] Recent investments in China, India and the former

Exhibit 6.2 Labour disputes

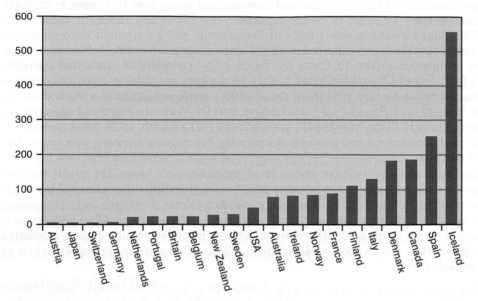

Source: based on *The Economist*, 'Labour Disputes', 24 April 2004, p. 120.

GOING INTERNATIONAL 6.2

South Korea and China: labour divide

South Korea, generally seen as offering one of the most lucrative investment opportunities for foreign companies in Asia, is in danger of losing the foreign investment to China unless its labour market is made more flexible and unions curbed. Foreign direct investment into South Korea fell from $15.22 billion in 2000 to $9.1 billion in 2001 and $2.66 billion in the first half of 2002. One of the main reasons underlying the fall in investment is worsening relations between foreign companies and local labour following the change of government and the economy's slide into recession.

Effigies of General Motors bosses are burnt as dismissed workers clash with police in Seoul
© Reuters newmedia Inc./ CORBIS

Nestlé, the Swiss food and drinks group, is considering withdrawing from South Korea because of labour unrest. The company's 450-strong workforce went on strike in July 2003 after the company refused to meet union demands for an inflation-busting 11.7 per cent pay rise and participation in management. Nestlé offered 5.6 per cent. Now the company is 'reviewing the necessity' of its factory in South Korea and investigating the legal procedures for closing it, following a 50-day strike that cost the company millions of dollars. The situation in China could not be more different. Increasing competition, falling transport costs and flagging consumer demand are forcing multinational companies to flock to the regions with lowest production costs, such as the Pearl river delta. In 2002 more goods were exported from China's Guangdong province, which encompasses the Pearl river delta, than during the entire 13-year period from 1978 to 1990. Total Chinese exports grew

GOING INTERNATIONAL 6.4

Indian court orders tests on Coca-Cola and Pepsi's soft drinks

Locals protest against Pepsi
© Sharad Saxena/
India Today)

A New Delhi court ordered independent testing of Pepsi soft drinks following allegations that they and those of Coca-Cola's Indian subsidiary were polluted with pesticides. The ruling, which follows a decision of the Indian Parliament to ban the two brands from its premises, was welcomed by PepsiCo.

The Centre for Science and Environment (CSE), the pressure group that made the allegations, said it also welcomed the ruling since it believed it would corroborate its own tests, which it says were conducted under US Government protocols. The CSE alleged that 12 soft drinks owned by the two companies contained traces of deadly pesticide, including DDT, from the groundwater that is used in the drinks.

The pressure group said the threat to public health extended far beyond the quality of soft drinks, since it was the broader contamination of water that was at issue. Indian law does not define clean water. However, the campaign to boycott Pepsi and Coke appears to be gaining momentum in parts of India. The youth wing of the Hindu nationalists has organised demonstrations where bottles of Coke and Pepsi were smashed. The Indian arms of Coca-Cola and PepsiCo hinted strongly that they were planning legal action against the CSE, a non-government body.

Four of the 30 state governments said they would test Pepsi and Coca-Cola for toxins. The two companies placed advertisements in the largest-circulation Indian newspapers seeking to counter the CSE's allegations. But many of the newspapers also carried editorials accusing the two of double standards. 'This is trial by media', said Rajeev Bakshi, chairman of Pepsi India. 'We are also concerned that there are other players [parliament and government] getting in on the act'. Pepsi said that its regular in-house tests showed that the quality of its products did conform to European Union norms. But India's standards left room for confusion. 'Our aim must surely be to get the Indian Government to establish transparent standards and procedures so that campaigns like this do not happen in this way again', said the chairman of Pepsi India.

● How should Pepsi and Coca-Cola handle this situation?

Sources: Edward Luce, 'Coca-Cola and Pepsi May Take Legal Action Over "Pesticide" Claim', *Financial Times*, 8 August 2003, p. 10; and Edward Luce, 'Indian Court Orders Further Tests on Pepsi's Soft Drinks', *Financial Times*, 12 August 2003, p. 8.

power of a third country. It is also a preferred entry strategy in countries with relatively higher political risk.

Expanding the Investment Base   Including several investors and banks in financing an investment in the host country is another strategy. This has the advantage of engaging the power of the banks whenever any kind of government takeover or harassment is threatened. This strategy becomes especially powerful if the banks have made loans to the host country; if the government threatens expropriation or other types of takeover, the financing bank has substantial power with the government.

Marketing and Distribution Controlling distribution in world markets can be used effectively if an investment should be expropriated; the expropriating country would lose access to world markets. This has proved especially useful for MNCs in the extractive industries where world markets for iron ore, copper and so forth are crucial to the success of the investment. Peru found that when Marcona Mining Company was expropriated, the country lost access to iron ore markets around the world and ultimately had to deal with Marcona on a much more favourable basis than first thought possible.

Licensing A strategy that some firms find eliminates almost all risks is to license technology for a fee. It can be effective in situations where the technology is unique and the risk is high. Of course, there is some risk assumed because the licensee can refuse to pay the required fees while continuing to use the technology.

Legal Environments

Laws governing business activities within and between countries are an integral part of the legal environment of international marketing. A Japanese company doing business with France has to contend with two jurisdictions (Japan and France), two tax systems, two legal systems and a third supranational set of European Union laws and regulations that may override French commercial law. Because no single, uniform international commercial law governing foreign business transactions exists, the international marketer must pay particular attention to the legal environment of each country within which it operates.

GOING INTERNATIONAL 6.5

Market-driven political reforms

There have long been two official perceptions of China in the United States: those who welcome economic engagement with the country and those who, by limiting contracts, would restrain its ascending power. Those committed to containment, represented mainly by the Republican Party's right wing, insist that economic engagement does not foster changes to China's repressive political system. The engagement school, on the other hand, holds that as the Chinese become wealthier, so their demands for political representation increase.

Important changes now under way in China support the case for engagement: cities in coastal China, motivated by foreign investors, are embarking on experiments to introduce checks and balances to single-party rule. Yu Youjun, mayor of Shenzhen, says that foreign companies, especially those establishing high-technology factories, are mindful of the need to protect intellectual property: 'Every multinational company and investor is influenced by the investment climate created by governments.' The 'hard environment' of roads, railways, ports and telecommunications was important, but more crucial was the 'soft environment', meaning a government that is 'democratic' and transparent.

www. adrianbradshaw. com

The crux of the current reform is a strict separation of the roles of the Communist Party, the executive government and the local legislature. The party would be responsible for setting the broad direction of policy, but would be prevented from interfering in its execution. The local legislature would be charged with reviewing and supervising the government's work. In addition, seizing on the trend for greater accountability, many cities last year opened themselves to criticism from local and

GOING INTERNATIONAL 6.6

Wal-Mart arm settles over fakes

© P. Ghauri

Sam's Club, a division of the US retailer Wal-Mart, has admitted selling fake Fendi bags and wallets and has agreed to pay an unspecified amount of money in order to make amends to the Italian fashion house's owner, LVMH. The settlement is the latest example of how luxury brand owners are becoming more publicly assertive in protecting themselves from counterfeiting.

Sam's Club operates on a membership system and promises customers 'name brands at warehouse savings'. Fendi was founded in Rome in 1925 and has become an important brand for LVMH, whose fashion and leather goods division is dominated by Louis Vuitton. Fendi sued Sam's Club last year. As part of the settlement announced yesterday afternoon, it will abandon this litigation. LVMH also sued eBay last year, alleging that the products sold on the auction site bearing the Louis Vuitton name were fakes in the vast majority of cases.

Doug McMillon, president and chief executive of Sam's Club, said in the same statement: 'We have programmes in place to protect the intellectual property rights of others. However, during this litigation, Fendi provided us with information that the 12 types of bags and wallets specifically listed in its complaint were not genuine. We accept this information.' He added: 'We recognise the importance of enforcing intellectual property rights. We expect our suppliers to respect these rights as well, and we will not tolerate deviation from that high standard.' Sam's Club members will be allowed to return any fake Fendi products that they might have bought from its stores and receive a full refund.

Source: FT, 7 June 2008, p. 25.

JURISDICTION
overall legal
authority

Determining whose legal system has **jurisdiction** when a commercial dispute arises is another problem of international marketing. A frequent error is to assume that disputes between citizens of different nations are adjudicated under some supranational system of laws. Unfortunately, no judicial body exists to deal with legal commercial problems arising between citizens of different countries. Confusion probably stems from the existence of international courts, such as the World Court in The Hague and the International Court of Justice, the principal judicial organ of the United Nations. These courts are operative in international disputes between sovereign nations of the world rather than between private citizens.

The most clear-cut decision can be made when the contracts or legal documents supporting a business transaction include a jurisdictional clause. A clause similar to the following establishes jurisdiction in the event of disagreements:

That the parties hereby agree that the agreement is made in London, UK, and that any question regarding this agreement shall be governed by the law of the United Kingdom.

Legal Recourse in Resolving International Disputes

Should the settlement of a dispute on a private basis become impossible, the foreign marketer must resort to more resolute action. Such action can take the form of conciliation, arbitration or, as a last resort, litigation. Most international business people prefer a settlement through arbitration rather than by suing a foreign company.

Conciliation

Although arbitration is recommended as the best means of settling international disputes, conciliation can be an important first step for resolving commercial disputes. **Conciliation** is a non-binding agreement between parties to resolve disputes by asking a third party to mediate the differences.

Conciliation is considered to be especially effective when resolving disputes with Chinese business partners because they are less threatened by conciliation than arbitration. The Chinese believe that when a dispute occurs, friendly negotiation should be used first to solve the problem; if that fails, conciliation should be tried. In fact, some Chinese companies may avoid doing business with companies that resort first to arbitration.

Conciliation can be either formal or informal. Informal conciliation can be established by both sides agreeing on a third party to mediate. Formal conciliation is conducted under the auspices of the Beijing Conciliation Centre, which assigns one or two conciliators to mediate. If agreement is reached, a conciliation statement based on the signed agreement is recorded. Although conciliation may be the friendly route to resolving disputes in China, it is not legally binding, so an arbitration clause should be included in all conciliation agreements.

Arbitration

International commercial disputes are often resolved by **arbitration** rather than litigation. The usual arbitration procedure is for the parties involved to select a disinterested and informed party or parties as referee(s) to determine the merits of the case and make a judgement that both parties agree to honour.

Tribunals for Arbitration Although the preceding informal method of arbitration is workable, most arbitration is conducted under the auspices of one of the more formal domestic and international arbitration groups organised specifically to facilitate the mediation of commercial disputes. These groups have experienced arbitrators available and formal rules for the process of arbitration. In most countries, decisions reached in formal mediation are enforceable under the law.

Among the formal arbitration organisations are:

1 the International Chamber of Commerce
2 the London Court of Arbitration; decisions are enforceable under English law and in English courts
3 the American Arbitration Association.

The procedures used by formal arbitration organisations are similar. Arbitration under the rules of the International Chamber of Commerce (ICC) affords an excellent example of how most organisations operate. When an initial request for arbitration is received, the chamber first attempts a conciliation between the disputants. If this fails, the process of arbitration is started. The plaintiff and the defendant select one person each from among acceptable arbitrators to defend their case, and the ICC Court of Arbitration appoints a third member, generally chosen from a list of distinguished lawyers, jurists and/or professors.

The history of ICC effectiveness in arbitration has been spectacular. An example of a case that involved arbitration by the ICC concerned a contract between an English business and a Japanese manufacturer. The English business agreed to buy 100 000 plastic dolls for 80 cents each. On the strength of the contract, the English business sold the

CONCILIATION
a non-binding agreement between parties to resolve disputes by asking a third party to mediate

ARBITRATION
mediation done by a third party in case of a commercial dispute

entire lot at $1.40 per doll. Before the dolls were delivered, the Japanese manufacturer had a strike; the settlement of the strike increased costs and the English business was informed that the delivery price of the dolls had increased from 80 cents to $1.50 each. The English business maintained that the Japanese firm had committed to make delivery at 80 cents and should deliver at that price. Each side was convinced that it was right. The Japanese, accustomed to code law, felt that the strike was beyond control, was an act of God, and thus compliance with the original provisions of the contract was excused. The English, accustomed to common law, did not accept the Japanese reasons for not complying because they considered a strike the normal course of doing business and not an act of God. The dispute could not be settled except through arbitration or litigation. They chose arbitration; the ICC appointed an arbitrator who heard both sides and ruled that the two parties would share proportionately in the loss. Both parties were satisfied with the arbitration decision and costly litigation was avoided. Most arbitration is successful, but success depends on the willingness of both parties to accept the arbitrator's rulings.

Litigation

LITIGATION
taking the other party to court

Lawsuits in public courts are avoided for many reasons. Most observers of **litigation** between citizens of different countries believe that almost all victories are spurious because the cost, frustrating delays and extended aggravation that these cases produce are more oppressive by far than any matter of comparable size. The best advice is to seek a settlement, if possible, rather than sue.

One authority suggests that the settlement of every dispute should follow three steps: first, try to placate the injured party; if this does not work, conciliate, arbitrate; and, finally, litigate. The final step is typically taken only when all other methods fail. Actually, this advice is probably wise whether one is involved in an international dispute or a domestic one.

GOING INTERNATIONAL 6.7

Counterfeit, pirated or the original: take your choice

© Dave Bartruff/
CORBIS

Intellectual properties – trademarks, brand names, designs, manufacturing processes, formulas – are valuable company assets that US officials estimate are knocked off to the tune of $800 million (€720 million) a year due to counterfeiting and/or pirating. Some examples from China are given below.

● Design rip-offs. Beijing Jeep Corporation, a Chrysler Corporation joint venture, found more than 2000 four-wheel-drive vehicles designed to look nearly identical to its popular Cherokee model.
● Product rip-offs. Exact copies of products made by Procter & Gamble, Colgate Palmolive, Reebok and Nike are common throughout southern China. Exact copies of any Madonna album are available for as little as $1, as are CDs and movies. One executive says, 'They'll actually hire workers away from the real factories'.
● Brand name ripoffs. Bausch & Lomb's Ray Ban sunglasses become Ran Bans. Colgate in the familiar bright red becomes Cologate. The familiar Red Rooster on Kellogg's Corn Flakes appears on Kongalu Corn Strips packages that state 'the trustworthy sign of quality which is famous around the world'.

- Book ripoffs. Even the rich and powerful fall prey to pirating. Soon after *My Father, Deng Xiaoping*, a biography written by Deng Rong, daughter of Deng Xiaoping, was published, thousands of illegal copies flooded the market.
- Original versions of the products mentioned above are also sold in China by the true owners.

While joining the WTO, China passed a law allowing customers to demand a double refund for fake merchandise sold in department stores. This led to a new business for some. Wang Hai claimed to have made $10 000 buying bogus phones and fax machines and then getting a double refund: 'If I had more money, I would have emptied out every store in Beijing.' The 'Wang Hai Phenomenon' is forcing department stores to stop stocking counterfeit products.

Sources: adapted from Marcus W. Brauchli, 'Chinese Flagrantly Copy Trademarks of Foreigners', *The Wall Street Journal*, 26 June 1994, p. B-1; Bob Davis, 'US Plans to Probe Piracy in China, Raising Possibility of Trade Sanctions', *The Wall Street Journal*, 28 June 1994, p. A-2; Chin-Ching Ni, 'Anti-counterfeit Law Allows Chinese Customer to Cash in', *Los Angeles Times*, 14 September 2002, p. A-3.

Protection of Intellectual Property Rights: a Special Problem

Companies spend millions of dollars establishing brand names or trademarks to symbolise quality and a host of other product features designed to entice customers to buy their brands to the exclusion of all others. Such intellectual or industrial properties are among the more valuable assets a company may possess. Names such as Philips, Sony, Swatch, Kodak, Coca-Cola and Gucci, and rights to processes such as xerography and computer software are invaluable.

TRADEMARKS registered 'mark' or 'logo' for a company or business

Estimates are that more than 10 million fake Swiss watches carrying famous brand names such as Cartier and Rolex are sold every year, netting illegal profits of at least €550 million ($600 million). Although difficult to pinpoint, lost sales from the unauthorised use of patents, **trademarks** and copyrights amount to more than €90 billion ($100 billion) annually. That translates into more than a million lost jobs. Software is an especially

GOING INTERNATIONAL 6.8

Protection of counterfeited pills

Packets of a Chinese version of the sex-enhancing Viagra pills were put on sale at a park in the Chinese city of Shenyang. The shape and composition of the fake Viagra pills, which has been declared as 'pearl calcium', were similar to the real thing. The Chinese police raided an underground crime ring that was churning out millions of counterfeit Viagra pills to hopeful men across the country's southeast. Since the real Viagra costs more than four times as much as the fake pills, many customers bought the fake pills for use as business gifts.

A Chinese version of the Viagra pill.
©AFP/CORBIS

attractive target for pirates because it is costly to develop but cheap to reproduce. Unauthorised software that sells for €450 ($500) in the United States and United Kingdom can be purchased for less than €9 ($10) in the Far East.

The failure to protect intellectual or industrial property rights adequately in the world marketplace can lead to the legal loss of these rights in potentially profitable markets. Because **patents**, processes, trademarks and copyrights are valuable in all countries, some companies have found their assets appropriated and profitably exploited in foreign countries without a licence or reimbursement. Further, they often learn that not only are other firms producing and selling their products or using their trademarks, but also that the foreign companies are the rightful owners in the countries where they are operating.

There have been many cases where companies have legally lost the rights to trademarks and have had to buy back these rights or pay royalties for their use. Such was the case with McDonald's in Japan. Its 'Golden Arches' trademark was registered by an enterprising Japanese company. Only after a lengthy and costly legal action with a trip to the Japanese Supreme Court was McDonald's able to regain the exclusive right to use the trademark in Japan. After having to 'buy' its trademark for an undisclosed amount, McDonald's maintains a very active programme to protect its trademarks.

Prior Use versus Registration

In many code-law countries, ownership is established by registration rather than by prior use – the first to register a trademark or other property right is considered the rightful owner. In the United States, a common-law country, ownership of intellectual property rights is established by prior use – whoever can establish first use is typically considered the rightful owner. In Jordan a trademark belongs to whoever registers it first in that country. Thus, you can find a 'McDonald's' restaurant, 'Microsoft' software and 'Safeway' groceries all legally belonging to a Jordanian.[21] A company that believes it can always establish ownership in another country by proving it used the trademark or brand name first is wrong and risks the loss of these assets. It is best to protect intellectual property rights through registration. Several international conventions provide for simultaneous registration in member countries.

International Conventions

Many countries participate in international conventions designed for mutual recognition and protection of intellectual property rights. There are three major international conventions.

1 The **Paris Convention** for the Protection of Industrial Property, commonly referred to as the Paris Convention, is a group of 100 nations that have agreed to recognise the rights of all members in the protection of trademarks, patents and other property rights. Registration in one of the member countries ensures the same protection afforded by the home country in all the member countries.
2 The **Madrid Arrangement** established the Bureau for International Registration of Trademarks. There are some 26 member countries in Europe that have agreed to automatic trademark protection for all members. Even though the United States is not a participant of the Madrid Arrangement, if a subsidiary of a US company is located in one of the member countries, the subsidiary could file through the membership of its host country and thereby provide protection in all 26 countries for the US company.
3 The **Inter-American Convention** includes most of the Latin American nations and the United States. It provides protection similar to that afforded by the Paris Convention.

With these three agreements, two multi-country patent arrangements have streamlined patent procedures in Europe. The Patent Cooperation Treaty (PCT) facilitates the

PATENT
any product or formula/ technology registered with the relevant office that establishes who possesses the right of ownership

PARIS CONVENTION
a group of 100 nations that have agreed to recognise the rights of all members in the protection of trademarks, patents and other property rights

MADRID ARRANGEMENT
some 26 member countries in Europe that have agreed to automatic trademark protection for all members

INTER-AMERICAN CONVENTION
provides protection similar to that afforded by the Paris Convention

application of patents among its member countries. The European Patent Convention (EPC) establishes a regional patent system allowing any nationality to file a single international application for a European patent. Once the patent is approved, it has the same effect as a national patent in each individual country designated on the application.

In addition, the European Union (EU) has approved its Trademark Regulation, which will provide intellectual property protection throughout all member states. Companies have a choice between relying on national systems, when they want to protect a trademark in just a few member countries, or the European system, when protection is sought throughout the EU. Trademark protection is valid for 10 years and is renewable. However, if the mark is not used for five years, protection is forfeited.[22]

Commercial Law within Countries

Marketing Laws

All countries have laws regulating marketing activities in promotion, product development, labelling, pricing and channels of distribution. In some, there may be only a few laws, with lax enforcement; in others, there may be detailed, complicated rules to follow that are stringently enforced. There often are vast differences in enforcement and interpretation among countries having laws covering the same activities. Laws governing sales promotions in the EU offer good examples of such diversity.

In Austria, **premium offers** to consumers come under the discount law that prohibits any cash reductions that give preferential treatment to different groups of customers. Because most premium offers would result in discriminatory treatment of buyers, they normally are not allowed. Premium offers in Finland are allowed with considerable scope as long as the word 'free' is not used and consumers are not coerced into buying products. France also regulates premium offers, which are, for all practical purposes, illegal because it is illegal to sell for less than cost price or to offer a customer a gift or premium conditional on the purchase of another product. Furthermore, a manufacturer or retailer cannot

PREMIUM OFFERS
special offers or
high-priced offers

GOING INTERNATIONAL 6.9

Chinese court hands victory to Nike in trademark case

Nike, the US sports clothing company, has won a controversial court order in China to prevent a Spanish company from manufacturing and exporting clothing from the mainland using the 'Nike' name. The Spanish company, Cidesport, owns the right to use the Nike name in Spain and had been planning to sell the goods made in China solely in its home country, according to evidence before the court. However, the court ruled that the sample of the goods in China had breached Nike's China registered trademark.

'The protection of the brand [in China] covers not only final consumption, but also the manufacturing of it,' said Tao Xinliang of Shanghai University.

© P. Ghauri

Despite the unusual circumstances, the decision reflects the growing propensity of Chinese courts to uphold the intellectual property rights of foreign brands.

one administration may find its activities completely undesirable under another. The EU may aid European business in its foreign operations and, if a company is considered vital to achieving national economic goals, the host country often provides an umbrella of protection not extended to others. An unfamiliar or hostile political environment does not necessarily preclude success for a foreign marketer if the marketer's plans are such that the company becomes a local economic asset.

Business faces a multitude of problems in its efforts to develop a successful marketing programme. Not the least of these problems are the varying legal systems of the world and their effect on business transactions. Just as political climate, cultural differences, local geography, different business customs and the stage of economic development must be taken into account, so must such legal questions as jurisdictional and legal recourse in disputes, protection of industrial property rights, extended law enforcement and enforcement of anti-trust legislation by foreign governments. A primary marketing task is to develop a plan that will be enhanced, or at least not adversely affected, by these and other environmental elements. The myriad questions created by different laws and different legal systems indicate that the prudent path to follow at all stages of foreign marketing operations is one leading to competent counsel well versed in the intricacies of the international legal environment.

Questions

1 Why would a country rather domesticate than expropriate?
2 How can government-initiated domestication be the same as confiscation?
3 What are the main factors to consider in assessing the dominant political climate within a country?
4 Why is a working knowledge of political party philosophy so important in a political assessment of a market? Discuss.
5 What are the most frequently encountered political risks in foreign business? Discuss.
6 What are the factors that influence the risk-reduction process in international marketing?
7 Discuss measures a company might take to lessen its political vulnerability.
8 Select a country and analyse it politically from a marketing viewpoint.
9 How does the international marketer determine which legal system will have jurisdiction when legal disputes arise?
10 Discuss some of the reasons why it is probably best to seek an out-of-court settlement in international commercial legal disputes rather than to sue.
11 Illustrate the procedure generally followed in international commercial disputes when settled under the auspices of a formal arbitration tribunal.
12 What are intellectual property rights? Why should a company in international marketing take special steps to protect them?

Further Reading

A. Lee Hadjikhani and P.N. Ghauri, 'Network view of MNCs socio-political behaviour', *Journal of Business Research*, 2008, 61, pp. 912–24.

L.S. Amine, 'Country-of-origin, animosity and consumer response: Marketing implications of anti-Americanism and Francophobia', *International Business Review*, 2008, 17(4), pp. 402–22.

P.-X. Meschi and L. Riccio, 'Country risk, national cultural differences between partners and survival of international joint ventures in Brazil', *International Business Review*, 2008, 17(3), pp. 250–66.

A. Hadjikhani and P. Ghauri, 'The Behaviour of International Firms in Socio-Political Environments in the European Union', *Journal of Business Research*, 2001, 52(3), pp. 263–75.

References

1 For an account of political change and potential effect on economic growth, see 'China: is Prosperity Creating a Freer Society?', *Business Week*, 6 June 1994, pp. 94–9.

2 Jean J. Boddewyn and Thomas L. Brewer, 'International-Business Political Behavior: New Theoretical Directions', *Academy of Management Review*, vol. 19, no. 1, 1994, pp. 119–43.

3 Niccolo d'Aguino, 'Italy's Political Future', *Europe*, June 1994, pp. 4–8.

4 Visit Pepsi's Russian website for the history of Pepsi in Russia: www.pepsi.ru.

5 Kent Granzin and John Painter, 'Motivational Influences on "Buy Domestic" Purchasing: Marketing Management Implications from a Study of Two Nations', *Journal of International Marketing*, 9(2), 2001, pp. 73–96.

6 Richard Whalen, 'The New Nationalism', *Across the Board*, January/February, 2002; and Harold James, *The End of Globalization: Lessons from the Great Depression* (Boston: Harvard University Press, 2001).

7 Amitaz Ghosh, 'The Mask of Nationalism', *Business India*, 1993 Anniversary Issue, pp. 47–50.

8 Peter J. Buckley and Pervez N. Ghauri (eds), *The Global Challenge for Multinational Enterprises* (Amsterdam: Elsevier, 1999).

9 Lars Oxelheim and Pervez Ghauri (eds), *European Union and the Race for Foreign Direct Investment in Europe* (Oxford: Elsevier, 2004).

10 Lars Oxelheim (ed.), *The Global Race for Foreign Direct Investment: Prospects for Future* (Berlin: Springer-Verlag, 1993).

11 Peter J. Buckley and Pervez N. Ghauri (eds), *The Global Challenge for Multinational Enterprises* (Amsterdam: Elsevier, 1999).

12 Sandeep Tyagi, 'The Giant Awakens: An Interview with Professor Jagdish Bhagwatti on Economic Reform in India', *Columbia Journal of World Business*, Spring 1994, pp. 14–23.

13 Rahul Jacob, 'Coke Adds Fizz to India', *Fortune*, 10 January 1994, pp. 14–15.

14 For a comprehensive review of political risk analysis, see Frederick Stapenhurst, 'Political Risk Analysis in North American Multinationals: An Empirical Review and Assessment', *The International Executive*, March–April 1995, pp. 127–45.

15 For a discussion of problems associated with hostile publics and infrastructure projects, see Amjad Hadjikhani, 'International Businesses and Political Crisis: Swedish MNCs in a Turbulent Market', *Acta Universitatis Uppsaliances*, series Studia Oeconomiae Negotiorum, no. 40, Uppsala, 1996.

16 Goran Therborn, 'The World's Trader, the World's Lawyer: Europe and Global Processes', *European Journal of Social Theory*, November 2002, pp. 403–17.

17 Industrial property rights and intellectual property rights are used interchangeably. The more common term used today is intellectual property rights to refer to patents, copyrights, trademarks and so forth.

Part 3

Assessing International Market Opportunities

Chapter 7
Researching International Markets

MARKETING
RESEARCH
the systematic
gathering,
recording and
analysing of data
to provide
information useful
in marketing
decision making

Exhibit 7.2 The marketing research process and the international dimension

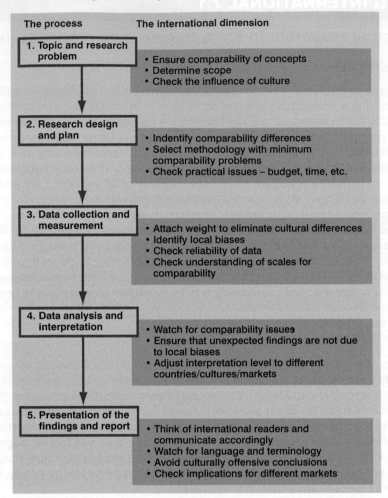

The process	The international dimension
1. Topic and research problem	• Ensure comparability of concepts • Determine scope • Check the influence of culture
2. Research design and plan	• Indentify comparability differences • Select methodology with minimum comparability problems • Check practical issues – budget, time, etc.
3. Data collection and measurement	• Attach weight to eliminate cultural differences • Identify local biases • Check reliability of data • Check understanding of scales for comparability
4. Data analysis and interpretation	• Watch for comparability issues • Ensure that unexpected findings are not due to local biases • Adjust interpretation level to different countries/cultures/markets
5. Presentation of the findings and report	• Think of international readers and communicate accordingly • Watch for language and terminology • Avoid culturally offensive conclusions • Check implications for different markets

UNFAMILIAR ENVIRONMENT
environment with which a company is not familiar, especially when it is a foreign market

PROBLEM DEFINITION
explaining the research problem

CONSUMPTION PATTERNS
how consumers buy a particular product

This first step in research is more critical in foreign markets since an **unfamiliar environment** tends to cloud problem definition. Researchers either fail to anticipate the influence of the local culture on the problem or fail to identify the self-reference criterion (SRC) and so treat the **problem definition** as if it were in the researcher's home environment. In assessing some foreign business failures it is apparent that research was conducted, but the questions asked were more appropriate for the home market than for the foreign one. For example, Unilever introduced a super-concentrated detergent to the Japanese market only to find out that a premeasured package on which it was trying to differentiate its product was unacceptable to the market because it didn't dissolve in the wash, the product was not designed to work in a new, popular low-agitation washing machine and the 'fresh smell' positioning of the detergent was not relevant in Japan since most consumers hang their washing outside to dry in the fresh air.[6] Did the company conduct research? Yes. Were appropriate questions asked? No.

Other difficulties in foreign research stem from a failure to establish problem limits broad enough to include all relevant variables. Information on a far greater range of factors is necessary to offset the unfamiliar cultural background of the foreign market. Consider proposed research about **consumption patterns** and attitudes towards hot milk-based drinks. In the United Kingdom hot milk-based drinks are considered to have

sleep-inducing, restful and relaxing properties, and are traditionally consumed prior to bedtime. People in Thailand, however, drink the same hot milk-based drinks in the morning on the way to work and see them as being invigorating, energy-giving and stimulating. If one's only experience is in the United States, the picture is further clouded since hot milk-based drinks are frequently associated with cold weather, either in the morning or the evening, and for different reasons at each time of day. The market researcher must be certain the problem definition is sufficiently defined to cover the relevant range of response possibilities and not be clouded by his or her SRC.

Developing a Research Plan

Once a research problem is clear and its objectives have been defined, it is important to plan the research process. This should be done irrespective of whether the company will undertake the work with its own resources or use outside agencies. The tasks to be undertaken should be specified and alternative methodologies should be evaluated. In this process an appropriate **methodology** should be selected. For example, which type of research, quantitative or qualitative, should be done. The theories/models we can use to find answers to research questions are also to be identified here. While selecting these methodologies, the comparability of research findings and their usefulness must be kept in mind.

METHODOLOGY
way of doing market research

Quantitative and Qualitative Research

Marketing research methods can be grouped into two basic types, quantitative and qualitative research. In both methods, the marketer is interested in gaining knowledge about the market.

In **quantitative research**, the respondent is asked to reply either verbally or in writing to structured questions using a specific response format such as 'yes' or 'no', or to select a response from a set of choices. Questions are designed to get a specific response to aspects of the respondent's behaviour, intentions, attitudes, motives and demographic characteristics. This type of quantitative or survey research provides the marketer with responses that can be presented with precise estimations. The structured responses received in a survey can be summarised in percentages, averages or other statistics. For example, 76 per cent of the respondents prefer product A over product B, and so on.

QUANTITATIVE RESEARCH
structured questioning, producing answers that can easily be converted to numerical data

Survey research is generally associated with quantitative research, and the typical instrument used is the questionnaire administered by personal interview, mail or telephone.

Qualitative research, on the other hand, is open-ended, in-depth and seeks unstructured responses that reflect the person's thoughts and feelings on the subject. Qualitative research interprets what the 'people in the sample are like, their outlooks, their feelings, the dynamic interplay of their feelings and ideas, their attitudes and opinions, and their resulting actions'.[7] The most often used forms of qualitative questioning are the focus group, interviews and case studies.

QUALITATIVE RESEARCH
open-ended and in-depth, seeking unstructured responses. Expresses the respondent's thoughts and feelings

Qualitative research is also used in international marketing research to formulate and define a problem more clearly and to determine relevant questions to be examined in subsequent research. It is used where interest is centred on gaining an understanding of a market, rather than quantifying relevant aspects.

When a British childrens-wear subsidiary of Sears was planning to enter the Spanish market, there was concern about the differences in attitudes and buying patterns of the Spanish from those in the United Kingdom, and about market differences that might possibly exist among Spain's five major trading areas of Barcelona, Madrid, Seville, Bilbao and Valencia. Because the types of retail outlet in Spain were substantially different from those in the United Kingdom, 'accompanied shopping interviews'[8] were used to explore shoppers' attitudes about different types of store. In the **interviews**, respondents were accompanied on visits to different outlets selling childrens-wear. During the visit to each shop, the respondent talked the interviewer through what she was seeing and feeling.

INTERVIEWS
when we talk to people to get information on specific matters

This enabled the interviewer to see the outlet through the eyes of the shopper, and to determine the criteria with which she evaluated the shopping environment and the products available. Information gathered in these studies and other focus group studies helped the company develop a successful entry strategy into Spain.

Qualitative research is also helpful in revealing the impact of sociocultural factors on behaviour patterns and to develop **research hypotheses** that can be tested in subsequent studies designed to quantify the concepts and relevant relationships uncovered in qualitative data collection. Research conducted by Procter & Gamble in Egypt offers an example of how qualitative research leads to specific points that can later be measured by using survey or quantitative research.

For years Procter & Gamble had marketed Ariel Low Suds brand laundry detergent to the 5 per cent of homes in the Egyptian market that had automatic washing machines. It planned to expand its presence in the Egyptian market and commissioned a study to (1) identify the most lucrative opportunities in the Egyptian laundry market and (2) develop the right concept, product, price, brand name, package and advertising copy once the decision was made to pursue a segment of the laundry market.

The 'Habits and Practices' study, P&G's name for this phase, consisted of home visits and discussion groups (qualitative research) to understand how the Egyptian housewife did her laundry. They wanted to know her likes, dislikes and habits (the company's knowledge of laundry practices in Egypt had been limited to automatic washing machines). From this study, it was determined that the Egyptian consumer goes through a very laborious washing process to achieve the desired results. Among the 95 per cent of homes that washed in a non-automatic washing machine or by hand, the process consisted of soaking, boiling, bleaching and washing each load several times. Several products were used in the process; bar soaps or flakes were added to the main wash, along with liquid bleach and bluing to enhance the cleaning performance of the poor-quality locally produced powders. These findings highlighted the potential for a high-performing detergent that would accomplish everything that currently required several products. The decision was made to proceed with the development and introduction of a superior-performing high-suds granular detergent.

Once the basic product concept (i.e. one product instead of several to do laundry) was decided on, the company needed to determine the best components for a marketing mix to introduce the new product. The company went back to **focus groups** to assess reactions to different brand names (they were considering Ariel, already in the market as a low-suds detergent for automatic washers, and Tide, which had been marketed in Egypt in the 1960s and 1970s) to get ideas about the appeal and relevant wording for promotions, and to test various price ranges, package design and size. Information derived from focus-group encounters helped the company eliminate ideas with low consumer appeal and focus on those that triggered the most interest. Further, the groups helped refine advertising and promotion wording to ensure clarity of communication through the use of everyday consumer language.

At the end of this stage, the company had well-defined ideas garnered from several focus groups, but did not have a 'feel' for the rest of those in the target market. Would they respond the same way the focus groups had? To answer this question, the company proceeded to the next step, a research programme to validate the relative appeal of the concepts generated from focus groups with a survey (quantitative research) of a large sample from the target market. Additionally, brand name, price, size and the product's intended benefits were tested in large sample surveys. Information gathered in the final **surveys** provided the company with the specific information used to develop a marketing programme that led to a successful product introduction and brand recognition for Ariel throughout Egypt.[9]

Qualitative and quantitative research is not always coupled as in the example of Procter & Gamble's research on Ariel. Qualitative research is also used alone where a small sample of carefully selected consumers is sufficient. For example, it is often difficult for

RESEARCH HYPOTHESIS
a theory that can be proved or rejected via research

FOCUS GROUPS
a group of people who are considered relevant for our product and can provide us with useful information

SURVEYS
when we collect information through a list of questions

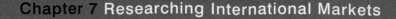

respondents to know whether a product, flavour, concept or some other new idea is appealing if they have no experience with the issue being studied. To simply ask in a direct way may result in no response or, worse, a response that does not reflect how respondents would react if they had more experience.

In another case, Cadbury's, a UK firm, was looking for a way to give its chocolate cream liqueur a unique flavour. One idea was to add a hint of hazelnut flavouring. Yet when the company suggested verbally that the liqueur should be changed in this way, consumers reacted negatively because they were unfamiliar with the mix of the two flavours. However, when taste tests were done without revealing what the extra flavours were, consumers loved the result.[10]

Gathering Secondary Data

The breadth of many foreign marketing research studies and the marketer's lack of familiarity with a country's basic socioeconomic and cultural data result in considerable demand for information generally available from secondary sources in the Western countries. Unfortunately, such data are not as available in foreign markets. Most Western governments provide comprehensive statistics for their home markets; periodic censuses of population, housing, business and agriculture are conducted and, in some cases, have been taken for over 100 years. Commercial sources, trade associations, management groups, and state and local governments also provide the researcher with additional sources of detailed market information.

While data collection has only recently begun in many countries, it is improving substantially through the efforts of organisations such as the United Nations and the Organisation for Economic Co-operation and Development (OECD). As a country becomes more important as a market, a greater interest in basic data and better collection methods develop. The problems of availability, reliability, comparability of data and validating **secondary data** are described below.

With the emergence of Eastern European countries as potentially viable markets, a number of private and public groups are funding the collection of information to offset a lack of comprehensive market data. Several Japanese consumer goods manufacturers are coordinating market research on a corporate level and have funded 47 research centres throughout Eastern Europe. As market activity continues in Eastern Europe and elsewhere, market information will improve in quantity and quality. To build a **database** on Russian consumers, one Western firm used a novel approach to conduct a survey. It ran a questionnaire in Moscow's *Komsomolskaya Pravda* newspaper asking for replies to be sent to the company. The 350 000 replies received (3000 by registered mail) attested to the willingness of Russian consumers to respond to market enquiries.

SECONDARY DATA
information that somebody else has collected, but that we can use for our purpose

DATABASE
a bank/storage of information on a particular issue

Availability of Data   A critical shortcoming of secondary data on foreign markets is the paucity of detailed data for many market areas. Much of the secondary data a Western marketer is accustomed to having about Western markets is just not available for many countries. Detailed data on the numbers of wholesalers, retailers, manufacturers and facilitating services, for example, are unavailable for many parts of the world; the same applies to data on population and income. Most countries simply do not have governmental agencies that collect, on a regular basis, the kinds of secondary data readily available in, say, the United States, the Netherlands, Germany and the Scandinavian countries. If such information is important, the marketer must initiate the research or rely on private sources of data.

Reliability of Data   Available data may not have the level of reliability necessary for confident decision making for many reasons. Official statistics are sometimes too optimistic, reflecting national pride rather than practical reality, while tax structures and fear of the tax collector often adversely affect data.

Gathering Primary Data

PRIMARY DATA
data that has been
collected for the
research at hand

If, after seeking all reasonable secondary data sources, research questions can still not be adequately answered, the market researcher must collect **primary data**. The researcher may question the firm's sales force, distributors, middlemen and/or customers to get appropriate market information. In most primary data collection, the researcher questions respondents to determine what they think about some topic or how they might behave under certain conditions.

The problems of collecting primary data in foreign countries are different only in degree from those encountered at home. Assuming the research problems are well defined and objectives are properly formulated, the success of primary research hinges on the ability of the researcher to get correct and truthful information that addresses the research objectives. Most problems in collecting primary data in international marketing research stem from cultural differences among countries, and range from the inability of respondents to communicate their opinions to inadequacies in questionnaire translation (see Exhibit 7.3).

PRIMARY DATA
data that has been
collected for the
research at hand

Exhibit 7.3 Problems with gathering primary data

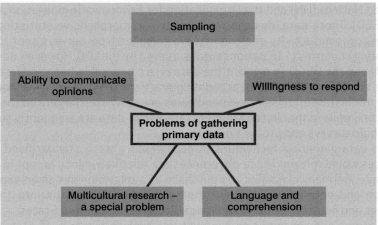

Ability to Communicate Opinions The ability to express attitudes and opinions about a product or concept depends on the respondent's ability to recognise the usefulness and value of such a product or concept. It is difficult for a person to formulate needs, attitudes and opinions about goods whose use may not be understood, that are not in common use within the community or that have never been available. For example, it may be impossible for someone who has never had the benefits of some type of air conditioning in the home to express accurate feelings or provide any reasonable information about purchase intentions, or likes and dislikes concerning electric air conditioning. The more complex the concept, the more difficult it is to design research that will help the respondent communicate meaningful opinions and reactions. Under these circumstances, the creative capabilities of the foreign marketing researcher are challenged.

Willingness to Respond Cultural differences offer the best explanation for the unwillingness or the inability of many to respond to research surveys. The role of the male, the suitability of personal gender-based enquiries, and other gender-related issues can affect willingness to respond. In some countries, the husband not only earns the money, but also dictates exactly how it is to be spent. Because the husband controls the spending, it is he, not the wife, who should be questioned to determine preferences and demand for

many consumer goods. In some cultures, women would never consent to be interviewed by a male or a stranger. A French Canadian woman does not like to be questioned and is likely to be reticent in her responses.

Anyone asking questions about any topic from which tax assessment could be inferred is immediately suspected of being a tax agent. Citizens of many Western countries do not feel the same legal and moral obligations to pay their taxes. So, tax evasion is an accepted practice for many and a source of pride for the more adept. Where such an attitude exists, taxes are arbitrarily assessed by the government, which results in much incomplete or misleading information being reported. One of the problems revealed by the government of India in a recent population census was the under-reporting of tenants by landlords trying to hide the actual number of people living in houses and flats. The landlords or tenants had been subletting accommodations illegally and were concealing their activities from the tax department.

Although such cultural differences may make survey research more difficult to conduct, it is possible. In some communities, locally prominent people could open otherwise closed doors; in other situations, professional people and local students have been used as interviewers because of their knowledge of the market.

Sampling in Field Surveys   The greatest problem of **sampling** stems from the lack of adequate **demographic data** and available lists from which to draw meaningful samples. If current reliable lists are not available, sampling becomes more complex and generally less reliable. In many countries, telephone directories, cross-index street directories, census tract and block data, and detailed social and economic characteristics of the population being studied are not available on a current basis, if at all.

To add to the confusion, in some South American, Mexican and Asian cities, street maps are unavailable, and, in some Asian metropolitan areas, streets are not identified or marked. In contrast, one of the positive aspects of research in Japan and Taiwan is the availability and accuracy of **census data** on individuals. In these countries, when a household moves it is required to submit up-to-date information to a centralised government agency before it can use communal services such as water, gas, electricity and education.

The effectiveness of various methods of communication (mail, telephone and personal interview) in surveys is limited. In many countries, telephone ownership is extremely low, making telephone surveys virtually worthless unless the survey is intended to cover only the wealthy. In some countries, fewer than 5 per cent of residents – only the wealthy – have telephones.

The problem of sampling was best summarised by one authority on research in Saudi Arabia who commented that probability sampling there was very difficult, if not impossible. The difficulties are so acute that non-probabilistic sampling becomes a necessary evil.[14] The kinds of problem encountered in drawing a random sample include:

- no officially recognised census of population
- no other listings that can serve as sampling frames
- incomplete and out-of-date telephone directories
- no accurate maps of population centres; thus, no cluster (area) samples can be made.

Furthermore, door-to-door interviewing in Saudi Arabia is illegal. While all the conditions described do not exist in all countries, they illustrate why the collection of primary data requires creative applications of research techniques when expanding into many foreign markets.[15]

Language and Comprehension   The most universal survey sampling problem in foreign countries is the language barrier. Differences in idiom and the difficulty of exact translation create problems in eliciting the specific information desired and in interpreting the respondents' answers. Equivalent concepts may not exist in all languages.[16]

SAMPLING
selection of potential respondents

DEMOGRAPHIC DATA
information on the demographics of a country/city/area

CENSUS DATA
a record of population and its breakdown

161

GOING INTERNATIONAL 7.4

France has stolen a march on the US in economic intelligence

© iStockphoto.com/
SteveStone

In a report to the US Congress earlier this month, the Central Intelligence Agency named the French services, along with the Israelis, as the most active in launching operations against American interests, both inside and outside the United States. Recently, the DGSE, the French secret service, has stepped up operations in areas such as Bosnia, Algeria and Russia.

The emphasis has continued to shift towards economic intelligence. The ability to intercept secret offers made by US armament firms to Middle Eastern countries has allowed French firms to propose better deals. In 1997 they broke into the lucrative Saudi defence market for the first time by signing a contract for the sale of 12 helicopters built by Eurocopter. The recent CIA report accused the French specifically of launching intelligence operations against US military contractors and high-technology firms. In the report, national security specialist David E. Cooper describes the intelligence-gathering of a particular country, clearly identifiable as France, which 'recruited agents at the European offices of three US computer and electronic firms'.

According to sources, IBM in Brussels and Texas Instruments were two of those targets. Clearly, France is not the only country to seek such information. In 1994, President Bill Clinton asked the FBI to launch an economic counter-intelligence programme. Former DGSE director Admiral Pierce Lacoste told *The European*:

> 'It is part of an indirect strategy by the US. They want all the trumps. Initially their target was Japan. But now it is France, for two main reasons. First, France is seen as one of the most vocal and active countries over the strengthening of the European Union and a single currency; and second, because this country is organizing a new economic intelligence system.'

While continuing with traditional intelligence, French President Jacques Chirac set up a special economic and technological intelligence coordination body, inspired by the highly effective Japanese Ministry of International Trade and Industry. The Comité pour la Competitivité et la Securité Économique (CCSE) is led by seven 'wise men', including banker Bernard Esambert, Matra boss Jean-Luc Lagardère and Henri Martre, former chairman of Aérospatiale and author of a detailed study on economic intelligence.

'This is essentially the start of a cultural shift on the part of French industrial and commercial intelligence. But this process will take some time to come to fruition,' said Lacoste. 'Obviously, the French and future European intelligence would play some role in this. They could not allow the CIA to be the only secret service operating in that field'.

● Do you think companies should have economic intelligence departments, to better forecast the demand?

Source: The European, 29 August–4 September 1996.

and demographic relationships. Some of the necessary but frequently unavailable statistics for assessing market opportunity and estimating demand for a product are current trends in market demand.

When the desired statistics are not available, a close approximation can be made using local production figures plus imports, with adjustments for exports and current inventory

levels. These data are more readily available because they are commonly reported by the United Nations and other international agencies. Once approximations for sales trends are established, historical series can be used as the basis for projections of growth.[21] In any straight extrapolation, however, the estimator assumes that the trends of the immediate past will continue into the future. For example, if there has been 10 per cent growth per year, on average, in the last five years, we can expect that market will grow by 10 per cent also next year. In a rapidly developing economy, extrapolated figures may not reflect rapid growth and must be adjusted accordingly.

GOING INTERNATIONAL 7.5

Marketing tool: the semantic differential

An important tool in attitudinal research, image studies and positioning decisions is the *semantic differential*. It was originally developed to measure the meaning that a concept – perhaps a political issue, a person, a work of art or, in marketing, a brand, product or company – might have for people in terms of various dimensions. As first presented, the instrument consisted of pairs of polar adjectives with a seven-interval scale separating the opposite members of each pair. For example:

    Extremely good   – – – – – –   Extremely bad

This instrument has been refined to obtain greater sensitivity through the use of descriptive phrases. Examples of such bipolar phrases for determining the image of a particular brand of beer are:

    Something special   – – – – – –   Just another drink

    Local flavour   – – – – – –   Foreign flavour

    Really peps you up   – – – – – –   Somehow doesn't pep you up

The number of word pairs varies considerably but may be as many as 50 or more. Flexibility and appropriateness to a particular study are achieved by constructing tailor-made word and phrase lists.

Semantic differential scales have been used in marketing to compare images of particular products, brands, firms and stores against competing ones. The answers of all respondents can be averaged and then plotted to provide a 'profile', as shown below for three competing beers on four scales (actually, a firm would probably use more scales in such a study).

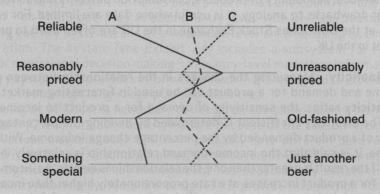

Exhibit 7.4 Multinational marketing information system

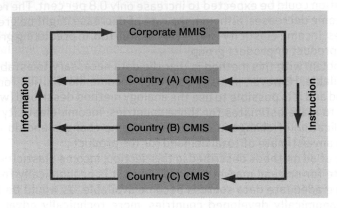

ultimately are transmitted to the MMIS to be included in overall planning decisions. Some of the most challenging tasks facing the developer of the MMIS are determining the kinds of data and the depth of detail necessary, and analysing how it should be processed. This implies that models for decision making have been thought through and are sufficiently specific to be functional.

An MMIS can be designed as a basic system that provides only a source of information or as a highly sophisticated system that includes specific decision models. Experience has shown that success is greater when a company begins with a basic system and continues perfecting it to the desired level of sophistication.

Summary

The basic objective of the market research function is providing management with information for more accurate decision making. This objective is the same for domestic and international marketing. In international marketing research, however, achieving that objective presents some problems not encountered on the domestic front.

Consumer attitudes about providing information to a researcher are culturally conditioned. Foreign market information surveys must be carefully designed to elicit the desired data and at the same time not offend the respondent's sense of privacy. The concepts and ideas might have different meanings in different cultures. It is therefore particularly important in cases where research data or results from different markets are compared with each other. Besides the cultural and managerial constraints involved in gathering information for primary data, many foreign markets have inadequate and/or unreliable bases of secondary information.

Three generalisations can be made about the direction and rate of growth of marketing research in foreign marketing. First, both home-based and foreign management are increasingly aware of and accept the importance of marketing research's role in decision making. Second, there is a current trend towards the decentralisation of the research function to put control closer to the area being studied. Third, the most sophisticated tools and techniques are being adapted to foreign information gathering with increasing success. They are so successful, in fact, that it has become necessary to develop structured information systems to appreciate and utilise effectively the mass of information available.

Appendix: Sources of Secondary Data

For almost any marketing research project, an analysis of available secondary information is a useful and inexpensive first step. Although there are information gaps, particularly for detailed market information, the situation on data availability and reliability is improving. The principal agencies that collect and publish information useful in international business are presented here, with some notations of selected publications.

International Organisations

A number of international organisations provide information and statistics on international markets. The **Statistical Yearbook**, an annual publication of the United Nations, provides comprehensive social and economic data for more than 250 countries around the world. Many regional organisations, such as the Organisation for Economic Co-operation and Development (OECD), the Pan American Union and the European Union, publish information, statistics and market studies relating to their respective regions. The United Nations *Investment Report* and *Development Report* present a lot of information every year. The European Union gathers information on all aspects of European trade issues that are public (see, for example, www.euromonitor.org).

Chambers of Commerce

In addition to government and organisational publications, many foreign countries maintain chamber of commerce offices in the European Union, functioning as permanent trade missions. These foreign chambers of commerce generally have research libraries available and are knowledgeable regarding further sources of information on specific products or marketing problems.

Trade, Business and Service Organisations

Foreign trade associations are particularly good sources of information on specific products or product lines. Many associations perform special studies or continuing services in collecting comprehensive statistical data for a specific product group or industry. Although some information is proprietary in nature and available only to members of an association, non-members frequently have access to it under certain conditions. Up-to-date membership lists providing potential customers or competitors are often available to anyone requesting them, and a listing of foreign trade associations is usually annotated at the end of a specific trade list.

Foreign service industries also supply valuable sources of information useful in international business. Service companies – such as commercial and investment banks, international advertising agencies, foreign-based research firms, economic research institutes, foreign carriers, shipping agencies and freight forwarders – generally regard the furnishing of current, reliable information as part of their service function. The banking industry in foreign countries is particularly useful as a source of information on current local economic situations. The Chase Manhattan Bank in New York periodically publishes a newsletter on such subjects as the European Union. There are several good independently published reports on techniques, trends, forecasts and other such current data. Many foreign banks publish periodic or special review newsletters relating to the local economy, providing a first-hand analysis of the economic situation of specific foreign countries. For example, the Krediet Bank in Brussels has published *Belgium, Key to the Common Market*, and the Banco National Commercio Exterior in Mexico has published *Mexico Facts, Figures and Trends*. Even though these publications are sometimes available without charge, they must usually be translated.

US Government

The US Government actively promotes the expansion of US business into international trade. In the process of keeping US businesses informed of foreign opportunities, the US

5 *The World Factbook* provides macro- and microeconomic data by the CIA, including economic overviews of 260 countries, sectoral briefings, government and defence information. This site can be reached at http://www.odci.gov/cia/publications/factbook.

6 The Web of Culture page is devoted to improving executives' understanding of cross-cultural communications, which is a 'critical success factor' in international marketing, while the other sites reviewed here focus on the economic, business and trade environments of different countries. The site is a useful starting point for those seeking to better their understanding of different national cultures before visiting overseas markets and for students studying the cultural aspects of international marketing. This site can be reached at http://www.webofculture.com.

7 The Organisation for Economic Co-operation and Development provides at its website statistics, economic indicators and other information on member countries. The site can be reached at http://www.oecd.org.

8 The World Bank has more than 14 000 documents containing economic, social, national and regional information on more than 200 countries. The site can be reached at http://www.worldbank.org.

9 The Census Bureau has extensive data at the US level and substantial data for states and counties, somewhat less for cities (e.g. incorporated places). It releases data for the very smallest areas (census tracts, block groups, and blocks). The US Bureau of Census provides several resources available on its Census 2000 Gateway to assist people to narrow their search for Census 2000 data including the release schedules by date, geography and subject. The site can be reached at http://www.census.gov.

10 The British Household Panel Survey began in 1991 and is conducted annually by interview and questionnaire with a national representative sample of some 5500 households and 10 300 individuals. It covers topics like labour market behaviour, income and wealth, housing, health and socioeconomic values. The site can be reached at http://www.iser.essex.ac.uk/bhps.

11 Euromonitor provides global consumer market intelligence. The website provides consumer industry market reports and online databases about manufacturers, retailers, distributors and suppliers. The databases can be a starting point for researching international markets. The site can be reached at http://www.euromonitor.com.

Questions

1 Discuss how the shift from making 'market entry' decisions to 'continuous operations' decisions creates a need for different types of information and data. What assistance does an MMIS provide?

2 Using a hypothetical situation, illustrate how an MMIS might be established and how it would be used at different levels.

3 Discuss the breadth and scope of international marketing research. Why is international marketing research generally broader in scope than domestic marketing research?

4 What is the task of the international market researcher? How is it complicated by the foreign environment?

5 Discuss the stages of the research process in relation to the problems encountered. Give examples.

6 Why is the formulation of the research problem difficult in foreign market research?

7 Discuss the problems of gathering secondary data in foreign markets.

8 What are some of the problems created by language and the ability to comprehend in collecting primary data? How can an international market researcher overcome these difficulties?

9 Discuss how 'decentring' is used to get an accurate translation of a questionnaire.

10 Discuss when qualitative research may be more effective than quantitative research.

11 Sampling offers some major problems in market research. Discuss.

12 Select a country. From secondary sources compile the following information for at least a 10-year period prior to the present:

- principal imports
- principal exports
- gross national product
- chief of state
- major cities and population
- principal agricultural crop.

13 'The foreign market researcher must possess three essential capabilities to generate meaningful marketing information.' Discuss.

Further Reading

P.N. Ghauri and K. Grønhaug, *Research Methods in Business Studies: A practical guide*, 3rd edn (London: FT Pearson), 2005.

Samuel Craig and Susan Douglas, 'Conducting International Marketing Research in the Twenty-first Century', *International Marketing Review*, 2001, 18(1), pp. 80–90.

Rudolf Sinkovics, Elfriede Penz and Pervez Ghauri, 'Analyzing Textual Data in International Marketing Research', *Qualitative Market Research: An International Journal*, 2005, 8(1), pp. 9–38.

References

1 Tamer Cavusgil, Pervez Ghauri and Milind Agarwal, *Doing Business in Emerging Markets: Entry and Negotiation Strategies* (Thousand Oaks: Sage, 2002).

2 For a complete discussion of marketing research in foreign environments, see Susan P. Douglas and C. Samuel Craig, *International Marketing Research* (Chichester/New York, 2000).

3 John Cantwell, 'The Methodological Problems Raised by the Collection of Foreign Direct Investment Data', *Scandinavian International Business Review*, 1(1), 1992, pp. 86–103.

4 Susan Douglas and Samuel Craig, 'The Changing Dynamic of Consumer Behavior: Implications for Cross-Cultural Research', *International Journal of Research in Marketing*, 1997, 14(4), pp. 373–95.

5 Pervez Ghauri and Kjell Grønhaug, *Research Methods in Business Studies: A Practical Guide*, 3rd edn, (Hemel Hempstead: Prentice Hall, 2005).

6 David Kiburn, 'Unilever Struggles with Surf in Japan', *Advertising Age*, 6 May 1991, p. 22.

Exhibit 8.2 Global light vehicles sales

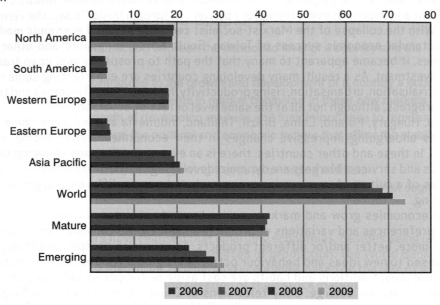

Units m

Legend: 2006, 2007, 2008, 2009

Categories: North America, South America, Western Europe, Eastern Europe, Asia Pacific, World, Mature, Emerging

Source: FT Special Report, 4 March 2008, p. 1.

Exhibit 8.3 Contribution to global assembly growth

By region, 2006–2011 (% and number of units)

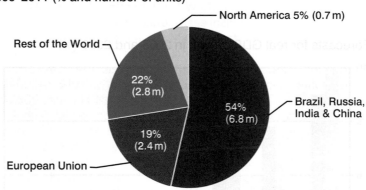

- North America 5% (0.7 m)
- Rest of the World 22% (2.8 m)
- European Union 19% (2.4 m)
- Brazil, Russia, India & China 54% (6.8 m)

Total global growth: 12.7 m units

Source: FT Special Report, 4 March 2008, p. 1.

Marketing and Economic Development

The economic level of a country is the single most important environmental element to which the foreign marketer must adjust the marketing task. The stage of economic growth within a country affects attitudes towards foreign business activity, the demand for goods, distribution systems found within a country and the entire marketing process. In static economies, consumption patterns become rigid, and marketing is typically nothing more than a supply effort. In a dynamic economy, consumption patterns change rapidly.

Marketing is constantly faced with the challenge of detecting and providing for new levels of consumption, and marketing efforts must be matched with ever-changing market needs and wants.

Economic development presents a two-sided challenge. First, a study of the general aspects of economic development is necessary to gain empathy for the economic climate within developing countries. Second, the state of economic development must be studied with respect to market potential, including the present economic level and the economy's growth potential. The current level of economic development dictates the kind and degree of market potential that exists, while a knowledge of the dynamism of the economy allows the marketer to prepare for economic shifts in emerging markets.

Economic development is generally understood to mean an increase in national production that results in an increase in the average per capita GDP.[3] Besides an increase in average per capita GDP, most interpretations of the concept also imply a widespread distribution of the increased income. The term 'emerging market', as commonly defined today, tends to mean a country with rapid economic growth – improvements achieved in decades rather than centuries – and considerable increases in consumer demand.

Stages of Economic Development

The best-known model for classifying countries by stage of economic development is that presented by Walt Rostow. He identified five stages of development; each stage is a function of the cost of labour, technical capability of the buyers, scale of operations, interest rates and level of product sophistication. Growth is the movement from one stage to another, and countries in the first three stages are considered to be economically underdeveloped. Briefly, the stages are as follows:

Stage 1: The traditional society. Countries in this stage lack the capability of significantly increasing the level of productivity. There is a marked absence of systematic application of the methods of modern science and technology. Literacy is low, as are other types of social overhead.

Stage 2: The preconditions for take-off. This second stage includes those societies in the process of transition to the take-off stage. During this period, the advances of modern science are beginning to be applied in agriculture and production. The development of transportation, communications, power, education, health and other public undertakings are begun in a small but important way.

Stage 3: The take-off. At this stage, countries achieve a growth pattern that becomes a normal condition. Human resources and social overhead have been developed to sustain steady development. Agricultural and industrial modernisation lead to rapid expansion in these areas.

Stage 4: The drive to maturity. After take-off, sustained progress is maintained and the economy seeks to extend modern technology to all fronts of economic activity. The economy takes on international involvement. In this stage, an economy demonstrates that it has the technological and entrepreneurial skills to produce not everything, but anything it chooses to produce.

Stage 5: The age of high mass consumption. The age of high mass consumption leads to shifts in the leading economic sectors towards durable consumer goods and services. Real income per capita rises to the point where a very large number of people have significant amounts of discretionary income.[4]

While Rostow's classification has met with some criticism because of the difficulty of distinguishing among the five stages, it provides the marketer with some indication of the relationship between economic development, the types of products a country needs, and the sophistication of its industrial infrastructure.

GOING INTERNATIONAL 8.2

Coke to squeeze more from China

Fruit juice drink growth in China

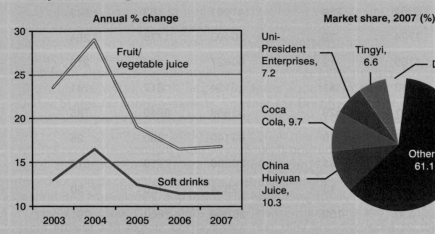

Coca-Cola's 47 products in China range from its trademark Coke to Ice Dew bottled water, and nearly everything in between. Muhtar Kent, the company's CEO, is now trying to fill it by making a $2.4 billion offer for China Huiyuan Juice Group, the country's biggest juice-maker. The acquisition would more than double Coke's market share in China's fruit juices market to about 20 per cent, far ahead of its next closest rival, according to market research firm Euromonitor International.

China's non-alcoholic drinks market has grown by 82 per cent in the past five years to $32.7 billion at the end of last year, but of that fruit juice sales have grown by 160 per cent over the same period. Two years ago Coke agreed to acquire its third major China bottler, Kerry Beverages, from Robert Kuok, the Chinese-Malaysian tycoon. The deal would also be the first major test of China's new anti-competition policy, enacted last month. An online poll conducted by internet portal sina.com, yesterday, showed 82 per cent of 52 000 respondents opposed the deal, saying it would be an example of foreign capital destroying a 'cultural pillar'.

Source: FT, 4 September 2008, p. 20.

Marketing in a Developing Country

A marketer cannot superimpose a sophisticated marketing programme on an underdeveloped economy. Marketing efforts must be keyed to each situation, custom tailored for each set of circumstances. A promotional programme for a population that is 60 per cent illiterate is vastly different from a programme for a population that is 80 per cent literate. Pricing in a subsistence market poses different problems than pricing in an affluent society. The distribution structure should provide an efficient method of matching productive capacity with available demand. An efficient marketing programme is one that provides for optimum utility at a single point in time, given a specific set of circumstances. In evaluating the potential in a developing country, the marketer must make an assessment of the existing level of marketing development within the country.[10]

GOING INTERNATIONAL 8.3

Carrefour profit rises on emerging markets

Carrefour SA, the world's second-largest retailer after Wal-Mart Stores Inc., posted a 3.1 per cent rise in first-half net profit as strong growth in emerging markets helped the French company offset weakness at home.

Net profit for the first six months of the year rose to €751.1 million ($1.1 billion) a year earlier. The company previous reported an 8 per cent rise in the first half sales to €41.95 billion. Carrefour shares closed up 7.2 per cent, or €2.43 at €36.13, outperforming a 0.5 per cent rise in the CAC-40 Paris index. The earnings were 'totally in line with our expectations,' said Cedric Lecasble, analyst with Landsbanki Kepler, noting that 'no spectacular announcements' such as a profit warning or management changes were made.

Dia – a supermarket in the Carrefour chain

The French retailer's solid results were a bright spot amid otherwise lacklustre retail earnings in Europe. Supermarket operators Ahold NV of the Netherlands and Casino Guichard-Perrachon SA of France posted a sharp decline in net profit from a year earlier, when earnings were boosted by gains from asset sales.

The retailer will redirect €200 million in capital to investments that it expects to generate high returns, such as investing in growth markets and increasing the proportion of its new store openings in countries like Brazil and China.

Level of Marketing Development

The more developed an economy, the greater the variety of marketing functions demanded, and the more sophisticated and specialised the institutions become to perform marketing functions. The evolution of the channel structure illustrates the relationship between marketing development and the stage of economic development of a country.

Advertising agencies, facilities for marketing research, repair services, specialised consumer financing agencies and storage and warehousing facilities are supportive facilitating agencies created to serve the particular needs of expanded markets and economies. It is important to remember that these institutions do not come about automatically, nor does the necessary marketing institution simply appear. Part of the marketer's task when studying an economy is to determine what in the foreign environment will be useful and how much adjustment will be necessary to carry out stated objectives. In some developing countries it may be up to the marketer to institute the foundations of a modern marketing system.

Demand in a Developing Country

Estimating market potential in less developed countries involves myriad challenges. Most of the difficulty arises from economic dualism – that is, the coexistence of modern and traditional sectors within the economy. The modern sector is centred in the cities and has airports, international hotels, new factories and a Westernised middle class. Alongside this modern sector is a traditional sector containing the remainder of the

country's population. Although the two sectors may be very close geographically, they are centuries away in terms of production and consumption. This dual economy affects the size of the market and, in many countries, creates two distinct economic and marketing levels. Indonesia, Pakistan and India are good examples. The 11th largest industrial economy in the world, India has a population of over 1 billion, more than 350 million of whom are part of an affluent middle class.[11] The modern sector demands products and services similar to those available in any industrialised country; the traditional sector demands items more indigenous and basic to subsistence. As one authority observed, a rural Indian can live a sound life with few products. Toothpaste, sugar, coffee, washing soap, bath soap and kerosene are bare necessities for those who live in semi-urban and urban areas.[12]

In countries with dual sectors, there are at least two different market segments. Each can prove profitable but each requires its own marketing programme and products appropriate for its market characteristics. Many companies market successfully to both the traditional and the modern market segments in countries with mixed economies. The traditional sector may offer the greatest potential initially, but as the transition from the traditional to the modern takes place (i.e. as the middle-income class grows) an established marketer is better able to capitalise on the growing market.

Tomorrow's markets will include expansion in industrialised countries and the development of the traditional side of emerging and less-developed countries, as well as continued expansion of the modern sectors of such countries. The greatest long-range growth potential is to be found in the traditional sector, where the realisation of profit may require a change in orientation and willingness to invest time and effort for longer periods. The development of demand in a traditional market sector means higher initial marketing costs, compromises in marketing methods and sometimes redesigning products, but market investment today is necessary to produce profits tomorrow. The companies that will benefit in the future from emerging markets in Eastern Europe, China, Latin America and elsewhere are the ones that invest when it is difficult and initially unprofitable.[13]

Emerging Markets

MARKET-DRIVEN ECONOMIES
economies/ countries that are following the free-market economic system

PUBLIC-SECTOR ENTERPRISES
government-owned organisations

The transition from socialist to **market-driven economies**, the liberalisation of trade and investment policies in developing countries, the transfer of **public-sector enterprises** to the private sector and the rapid development of regional market alliances are changing the way countries will trade and prosper in the next century.

The US Department of Commerce estimates that over 75 per cent of the expected growth in world trade over the next two decades will come from the more than 130 developing and emerging countries. A small core of these countries will account for more than half of that growth.[14] It predicts that the countries identified as big emerging markets (BEMs) alone will be a bigger import market by the end of this decade than the European Union (EU) and, by 2015, will be importing more than the EU and Japan combined.[15] These BEMs, as the US Department of Commerce refers to them, share a number of important traits. They:

- are all physically large
- have significant populations
- represent considerable markets for a wide range of products
- all have strong rates of growth or the potential for significant growth
- have all undertaken significant programmes of economic reform
- are all of major political importance within their regions
- are 'regional economic drivers'
- will engender further expansion in neighbouring markets as they grow.

GOING INTERNATIONAL 8.4

Multinational brands face tough competition from local brands in emerging markets

India has a billion-plus customers and the climate is hot, but Coca-Cola is having a tough time there. After years of mistakes, in 2002 it had 16.5 per cent of the market, behind Pepsi Cola (23.5 per cent) and the number two local rival, Thums Up. Coca-Cola acquired Thums Up in 1993 when it entered India with big plans. In its early years it made all the classic mistakes, overestimating the size of market, misreading consumers and fighting with government rules and regulations. A big dispute with Pepsi, where Coke bottlers hoarded empty Pepsi bottles, gave it a very bad reputation. In the past 10 years it has had five expatriate CEOs. Pepsi, on the other hand, has had three local CEOs in its 15 years. Coke suffered undeclared losses in the first 10 years and had written off its assets in India by $405 million.

In 2003, however, Coke decided to sell 49 per cent of its Indian bottler, Hindustan Coca-Cola Beverages, for $41 million. The company's overall sales jumped 24 per cent in the same year. India has huge potential. At present soft drink consumption is seven (250 millilitres) servings per head, while in neighbouring Pakistan it is 14 servings per head; in China it is 89 and in Mexico it is 1500 servings. Thus, the potential is huge (see graph).

The key to the new strategy is the new local CEO, who fought with Atlanta to revive the local brand, Thums Up (owned by Coke): $3.5 million was spent on advertising and improving distribution of Thums Up, which within a year jumped to the number two position. Coca-Cola then launched a new 200 ml bottle, selling for 10 cents and aimed at the lower market segments, and the price for normal Coke (300 ml) was dropped to 17 cents from 24 cents. For advertising, a Bollywood movie star, Amir Khan, was hired.

● Do you think Coca-Cola is on the right path?

Source: Business Week, 10 February 2003, p. 23.

Local brand Thums Up is now owned by Coca-Cola

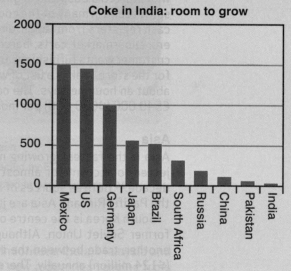

Coke in India: room to grow

■ Annual per capita consumption of soft drinks, 8 oz serving, all brands

These emerging markets differ from other developing countries because they import more than smaller markets and more than economies of similar size. As they embark on economic development, demand for capital goods to build their manufacturing base and develop infrastructure increases. Increased economic activity means more jobs and more

GOING INTERNATIONAL 8.7

The benefits of information technology in village life

Delora Begum's home office is a corrugated metal and straw hut in Bangladesh with a mud floor, no toilet, and no running water. Yet, in this humble setting, she reigns as the 'phone lady', a successful entrepreneur and a person of standing in her community. It's all due to a sleek Nokia cellphone. Mrs Begum acquired the handset in 1999. Her telephone 'booth' is mobile: during the day, it's the stall on the village's main dirt road; at night, callers drop by her family hut to use the phone.

After the phone hookup was made, incomes and quality of life improved almost immediately for many villagers. For as long as he can remember, a brick factory manager had to take a two-and-a-half-hour bus ride to Dhaka to order furnace oil and coal for the brick factory. Now he avoids the biweekly trip: 'I can just call if I need anything, or if I have any problems.' The local carpenter uses the cellphone to check the current market price of wood, so he ensures a higher profit for the furniture he makes.

The only public telecom link to the outside world, this unit allows villagers to learn the fair value of their rice and vegetables, cutting out the middlemen notorious for exploiting them. They can arrange bank transfers or consult doctors in distant cities and, in a nation where only 45 per cent of the population can read and write, the cellphone allows people to dispense with a scribe to compose a letter. It also earns some $600 a year for its owner – twice the annual per capita income in Bangladesh.

When members of the Grand Coast Fishing Operators Cooperative salt and smoke the day's catch to prepare it for market, it may seem light years away from cyberspace, but for these women the Internet is a boon. The cooperative set up a website that enables its 7350 members to promote their produce, monitor export markets and negotiate prices with overseas buyers before they arrive at markets in Senegal. Information technology has thus improved their economic position.

Finally, it seems that new technology can also breed new economic disputes. A disagreement over an unpaid $50 phone bill in a village 110 kilometres northeast of Dhaka, Bangladesh turned into a gunfight between two groups of villagers that left 5 dead and 25 injured.

● What do we learn from this example?

Sources: Miriam Jordan, 'It Takes a Cell Phone', *Wall Street Journal*, 25 June 1999, p. B-1; 'A Great Leap: Developing Countries are Finding Ways to Leverage Advances in Information Technology and Help Narrow the North–South Divide', *Time International*, 31 January 2000, p. 42; 'Bangladesh – Five Killed in Shootout over Telephone Bill', *Los Angeles Times*, 31 March 2003, p. A17.

The Americas

The North American Free Trade Agreement (NAFTA) marks the high point of a silent political and economic revolution that has been taking place in the Americas (see Exhibit 8.9) over the past decade. Most of the countries have moved from military dictatorships to democratically elected governments, while sweeping economic and trade liberalisation is replacing the economic model most Latin American countries followed for decades. Today many of them are at roughly the same stage of liberalisation that launched the dynamic growth in Asia during the last two decades.[24]

New leaders have turned away from the traditional closed policies of the past to implement positive market-oriented reforms and seek ways for economic cooperation.

Exhibit 8.9 The Americas

Privatisation of state-owned enterprises (SOEs) and other economic, monetary and trade policy reforms show a broad shift away from inward-looking policies of import substitution (that is, manufacture products at home rather than import them) and protectionism that were so prevalent earlier. In a positive response to these reforms, investors are spending billions of dollars to buy airlines, banks, public works and telecommunications systems.

Argentina, Brazil, Chile and Mexico are among the countries that have quickly instituted reforms. Mexico has been the leader in privatisation and in lowering tariffs even before entering NAFTA. Over 750 businesses, including the telephone company, steel mills, airlines and banks, have been sold. Pemex, the national oil company, is the only major industry Mexico is not privatising, although restrictions on joint projects between Pemex and foreign companies have been liberalised.

PRIVATISATION
when a government company is sold to private investors

communist-bloc countries to foreign direct investments and international trade. And although emerging markets present special problems, they are promising markets for a broad range of products.

This ever-expanding involvement of more and more of the world's people with varying needs and wants will test old trading patterns and alliances. The foreign marketer of today and tomorrow must be able to react to market changes rapidly and to anticipate new trends within constantly evolving market segments that may not have existed as recently as last year. Many of today's market facts will probably be tomorrow's historical myths.

Questions

1 Is it possible for an economy to experience economic growth as measured by total GNP without a commensurate rise in the standard of living? Discuss fully.

2 Discuss each of the stages of evolution in the marketing process. Illustrate each stage with the example of a particular country.

3 As a country progresses from one economic stage to another, what in general are the marketing effects?

4 Discuss the impact of IT on the emerging markets. How can it influence company strategies?

5 Discuss the significance of economic development to international marketing. Why is the knowledge of economic development of importance in assessing the world marketing environment? Discuss.

6 Considering the developments in the two biggest markets (India and China), discuss the opportunities and threats in these two markets from a foreign company's perspective.

7 The infrastructure is important to the economic growth of an economy. Comment.

8 What is marketing's role in economic development? Discuss marketing's contributions to economic development.

9 Discuss the economic and trade importance of the big emerging markets.

10 What are the traits of those countries considered to be big emerging markets? Discuss.

11 The importance of China as a market and as a competitor to Western companies is widely discussed. You are required to analyse China's emergence as a competitor to the Western markets; would it be able to surpass the US and/or the EU in terms of trade and GDP? Discuss with arguments and examples.

12 What are global market segments? Why are they important to global companies? Discuss.

Further Reading

S.T. Cavusgil, P. Ghauri and M. Agarwal, *Doing Business in Emerging Markets* (Thousand Oaks: Sage, 2002), Chapters 1 and 2.

S. Estrin, K.E. Meyer, M. Wright and F. Foliano, 'Export propensity and intensity of subsidiaries in emerging economies', *International Business Review*, 2008, 17(5), pp. 574–86.

P. Krugman, 'Does Third World Growth Hurt First World Prosperity?', *Harvard Business Review*, 1994 (July–August), p. 153.

References

1 'The Big Emerging Markets', *Business America*, March 1994, pp. 4–6.

2 S. Tamer Cavusgil, Pervez Ghauri and Milind Agarwal, *Doing Business in Emerging Markets* (Thousand Oaks: Sage, 2002).

3 Gross domestic product (GDP) and gross national product (GNP) are two measures of a country's economic activity. GDP is a measure of the market value of all goods and services produced within the boundaries of a nation, regardless of asset ownership. Unlike GNP, GDP excludes receipts from that nation's business operations in foreign countries, as well as the share of reinvested earnings in foreign affiliates of domestic corporations.

4 Walt W. Rostow, *The Stages of Economic Growth*, 2nd edn (London: Cambridge University Press, 1971), p. 10. For an interesting discussion, see Peter Buckley and Pervez Ghauri, *The Global Challenge for Multinational Enterprises* (Oxford: Pergamon Press, 1999).

5 'The Battle for Brazil', *Fortune*, 20 July 1998, pp. 48–53.

6 For a description of how competitive South Korea has become, see David P. Hamilton and Steve Glain, 'Silicon Duel: Koreans Move to Grab Memory-chip Market from the Japanese', *Wall Street Journal*, 14 March 1995, p. A-1.

7 For a discussion of the billions of dollars being invested in infrastructure, see Dave Savona, 'Remaking the Globe', *International Business*, March 1995, pp. 30–6.

8 Goitom Tesfom, Clemens Lutz and Pervez Ghauri, 'Comparing Export Marketing Channels: Developed versus Developing Countries', *International Marketing Review*, 2004, 21(4/5), pp. 409–22.

9 For a comprehensive review of one country's move towards a more open economy, see 'Argentina Survey', *The Economist*, 26 November 1994, 18 pages unnumbered beginning on p. 62.

10 For a comprehensive review of channels of distribution in developing countries, see Saeed Samiee, 'Retailing and Channel Considerations in Developing Countries: A Review and Research Propositions', *Journal of Business Research*, vol. 23, 1993, pp. 103–30; and Janeen E. Olsen and Kent L. Granzin, 'Vertical Integration and Economic Development: An Empirical Investigation of Channel Integration', *Journal of Global Marketing*, vol. 7, no. 3, 1994, pp. 7–39.

11 'India: The Poor Get Richer', *The Economist*, 5 November 1994, pp. 39–40.

12 *Business Week*, 'India: How a Thirst for Energy Lead to a Thaw', 15 November 2004, p. 63.

13 When the US Government lifted the trade embargo against Vietnam, many US companies found that their competitors had already made inroads in that market. See Marita Van Oldenborgy; 'Catch-Up Ball', *International Business*, March 1994, pp. 92–4.

14 'Big Emerging Markets', *Business America*, March 1994, pp. 4–6.

15 'Big Emerging Markets' Share of World Exports Continues to Rise', *Business America*, March 1994, p. 28.

16 John Naisbitt, *Megatrends Asia: Eight Asian Megatrends that are Reshaping Our World* (New York: Simon & Schuster, 1996).

17 Jim Rohwer, *Asia Rising, Why America will Prosper while Asia's Economics Boom* (New York: Simon & Schuster, 1995).

18 'As Japan Goes?' *The Economist*, 20 June 1998, pp. 17–8; and 'Three Futures for Japan', *The Economist*, 21 March 1998, pp. 29–30.

19 Dan Biers, 'Now in First World, Asia's Tigers Act Like It', *Wall Street Journal*, 28 February 1995, p. A-15.

20 'The China Connection', *Business Week*, 5 August 1996, pp. 32–5; and 'China's WTO Accession', *Far Eastern Economic Review*, 2 July 1998, p. 38.

21 China is divided into 23 provinces (including Taiwan) and five autonomous border regions. The provinces and autonomous regions are usually grouped into six large administrative regions: Northeastern Region, Northern Region (includes Beijing), Eastern Region (includes Shanghai), South Central Region, Southwestern Region, and the Northwestern Region. After Hong Kong's reversion to China, it is considered the seventh autonomous region.

22 'The China Connection', *Business Week*, 5 August 1996, pp. 32–3.

23 'India's Political Struggle', *The Economist*, 5 April 1997, p. 66.

24 Matt Moffett, 'Seeds of Reform: Key Finance Ministers in Latin America are Old Harvard-MIT Pals', *Wall Street Journal*, 1 August 1994, p. 1.

25 S. Tamer Cavusgil, Pervez N. Ghauri and Milind R. Agarwal, *Doing Business in Emerging Markets* (Thousand Oaks: Sage, 2002).

26 Paul Magnusson, 'With Latin America Thriving, NAFTA Might Keep Marching South', *Business Week*, 24 July 1994, p. 20.

Chapter 9
Multinational Market Regions and Market Groups

Chapter Outline

Food definition problems in particular have impeded progress in guaranteeing free circulation of food products within the EU. For example, several member states maintain different definitions of yoghurt. The French insist that anything called *yogurt* must contain live cultures; thus, they prohibited the sale of a Dutch product under the name *yoghurt* because it did not contain live cultures, as does the French product. In March 1996, the European Commission decided that only goat's-milk or ewe's-milk cheese produced in Greece was entitled to be called feta. The ruling brought storms of protest from Danes, who now have five years to rename their cow's-milk feta. Greeks have a solid claim of name, backed by a thousand years of history.[12]

Some of the first and most welcome reforms were the single customs document that replaced the 70 forms originally required for transborder shipments to member countries, the elimination of sabotage rules (which kept a trucker from returning with a loaded truck after delivery), and EU-wide transport licensing. These changes alone were estimated to have reduced distribution costs by 50 per cent for companies doing cross-border business in the EU.

GOING INTERNATIONAL 9.2

How to prevent old Europe becoming a dying continent

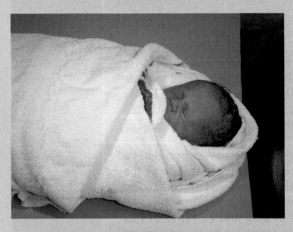

More babies are needed to boost birth rates in Europe

The evidence from the UN population division shows that Europe is a continent that has a high degree of population growth. It implies that Europe could become a huge old people's home. There are still high birth rates in northern and western Europe. The fertility rates vary from 1.6 children per woman in the UK to 1.9 for Ireland. The forecast is of a UK population increase of 13 per cent at 136 000 a year. There are low birth rates in southern Europe: 1.27 children per woman in Greece, 1.23 in Italy and 1.15 in Spain. The birth rate is also low in the central European countries: 1.35 in Germany, 1.28 in Austria and 1.41 in Switzerland. The forecast is that the population will drop by 19 per cent in Switzerland and 9 per cent in Austria. Those countries joining the European Union have low birth rates, varying from 1.1 in Latvia to 1.32 in Romania.

This ageing population has a negative impact on potential economic growth. The overall economic growth rate in the EU declines from 2–2.25 per cent a year to about 1.25 per cent* according to the European Commission. The percentage of people over 60 is 40 per cent, which is significantly more than the percentage of people under 14 (13 per cent). The fertility rate is declining while immigration continues to grow, leading to a threat against cultural continuity.

The solution to these challenges could include promoting more provision for childcare; pension reform to reduce the burden on state welfare provision; governments could reduce large fiscal deficits in order to contribute more towards the accumulation of capital; and immigration could be better managed.

* 'Economic and Financial Market Consequences of Ageing Populations', the EU Economy: 2002 Review, www.europa.eu.int/comm/economy_finance.

Source: adapted from Martin Wolf, 'How to Prevent Old Europe Becoming a Dying Continent', *Financial Times*, 5 March 2003, p. 21.

EU Structure   The European Union was created as a result of three treaties that established the European Coal and Steel Community, the European Economic Community and the European Atomic Energy Community. These three treaties are incorporated within the European Union and serve as the community's constitution. They provide a policy framework and empower the commission and the Council of Ministers to pass laws to carry out EU policy. The union uses three legal instruments: (1) regulations binding the member states directly and having the same strength as national laws; (2) directives also binding the member states but allowing them to choose the means of execution; and (3) decisions addressed to a government, an enterprise or an individual binding the parties named.

GOING INTERNATIONAL 9.3

Benefits of EU expansion

1 **Stability**   Expansion will promote democracy and rule of law in economies in Eastern Europe and provide the EU region with wider stability.
2 **Bigger market**   The new EU will have almost 500 million citizens, creating the biggest single market of affluent customers. Both old and new members will benefit.
3 **More investment**   The new EU members have already attracted billions of € of foreign capital. The bigger EU will become even more attractive for foreign investors.
4 **Reforms in Central and Eastern Europe**   The accession countries have fully privatised most state industries and have achieved market economies. It will help modernise infrastructure, clean environment and promote efficient industries.
5 **Structural reforms in Western Europe**   The 10 new members will stimulate economies in the smaller (older) EU members. Most countries will reform labour markets, thus restructuring industries and economies toward greater efficiencies.

© iStockphoto.com/
invictus999

Source: Business Week, Special Report: 'Mega Europe', 18 November 2002, pp. 24–40.

EU Authority   Over the years the European Union has gained an increasing amount of authority over its member states. The Union's institutions (the European Commission, the Council of Ministers, the European Parliament and the European Court of Justice) and their decision-making processes have legal status and extensive powers in fields covered by common policies. Union institutions have the power to make decisions and execute policies in specific areas. They form a federal pattern with executive, parliamentary and judicial branches. A number of private consultant companies specialise in lobbying the different EU institutions (see Exhibit 9.5).

● The European Commission is a group that initiates policy and supervises its observance by member states. It proposes and supervises the execution of laws and policies. The Commission has a president and four vice presidents; each of its members is appointed for a four-year term by mutual agreement of EU governments. Commission members act only in the interest of the EU. They may not receive instructions from any national government and are subject to the supervision of the European Parliament. Their responsibilities are to ensure that EU rules and the principles of the common market are respected.
● The Council of Ministers, one from each member country, passes laws based on commission proposals. Because the council is the decision-making body of the EU, it is its

that their already dominant trading positions in each other's markets are safe from protectionist pressures. When the NAFTA agreement was ratified and became effective in 1994, a single market of 360 million people with a €5.4 trillion ($6 trillion) GNP emerged.

NAFTA requires the three countries to remove all tariffs and barriers to trade, but each will have its own tariff arrangements with non-member countries. Some of the key provisions of the agreement follow.

Market Access   Within 10 years of implementation, all tariffs will be eliminated on North American industrial products traded between Canada, Mexico and the United States. All trade between Canada and the United States is duty free as provided for in CFTA. Mexico immediately eliminated tariffs on nearly 50 per cent of all industrial goods imported from the United States, and remaining tariffs will be phased out entirely within 15 years.

Non-tariff Barriers   In addition to the elimination of tariffs, countries will eliminate non-tariff barriers and other trade-distorting restrictions. NAFTA also eliminates a host of other Mexican barriers such as local content, local production and export performance requirements that have limited US exports.

Rules of Origin   NAFTA reduces tariffs only for goods made in North America. Tough rules of origin will determine whether a good qualifies for preferential tariff treatment under NAFTA. Rules of origin are designed to prevent 'free riders' from benefiting through minor processing or transshipment of non-NAFTA goods. For example, Japan could not assemble cars in Mexico and avoid US or Canadian tariffs and quotas unless the car had a specific percentage of Mexican (i.e. North American) content. For goods to be traded duty free, they must contain substantial (62.5 per cent) North American content.

Customs Administration   Under NAFTA, Canada, Mexico and the United States have agreed to implement uniform customs procedures and regulations. Uniform procedures ensure that exporters who market their products in more than one NAFTA country will not have to adapt to multiple customs procedures. Most procedures governing rules of origin documentation, record keeping and origin verification will be the same for all three NAFTA countries.

Investment   NAFTA will eliminate investment conditions that restrict the trade of goods and service among the three countries. Among conditions eliminated are the requirements that foreign investors export a given level or percentage of goods or services, use domestic goods or services, transfer technology to competitors, or limit imports to a certain percentage of exports.

Services   NAFTA establishes the first comprehensive set of principles governing services trade. Financial institutions are permitted to open wholly owned subsidiaries in each other's markets, and all restrictions on the services they offer had been lifted by 2000.

Intellectual Property   NAFTA will provide the highest standards of protection of intellectual property available in any bilateral or international agreement. The agreement covers patents, trademarks, copyrights, trade secrets, semiconductor integrated circuits, copyrights for North American movies, computer software and records.

Government Procurement   NAFTA guarantees businesses fair and open competition for procurement in North America through transparent and predictable procurement procedures.

In the first six months after NAFTA's inception, for example, US exports to Mexico rose to $24.5 billion, an increase of 16 per cent over the previous 12 months. Mexican exports

GOING INTERNATIONAL 9.7

Mexico and NAFTA: was it worth it?

On 1 January 2004 NAFTA celebrated its 10th birthday. If we assess the 10 years, NAFTA has been a great success in some areas. The investments flooded in at a rate of $12 billion per year and Mexico's exports grew threefold, from $52 billion to $161 billion. Mexico's per capita income rose by 24 per cent to $4000, which is about 10 times that of China. Mexico's economy was number 15 in the world before NAFTA; now it is the ninth largest economy.

Most Mexicans are, however, soured over NAFTA. Many think that it was oversold and, 10 years on, it has stopped creating any value added. They feel that America, consumed by the so-called 'war on terror', has neglected Mexico. The Mexican envoy to the UN characterised NAFTA as a 'weekend fling'. One recent survey showed that only 45 per cent of Mexicans think that NAFTA has benefited Mexico's economy.

Mexico thought it would become America's biggest workshop, but the job went to China. Local producers of goods from toys to shoes are struggling to survive due to cheaper imports. Mexico has not been able to generate enough jobs to accommodate its fast-growing workforce. Although a lot of investments came in the early years, since 2000 850 factories have been shut down due to decreased demand for their products, partly because many companies are relocating their production to China. Although exports to the US tripled, only a handful of companies enjoyed big gains. Wages have dropped due to the peso crash and government relations have not improved.

The countries around Mexico have gained equally well or more in some cases. Less than 3 per cent of industry parts and components are sourced in Mexico. The infrastructure has not improved; the country needs $50 billion to upgrade its power grid. Moreover, Mexico's gas and energy costs are 40 per cent higher than China's and the availability of skilled (educated) workers is much better in India. India graduates 314 000 science students per annum and China 363 000 as compared to Mexico's 13 300. However, Mexico knows that it has burnt its boats and there is no turning back from NAFTA.

Along with NAFTA came two of Mexico's biggest brand names, Gigante (Mexico's largest supermarket chain) and Grupo Bimbo (a Mexican multinational).

● Do you think Mexico has benefited from NAFTA? What do you think can be done to enhance the benefits of NAFTA for Mexico?

Source: abridged from Geri Smith and Cristina Lindblad, 'A Tale of What Free Trade Can and Cannot Do', Special Report, *Business Week*, 22 December 2003, pp. 36–43.

to the United States rose 21 per cent in those first six months to €20.2 billion ($23.4 billion). Equally impressive is the increase in trade between Mexico and Canada during the same period: exports from Canada to Mexico increased 33 per cent and Mexican exports to Canada increased by 31 per cent. Trade between Canada and the United States has been increasing steadily since 1989 when the Canada Free Trade Agreement (CFTA is now part of NAFTA) became effective.

Latin American Economic Cooperation

Prior to 1990, most Latin American market groups (see Exhibit 9.6) had varying degrees of success. The first and most ambitious, the Latin American Free Trade Association (LAFTA) gave way to the LAIA (Latin American Integration Association). Plagued with tremendous

unofficially referred to as the Chinese Economic Area (CEA), has advanced rapidly in recent years. The current expansion of the triangular economic relationship can be attributed to a steady transfer of labour-intensive manufacturing operations from Taiwan and Hong Kong to the Chinese mainland. China provides a supply of cheap, abundant labour, and Taiwan and Hong Kong provide capital, technology and management expertise. Hong Kong, now formally part of China, also plays an important role as the financier, investor, supplier and provider of technology, and as a port of entry for China as a whole.[30]

As an economic region, the CEA's economic importance should not be undervalued. Combined exports of the CEA were valued at €254.1 billion ($281.5 billion), accounting for 7.6 per cent of the world's exports and ranking fourth worldwide, behind the United States, Germany and Japan. Their combined imports totalled €240 billion ($266 billion), accounting for 6.9 per cent of the world's imports and ranking third, behind the United States and Germany.[31] The Chinese business empire extends beyond Hong Kong, Taiwan and China itself (see Exhibit 9.11).

Exhibit 9.11 The Chinese empire overseas

	Chinese population as % total of local population	Chinese population (millions)	Business output as % of total local population	GDP contribution ($ billions)
Hong Kong	98	6	80	120
Singapore	76	2	76	62
Taiwan	99	21	95	255
Malaysia	32	6	60	48
Indonesia	4	8	50	98
Philippines	1	1	40	30
Thailand	10	6	50	80
Vietnam	1	1	20	4
Total		51		697

Source: based on 'A Survey of Business in Asia', *The Economist*, 9 March 1996, p. 10.

Strategic Implications for Marketing

The complexion of the entire world marketplace has been changed significantly by the coalition of nations into multinational market groups. To international business firms, multinational groups spell opportunity writ large through access to greatly enlarged markets with reduced or abolished country-by-country tariff barriers and restrictions. Production, financing, labour and marketing decisions are affected by the remapping of the world into market groups.

As goals of the EEA and NAFTA are reached, new marketing opportunities are created; so are new problems. World competition will intensify as businesses become stronger and more experienced in dealing with large market groups. European and non-European multinationals are preparing to deal with the changes in competition in a fully integrated Europe. In an integrated Europe, industries and markets are being restructured. Mergers, acquisitions and joint ventures consolidate operations of European firms in anticipation of the benefits of a single European market. International managers will still be confronted by

individual national markets with the same problems of language, customs and instability, even though they are packaged under the umbrella of a common market.

Opportunities

Economic integration creates large mass markets for the marketer. Many national markets, too small to bother with individually, take on new dimensions and significance when combined with markets from cooperating countries. Large markets are particularly important to businesses accustomed to mass production and mass distribution because of the economies of scale and marketing efficiencies that can be achieved. In highly competitive markets, the benefits derived from enhanced efficiencies are often passed along as lower prices, which lead to increased purchasing power.

Another major saving will result from the billions of dollars wasted in developing different versions of products to meet a hotchpotch of national standards. Philips and other European companies invested a total of €18 billion ($20 billion) to develop a common switching system for Europe's 10 different telephone networks. This compares with €2.7 billion ($3 billion) spent in the United States for a common system and €1.35 billion ($1.5 billion) in Japan for a single system.

Market Barriers

The initial aim of a multinational market is to protect businesses that operate within its borders. An expressed goal is to give an advantage to the companies within the market in their dealings with other countries of the market group. Analysis of the intra-regional and international trade patterns of the market groups indicates that such goals have been achieved. Trade does increase among member nations and decrease with non-member nations.

Local preferences certainly spell trouble for the exporter located outside the market. Companies willing to invest in production facilities in multinational markets may benefit from such protection as they become a part of the market. Exporters, however, are in a considerably weaker position. This prospect confronts many US exporters faced with the possible need to invest in Europe to protect their export markets in the European Union. Recent heavy investments by Japanese (Toyota, Honda and Nissan), American (MCI, GM and Procter & Gamble) and Korean companies (Lucky Goldstar and Samsung) are good examples of such investments.

Ensuring EU Market Entry

Whether or not the European Union will close its doors to outsiders, firms who want to be competitive in the EU will have to establish a presence there. There are four levels of involvement that a firm may have *vis-à-vis* the EU: (1) firms based in Europe with well-established manufacturing and distribution operations in several European countries; (2) firms with operations in a single EU country; (3) firms that export manufactured goods to the EU from an offshore location; and (4) firms that have not actively exported to EU countries. The strategies for effective competitiveness in the EU are different for each type of firm.

The first firm, fully established in several EU countries with local manufacturing, is the best positioned. However, the competitive structure will change under a single Europe. Marketers will have to exploit the opportunities of greater efficiencies of production and distribution that result from lowering the barriers. They will also have to deal with increased competition from European firms as well as other MNCs that will be aggressively establishing market positions. A third area of change will require companies to learn how their customers are changing and, thus, how best to market to them.

European retailers and wholesalers as well as industrial customers are merging, expanding and taking steps to assure their success in this larger market. Nestlé has bought Rowntree, a UK confectionery company, and Britone, the Italian food conglomerate, to strengthen its ties to EU market firms. European banking is also going through a stage of mergers. In one 18-month period, 400 banks and finance firms merged, took stock in one

Further Reading

B. Lévy, 'The interface between globalization, trade and development: Theoretical issues for international business studies', *International Business Review*, 2007, 16(5), pp. 594–612.

P. Gabrielsson, M. Gabrielsson and H. Gabrielsson, 'International advertising campaigns in fast-moving consumer goods companies originating from a SMOPEC country', *International Business Review*, 2008, 17(6), pp. 714–28.

Andrew Delios, 'The Race for Japanese FDI in the European Union', in Lars Oxelheim and Pervez Ghauri (eds), *European Union and the Race for Foreign Direct Investment in Europe* (Oxford: Elsevier, 2004), pp. 185–208.

References

1   UNCTAD, *Companies without Borders: Transnational Corporations in the 1990s* (London: Thomson Business Press, 1996).

2   Jay L. Camillo, 'Mexico: NAFTA Opens Door to US Business', *Business America*, March 1994, pp. 14–21.

3   Sabrina Tavernise, 'Buying on Credit is the Latest Rage in Russia', *New York Times*, 20 January 2003, p. 1.

4   The following website provides information on a number of trade blocs: www.mac.doc.org.

5   Kenichi Ohmae, *Triad Power* (New York: The Free Press, 1985), p. 220.

6   The European Community still exists as a legal entity within the broader framework of the European Union.

7   Keith Perry, *Business and the European Community* (Oxford: Butterworth-Heinemann, 1994).

8   James Mehring, 'High Hurdles for New EU Members to Clear', *Business Week*, 5 May 2003, p. 26.

9   *The Economist,* 'Britain and Euro, What a Pity, What a Relief', 14 June 2003, p. 46.

10   Lionel Barber, 'From the Heart of Europe', *Europe*, July–August 1994, pp. 14–17; and 'Pondering Europe's Union', *The Economist*, 20 June 1998, p. 32.

11   T. Buck and R. Waters, 'Commission Talk Tough over Microsoft "Abuses"', *Financial Times*, 7 August 2003, p. 25.

12   *The Economist*, 'All Aboard the EuroTrain', 5 April, 2003, p. 50.

13   F. Guerrera and B. de Jonquieres, 'Something is Rotten Within our System: Europe's Mighty Competition Authorities are Cut Down to Size', *Financial Times*, 28 October 2002, p. 25.

14   'Advertising: Awaiting the Commission's Green Paper', *Business Europe*, 28 March–3 April 1994, pp. 2–3.

15   'The Euro: Will it Create a New European Economy?', *Business Week*, Special Issue, 27 April 1998.

16   *Financial Times*, 'A Year of Planes, Jeans and Price-fixing Deals', 20 March 2002, p. 23.

17   EFTA countries joining the EEA were Austria, Finland, Iceland, Norway and Sweden.

18   The 12 republics of the former USSR, collectively referred to as the Newly Independent States (NIS), are: Russia, Ukraine, Belarus (formerly Byelorussia), Armenia, Moldova (formerly Moldavia), Azerbaijan, Uzbekistan, Turkmenistan, Tajikistan, Kazakhstan, Kyrgystan (formerly Kirghiziya) and Georgia. These same countries, the NIS, are also members of the CIS.

19   For more information on NAFTA, see the following website: www.mac.doc.gov.

20   C.J. Chippello, 'NAFTA's Benefits to Firms in Canada May Top Those for Mexico', *Wall Street Journal*, 23 February 2003, p. A2.

21   Paul Magnusson, 'With Latin America Thriving, NAFTA Might Keep Marching South', *Business Week*, 24 July 1994, p. 20.

22   Richard Lapper, 'South American Unity Still a Distant Dream', *Financial Times*, 12 December 2004, p. 8.

23   John Naisbitt, *Mega Trends in Asia* (New York: Simon & Schuster, 1996).

24   ASEAN countries are: Brunei, Indonesia, Malaysia, the Philippines, Singapore and Thailand. Vietnam entered ASEAN in 1996.

25 'A Great Slide Backward in Southeast Asia', *Business Week*, 5 August 1996, p. 23.

26 For details see: www.aseansec.org.

27 APEC members are: Australia, Brunei, Canada, Chile, China, Hong Kong, Indonesia, Japan, the Republic of Korea, Malaysia, Mexico, New Zealand, the Philippines, Papua New Guinea, Singapore, Chinese Taipei (Taiwan), Thailand and the United States.

28 'Opening South Africa: It Should Act Now to Rid Itself and the Region of Apartheid's Economic Remnants', *The Economist*, 8 March 1997, p. 17.

29 'ECOWAS: Last Month ECOWAS Celebrated its 19th Anniversary', *West Africa*, 18 July 1994, pp. 1258–63.

30 For more on China and the Pacific Rim, see www.apec.org.

31 Kenichi Ohmae, 'The New World Order: The Rise of the Region-State', *The Wall Street Journal*, 8 August 1994, p. A-12.

Part 4
Developing International Marketing Strategies

Chapter 10
International Marketing Strategies

Positioning

Positioning is not what you do with the product, but what you do to the customer's mind. The better you understand the mind, the better you understand how positioning works. This means that companies are battling to capture the mind of the customer. This task has become more difficult due to an overload of information and communication by companies and other organisations such as Greenpeace and the WTO. The market is no longer responsive to old strategies due to the fact that there are simply too many companies, too many products and too much communication/information in the market.

The most effective way of positioning a company/product is to know your customer segment and concentrate on understanding this target group, and create an image that matches with their needs/wants. Advertising is only one way to communicate with customers; companies communicate with their markets in many ways. Positioning is thus considered a systematic way to find a window into the customer's mind. It has to be done at the right time and under the right circumstances. Moreover, it has to be done constantly and consistently. Companies such as Sony and Gillette try to position themselves as most innovative and leaders in their industries, and they have consistently tried to do that through communication.

GOING INTERNATIONAL 10.3

Sony's mission: make its own products obsolete

Sony, the creator of the Walkman and the Play-Station, has been synonymous with consumer electronics for most of the past five decades. However, while facing the increasing competition from lower-priced manufacturers in South Korea and China, Sony is frank about the size of the challenge and realises it has to redefine its market strategies. More pressure comes from the digital product industry, where companies with little or no expertise rush into this market due to the rapid commoditisation of hardware products and the ease of access to gain the technologies and know-how.

Kunitake Ando, Sony's president, points out that a networked world influences the consumer electronics industry, and believes that 'Sony's mission is to make our own products obsolete. Otherwise somebody else will do it.' Senior executives aim to transform stand-alone Sony's products (TVs, PCs, camcorders and mobile phones) into the Internet, what they call 'gateways to networks'.

Sony's unique position, based on its broad portfolio of business, enables it to fashion the next generation of high-tech products according to its own vision. Television is believed to be at the heart of Sony's business combination because 'TV is about to be reborn as the centre of broadband entertainment'. Seeking to keep the costs down and to optimise technological gains, the new strategy also centres on software and hardware, an approach that requires better coordination between different divisions. The integration of its audio-visual and IT operations is a good example of the transformation.

Even though Sony is on the way to its new mission, it faces a tough fight on three fronts: against all the other movie studios and music companies; against the might of Microsoft and others in software; and every other electronics company in hardware. And, finally, it will still be a long time before Sony can see whether the new products can survive and compete in the 'networked world'.

● Do you think it is a good strategy to cannibalise your own product?

Source: 'Sony's Mission is to Make Our Own Products Obsolete. Otherwise Somebody Else Will Do It', an interview with the CEO, *Financial Times*, 10 February 2003.

Every now and then companies need to reposition themselves due to changes in the marketplace or changes in customer tastes. There are several such examples: McDonald's has been trying to reposition itself from a company perceived to be selling 'fast food' or 'junk food' or 'unhealthy food' towards a company selling healthy food. Digital photography has forced Kodak to reposition itself as more and more customers have moved from film cameras to digital cameras. Toyota had to reposition itself, or create a new positioning, when it wanted to cover the luxury car market, initially in the United States, by introducing the Lexus.

Due to constant changes in technology, consumer tastes and competition, companies are increasingly in danger of losing their positioning. If companies are not proactive in analysing their positioning and repositioning, whenever needed, they lose their markets. The American automobile industry, Sega and Nintendo game consoles, Word Perfect and Lotus spreadsheet software are good examples of companies that lost their positioning. While Macintosh (Apple), IBM and Nokia are good examples of successfully repositioning companies and products.

Product Life Cycle and International Marketing Strategy

Most products go through the different stages of a life cycle; each stage demands different marketing strategies due to different market conditions. There is no fixed length of a **product life cycle (PLC)**, it represents a sale history of a particular product following an S-shaped curve, which is divided into four **PLC stages**: introduction, growth, maturity and decline (see Exhibit 10.4). However, all products do not necessarily follow the S-shape through all four stages. Some products die after the first stage, introduction, while others mature very quickly.

Different stages of the PLC have different characteristics and the marketing objectives in each stage are different. Due to these differences, a marketer has to apply different marketing strategies in different stages. The intensity of competition increases with the stages and finally reaches a point where the market starts declining. At this point, companies can revive the PLC by introducing new features to the product. This is done successfully by automobile companies, by introducing new models every four or five years. Gillette razors are good examples of this strategy, when the company keeps introducing the next generation of shaving razors, from Gillette Sensor to Mach 3 to Mach 3 Turbo and Mach 3 Power to six blade Fusion.

Strategic Planning

Strategic planning is a systematised way of relating to the future. It is an attempt to manage the effects of external, uncontrollable factors on the firm's strengths, weaknesses, objectives and goals to attain a desired end. Further, it is a commitment of resources to a country market to achieve specific goals. In other words, planning is the job of making things happen that may not otherwise occur. There is a lot of discussion on the

PRODUCT LIFE CYCLE (PLC)
different stages in a product's life, from introduction to death

PLC STAGES
stages in the product life cycle: introduction, growth, maturity and decline

STRATEGIC PLANNING
a systematised way of relating to the future

Exhibit 10.5 Mergers and cooperation in the auto industry

The auto industry has been consolidating since the 1960s when there were 42 companies. The number of companies decreased to 11 in 2000 and the consolidation is still going on. In 2004 the following groups were present.

1	GM	General Motors, Fiat, Alfa Romeo, Ferrari, Subaru, Suzuki, Daewoo, Kia, Lotus, Opel, Cadillac, Chevrolet, Pontiac, Saab, Buick, Saturn, Vauxhall and Isuzu
2	Ford	Ford, Mazda, Volvo, Land Rover, Jaguar, Aston Martin and Lancia
3	VW	VW, SEAT, Audi, Skoda and Bentley
4	Toyota	Toyota, Lexus and Daihatsu
5	Daimler-Chrysler	Mercedes, Chrysler, Mitsubishi, Hyundai and Smart
6	BMW	BMW, Rolls-Royce and Mini
7	Peugeot	Peugeot and Citroën
8	Renault	Renault, Nissan and Samsung
9	Rover	Rover and MG
10	Honda	Honda
11	Porsche	Porsche

Source: compiled from Geutz, M., 'Turning Wheels between Europe, America and Asia: Mergers, Acquisition and Cooperation', paper presented at Carnegie Bosch Institute, Conference, Berlin, October 2001, and Auto Intelligence, 2002.

Company Objectives and Resources

Evaluation of a company's objectives and resources is crucial in all stages of planning for international operations. Each new market entered can require a complete evaluation, including existing commitments, relative to the parent company's objectives and resources. As markets grow increasingly competitive, as companies find new opportunities, and as the cost of entering foreign markets increases, companies need such planning.

Foreign market opportunities do not always parallel corporate objectives; it may be necessary to change the objectives, alter the scale of international plans or abandon them. One market may offer immediate profit but have a poor long-run outlook, while another may offer the reverse. Only when corporate objectives are clear can such differences be reconciled effectively.

International Commitment

The strategic planning approach taken by an international firm affects the degree of internationalisation to which management is philosophically committed. Such commitment affects the specific international strategies and decisions of the firm. After company objectives have been identified, management needs to determine whether it is prepared to make the level of commitment required for successful international operations – commitment in terms of resources to be invested, personnel for managing the international organisation and determination to stay in the market long enough to realise a return on these investments.

The Planning Process

Whether a company is marketing in several countries or entering a foreign market for the first time, planning is a major factor of success. The first-time foreign marketer must decide what products to develop, in which markets, and with what level of resource commitment. For the company already committed, the key decisions involve allocating effort and resources among countries and products, deciding on new markets to develop or old ones to withdraw from, and which products to develop or drop. Guidelines and systematic procedures are essential for evaluating international opportunities and risks and for developing strategic plans to take advantage of such opportunities. The process illustrated in Exhibit 10.6 offers a systematic guide to planning for the multinational firm operating in several countries.

Exhibit 10.6 The international planning process

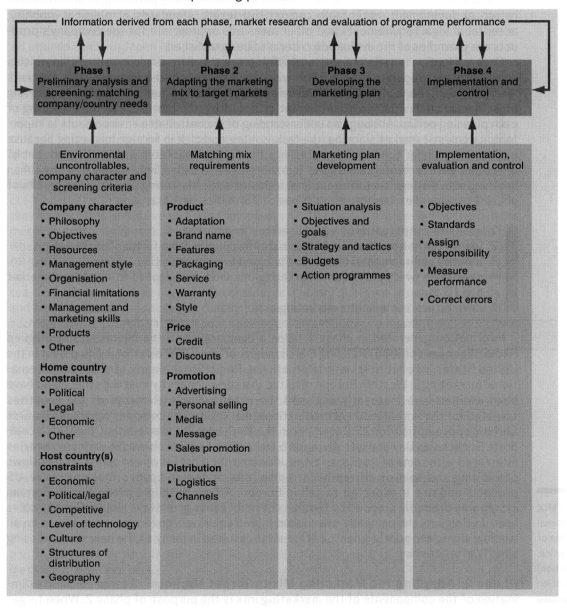

possible? (2) Which cultural/environmental adaptations are necessary for successful acceptance of the marketing mix? (3) Will adaptation costs allow profitable market entry? Based on the results in phase 2, a second screening of countries may take place with some countries dropped from further consideration. The next phase in the planning process is development of a marketing plan.

Phase 3: Developing the Marketing Plan   At this stage of the planning process, a marketing plan is developed for the target market – whether a single country or a global market set. It begins with a situation analysis and culminates in a specific action pro-gramme for the market. The specific plan establishes what is to be done, by whom, how it is to be done and when. Included are budgets and sales and profit expectations. Just as in phase 2, a decision not to enter a specific market may be made if it is determined that company marketing objectives and goals cannot be met.

Phase 4: Implementation and Control   A 'go' decision in phase 3 triggers imple-mentation of specific plans and anticipation of successful marketing. However, the plan-ning process does not end at this point. All marketing plans require coordination and control (phase 4) during the period of implementation. Many businesses do not control marketing plans as thoroughly as they could, even though continuous monitoring and con-trol could increase their success. An evaluation and control system requires performance objective action, that is, to bring the plan back on track should standards of performance fall short. A global orientation facilitates the difficult but extremely important manage-ment tasks of coordinating and controlling the complexities of international marketing.

While the model is presented as a series of sequential phases, the planning process is a dynamic, continuous set of interacting variables with information continuously building among phases. The phases outline a crucial path to be followed for effective, systematic planning. Furthermore, it provides the basis for viewing all country markets and their interrelationships as an integrated global unit.[18] By following the guidelines presented in Section 6, 'The Country Notebook – A Guide for Developing a Marketing Plan', the interna-tional marketer can put the strategic planning process into operation.[19]

Summary

Expanding markets around the world have increased competition for all levels of inter-national marketing. To keep abreast of the competition and maintain a viable position for increasingly competitive markets, a global perspective is necessary. Global competition also requires quality products designed to meet ever-changing customer needs and rap-idly advancing technology. Cost containment, customer satisfaction and a greater num-ber of players mean that every opportunity to refine international business practices must be examined in the light of company goals. Collaborative relationships, strategic international alliances and strategic planning are important avenues to global marketing that must be implemented in the planning of global marketing management.

Companies normally follow generic strategies as overall corporate strategies. These strategies are differentiation strategy or focus strategy. The choice of these strategies leads to sub-strategies for each and every product and market. These sub-strategies are influenced by a number of factors, such as branding, positioning and customer segments, the life cycle of the particular product and the market environment. This is achieved through a systematic marketing planning process.

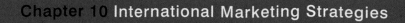

Questions

1 Define strategic planning. How does strategic planning for international marketing differ from domestic marketing?
2 Discuss the benefits to an MNC of accepting the global market concept.
3 Define the concept of quality. How do the concept of quality and TQM relate?
4 Cost containment and technological improvement are said to be the basis for competition. Why? Discuss.
5 What is meant by positioning? Explain.
6 Explain the three points that define a global approach to international marketing.
7 Branding is considered a part of strategy – discuss how valuable branding is for a consumer products company. Give examples.
8 What is the importance of collaborative relationships to competition?
9 Discuss what is meant by relationship marketing and how it differs from traditional marketing.
10 In phases 1 and 2 of the international planning process, countries may be dropped from further consideration as potential markets. Discuss some of the conditions in each phase that may exist in a country that would lead a marketer to exclude it.
11 Assume that you are the director of international marketing for a company producing refrigerators. Select one country in Asia and one in Europe and develop screening criteria to use in evaluating the two countries. Make any additional assumptions that are necessary about your company.

Further Reading

Peter J. Buckley and Pervez N. Ghauri, 'Globalisation, Economic Geography and the Strategy of Multinational Enterprises', *Journal of International Business Studies*, 2004, 35(2), pp. 81–98.

U. Elg, P.N. Ghauri and V. Tarnovskaya, 'The role of networking and matching in market entry to emerging retail markets', *International Marketing Review*, 2008, 25(6), pp. 674–99.

G. Hamel and C.K. Prahalad, 'Do You Really Have a Global Strategy?', *Harvard Business Review*, 1985, 63(4), pp. 139–48.

References

1 John Dunning, *Making Globalization Good: The Moral Challenges of Global Capitalism* (Oxford: Oxford University Press, 2003).
2 S. Ghoshal and C.A. Bartlett, 'Integrating the Enterprise', *Sloan Management Review*, 2002, 44(1), pp. 31–8.
3 John Dunning and J.-L. Muschielli (eds), *Multinational Firms: The Global–Local Dilemma* (London: Routledge, 2002).
4 Cyndee Miller, 'Chasing the Global Dream', *Marketing News*, 2 December 1996, pp. 1–2.
5 Peter Buckley, *Multinational Firms, Cooperation and Competition in the World Economy* (Houndsmill, Basingstoke: Macmillan).
6 A.K. Kohli and B.J. Jaworski, 'Market Orientation: The construct, research proposition and management implications', *Journal of Marketing*, 1990, 54/2, pp. 1–18.

7 B.J. Jaworski, A.K. Kohli and A. Sahay, 'Market Driven versus Market Driving Firms', *Journal of the Academy of Marketing Science*, 2000, 28/1, pp. 45–54.

8 P.N. Ghauri, V. Tarnovskaya and U. Elg, 'Market Driving Multinationals and their Global Sourcing Network', *International Marketing Review*, 2008, 25/5, pp. 504–19.

9 U. Elg, P.N. Ghauri and V. Tarnovskaya, 'The role of Networks and Matching in Market Entry to Emerging Retail Markets', *International Marketing Review*, 2008, 25/6, pp. 674–99.

10 'Tearing Up Today's Organization Chart', *Business Week*, 21st Century Capitalism Issue, 1994, pp. 80–2.

11 This section draws from Robert M. Morgan and Shelby D. Hunt, 'The Commitment-Trust Theory of Relationship Marketing', *Journal of Marketing*, July 1994, pp. 20–38.

12 David Whitwam, Regina Fazio Maruca, 'The Right Way to Go Global: An Interview with Whirlpool CEO David Whitwam', *Harvard Business Review*, March–April 1994, 72(2), pp. 135–43.

13 The authors prefer to use the term *collaborative relationship* to refer to all forms of collaborative effort between a company and its customers, markets, suppliers, manufacturing partners, research and development partners, government agencies and all other types of alliance. Consumer orientation, *Keiretsu* and strategic alliances can all be grouped under the broad rubric of collaborative relationships. All seek similar universal 'truths': participant satisfaction, long-term ties, loyalty and mutually beneficial exchanges, yet there are some fundamental differences among them.

14 Jagdish Seth and Atul Parvatiyar, 'The Evolution of Relationship Marketing', *International Business Review*, 1995, 5(4), pp. 625–45.

15 Saeed Smiee and Peter Walters, 'Relationship Marketing in an International Context', *International Business Review*, 2003, 12(2), pp. 193–214.

16 For a complete discussion of the logic of SIAs, see Kenichi Ohmae, *The Borderless World* (New York: Harper Business, 1990), Chap. 8, 'The Global Logic of Strategic Alliances', pp. 114–36; and Kenichi Ohmae, 'Putting Global Logic First', *Harvard Business Review*, January 1995, 73(1), pp. 119–25.

17 This section draws on Michael Porter, *Competitive Advantage; Creating and Sustaining Superior Performance* (The Free Press, 1985); and Harold Chee and Rod Haris, *Global Marketing Strategy* (FT Management, 1998).

18 Roger Kashlak, Rajan Chandran and Anthony Di Benedetto, 'Reciprocity in International Business: A Study of Telecommunications Alliances and Contracts', *Journal of International Business Studies*, vol. 29, no. 2, 1998, pp. 281–304.

19 C.K. Prahalad and K. Lieberthal, 'The End of Corporate Imperialism', *Harvard Business Review*, 1998, 81(8), pp. 109–17.

Chapter 11
International Market Entry Strategies

Chapter Outline

systems to capitalise on global demand, have cost-effective manufacturing and have capital to build new systems as necessary. Other reasons to enter into strategic alliances are to:[8]

1 acquire needed current market bases
2 acquire needed technological bases
3 utilise excess manufacturing capacity
4 reduce new market risk and entry costs
5 accelerate product introductions demanded by rapid technological changes and shorter product life cycles
6 achieve economies of scale in production, research and development or marketing
7 overcome cultural and trade barriers
8 extend the existing scope of operations.

The scope of what a company needs to do and what it can do is at a point where even the largest firms engage in alliances to maintain their competitiveness. Exhibit 11.5 shows the different alliances in the airline industry and in the European television broadcast market.

STRATEGIC ALLIANCE
when two companies cooperate for a certain purpose

A company enters a **strategic alliance** to acquire the skills necessary to achieve its objectives more effectively, and at a lower cost or with less risk than if it acted alone.[9] For example, a company strong in research and development skills and weak in the ability or capital to successfully market a product will seek an alliance to offset its weakness – one partner to provide marketing skills and capital and the other to provide technology and a product. The majority of alliances today are designed to exploit markets and/or technology.

Of course, not all SIAs are successful; some fail and others are dissolved after reaching their goals. Failures can be attributed to a variety of reasons, but all revolve around lack of perceived benefits to one or more of the partners. Benefits may never have been realised in some cases, and different goals and management styles have caused dissatisfaction in other alliances. Such was the case with an alliance between Rubbermaid and the Dutch chemical company DSM; the two differed on management and strategic issues.

Exhibit 11.5 The biggest airline alliances

Alliance	Aircraft Fleet	Turnover (€ billion) ($)	GDP Passenger (million)	Kilometre* (million)	Close relationships with:

Oneworld
  American Airlines
  British Airways
  Cathay Pacific (Hong Kong)
  Qantas (Australia)
  Canadian Airlines
  Finnair
  Iberia
  Japan Airlines
  Lan
  Malev
  Royal Jordanian
	2226	64 (71)	159.4	390	Aerolineas (Arg.); Avianca (Col.); Taca, Tam (Brazil); US Airways

Exhibit 11.5 (The biggest airline alliances, continued)

Alliance	Aircraft Fleet	Turnover (€ billion) ($)	GDP Passenger (million)	Kilometre* (million)	Close relationships with:
Star Alliance USAirways (US) Lufthansa (Germany) SAS (Sweden) Air Canada Austrian Air China Asiana Airlines All Nippon Airways Air New Zealand BMI Egypt Air LOT Polish Airlines Shanghai Airlines South African Airways Spanair Swiss Singapore Airlines TAP Portugal Thai Airways Turkish Airlines Varig (Brazil)	3325	58.7 (65)	188.5	335	Air New Zealand; Ansett (Australia)
Sky Team Northwest KLM Air France Alitalia Aeroflot China Southern Continental Korean Air Delta CSA – Czech Airlines Aero Mexico	2496	31 (34.4)	134.0	253	Kenya Airways (35 per cent); Japan Air System, Nippon Cargo Japan); Malaysian Airline System (*16 mn passengers*); America West; Aces (Col.); Eurowings (Ger.); (Southern China Airlines); AirEurope; Copa Airlines

*A 'passenger/kilometre' is 1 kilometre flown with one passenger. The figures give the total amount of passenger/kilometres flown by the alliance.

Sources: based on 'Vier Allianties Beheersen Helft van Luchtvaart', *De Volkskrant*, 22 September, p..16; and 'Clubable Class Books Slots for Take-off', *The European*, 28 September–4 October 1998, pp. 18–19. www.skyteam.com; www.oneworld.com, www.staralliance.com, 2009.

messenger bag and several Vuitton accessories, and now covets high-heeled Vuitton sandals – even though she'll have to put her name on a waiting list. 'Louis Vuitton never goes out of style,' she says as she leaves its Fifth Avenue store.

● Would the Louis Vuitton machine ever run out of steam?

Source: Business Week, 'Money Machine', 22 March 2004.

Franchising

Franchising is a rapidly growing form of licensing in which the franchiser provides a standard package of products, systems and management services, and the franchisee provides market knowledge, capital and personal involvement in management. The combination of skills permits flexibility in dealing with local market conditions and yet provides the parent firm with a reasonable degree of control. The franchiser can follow through on marketing of the products to the point of final sale. It is an important form of vertical market integration. Potentially, the franchise system provides an effective blending of skill centralisation and operational decentralisation, and has become an increasingly important form of international marketing. In some cases, franchising is having a profound effect on traditional businesses. In England, for example, it is estimated that annual franchised sales of fast foods is nearly €1.8 billion ($2 billion), which accounts for 30 per cent of all foods eaten outside the home.

By the 1990s more than 30 000 franchises of US firms were located in countries throughout the world. Franchises include soft drinks, motels, retailing, fast foods, car rentals, automotive services, recreational services and a variety of business services from print shops to sign shops. Franchising is the fastest-growing market entry strategy. It is often among the first types of foreign retail business to open in the emerging market economies of Eastern Europe, the former republics of Russia and China. McDonald's is in Moscow (its first store seats 700 inside and has 27 cash registers), and Kentucky Fried Chicken is in China (the Beijing KFC store has the highest sales volume of any KFC store in the world).

There are three types of franchise agreement used by franchising firms – master franchise, joint venture and licensing – any one of which can have a country's government as one partner. The master franchise is the most inclusive agreement and the method used in more than half of the international franchises. The master franchise gives the franchisee the rights to a specific area (many are for an entire country) with the authority to sell or establish subfranchises. The McDonald's franchise in Moscow is a master agreement owned by a Canadian firm and its partner, the Moscow City Council Department of Food Services.

Joint Ventures

Joint ventures (JVs), one of the more important types of collaborative relationship, have accelerated sharply during the past 20 years. Besides serving as a means of lessening political and economic risks by the amount of the partner's contribution to the venture, joint ventures provide a less risky way to enter markets that pose legal and cultural barriers than would be the case in the acquisition of an existing company.

Local partners can often lead the way through legal mazes and provide the outsider with help in understanding cultural nuances. A joint venture can be attractive to an international marketer:

1 when it enables a company to utilise the specialised skills of a local partner
2 when it allows the marketer to gain access to a partner's local distribution system

3 when a company seeks to enter a market where wholly owned activities are prohibited

4 when it provides access to markets protected by tariffs or quotas, and

5 when the firm lacks the capital or personnel capabilities to expand its international activities.

In China, a country considered to be among the riskiest in Asia, there have been 49 400 joint ventures established in the first 15 years since they began allowing JVs. Among the many reasons JVs are so popular is that they offer a way of getting around high Chinese tariffs, allowing a company to gain a competitive price advantage over imports. By manufacturing locally with a Chinese partner rather than importing, China's high tariffs (the tariff on motor vehicles is 200 per cent, 150 per cent on cosmetics and the average on miscellaneous products is 75 per cent) are bypassed and additional savings are achieved by using low-cost Chinese labour.[13]

A joint venture is differentiated from other types of strategic alliance or collaborative relationship in that a joint venture is a partnership of two or more participating companies that have joined forces to create a separate legal entity. Joint ventures should also be differentiated from minority holdings by an MNC in a local firm. Four factors are associated with joint ventures:

1 JVs are established, separate, legal entities

2 they acknowledge intent by the partners to share in the management of the JV

3 they are partnerships between legally incorporated entities, such as companies, chartered organisations or governments, and not between individuals

4 equity positions are held by each of the partners.

Nearly all companies active in world trade participate in at least one joint venture somewhere; many number their joint ventures in the dozens. A recent Conference Board study indicated that more than 50 per cent of *Fortune* 500 companies were engaged in one or more international joint ventures. In Japan alone, Royal Dutch Shell has more than 30 joint ventures; IBM has more than 35.

Consortia

The consortium and syndicate are similar to the joint venture and could be classified as such except for two unique characteristics: (1) they typically involve a large number of participants; (2) they frequently operate in a country or market in which none of the participants is currently active. Consortia are developed for pooling financial and managerial resources and to lessen risks. Often, huge construction projects are built under a consortium arrangement in which major contractors with different specialities form a separate company specifically to negotiate for and produce one job. One firm usually acts as the lead firm or the newly formed corporation may exist quite independently of its originators.

Manufacturing

Another means of foreign market development and entry is manufacturing, also called a wholly owned subsidiary within a foreign country. A company may manufacture locally to capitalise on low-cost labour, to avoid high import taxes, to reduce the high costs of transportation to market, to gain access to raw materials, and/or as a means of gaining market entry. Seeking lower labour costs offshore is no longer an unusual strategy. A hallmark of global companies today is the establishment of manufacturing operations throughout the

Questions

1 How will entry into a developed foreign market differ from entry into a relatively untapped market?
2 Explain the popularity of joint ventures.
3 Assume you are marketing director of a company producing refrigerators. Select one country in Asia and one in Latin America and develop screening criteria to evaluate the two markets. On the basis of these criteria make an analysis and select the country you should enter.
4 What are the factors that influence the attractiveness of a country as a market? How can you do the analysis to select a market to enter?
5 Explain the popularity of strategic alliances – why do companies enter these agreements?

Further Reading

F.R. Root, *Entry Strategies for International Markets* (Lexington, MA: Lexington Books, 1994).

H. Agndal, S. Chetty, H. Wilson, 'Social capital dynamics and foreign market entry' *International Business Review*, 2008, 17(6), pp. 663–75.

R. Mudambi and S.M. Mudambi, 'Diversification and Market Entry Choices in the Context of Foreign Direct Investment', *International Business Review*, 2002, 11(1), pp. 35–55.

References

1 This section draws on Peter Buckley and Pervez Ghauri (eds), *The Internationalization of the Firm: A Reader* (London: Thomson Learning, 2004).
2 Jan Johanson and Finn Wiethersheim-Paul, 'The Internationalization of the Firm: Four Swedish Cases', *Journal of Management Studies*, 1975 (October), pp. 305–22.
3 J. Johanson and J.E. Vahlne, 'The Internationalisation Process of the Firm: a Model of Knowledge Development and Increasing Foreign Market Commitments', *Journal of International Business Studies*, 1977, 8(1), 23–32.
4 This section draws on Pervez Ghauri and Peter Buckley, 'Globalization and the End of Competition', in V. Havila, M. Forsgren and H. Håkansson (eds), *Critical Perspectives on Internationalisation* (Oxford: Elsevier, 2002), pp. 7–28.
5 Lars Oxelheim and Pervez Ghauri (eds), *European Union and the Race for Foreign Direct Investment in Europe* (Oxford: Elsevier, 2004).
6 G.D. Harrel and R.O. Kiefer, 'Multinational Strategic Portfolios', *MSU Business Topics*, 1981 (winter), pp. 51–5.
7 This section draws on G. Albaum, J. Strandskov and E. Duerr, *International Marketing and Export Management* (London: FT-Prentice Hall, 2002).
8 Pontus Braunerhjelm, Lars Oxelheim, and Per Thulin, 'The relationship between domestic and outward foreign direct investment: The role of industry-specific effects' *International Business Review*, 2005, 14(6), pp. 67–76.
9 U. Elg, P.N. Ghauri and V. Tarnovskaya, 'The Role of Networks and Matching in Market Entry to Emerging Retail Markets', *International Marketing Review*, 2008, 25(6), 674–99.

10 Raju Narisetti, 'Rubbermaid Brings to End Europe Venture', *Wall Street Journal*, 1 June 1994, p. A-4.

11 Roger Kashlak, Rajan Chandran and Anthony Di Benedetto, 'Reciprocity in International Business: A Study of Telecommunications Alliances and Contracts', *Journal of International Business Studies*, 1998, 29(2), pp. 281–304.

12 Preet Aulakh, Tamer Cavusgil and M.B. Sarkar, 'Compensation in International Licensing Agreements', *Journal of International Business Studies*, 1998, 29(2), pp. 409–20.

13 Dana B. Minbaeva, 'HRM practices affecting extrinsic and intrinsic motivation of knowledge receivers and their effect on intra-MNC knowledge transfer', *International Business Review*, 2008, 17(6), pp. 703–13.

14 For further details on this topic see Michael Row, *Countertrade* (London: Euromoney Books, 1989).

The transaction brings to an end an unhappy association between E-Land and Homever. E-Land bought Korea's fourth biggest discounter back in 2006 from French retailer Carrefour for $1.85 billion, but it posted a W200 billion net loss last year. E-Land had re-designed the unpopular warehouse-style stores and given them a new brand name. But labour unrest over contract workers disrupted operations at some of its outlets and created a public relations disaster. European private equity fund Permira came to the rescue earlier this month, agreeing to pump W400 billion into the ailing subsidiary — although that deal will now not take place.

Tesco entered Korea in 1999 and the country is now its most profitable overseas market. The company is continuing to expand outside the UK as profits from its local market, in which it is dominant, come under pressure as consumer spending falls, and also as the government threatens to restrict further domestic expansion. But it is one of the few foreign companies in the sector to stay in Korea, let alone grow. Carrefour and Walmart, for instance, have already given up competing with market leader E-mart, which is owned by Shinsegae, and decided to focus on China instead.

Source: Business Week, 15 May 2008.

own-brand labels that chains such as Sainsbury boast about helps explain why their operating profit margins are as high as 8 per cent, or eight times the profit margins of their US counterparts.

Own-brand penetration has traditionally been high in Britain and, more recently, high in Europe as well. Own brands, with their high margins, will become even more important as the trend in consolidation of retailers continues and as discounters such as Ahold of the Netherlands, Aldi of Germany, Wal-Mart of the United States and Carrefour of France expand throughout Europe, putting greater pressure on prices.

As it stands now, own brands are formidable competitors. They provide the retailer with high margins, they receive preferential shelf space and strong in-store promotion and, perhaps most important for consumer appeal, they are quality products at low prices. Contrast this with manufacturers' brands, which are traditionally premium priced and offer the retailer lower margins than they get from their own brands. Exhibit 12.2 shows the market share and growth rate for own brands.

Exhibit 12.2 Market share and growth rate for own brands

	Market share (%)	Growth rate (annual % 2003)
Global	15	4
Europe	22	6
North America	16	0
Asia Pacific	4	14
Emerging markets	4	48
Latin America	1	16

Source: compiled from Gary Silverman, 'Retailers Pack New Punch in Battle with Brands', *Financial Times*, 15 November 2004, p. 20.

To maintain market share, global brands will have to be priced competitively and provide real consumer value. Global marketers must examine the adequacy of their brand strategies in the light of such competition. This may make the cost and efficiency benefits of global brands even more appealing.

Brand Elements

Twelve main elements are identified on branding that represent the broad range of definitions and elements of a brand; such as: *legal instrument; logo; company; shorthand; risk reducer; identity system; image in consumers' minds; value system; personality; relationship; adding value; and evolving entity.*[16] The twelve elements present a certain degree of overlapping among the tangible and intangible contents of the brand. Exhibit 12.3 shows these elements and lists their antecedents and consequences:

Exhibit 12.3 Elements of a brand and its functions

Brand elements	Contents	Functions
Legal Instrument	- Mark of ownership - Name, logo, design - Trademark	- Prosecute infringers
Logo	- Name, term, symbol, design - Product characteristics	- Indentify, differentiate through visual identity and name - Quality assurance
Company	- Recognisable corporate name and image - Programs of organisation define corporate personality	- Product lines benefit from corporate personality - Convey consistent message to stakeholders - Differentiation: establish relationship
Shorthand	- Firm stresses quality not quantity of information	- Recognisable brand association - Facilitate information processing - Speed decision
Risk Reducer	- Confidence that expectation being fulfilled	- Brand as a contract
Identity System	- More than just a name - Holistic structure including brand's personality	- Meaning - Strategic positioning - Communicate essence to stakeholders
Image	- Consumer centred - Image in consumers' mind is brand 'reality'	- Feedback of image to change identity - Market research - Manage brand concept over time
Value System	- Consumer relevant values imbue the brand	- Brand values match relevant consumer values
Personality	- Psychological values, communicated through advertising and packaging define brands personality	- Differentiation from symbolism: human values projected - Stress added values beyond functional

Exhibit 12.5 Components of brand equity

```
                    ┌──────────────────────────┐
                    │ • Reduced Marketing      │
        ┌─────────┐ │   Costs                  │
        │ Brand   │→│ • Attracting New         │
        │ Loyalty │ │   Customers              │──┐
        └─────────┘ │ • Time to Respond to     │  │   ┌──────────────────────┐
                    │   Competitive Threats    │  │   │ Provides Value to    │
                    └──────────────────────────┘  ├──→│ Customer by          │
                    ┌──────────────────────────┐  │   │ Enhancing Customer's:│
                    │ • Anchor to Which Other  │  │   │ • Processing of      │──┐
        ┌─────────┐ │   Associations Can Be    │  │   │   Information         │  │
        │ Brand   │ │   Attached               │  │   │ • Confidence in the  │  │
        │Awareness│→│ • Familiarity-Linking    │──┤   │   Purchase Decision  │  │
        └─────────┘ │ • Signal of             │  │   │ • Satisfaction       │  │
                    │   Commitment             │  │   └──────────────────────┘  │
┌────────┐          └──────────────────────────┘  │              ↑↓             │  ┌──────────────┐
│ Brand  │          ┌──────────────────────────┐  │   ┌──────────────────────┐  ├─→│ Competitive  │
│ Equity │          │ • Reason-to-Buy          │  │   │ Provides Value to Firm│ │   │  Advantage   │
└────────┘ ┌─────────┐ • Differentiate/Position│──┤   │ by Enhancing:        │  │  └──────────────┘
        │Perceived│ │ • Price                  │  │   │ • Brand Loyalty      │──┘
        │ Quality │→│                          │  ├──→│ • Prices/Margins     │
        └─────────┘ └──────────────────────────┘  │   │ • Brand Extensions   │
                    ┌──────────────────────────┐  │   └──────────────────────┘
        ┌─────────┐ │ • Help Process           │  │
        │ Brand   │ │   Information            │  │
        │Associa- │→│ • Create Positive Attitude│─┘
        │ tions   │ │ • Extensions             │
        └─────────┘ └──────────────────────────┘
```

Source: based on Aaker (1991 and 1992).

GOING INTERNATIONAL 12.5

Developing a new brand

The sports apparel maker is sprinting into footwear – and trying to take on Nike – with the help of software and science.

The Baltimore headquarters of sports apparel maker Under Armour don't look much like the offices of a technology company.

Don't be fooled by the jock paraphernalia – or all the jocks working at the company: Under Armour is very much a high-tech place. It uses sophisticated design software, new manufacturing techniques, the latest in material engineering, and robust information technology systems to produce virtually everything it makes, from its original moisture-wicking T-shirts to kneepads to cleats. 'We try to be on the bleeding edge,' says CEO Kevin Plank, a former University of Maryland football player who founded the company in 1996. 'We're willing to look at wild, out-there ideas if they can make our products perform better.'

Executives at Under Armour, which had more than $700 million in revenue last year, knew that making a run at $19-billion-a-year Nike wouldn't be easy, so they set out to build state-of-the-art gear. A look at the process shows just how much innovation and technology companies have to pour into product development today – even for something as seemingly simple as a pair of athletic shoes.

Thinking in 3-D. Ask Under Armour management to talk about the technology in the new running shoes, and they'll tick off a list of advances in the composition of the foam in the sole or mention the moisture-resistant fabric used in the shoe's upper. But Under Armour wouldn't have been able to enter the running-shoe business if not for a game-changing upgrade in its enterprise software package implemented in 2006, not long after the company went public.

● Can Under Armour gain some market shares from Nike & Adidas? How?

Source: Stephanie N. Mehta, *Fortune*, 2 February 2009, p. 13.

Exhibit 12.6 The process of creating a brand

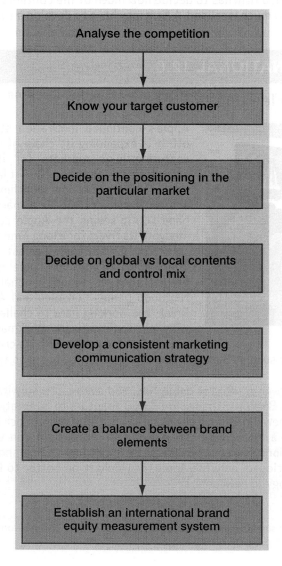

Further Reading

L. Chernatony and M. McDonald (1998), *Creating Powerful Brands – in Consumer Service and Industrial Markets*, Oxford: Butterworth-Heinemann, 2nd edn, p. 20.

D.A. Aaker and R. Jacobson (2001), 'The Value Relevance of Brand Attitude in High-Technology Markets', *Journal of Marketing Research* 38(4), 485–94.

D.A. Aaker (2004), *Brand Portfolio Strategy: Creating Relevance, Differentiation, Energy, Leverage, and Clarity*, New York: Free Press.

K.L. Keller (2008), *Strategic Brand Management: A European Perspective*, Harlow, UK: Pearson Education.

P. Wang, X.-P. Zhang and M. Ouyang (2009), 'Does advertising create sustained firm value? The capitalization of brand intangible', *Journal of Academy of Marketing Science*, 37/2, pp. 130–43.

References

1 P. Kotler (1997), *Marketing Management-analysis, planning, implementation and control* (New Jersey: Prentice-Hall).

2 L. Chernatony and M. McDonald (1998), *Creating Powerful Brands – in Consumer Service and Industrial Markets* (Oxford: Butterworth-Heinemann, 2nd edn, p. 20).

3 S. Hart and J. Murphy (1998), *Brands: The New Wealth Creators* (London: Macmillan Press).

4 N. Klein (2000), *No Logo* (Stockholm: Ordfront Förlang) and, E. Delgado-Ballester and M. Hernandez-Espallardo (2008), 'Building online brands through brand alliances in Internet', *European Journal of Marketing*, 42/9–10, pp. 954–76.

5 L. Chernatony and F.D.O. Riley (1998a), 'Defining A "Brand": Beyond The Literature With Experts' Interpretations', *Journal of Marketing Management*, 14(4/5), 417–43.

6 L. Chernatony and F.D.O. Riley (1998b), 'Modelling the Components of the Brand', *European Journal of Marketing*, 32(11/12), 1074–90.

7 'Unilever Chief: Refresh Brands', *Advertising Age*, 19 July 1994, pp. 1–20.

8 For a comprehensive review of the literature on country-of-origin effects, see e.g. Warren Bilky and Erik Nes, 'Country-of-origin Effects in Product Evaluations', *Journal of International Business Studies*, 1982, vol. 13, no. 1, pp. 89–99; Aysegul Ozsomer and Tamer Cavusgil, 'Country-of-origin Effects on Product Evaluation: A Sequel to Bilky and Nes Review', in M.C. Gilly *et al.* (eds), *Proceedings of the American Marketing Association, Annual Conference, 1991*, pp. 69–77; and Robert Peterson and Alain Jolibert, 'A Meta Analysis of Country-of-origin Effects', *Journal of International Business Studies*, vol. 26, no. 4, 1996, pp. 883–900.

9 David Strutton, Lou E. Pelton and James R. Lumpkin, 'Internal and External Country of Origin Stereotypes in the Global Marketplace for the Domestic Promotion of US Automobiles', *Journal of Global Marketing*, vol. 7, no. 3, 1994, pp. 61–77.

10 Jerome Witt and C.P. Rao, 'The Impact of Global Sourcing on Consumers: Country-of-origin Effects on Perceived Risk', *Journal of Global Marketing*, vol. 6, no. 3, 1992, pp. 105–28.

11 'Czech Republic: Consumers Think Foreign Goods are Overpriced', *Crossborder Monitor*, 3 August 1994, p. 4.

12 Dana Milbank, 'Made in America Becomes a Boast in Europe', *Wall Street Journal*, 19 January 1994, p. B1.

13 Sheila Tefft, 'China's Savvy Shoppers Load Carts with Expensive Imported Goods', *Advertising Age*, 20 June 1994, pp. 1–21.

14 See Frank Alpert and Michael Kamins, 'An Empirical Investigation of Consumer Memory, Attitude, and Perceptions Towards Pioneer and Follower Brands', *Journal of Marketing*, vol. 59, no. 4, 1995, pp. 34–45.

15 Eleena de Lisser and Kevin Helliker, 'Private Labels Reign in British Groceries', *Wall Street Journal*, 3 March 1994, p. B1.

16 P. Håkansson, R. Wahlund *et al.* (1996), *Varumarken-fran teori till praktik*, Stockholm: Stockholm School of Economics.

17 S. Moorthy and B.T. Ratchford (1997), 'Consumer Information Search Revisited: Theory and Empirical Analysis', *Journal of Consumer Research*, 23(4), 263–78.

18 M.D. Smith (2002), 'The Impact of Shopbots on Electronic Markets', *Journal of the Academy of Marketing Science*, 30(4), 446.

19 R.N. Stone and K. Gronhaug (1993), 'Perceived Risk: Further Considerations for the Marketing Discipline', *European Journal of Marketing*, 27(3), 39.

20 D.A. Aaker and R. Jacobson (2001), 'The Value Relevance of Brand Attitude in High-Technology Markets', *Journal of Marketing Research*, 38(4), 485–94.

21 D.A. Aaker and K.L. Keller (1990), 'Consumer evaluations of brand extensions', *Journal of Marketing*, 54(Winter), 27–41.

22 R. Ahluwalia, H.R. Unnava *et al.* (2001), 'The Moderating Role of Commitment on the Spillover Effect of Marketing Communications', *Journal of Marketing Research*, 38(4), 458–71.

23 T. Ambler, C.B. Bhattacharya *et al.* (2002), 'Relating Brand and Customer Perspectives on Marketing Management', *Journal of Service Research*, 5(1), 13–26.

24 P. Kotler (1996), 'Crisis in the Arts: The Marketing Response', *California Management Review*, 39(1), 28–52.

25 N. Kochan (1996), *The World's Greatest Brands* (London: Macmillan).

26 C.J. Simon and M.W. Sullivan (1993), 'The Measurement and Determinants of Brand Equity: A Financial Approach', *Marketing Science*, 12(Winter), 28–52.

27 D.A. Aaker (2004), *Brand Portfolio Strategy: Creating relevance, differentiation, energy, leverage, and clarity* (New York: Free Press).

28 P. Barwise, (1993), 'Brand Equity: Snark or boojum?', *International Journal of Research in Marketing*, 10(1), 93–104.

29 S.C. Bahadir, S.G. Bharadwaj and R.K. Shivastava (2008), 'Financial Value of Brands in Mergers and Acquisitions: Is Value in the Eye of the Beholder', *Journal of Marketing*, 72/6, pp. 49–64.

30 D.A. Aaker (1991), *Managing Brand Equity* (New York: Free Press).

31 D.A. Aaker (1992), 'Managing the most important asset: brand equity', *Planning Review*, 20, 56–68.

32 K.L. Keller (2008), *Strategic Brand Management: A European Perspective*, Pearson Education Limited.

33 D.A. Aaker and E. Joachimsthaler (2006), 'The Brand Relationship Spectrum: The key to brand architecture challenge', *California Management Review*, 42(4).

34 W. Olins (1989), *Corporate Identity* (London: Thames and Hudson).

35 J.N. Kapferer (1997), *Strategic Brand Management – creating and sustaining brand equity long term* (London: Kogan Page Limited).

36 J.N. Kapferer (2001), *Re inventing the brand* (London: Kogan Page Limited).

37 P. Kotler (1996), 'Crisis in the Arts: The Marketing Response', *California Management Review*, 39(1), 28–52.

38 P.J. Kitchen and D.E. Schultz (2001), 'Raising the Corporate Umbrella: Corporate Communication in the 21st century', p.121, and P. Wang, X.-P. Zhang and M. Ouyang (2009), 'Does advertising create sustained firm value? The Capitalization of brand intangible', *Journal of Academy of Marketing Science*, 37/2, pp. 130–43.

39 J.M. Handelman (2006), 'Corporate Identity and the Societal Constituent', *Journal of the Academy of Marketing Science*, 34(2), 107–14.

40 H. Itami and T.W. Roehl (1987), *Mobilizing Invisible Assets* (Cambridge, MA: Harvard University Press).

41 R. Hall (1993), 'A framework linking intangible resources and capabilities to sustainable competitive advantage', *Strategic Management Journal*, 14, 607–18.

42 L. Chernatony and F.D.O. Riley (1998b), 'Modelling the Components of the Brand', *European Journal of Marketing*, 32(11/12), 1074–90.

43 C.J. Fombrun and M. Shanley (1990), 'What's in a name? Reputation building and corporate strategy', *Academy of Management Journal*, 33, 233–58.

44 M. Hatch and M. Schultz (2000), 'Scaling the Towers of Babel: relational differences between identity, image and culture in organizations', in M. Schultz and M.H. Larsen (eds) *The Expressive Organization* (Oxford: Oxford University Press).

GOING INTERNATIONAL 13.2

US could clash with EU on tech trade tariffs

The US was poised to launch a fresh trade dispute against the European Union over tariffs on several technology products such as flat-screen monitors and printers. People familiar with the matter said the US was preparing to file the case at the World Trade Organisation barring an 11th-hour change of heart.

The dispute centres on the EU's interpretation of the Information Technology Agreement (ITA), a decade-old, 70-nation pact, which prohibits countries from imposing tariffs on many high-tech products. Washington says the EU is violating the ITA by placing tariffs of 14 per cent on items such as large flat-screen monitors and cable television set-top boxes, and tariffs of 6 per cent on multi-function printers.

As the prospects of a trade dispute with the EU over the ITA have grown, so has speculation that other leading technology producers, such as Japan, may flank the US in its case. The Japanese embassy in Washington declined to comment.

If the US were to file a WTO case against the EU over the ITA, it would start a 60-day consultation period, during which the sides would try to reach a settlement before the case moved to a dispute panel. In March, the US and EU joined forces to file a WTO claim against China for what they saw as unfair restrictions on providers of financial information.

Source: Financial Times, 28 May 2008.

Exhibit 13.2 World's 10 largest exporters and importers ($ billions)

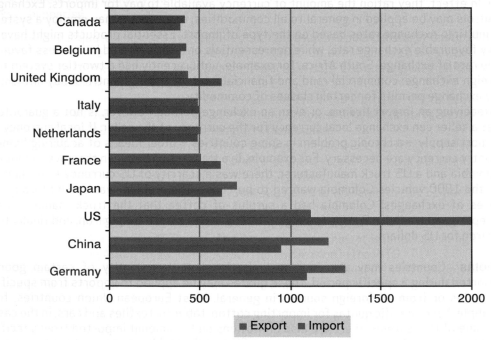

Source: WTO, 2007.

Import Licences   As a means of regulating the flow of exchange and the quantity of a particular imported commodity, countries often require import licences. The fundamental difference between quotas and import licences as a means of controlling imports is the greater flexibility of import licences over quotas. Quotas permit importing until the quota is filled; licensing limits quantities on a case-by-case basis.

Boycott   A boycott is an absolute restriction against trade with a country, or trade of specific goods. Countries can refuse to trade (buy or sell) with other countries; for example, the United States imposed, with the help of the United Nations, a boycott on trade with Libya, which was respected by most countries. This was, however, taken away after Libya gave up its plan to develop nuclear weapons. The United Nations also imposed a boycott on trade with Iraq after the first Gulf War. Similarly, the United States has had a boycott on trade with Cuba, due to the latter's communist regime. This boycott was also respected by Western European countries. However, lately the WTO and the European Union have expressed the wish to open trade with Cuba, but America is pushing against it.

Standards   Health standards, safety standards and product quality standards are necessary to protect the consuming public, and imported goods are required to comply with local laws. Unfortunately, standards can also be used to slow down or restrict the procedures for importing to the point that the additional time and cost required to comply become, in effect, trade restrictions. Safety standards are a good example. Most countries have safety standards for electrical appliances and require that imported electrical

GOING INTERNATIONAL 13.3

Export restrictions on technology

Most Western countries impose restrictions on the export of sensitive advanced technology to a number of countries. For example, while India and Pakistan were working to develop uranium enrichment capabilities, all export of technology related to uranium enrichment could not be exported to these countries. Libya has had total export restrictions for similar reasons. However, now that Libya has promised to give up its nuclear ambitions, these restrictions have been relaxed.

© Roger Ressimeyer/ CORBIS

China successfully fired a new type of long-range, ground-to-ground missile and is running an extensive training programme for air force officers. At the same time, tensions between China and Taiwan have intensified after Taiwan's president declared that relationships between Taipei and Beijing should be based on 'state-to-state' relationship principles.

The United States, being an ally of Taiwan, has restrictions on technology export to China, particularly technology that can be used in military applications. While most of the technology can be used for both civilian and military applications, it's the responsibility of the exporters to ensure that the technology exported is not used for military purposes.

● Is it justified to impose restrictions on technology exports?

Source: compiled from various sources.

GOING INTERNATIONAL 13.6

You don't look like a Mexican peanut to me!

The US Government is serious about its import restrictions, especially on agricultural products. It doesn't look kindly, for example, on peanuts from China being shipped as Mexican peanuts. But how do you tell where peanuts, orange juice and other agricultural products come from? With an 'inductively coupled plasma mass spectrometer', that's how.

The US Customs Service uses such a machine to determine whether a peanut headed for Safeway matches a peanut grown in Mexico or Georgia. It's a little like DNA testing for plants. While the machine can't tell exactly whether the peanuts come from a specific country, it can tell if the peanuts in a sample match a sample of peanuts known to come from a specific country. This process began about 10 years ago with the analysing of frozen orange juice. Since frozen orange juice from different countries has different tariff schedules, transshipment through a lower-tariff country can make a big difference in tariffs paid.

In a little over a year, with the help of the machine, US Customs was able to build a case of 'dumping' against Chinese garlic, an illegal transshipment case against Argentine peanuts, and a case against a California coffee distributor who was adulterating Hawaiian Kona coffee with cheaper Central American beans and selling the result as pure Kona.

Sources: Guy Gugliotta, 'High-tech Trade Enforcement Tracks Peanuts Across Borders', *Washington Post*, 4 December 1997, p. A21; and Bob Dart, 'US Takes Aim at Peanut Traffickers: High-tech Equipment is Helping to Detect Illegal Over-the-border Shipments: Undercutting NAFTA', *Atlanta Journal and Constitution*, 9 December 1997, p. A12.

of international trade transaction. When quoting prices, it is important to make them meaningful. The most commonly used international trade terms include the following.

CIF (cost, insurance, freight) to a named overseas port of import. A CIF quote is more meaningful to the overseas buyer because it includes the costs of goods, insurance, and all transportation and miscellaneous charges to the named place of debarkation.

C&F (cost and freight) to named overseas port. The price includes the cost of the goods and transportation costs to the named place of debarkation. The cost of insurance is borne by the buyer.

FAS (free alongside) at a named port of export. The price includes cost of goods and charges for delivery of the goods alongside the shipping vessel. The buyer is responsible for the cost of loading on to the vessel, transportation and insurance.

FOB (free on board) at a named inland point of origin; at a named port of exportation; or a named vessel and port of export. The price includes the cost of the goods and delivery to the place named.

EX (named port of origin). The price quoted covers costs only at the point of origin (for example, EX Factory). All other charges are the buyer's concern.

A complete list of terms and their definitions can be found in *Incoterms*, a booklet published by the International Chamber of Commerce. It is important for the exporter to

Exhibit 13.3 Who is responsible for costs under various terms

Cost items/terms	FOB (free on board) inland carrier at factory	FOB (free on board) inland carrier at point of shipment	FAS (free alongside) vessel or plane at port of shipment	CIF (cost, insurance, freight) at port of destination
Export packing*	Buyer	Seller	Seller	Seller
Inland freight	Buyer	Seller	Seller	Seller
Port charges	Buyer	Buyer	Seller	Seller
Forwarder's fee	Buyer	Buyer	Buyer	Seller
Consular fee	Buyer	Buyer	Buyer	Buyer†
Loading on vessel or plane	Buyer	Buyer	Buyer	Seller
Ocean freight	Buyer	Buyer	Buyer	Seller
Cargo insurance	Buyer	Buyer	Buyer	Seller
Customs duties	Buyer	Buyer	Buyer	Buyer
Ownership of goods passes	When goods on board an inland carrier (truck, rail, etc.) or in hands of inland carrier	When goods unloaded by inland carrier	When goods alongside carrier, in hands of air or ocean carrier	When goods on board air or ocean carrier at *port of shipment*

* Who absorbs export packing? This charge should be clearly agreed on. Charges are sometimes controversial.

† The seller has responsibility to arrange for consular invoices (and other documents requested by the buyer's government). According to official definitions, buyer pays fees, but sometimes, as a matter of practice, seller includes in quotations.

understand exactly the meanings of terms used in quotations. A simple misunderstanding regarding delivery terms may prevent the exporter from meeting contractual obligations or make that person responsible for shipping costs he or she did not intend to incur. Exhibit 13.3 indicates who is responsible for a variety of costs under various terms.

Letters of Credit   These days most import and export is done through **letters of credit (LC)**. The letter of credit shifts the buyer's credit risk to the bank issuing the LC. When an LC is issued, the seller draws a draft against the bank issuing the credit and receives money by presenting shipping documents to show that he has already shipped the goods. The LC provides the greatest degree of protection to the seller – that he will receive his money once he has shipped the goods.

The procedure for LC starts at the signing of the contract, as it stipulates how the cash will be paid for goods (see Exhibit 13.4). The buyer/importer goes to the local bank and arranges for the letter of credit, the buyer bank notifies its corresponding bank in the seller's country (seller's bank) with the conditions set forth in the LC. The seller can draw a draft against the LC for the payment of goods.

LETTERS OF CREDIT (LC)
shifts the buyer's credit risk to bank issuing the LC

Packing and Marking

Special packing and marking requirements must be considered for shipments destined to be transported over water, subject to excessive handling or destined for parts of the world

With paperwork completed, the physical movement of goods must be considered. Transportation mode affects total product cost because of the varying requirements of packing, inventory levels, time requirements, perishability, unit cost, damage and pilfering losses, and customer service. Transportation for each product must be assessed in view of the interdependent nature of all these factors. To assure optimum distribution at minimal cost, a physical distribution system determines everything from plant location to final customer delivery in terms of the most efficient use of capital investment, resources, production, inventory, packing and transportation.

Questions

1 Explain the reasoning behind the various regulations and restrictions imposed on the exportation and importation of goods.
2 What is the purpose of an import licence? Discuss.
3 Explain foreign-trade zones and illustrate how they may be used by an exporter/by an importer. How do foreign-trade zones differ from bonded warehouses?
4 Explain each of the following export documents:
   a bill of lading
   b consular invoice or certificate of origin
   c commercial invoice
   d insurance certificate.
5 Why would an exporter use the services of a foreign-freight forwarder? Discuss.
6 Besides cost advantages, what are the other benefits of an effective physical distribution system?

Further Reading

S. Estrin, K.E. Meyer, M. Wright, F. Foliano, 'Export propensity and intensity of subsidiaries in emerging economies', *International Business Review*, 2008, 17(5), pp. 574–86.

S.T. Cavusgil, 'Differences Among Exporting Firms Based on Degree of Internationalization', *Journal of Business Research*, 1984, 12(2), pp. 195–208.

C.A. Solberg and E. Nes, 'Export Trust, Commitment and Marketing Control in Integrated and Independent Export Channels', *International Business Review*, 2002, 11(4), pp. 385–405.

References

1 S.T. Cavusgil, 'Guidelines for Export Market Research', *Business Horizon*, 1985, November/December, pp. 283–95.
2 Fahri Karakaya, 'Barriers to Entry in International Markets', *Journal of Global Marketing*, vol. 7, no. 1, 1993, p. 10.
3 Alan Rugman and Alain Verbeke, 'Multinational Enterprises and Public Policy', *Journal of International Business Studies*, vol. 29, no. 1, 1998, pp. 115–36.
4 John Gorsuch, 'Air Cargo', *Trade and Culture*, March–April 1995, pp. 21–6.
5 G. Albaum, J. Strandkov and E. Derr, *International Marketing and Export Management* (Harlow: FT Prentice Hall, 2002).

Chapter 14
Ethics and Social Responsibility in International Marketing

Chapter Outline

Chapter Learning Objectives

What you should learn from Chapter 14

● To understand the importance of ethics in international marketing
● To be able to evaluate the impact of ethical issues on marketing
● To be able to analyse factors that influence a responsible marketing strategy
● How to use social responsibility as a marketing tool

Ethical issues and social responsibility together comprise a difficult but important task for international marketers. Consumer awareness about ethics, particularly in the case of multinational companies (MNCs) and foreign firms has increased. In addition a number of organisations (such as Greenpeace), consumer associations and national health organisations have entered the debate and are questioning MNC strategies and operations in different countries. Although most of the criticism is directed towards the strategic level of the companies, it is normally the marketing department that has to convince the market that the company is socially responsible and follows ethical principles.

Ethical Environment

Multinational companies (MNCs) operate in a number of countries, where legal and ethical standards may differ. There are huge differences as to right and wrong between the United States and Europe. Different countries in Europe also have different rules and regulations regarding Green marketing, marketing of cigarettes and alcoholic drinks, and packaged food. Huge investments made by MNCs in developing countries contribute towards their economic development but may have a huge impact on the environment (pollution) and other social issues. Some MNCs believe that while in developing countries, they do not have to follow the same standards of social responsibility as in their home markets, which is in itself morally wrong. Depending on history, geography, religion and economic systems, countries such as the US and Japan do have different attitudes towards work, leisure and pollution.

The existence of diverse nationalities within Europe means that attitudes are not quite homogeneous. In contrast to the Protestant values of hard work, self-control and saving for the future, four-week vacations, two-hour lunch breaks, 35-hour working weeks and excessive spending based on borrowing are quite common. This from an American or Japanese perspective can be considered lazy or perhaps even immoral. In Japan, for a senior executive to leave a company and join a competing firm is considered unethical.

Managers have also realised that instead of being defensive and reactive, they can use ethical issues proactively as marketing tools in many countries. Royal Shell, for example, has used this strategy for a number of years, where most of its advertising campaigns emphasise the role it is playing in the development of societies, particularly in developing countries. McDonald's has also changed its marketing strategies after being accused of selling 'junk food' to children. Not only did it change its product mix (e.g. adding fruit to its happy meals and salads to normal offerings), but it also ran an advertising campaign throughout 2004, aiming to convince the market that it is a socially responsible company. One study asserts that two-thirds of consumers claim that their purchasing decision is influenced by ethical considerations.

Conversely, firms marketing products not considered high priority or that fall from favour often face unpredictable government restrictions. Continental Can Company's joint venture to manufacture cans for the Chinese market faced a barrage of restrictions when

GOING INTERNATIONAL 14.1

Who is responsible for social responsibility?

Managers often complain of being held responsible for the well-being of society. They claim that according to the free market economic system (capitalism), by running a profitable company, they are advancing the public good. They also claim that by having 'good management', i.e. dealing honestly with employees, customers and suppliers, they are doing their job. They have responsibility towards their investors (owners) and if they reduce profits to raise social welfare then perhaps they are not being honest with their investors.

Rich multinationals operating in developing countries also claim that they in fact typically want to employ local people, and pay substantially higher wages and provide better benefits than the local norms. But how much more of this is required in order to be labelled a good corporate citizen? According to Joel Bakan, a professor at the University of Columbia:

> Today, corporations govern our lives. They determine what we eat, what we watch, what we wear, where we work and what we do. We are inescapably surrounded by their culture, iconography and ideology. And, like the church and the monarchy in other times, they posture as infallible and omnipotent, glorifying themselves in imposing buildings and elaborate displays. Increasingly, corporations dictate the decisions of their supposed overseers in government and control domains of society once firmly embedded in the public sphere. Corporations now govern society, perhaps more than governments themselves do; yet ironically it is their very power, much of which they have gained through economic globalisation, that makes them vulnerable. As is true of any ruling institution, the corporation now attracts mistrust, fear and demands for accountability from an increasingly anxious public. Today's corporate leaders understand, as did their predecessors, that work is needed to regain and maintain the public's trust. And they, like their predecessors, are seeking to soften the corporation's image by presenting it as human, benevolent and socially responsible.

Economist and philosopher Adam Smith
© Bettmann

According to Adam Smith, the father of the free market economic system:

> Every individual necessarily labours to render the annual revenue of the society as great as he can. He generally, indeed, neither intends to promote the public interest, nor knows how much he is promoting it; he intends only his own gain, and he is in this, as in many other cases, led by an invisible hand to promote an end which was no part of his intention. Nor is it always the worse for the society that it was no part of it. By pursuing his own interest he frequently promotes that of the society more effectually than when he really intends to promote it. I have never known much good done by those who affected to trade for the public good.
>
> It is not from the benevolence of the butcher, the brewer, or the baker, that we expect our dinner, but from their regard to their own interest. We address ourselves, not to their humanity but to their self-love, and never talk to them of our own necessities but of their advantages.

(According to Milton Friedman: The only responsibility of business is to make profit and grow, as long as it stays within the rules and regulations.)

Although Adam Smith promotes selfishness, he admires benevolence. But his main thesis is that benevolence is not necessary to advance public interest, as long as people are free to engage with each other in voluntary economic interactions.

● Does Adam Smith's invisible hand, the private search for profit, advance public interest? Who, in your opinion, should be responsible for the well-being of society?

Source: The Economist, 'A Survey of Corporate Responsibility: The Good Company', 22 January 2005, pp. 1–18.

the Chinese economy weakened. China decreed that canned beverages were wasteful and must be banned from all state functions and banquets. Tariffs on aluminium and other materials imported for producing cans were doubled and a new tax was imposed on canned drink consumption. An investment that had the potential for profit after a few years was rendered profitless by a change in the attitude of the Chinese Government.

Multinational corporations are facing a growing variety of legislation designed to address environmental issues. Global concern for the environment extends beyond industrial pollution, hazardous waste disposal and rampant deforestation to include issues that focus directly on consumer products. **Green marketing** laws focus on product packaging and its effect on solid waste management and environmentally friendly products.

Germany has passed the most stringent green marketing laws that regulate the management and recycling of packaging waste. The new packaging law was introduced in three phases. The first phase requires all transport packaging such as crates, drums, pallets and Styrofoam containers to be accepted back by the manufacturers and distributors for recycling.

The second phase requires manufacturers, distributors and retailers to accept all returned secondary packaging, including corrugated boxes, blister packs, all packaging designed to prevent theft, packaging for vending machine applications and packaging for promotional purposes. The third phase requires all retailers, distributors and manufacturers to accept returned sales packaging including cans, plastic containers for dairy products, foil wrapping, Styrofoam packages and folding cartons such as cereal boxes.[1]

The **green dot programme** mandates that the manufacturer must ensure a regular collection of used packaging materials directly from the consumer's home or from designated local collection points. A green dot on a package will identify those manufacturers participating in this programme. France, Belgium, Denmark and Austria have similar regulations to deal with solid waste disposal.[2]

Anti-trust: an Evolving Issue

With the exception of the United States and some European countries, **anti-trust laws** have been either non-existent or unenforced in most of the world's countries for the better part of the twentieth century. However, the European Union has begun to actively enforce its anti-trust laws. Anti-monopoly, price discrimination, supply restrictions and full-line forcing are areas in which the **European Court of Justice** has dealt severe penalties. For example, before Procter & Gamble was allowed to buy VP-Schickedanz AG, a German hygiene products company, it had to agree to sell off one of the German company's divisions that produced Camelia, a brand of sanitary napkin. P&G already marketed a brand in Europe, and the Commission was concerned that allowing it to keep Camelia would give it a controlling 60 per cent of the German sanitary products market and 81 per cent of Spain's.[3] In another instance, Michelin was fined €630 000 ($700 000) for operating a

GREEN MARKETING marketing decisions that take the environment into consideration

GREEN DOT PROGRAMME a sign (logo) that shows that the product adheres to Green marketing

ANTI-TRUST LAWS prevent businesses from creating unjust monopolies or competing unfairly in the marketplace

EUROPEAN COURT OF JUSTICE an institution of the European Union

system of discriminatory rebates to Dutch tyre dealers. Similar penalties have been assessed against such companies as United Brands for price discrimination and F. Hoffmann-LaRoche for non-cost-justified fidelity discounts to its dealers.

What is Social Responsibility?

Ethics and social responsibility go hand in hand. If a company is misleading its consumers, not telling the truth about the serious negative impact of its products (e.g. in case of pharmaceutical and food companies) or, once realising that its product has caused damage to consumer health or well-being, refuses to accept and take responsibility, then that company has not been socially responsible. The different views on these two concepts have been summarised by Fisher (2004) as follows.

- Social responsibility is ethics in an organisational context.
- Social responsibility focuses on the impact that business activity has on society while ethics is concerned with the conduct of people within organisations.
- Social responsibility and ethics are unrelated concepts.
- Social responsibility has various dimensions, one of which is ethics.

One problem is understanding what social responsibility is, and that ideas about right and wrong and what is ethical and what is not may differ from country to country. For instance, even within Europe there are different opinions on under-age sex, bribes and lying to serve self-interest. These standards differ from Scandinavia in the north to Italy and Greece in the south. Some countries stress individual responsibility while others think it is society's responsibility to ensure that companies operate in a socially responsible manner.

Social responsibility thus means that a company plays a role in society that is beyond its economic goals and that makes a constructive contribution towards society's well-being in the long term. A few decades ago, a number of authors stated that the main responsibility

SOCIAL RESPONSIBILITY
when a company is concerned about the implications of its decisions on society in general

---

GOING INTERNATIONAL 14.2

The US takes on global standards to fight obesity: 'personal responsibility'

How do you change the eating habits of several hundred million people? That's the daunting problem the World Health Organization (WHO) is trying to solve with a proposal for fighting obesity worldwide. It's a bold and necessary effort but, unfortunately, it may be undermined by the world's fattest nation: the US.

The UN estimates that 300 million people worldwide are obese and a further 750 million are overweight, including 22 million children under five. Health experts around the world are unanimous in saying that something must be done. But that's where the unanimity ends. The WHO has spent the past year hammering out a series of non-binding actions that governments could undertake. The initiative is scheduled for adoption in May, but the US, with backing from the powerful food lobby, is working furiously to water down the proposals. These include restrictions on advertising, changes in labelling, increased taxes on junk food and the elimination of sugar subsidies.

The playbook for the Administration's attack is much the same as the one it used to block international action on global warming. It is charging that the WHO's conclusions are not supported by 'sufficient scientific evidence' that fats and sugars cause obesity. Technically, the US has a point. William R. Steiger, the lead delegate to the WHO from the Health and Human Services Dept (HHS), complained in a letter to the organisation that the evidence linking sugar and fats to obesity comes from epidemiological studies rather than stringently controlled clinical trials. 'In this country, you can't make a scientific claim unless you have the evidence to back it up', argues an HHS spokesman.

Even the US does not advocate doing nothing. The Center for Disease Control estimates that one in every three adults in the US is obese, and 15 per cent of children are over-weight – double the rate of 10 years ago. Poor self-control is only one aspect of the obesity problem, however. There are huge obstacles to making healthier choices. Among them: larger portions, inadequate nutritional information on food labels, fast foods sold in schools, and cutbacks in physical education programmes. 'Food is something we need to live', says Dr C. Ronald Kahn, president of the Joslin Diabetes Center in Boston. 'What we really need to do is eat less of it.'

The WHO, however, does recommend restrictions on advertisements that exhort us to eat more, particularly those aimed at children. 'Advertising junk food to children is unethical and immoral', says Dr Walter C. Willett, head of the Department of Nutrition at Harvard University's School of Public Health.

Ultimately, the WHO proposals form a multifaceted approach, combining education and regulations. With the same combination, the US was able to cut the smoking rate in half, even though it took 40 years. 'It will take at least that long to cut obesity rates by half', Willet predicts, and then only if the US Government gets serious about tackling the problem. So far, there is little scientific evidence proving that it is.

● Do you think it is government's responsibility to control the food industry?

Source: Business Week, 'Let Them Eat Cake – if They Want to', 23 February 2004.

---

of a company is to maximise its profits within the rules of law.[4] Some even stated that if a company engages in activities other than profit maximisation, it is working against share-holder interests. They believe that society's well-being is the responsibility of the state.[5]

Later studies, however, stress that the role played by a company has to go beyond profit maximisation and self-interest. This view believes that the more a company behaves responsibly, the more it will create goodwill and its positive corporate image will help its positioning in customers' minds and thus its competitive advantage.[6]

As Friedman (1970: 2, see reference 6) comments, 'there is only one social responsibil-ity of business, to use its resources and engage in activities designed to increase profits so long as it stays within the rules of the game, and engages in open and free competition without deception or fraud'.

From the marketer's point of view we believe in the latter. It is important to realise that each company has its **stakeholders** who benefit or are harmed or whose rights are violated or respected by its actions.[7] Just as owners have a right to demand that a company does not jeopardise their interests, so do other stakeholders have the right to demand the same. Even in the 'narrow definition', the stakeholders include owners, employees, management, suppliers, customers and the local community (see Exhibit 14.1).

Owners are the investors and they want some return on their investment. Sometimes pension funds or other organisational advisers also invest in corporations. This means that the future well-being of lots of people is dependent on how the company performs. *Employees* have their own, and often their families', livelihoods to support and expect wages, security and other benefits. Employers have to follow management instructions

STAKEHOLDERS
parties that have an interest in the company's activities

Exhibit 14.1 Stakeholders of a firm

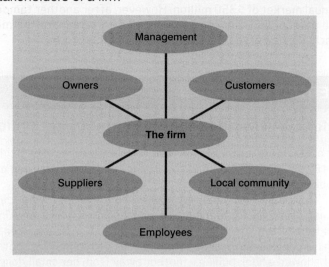

Source: Freeman, 2002, p. 175 (see reference 8).

and they represent the company with their behaviour inside and outside the firm. *Suppliers* are important for firms and this relationship is in fact mutual and reciprocal. While suppliers' components and materials influence the quality and reputation of the firm, the firm's performance influences supplier success.

Customers are involved in the actual exchange with the firm as they pay to acquire its products. This payment is the lifeblood of the firm as it provides it with revenue. Understanding and satisfying customers' needs and wants are the main tasks of marketers. The better a firm can satisfy its customers, the more successful it will be and the better it can serve the interests of other stakeholders. The *local community* benefits from the activities of the firm as it pays tax and provides job opportunities; it thus contributes towards the economic and social well-being of the local community. From a resident's perspective, the firm is expected to be a good citizen, just like all other citizens, individuals as well as organisations. It cannot endanger the community by its anti-social behaviour, such as causing pollution, dumping toxic waste or not paying taxes.

In case companies are not taking due care of their stakeholders or are violating the rules of good citizenship, the government intervenes and/or regulates company behaviour through industrial policy and taxation.

Analysing Ethical Issues and Social Responsibility

In international marketing, there is a tendency to find reasons to support company decision making. In the case of a company deciding to enter a particular market, its marketing research will show how lucrative the market is. It can make even small numbers look good. The dilemmas and temptations in market research to give in to unethical behaviour are well documented.[8]

Respecting the rights of respondents in marketing research is a matter of ethics. Collecting information on consumers without their consent (e.g. through observations) is considered unethical.

After a poisoning scandal in 1982, where several deaths were reported from taking cyanide-laced, Tylenol-extra-strength pain reliever capsules, Johnson & Johnson learnt its lesson. The company convinced the market that the cyanide had been placed in the capsules by criminals. Johnson & Johnson was able to do this thanks to the trust it had developed with the market and local communities. As a result, it now openly states its code of conduct.

The company continued to market Tylenol-extra-strength, as it was a very successful brand with an annual market of $350 million. However, after another tampering incident in 1986, where one person died, the company decided to terminate the marketing of this product and launched a new brand, Tylenol-caplets, in tablet form.[9]

GOING INTERNATIONAL 14.3

Reprimand for Government over ads that upset children

The Department of Health is to be reprimanded formally by the Advertising Standards Authority over its £7 million anti-smoking advertising campaign, which depicted smokers with giant fishhooks piercing their mouths.

It attracted 771 complaints, most of them from parents who described the advertisements as offensive, frightening and distressing to children. One television advert, screened before the 9 p.m. watershed, showed an office worker with a giant fishhook through his cheek being dragged from his desk to a smoking spot in a freezing car park. Another showed a hook pulling a mother away from her small daughter. A third depicted a man being dragged through traffic and into a newsagent's shop to buy cigarettes. The Advertising Standards Authority is to recommend that the adverts breached strict codes that are designed to protect children and that therefore the authority should uphold the complaints against the posters and television adverts and reprimand the Department of Health.

Source: The Times, 7 April 2007.

Social responsibility refers to voluntary responsibilities that go beyond the purely economic and legal responsibilities of a firm. This means that the firm is willing to sacrifice part of its profit for the benefit of its stakeholders. It can thus be defined as corporate behaviour up to a level where it is congruent with the prevailing social norms, values and expectations of performance.[10]

These responsibilities can be presented at different levels (Exhibit 14.2). The inner circle in Exhibit 14.2 refers to the absolute minimum responsibility of a firm, where it has to efficiently perform the economic functions such as products, job creation and growth. The second circle refers to the awareness of changing social values and priorities with regard to the environment, safety of employees and customers, and relationships with employees. The third circle refers to emerging priorities that a firm should adhere to. This includes improving the life of local communities and helping them solve problems such as poverty and injustice. Companies can make a considerable contribution in this respect.

Business Ethics

In the real world of business, companies do generally behave.[11] With an increasing awareness of ethics among all the stakeholders, those companies that are more ethical are believed to perform better. Ethics refers to a standard of behaviour or code of conduct that is based on moral duties and obligations. These standards are based on values, beliefs, industry, society and government regulations.

There are two views on ethics: one is that you follow some absolute principles (e.g. based on religion); the other is that you follow a more consequential approach – you evaluate the consequences of your decisions and if they do not violate the ethical standards then they are fine. Many managers follow this approach as it fits into their normal decision-making models.[12] In reality, however, managers use a mixed approach.

Exhibit 14.2 Levels of social responsibility

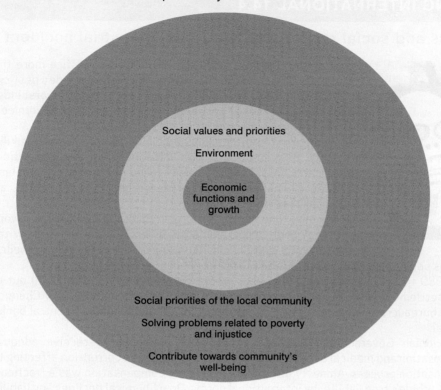

Social values and priorities

Environment

Economic functions and growth

Social priorities of the local community

Solving problems related to poverty and injustice

Contribute towards community's well-being

Source: based on J.R. Boatright, 2003, pp. 374–5.

Ethics have also become a matter of not violating basic human rights. The norms of morality are time and place bound. This means that they can change with time and increased awareness. For example, some decades ago it was considered all right for factories to throw their liquid waste into lakes and rivers, while at present it is considered totally wrong and unethical. In Europe, a couple of decades ago, all such factories were required to install anti-pollution systems to clean any such waste before dumping it into natural surroundings. No longer can ethics be confused with legality. Law and written codes of conduct are the minimum requirements; they provide only basic guidelines. All that is legal is not necessarily ethical. If a company is acquitted of any wrongdoing, this does not necessarily mean that it has been ethical.[13] An ethical company is not looking to meet minimum standards but instead is looking to do the maximum it can for the well-being of its stakeholders.

Ethics and International Marketing

Consumers and societies have become increasingly wary (read sceptical) of the marketing activities of firms. The main purpose of marketing and advertising is to communicate with consumers and make them aware of the existence and characteristics of products. However, the type of information conveyed in these advertisements, and whether the claims made (e.g. Coke is the real thing or that a certain cosmetic will make you look 10 years younger) are correct, realistic and justified, is often questioned. It was once a common view that companies not only satisfy consumer demands but they also create consumer demand: the 'dependence effect'. A number of scholars regard excessive advertising campaigns for cigarettes as an example of this unnecessary or 'unethical' demand creation.[14]

GOING INTERNATIONAL 14.4

Ethics and social responsibility after an industrial accident

Activists of the Bharatiya Janata Party wearing mask protest in Bhopal on the eve of World Environment Day, 2003

© Reuters NewMedia, Inc./ CORBIS

Victims of the Bhopal disaster are still awaiting justice more than 20 years after a gas leak from US company Union Carbide's pesticide plant, which killed more than 7000 people in the world's worst industrial accident. Almost all parties, including the Indian Government, continue to evade their responsibilities.

The gas leaked into the slums adjoining the plant and has killed another 15 000 in the last two decades. Amnesty International estimates that fatalities have been caused by respiratory problems, breakdown of immune systems, breast and cervical cancer, and neurological disorders.

Yet the site, Union Carbide's largest plant in the developing world, has still not been decontaminated. Independent studies show that the groundwater system, which continues to be used by slum-dwellers, remains polluted and that numerous health disorders continue to arise.

In 1989 the government of India negotiated a €353 million (£248 million) out-of-court settlement with Union Carbide, which has since been bought by Dow Chemical. Due to bureaucratic slowness, most of the money is still held in India's central bank in Mumbai.

The Indian Government has failed to ensure that survivors receive adequate compensation and medical assistance or to prevent widespread corruption affecting the compensation process. Amnesty International says the compensation was a fraction of Union Carbide's true liability by international norms; Dow Chemical declines any liability. India continues to press for the extradition of Warren Anderson, Union Carbide's CEO. His whereabouts are disputed. Amnesty says the tragedy underlines the need to develop an international human rights framework that could govern the duties and liabilities of private companies.

● Do you think Union Carbide has behaved ethically in this case? Has it been socially responsible?
● Who, do you think is to be blamed for the misery of the victims and the fact that majority of them still haven't received compensation or medical assistance?

Source: Edward Luc, 'Victims of Bhopal Disaster Still Awaiting Justice', *Financial Times*, 29 November 2004, p. 8.

In recent years, however, it has been widely accepted that marketing and advertising are essential parts of company activities and play important roles in modern society. Marketing should not, however, be deceiving, manipulating or exaggerative. Failure to tell the whole truth about a product, and misleading or unjustified pricing or packaging are considered unethical marketing practices. Product safety is a responsibility of the manufacturing company and if there are any dangers, it is the company's responsibility to properly inform the customer. Moreover, despite being careful, if the company has not properly conveyed the dangers or possible risks of a product usage, it will be held responsible for any hardship caused to anyone.[15] That is why car companies often call back a particular model to replace parts, if they suspect they might malfunction and hurt someone.

GOING INTERNATIONAL 14.5

The tale of a twenty-first century car

In 13 years the Prius has gone from a brainstorming session about the future of the automobile to a vehicle that is changing the way the world drives.

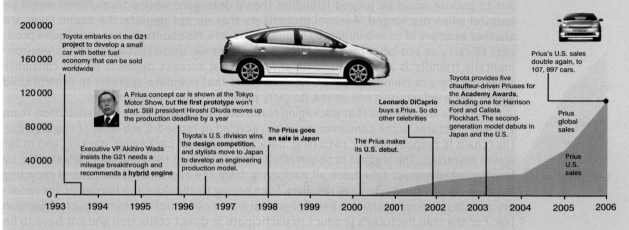

Toyota embarks on the **G21 project** to develop a small car with better fuel economy that can be sold worldwide

A Prius concept car is shown at the Tokyo Motor Show, but **the first prototype won't start**. Still president Hiroshi Okuda moves up the production deadline by a year

Executive VP Akihiro Wada insists the G21 needs a mileage breakthrough and recommends a **hybrid engine**

Toyota's U.S. division wins the **design competition**, and stylists move to Japan to develop an engineering production model.

The Prius goes on sale in Japan

The Prius makes its U.S. debut.

Leonardo DiCaprio buys a Prius. So do other celebrities

Toyota provides five chauffeur-driven Priuses for the **Academy Awards**, including one for Harrison Ford and Calista Flockhart. The second-generation model debuts in Japan and the U.S.

Prius's U.S. sales double again, to 107, 897 cars.

Prius global sales

Prius U.S. sales

Source: Fortune, 6 March 2006, pp. 65–8.

Green Marketing

The twenty-first century has been dubbed 'the century of environmental awareness'. Consumers, business people and public administrators must now demonstrate a sense of 'Green' responsibility by integrating environmental habits into individual behaviour.

Europe has been at the forefront of the '**Green movement**' (www.greendot.ie), with strong public opinion and specific legislation favouring environmentally friendly marketing. Green marketing is a term used to identify concern with the environmental consequences of a variety of marketing activities. The European Union, concerned that national restrictions on waste would create 15 different codes that could become clear barriers to trade, has passed legislation to control all kinds of packaging waste throughout the EU. Two critical issues that affect product development are the control of the packaging component of solid waste and consumer demand for environmentally friendly products.[16]

Germany has a strict **eco-labelling** programme to identify, for the concerned consumer, products that have a lesser impact on the environment than similar products. Under German regulation a manufacturer is permitted to display a logo, called the 'Blue Angel', on all products that comply with certain criteria that make them environmentally friendly. More than 3400 products in 85 product categories have been examined and awarded the Blue Angel logo (www.blauerengel.de), while for the European eco-label there are 23 product groups with 236 companies being awarded the label. While it is difficult to judge the commercial value of a Blue Angel designation, manufacturers are seeking the eco-label for their products in response to growing consumer demand for environmentally friendly products. Similar national labels exist in France, Denmark, the Netherlands, Finland, Norway, Austria, the Czech Republic and Hungary.

Partly to offset an onrush of eco-labels from every European country, the European Commission issued guidelines for eco-labelling that became operational in October 1992. Under the EC directive, a product is evaluated on all significant environmental effects throughout its life cycle, from manufacturing to disposal – a cradle-to-grave approach.[17]

GREEN MOVEMENT
political/consumer movement favouring environment-friendly approaches

ECO-LABELLING
a label or logo to show that a company is socially responsible

product. This is true for cigarette and liquor advertising and its impact on younger members of the market.

In salesman/buyer relationships, bribery and other illegal/immoral payments are common issues. It is quite prevalent in many societies. In Hong Kong, it is said to be around 5 per cent, in Russia around 20 per cent and in Indonesia it can sometimes be as high as 30 per cent.[21] In many countries there is a formal way of doing business and there is also an informal way of doing business. The informal way often works faster, but might include bribes or 'commission' to be paid to 'experts'.[22]

GOING INTERNATIONAL 14.6

Donors still paying for access

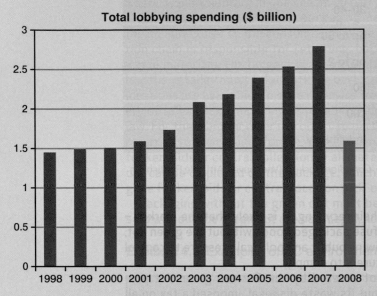

Total lobbying spending ($ billion)

In restaurants and hotels, lawmakers mingled with lobbyists and other donors just as they do in Washington, out of the view of the general public, and seemingly unconcerned by Mr Obama's stance against lobbyists – he has banned them from donating or taking paid positions on his campaign. Among the dozens of parties were JPMorgan's salute to women governors, the Recording Industry Association of America's concert featuring Kanye West, and a brunch hosted by Billy Tauzin, a former congressman who is now chief executive of the pharmaceutical lobby group PhRMA.

Lawmakers seen at a party hosted by Washington lobbyists Heather and Tony Podesta appeared visibly uncomfortable when asked what they thought about Mr Obama's stance on lobbyists.

Carl Levin, the Michigan senator, shrugged and said he had not followed the lobbying debate. 'They are old friends of mine,' he said of the Podestas.

Experts say that every election cycle raises the cost of access. When President George W. Bush ran for office in 2000, individuals who bundled donations on his behalf were given special status if they raised $100 000 (€68 000; £55 000). Today, campaign finance experts say bundlers are raising as much as $500 000 for the presidential candidates.

In all, private donations exceeding $112 million will pay for about 80 per cent of the combined convention costs in Denver and St Paul, according to a study by the Campaign Finance Institute.

'Both candidates have talked a big game about reducing the influence of special interests,' says Massie Ritsch of the Center for Responsive Politics, which tracks political donations. 'But they don't seem to have done much to rein in their political parties and the corporate subsidies underwriting the conventions that nominate them.'

● Is lobbying ethical?

Source: FT, 30 August 2008, p. 2.

Exhibit 14.5 OECD anti-bribery convention: signatory countries

Argentina	Germany	Norway
Australia	Greece	Poland
Austria	Hungary	Portugal
Belgium	Iceland	Slovak Republic
Brazil	Ireland	Slovenia
Bulgaria	Italy	Spain
Canada	Japan	Sweden
Chile	Korea	Switzerland
Czech Republic	Luxembourg	Turkey
Denmark	Mexico	United Kingdom
Finland	The Netherlands	United States
France	New Zealand	

Source: Report on Anti-Bribery Convention 2003. Cited in Blythe and Zimmerman, 2005, p. 361 (see reference 13).

A number of countries have signed a convention against bribery (see Exhibit 14.5) but, as it is an illegal activity, there is no guarantee that in these countries bribery does not take place.

Product safety is a major issue in marketing ethics. Consumers have the right to be protected from harmful products. It is the responsibility of the marketer to ensure that the products meet these criteria. Consumers need to be informed sufficiently (e.g. on the package) to make a rational decision. The package must include crucial information about the product, e.g. the net quantity/weight and value comparison. Food articles should also include nutrition values and contents. Exhibit 14.6 explains non-ethical behaviour in international marketing activities.

These days the usage of universal price codes (UPCs) or barcodes does not always allow the customer to see and compare the price. It is the duty of the seller/retailer to provide information on price on each product. In case there is an operational cost (e.g. electric appliances, tyres, etc.) the customer has to be informed about these 'hidden costs'.

Advertising is considered the most crucial aspect of marketing with regard to ethical issues. Quite often advertising is misleading or deceptive and customers are led to believe a false claim. Advertising is deceptive when it shows packaging that does not correspond with the price mentioned, e.g. the size and quantity versus price. A number of countries find slogans such as 'buy one, get one free' or '30 per cent free' manipulative and misleading.[23]

Moreover, it is unethical to market food knowing that it is unhealthy or harmful. It is not the customer's responsibility to check before buying.

In terms of guidelines for future managers, the ethical test, shown below, drawn up by the Institute of Business Ethics is useful because of its simplicity and clarity.

Exhibit 14.6 Ethical issues in international marketing activities

Marketing activity	(Un)Ethical issues
Positioning	Positioning a low-quality product as a high-quality product
	Product positioned to perform a function that is not true, e.g. cholesterol-reducing food, anti-ageing cosmetics
	Blackmailing customers that if they do not use the product they will be harmed/disadvantaged in some way
Product	Product that can cause harm to customers/users, e.g. children's toys
	Products that pose a safety risk for the users, e.g. electric goods, automobiles
	Products that can cause health problems, e.g. side-effects of medicines
	When customers are not fully informed about product content, e.g. in food articles, nuts, GM ingredients or sugar/salt level
	Use of environment-friendly packaging
Price	Price cartels, where two or more competitors fix a price that is higher than competitive pricing
	Charging discriminatory prices without any extra value provided
	Transfer pricing; over/underpricing internal invoices for taxation purposes
	Charging high monopolistic prices, e.g. medicines for epidemic diseases, such as AIDS in Africa
	Pay bribery/illegal payments or gifts to acquire sales
Promotion	Claiming inaccurate product benefits through advertising
	Not informing the customer fully through different communication
	Using inappropriate language in advertising
	Using discriminatory or degrading slogans
	Advertising directed towards younger children
	Paying illegal kickbacks to promote the product
Place/distribution	Discriminatory distribution, e.g. forcing wholesalers and retailers to discriminate among customers (to whom the product can be sold)
	Demanding unfair benefits/kickbacks/advances from retailers or suppliers
	Taking responsibility for after-sales service, e.g. in electronic goods

Simple ethical test for a business decision:

- *Transparency*
  Do I mind others knowing what I have done?
- *Effect*
  Who does my decision affect or hurt?
- *Fairness*
  Would my decision be considered fair by others?
- *Check*
  Should I check the consequences of my decision on public/customer?

GOING INTERNATIONAL 14.7

Should multinationals be held responsible?

The first Coca-Cola worker and trade unionist in Carepa to be assassinated was José Eleazar Manco, in April 1994. The second was killed days later on April 20. He was Giraldo's brother, Enrique. In the mornings, Enrique travelled to work on the back of a friend's motorbike. Three men emerged from the side of the road and aimed guns at the bike, forcing it to stop. Enrique was dragged off into the bushes. Enrique's body dumped at the side of the road.

The Colombian paramilitary groups were spawned in the conflict between the state and revolutionary guerrillas. In 1982 officers under General Landazábal, the defence minister, worked with multinationals and cattle ranchers to organise and fund 'defence groups'. Ostensibly they were to fight left-wing insurgent groups, but increasingly the paras, as they are known, became entwined with the drug cartels and the army. They formed death squads, attacking and killing anyone considered to support the left-wing guerrillas – basically anyone working in human rights or trade unions. It is a common refrain among the establishment and security forces that the guerrillas and trade unionists are one and the same.

When the surviving union leaders were threatened and intimidated, it became blindingly obvious that there was a campaign against the union at the Coca-Cola plant. These men were followed as they left work, cards were delivered to their homes saying, 'Go now or face death!'

The body of Isidro Gil lay inside the plant. The first bullet had hit him between the eyes. The remaining five shots were fired out of spite or bravado. Another Coca-Cola union leader had been disposed of.

The union in Carepa was smashed. The leadership was in hiding, exiled or dead. The members, cowed by guns, threats and intimidation, had signed away their rights. Meanwhile, the managers of the plant introduced a pay cut – according to Sinaltrainal, the wages for experienced workers dropped from between $380 and $450 a month to $130 a month: Colombia's minimum wage. When asked about this, Coca-Cola failed to respond. What was the Coca-Cola Company's response?

From the outset, the company's Atlanta headquarters denied 'any connection to any human-rights violations' and distanced itself from the bottlers, saying, 'The Coca-Cola Company does not own or operate any bottling plants in Colombia.' This is the standard use of the 'Coca-Cola system', operating as an entity but claiming no legal lines of accountability to the Coca-Cola Company. Coca-Cola does not own the bottling plants; the bottlers operate under a franchise. But the case here is similar to that of Gap and Nike in the 90s. In these instances, the clothes giants had outsourced their production to factories in the developing world that operated sweatshop conditions. It was not Nike or Gap that forced the workers to do long hours for poor pay, it was the contractors. However, campaigners insisted the companies should have enforceable human rights standards applied throughout the supply chain, compelling the companies to take action. The argument was then, and is now, that no matter where the human rights abuse occurred, if it's your name on the label, then you're responsible for sorting it out.

In the Coca-Cola Company's case, the argument is made more compelling by the fact that although it franchised Coke production to Bebidas y Alimentos and Panamerican Beverages (Panamco), Coca-Cola held 24 per cent of Panamco's shares – a controlling interest. Which gives it considerable clout in how the business is run.

Across the world, the Coca-Cola boycott had mixed results. In Dublin, Trinity College and University voted to 'Kick Coke off Campus' and refused to stock its products in student-run facilities, as did New York University and Michigan University in the US. They were joined in the UK by Sussex, Manchester and Middlesex universities, and London's School of Oriental and African Studies. Even though the contracts with US universities are usually worth millions, kicking Coca-Cola off campuses is unlikely to dent the balance sheet of a company that last year made $5.98 billion profit. But the accompanying media attention, and headlines such as 'Has Coke become the new McDonald's' in the *Guardian*, and the *Nation* calling Coke 'the new Nike', must surely be part of the reason it has seen its 'brand value' drop. (Brand value is what turns a sweet, fizzy brown liquid into a product that is desirable and saleable worldwide. In 2007, Coca-Cola's brand value was estimated by *Business Week*/Interbrand at $65 324 million – top of the league, but $2201 million less than in 2005.)

- Should Coca-Cola be held responsible? Discuss.

Source: The Guardian Weekend, 20 September 2008, pp. 18–27.

Summary

The classic view about the responsibilities of a firm believes that its main goals and obligations refer to economic behaviour. The firm has to be concerned about performance and growth, including innovations and technology. The modern view, however, states that a firm has to be responsible beyond its economic goals. It has to be responsible for the well-being and interest of its stakeholders: owners, employee, suppliers, customers, managers and local communities. Thus, it is a firm's responsibility to be fair and impartial towards its employees and to help society in eradicating poverty and injustice.

Ethics and social responsibility become particularly important for marketers as they are the ones who have to convey this to the market. Moreover, it is quite often the marketing function that has to take the major responsibility, at least towards the customers, and to ensure the positive performance of the company. Product safety, packaging and labelling has to be undertaken in a responsible way. The marketing message (advertising, etc.) has to be honest and clean, and not manipulative or deceptive. The same is true for pricing – customers should be able to compare prices with competing products. Finally, the company has to participate in the community's social programmes such as education and equality.

Questions

1 Can a company behave legally and still be unethical? Give examples.
2 What is meant by Green marketing. How is it enforced?
3 What are the three levels of social responsibility? How can society evaluate whether a company is behaving in a responsible manner or not?
4 What are the implications of ethics and social responsibility for the marketing mix of a company? Discuss.
5 How can advertising be unethical? Give examples.

Further Reading

D. Holtbrügge, N. Berg and J.F. Puck, 'To bribe or to convince? Political stakeholders and political activities in German multinational corporations', *International Business Review*, 2007, 6(1), pp. 47–67.

J.M. Aurifelle and P.G. Quester, 'Predicting Business Ethical Tolerance in International Markets: A Concomitant Clusterwise Regression Analysis', *International Business Review*, 2003, 12(2), pp. 253–72.

J. Fisher, 'Social Responsibility and Ethics: Clarifying the Concepts', *Journal of Business Ethics*, 2004, 52, pp. 391–400.

References

1 Steve Zwick, 'A Better Package Deal? Germany's Green Dot – a Symbol of Success in Re-cycling Business', *Time International*, 21 May 2001, p. 55.
2 Brandon Mitchener, 'Increasingly, Rules of Global Economy are set in Brussels', *The Wall Street Journal*, 23 April 2002, p. A1.
3 'P&G Will Drop Brand to Gain EU Takeover Clearance', Reuters News Service, 17 June 1994.
4 B. Schlegelmich, *Marketing Ethics: An International Perspective* (London: Thomson, 1998).
5 C. Stone, 'Why Shouldn't Corporations Be Socially Responsible?', in W.M. Hoffman and J.M. Moore (eds), *Business Ethics: Readings and Cases in Corporate Morality* (New York: McGraw-Hill, 1990).
6 M. Friedman, 'The Social Responsibility of Business is to Increase its Profits', *New York Times*, 14 September 1970.
7 H. Mintzberg, 'The Case for Corporate Social Responsibility', *Journal of Business Strategy*, 1983, 4(2), pp. 65–74.
8 J.M. Aurifielle and P.G. Quester, 'Predicting Business Ethical Tolerance in International Markets: A Concomitant Cluster-wise Regression Analysis', *International Business Review*, 2003, 12(2), pp. 253–72.
9 J.R. Boatright, *Ethics and the Conduct of Business* (New Jersey: Pearson, 2003).
10 S.P. Sethi, 'Dimensions of Corporate Social Performance: An Analytical Framework for Measurement and Analysis', *California Management Review*, 17(Spring), pp. 62–72.
11 This section draws on R.E. Freeman, 'A Stakeholder Theory of the Modern Corporation', in L.P. Hartman (ed.), *Perspectives in Business Ethics*, 2nd edn (New York: McGraw-Hill, 2002), pp. 177–204.
12 N. Bowie, 'It Seems Right in Theory but Does it Work in Practice?', in L.P. Harman (ed.), *Perspectives in Business Ethics*, 2nd edn (New York: McGraw-Hill, 2002), pp. 83–6.
13 J. Blythe and A. Zimmerman, *Business to Business Marketing Management: A Global Perspective* (London: Thomson, 2005).

14 M. Josephson, 'Ethics and Business Decision Making', in W. Hoffman, R. Fredrick and M. Schwartz (eds), *Business Ethics: Readings and Cases in Corporate Morality*, 4th edn (Boston: McGraw-Hill, 2001), pp. 87–116.

15 J.K. Galbraith, *The Affluent Society* (Boston: Houghton Mifflin, 1958).

16 Lynn S. Amine, 'The Need for Moral Champions in Global Marketing', *European Journal of Marketing*, vol. 30, no. 5, 1996, pp. 81–94.

17 'EC Wants Public as Environmental Watchdogs', *Business Europe*, 10 January 1992, pp. 1–2.

18 Kirsten Bergstrom, 'The Eco-Label and Exporting to Europe', *Business America*, 29 November 1993, p. 21.

19 Stephen Kinzer, 'Germany Upholds Tax on Fast-food Containers', *New York Times*, 22 August 1994, p. C2.

20 G.G. Brenkest, 'Marketing to Inner-city Blacks: Power Master and Moral Responsibility', in W.M. Hoffman, R.E. Fredrick, and M.S. Schwartz (eds), *Business Ethics: Readings and Cases in Corporate Morality*, 4th edn (Boston: McGraw-Hill, 2001), pp. 394–403.

21 Hoffman *et al.* (ibid.), p. 360.

22 V. Terpstra and K. David, *The Cultural Environment of International Business* (Cincinnati, OH: South Western Publishing).

23 Hoffman *et al.* (ibid.), pp. 277–82.

Part 5
Developing International Marketing Strategies

Part 5

Developing International Marketing Strategies

12 Product Decisions for International Markets

13 Marketing Industrial Products and Business Services

14 International Distribution and Retailing

15 Pricing for International Markets

16 International Promotion and Advertising

17 Personal Selling and Negotiations

Chapter 15

Product Decisions for International Markets

Chapter Learning Objectives

What you should learn from Chapter 15

- How important it is to offer a product suitable to the intended market
- The current dichotomy of standardised versus adapted products in international marketing
- How to manage the relationship between product acceptance and the market into which it is introduced
- How to identify physical, mandatory and cultural requirements for product evaluation
- How to identify and comply with physical, mandatory and cultural requirements for product adaptation
- To comprehend the need to view all attributes of a product in order to overcome or modify resistance to its acceptance
- To understand the impact of environmental awareness on product decisions

CONSUMER GOODS

goods that consumers buy to consume

DIFFERENTIATED PRODUCTS

products that are considered different from other similar products

The opportunities and challenges for international marketers of **consumer goods** today have never been greater or more diverse. New consumers are springing forth in emerging markets from Eastern Europe, the Commonwealth of Independent States, China, India, other Asian countries and Latin America – in short, globally.[1] Emerging markets promise to be huge markets in the future.[2] In the more mature markets of the industrialised world, opportunity and challenge also abound as consumers' tastes become more sophisticated and complex, and as increases in purchasing power provide them with the means of satisfying new demands.

Never has the question 'Which products should we sell?' been more critical than it is today. For the company with a domestic-market-extension orientation, the answer generally is, 'Whatever we are selling at home'. The company with a multidomestic-market orientation develops different products to fit the uniqueness of each country market; the global orientation seeks commonalties in needs among sets of country markets and responds with a somewhat global product.

All three strategies are appropriate somewhere but, because of the enormous diversity in international markets, the appropriate strategy for a specific market is determined by the company's resources, the product and the target market. Consequently, each country market must be examined thoroughly, or a firm risks marketing poorly conceived products in incorrectly defined markets with an inappropriate marketing effort.[3]

The trend for larger firms is towards becoming global in orientation and strategy. However, product adaptation is as important a task in a smaller firm's marketing effort as it is for global companies. As competition for world markets intensifies and as market preferences become more global, selling what is produced for the domestic market in the same manner as it is sold at home proves to be increasingly less effective. Most products cannot be sold at all in foreign markets without modification; others may be sold as is but their acceptance is greatly enhanced when tailored specifically to market needs. In a competitive struggle, quality products that meet the needs and wants of a market at an affordable price should be the goal of any marketing firm. For some product category groups and some country markets, this means **differentiated products** for each market. Other product groups and country market segments do well competitively with a global or standardised product but, for both, an effective marketing strategy is essential. Even standardised products may have to be sold by different and adapted marketing strategies.

This chapter explores some of the relevant issues facing an international marketer when planning and developing consumer products for international markets. The questions about product planning and development range from the obvious – which product to sell – to the more complex – when, how and if products should be adapted for different markets.

International Markets and Product Decisions

There is a recurring debate about product planning and development that focuses on the question of standardised or **global products** marketed worldwide versus differentiated products adapted, or even redesigned, for each culturally unique market. One extreme position is held by those with strong production and unit-cost orientation who advocate global standardisation, while at the other extreme are those, perhaps more culturally sensitive, who propose a different or adapted product for each market.[4]

Underlying the arguments offered by the proponents of standardised products is the premise that global communications and other worldwlde socialising forces have

GLOBAL PRODUCTS
standardised products

GOING INTERNATIONAL 15.1

Wii fit puts the fun in fitness

Nintendo's Wii strategy was conceived from the get-go to encourage a less sedentary form of gaming. Now the company is unveiling its calorie-burning coup, Wii Fit.

Wii Fit is Nintendo's second act to the wildly popular Wii console, which has sold nearly 10 million units in the US since its launch in 2006. The $90 pressure-sensitive plastic slab, released on 19 May, comes packaged with sophisticated exercise and fitness-tracking software. It is yet another piece of hardware in the company's expanding ecosystem of unconventional gaming products related to the Wii, which also includes the Wii Wheel for racing and the Wii Zapper for shoot-'em-ups.

The brainchild of Mario creator Shigeru Miyamoto, Wii Fit is a sturdy board slightly larger than a bathroom scale, about an inch high, that communicates with the Wii console wirelessly. Players step onto the board, which senses their movements, balance, and centre of gravity. Included software features dozens of activities based on strength training, aerobics, and yoga, as well as a calendar that tracks goals such as weight loss or improved flexibility. Players employ the board differently depending on the activity: standing on it to do a tree pose in yoga, for instance, or stepping on and off it for aerobics.

Some minor ego-bruising aside, Wii Fit accomplishes its mission. It may not replace your trainer, but it will allow beginners to start at their own pace and give fitness freaks yet another exercise outlet. Ultimately, Wii Fit shines because the bar to entry – and enjoyment – is extremely low: almost anybody can unpack and play. For the moment at least, Sony and Microsoft have nothing like it – more important, dovetailing nicely with its mission to improve general fitness.

● Could the Wii Fit replace a personal trainer?

Source: Business Week, 21 May 2008.

Its **physical attributes** generally are required to create the primary function of the product. The primary function of a car, for example, is to move passengers from point A to point B. This ability requires an engine, transmission and other physical features to achieve its primary purpose. The physical features and primary function of a car are generally in demand in all cultures where there is a desire to move from one point to another, other than on foot or by animal power. Few changes to the physical attributes of a product are required when moving from one culture to another. However, a car has a bundle of psychological features as important in providing consumer satisfaction as its physical features. Within a specific culture, other features (colour, size, design, brand name) have little to do with the car's primary function, the movement from point A to B, but do add value to the satisfaction received.

The meaning and value imputed to the psychological attributes of a product can vary among cultures and are perceived as negative or positive. To maximise the bundle of satisfactions received and to create positive product attributes rather than negative ones, adaptation of the **non-physical features** of a product may be necessary.

Coca-Cola, frequently touted as a global product, found it had to change Diet Coke to Coke Light when it was introduced in Japan and a number of European countries. Japanese women do not like to admit to dieting and, further, the idea of diet implies sickness or medicine. This also applies in some European countries. So, instead of emphasising weight loss, 'figure maintenance' is stressed.

The adoption of some products by consumers can be affected as much by how the product concept conflicts with norms, values and behaviour patterns as by its physical or mechanical attributes. As one authority states:

> In short, it is not just lack of money, nor even differences in the natural environment, that constitutes major barriers to the acceptance of new products and new ways of behaving. A novelty always comes up against a closely integrated cultural pattern, and it is primarily this that determines whether, when, how and in what form it gets adopted. The Japanese have always found all body jewellery repugnant. The Scots have a decided resistance to pork and all its associated products, apparently from days long ago when such taboos were decided by fundamentalist interpretations of the Bible.

When analysing a product for a second market, the extent of adaptation required depends on cultural differences in product use and perception between the market the product was originally developed for and the new market. The greater these cultural differences between the two markets, the greater the extent of adaptation necessary.

An example of this involves an undisputed American leader in cake mixes, which tacitly admitted failure in the English market by closing down operations after five unsuccessful years. Taking its most successful mixes in the US market, the company introduced them into the British market. A considerable amount of time, money and effort was expended to introduce its variety of cake mixes to this new market. Hindsight provides several probable causes for the company's failure. The British eat most of their cake with tea instead of dinner and have always preferred dry sponge cake, which is easy to handle; the fancy, iced cakes favoured in the United States were the type introduced. Fancy, iced cakes are accepted in Britain, but they are considered extra special and purchased from a bakery or made with much effort and care at home. Homemakers felt guilty about not even cracking an egg, and there was suspicion that dried eggs and milk were not as good as fresh ones. Therefore, when the occasion called for a fancy cake, an easy cake mix was simply not good enough.

When instant cake mixes were introduced in Japan, consumers' response was less than enthusiastic. Not only do Japanese reserve cakes for special occasions, they prefer them to be beautifully wrapped and purchased in pastry shops. The acceptance of instant cakes was further complicated by another cultural difference – most Japanese homes do not have ovens.

GOING INTERNATIONAL 15.4

Why Coca-Cola became so popular

When Atlanta pharmacist John Pemberton invented Coca-Cola in 1886, he named it that for a reason. His 'brain tonic' included extracts of the kola nut, a high-caffeine stimulant thought to be an aphrodisiac, and coca leaf extract, containing a small amount of cocaine. It's been a hundred years since Coke included that particular ingredient.

Before Coca-Cola, Pemberton had created a version of coca wine, a popular cocaine-laced beverage endorsed by Queen Victoria and Pope Leo XIII. In his new cola beverage, he eliminated alcohol in a nod to the temperance movement but kept the coca extract. When pharmacies began mixing his syrup with carbonated water, sales bubbled up.

In the late nineteenth century cocaine was hailed as a pain-killing breakthrough and found in dozens of products, from throat lozenges to suppositories. But public concern began to grow about its safety, and by 1904 Coca-Cola was completely 'decocainised' (though coca extract, with all traces of the drug removed, remains an ingredient to this day).

Despite the omission, Coke's popularity continued to rise, owing in part to a successful promotion campaign. Growing suspicious of the drink's success, officials at the US Bureau of Chemistry (precursor to the Food and Drug Administration) had a shipment of Coke syrup seized in Chattanooga, Tennessee, in 1909. The product, they charged, violated the Pure Food and Drug Act of 1906, prohibiting sale of 'adulterated or misbranded' foods. The 'adulterating' chemical: caffeine. The government lost its case.

● Should companies be allowed to continue with established products and brands, if proven harmless?

Source: M.G. Zackowitz, 'More Than Just a Sugar Buzz', *National Geographic*, October 2004, p. 4.

Innovative Products and Adaptation

An important first step in adapting a product to a foreign market is to determine the degree of newness perceived by the intended market. How people react to newness and how new a product is to a market must be understood. In evaluating the newness of a product, the international marketer must be aware that many products successful in Western countries, having reached the maturity or even decline stage in their life cycles, may be perceived as new in another country or culture and, thus, must be treated as innovations. A new product would therefore demand a different type of marketing strategy than the one used at home for a rather mature product.

Whether or not a group accepts an **innovation**, and the time it takes, depends on its characteristics. Products new to a social system are innovations, and knowledge about the diffusion (i.e. the process by which innovation spreads) of innovation is helpful in developing a successful product strategy.

INNOVATION
new product/
technology/
method

Another US cake-mix company entered the British market but carefully eliminated most of the newness of the product. Instead of introducing the most popular American cake mixes, the company asked 500 British housewives to bake their favourite cake. Since the majority baked a simple, very popular dry sponge cake, the company brought to the market a similar easy mix. The sponge cake mix represented familiar tastes and habits that could be translated into a convenience item, and did not infringe on the emotional aspects of

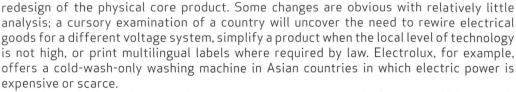

redesign of the physical core product. Some changes are obvious with relatively little analysis; a cursory examination of a country will uncover the need to rewire electrical goods for a different voltage system, simplify a product when the local level of technology is not high, or print multilingual labels where required by law. Electrolux, for example, offers a cold-wash-only washing machine in Asian countries in which electric power is expensive or scarce.

Legal, economic, technological and climatic requirements of the local marketplace often dictate product adaptation. Specific package sizes and safety and quality standards are usually set by laws that vary among countries. To make a purchase more affordable in low-income countries, the number of units per package may have to be reduced from the typical quantities offered in high-income countries. Razor blades, cigarettes, chewing gum and other multiple-pack items are often sold singly or two to a pack instead of the more customary 10 or 20.

Changes may also have to be made to accommodate climatic differences. General Motors of Canada, for example, experienced major problems with several thousand Chevrolet cars shipped to a Middle East country; it was quickly discovered they were unfit for the hot, dusty climate. Supplementary air filters and different clutches had to be added to adjust for the problem. Even peanuts and crackers have to be packaged in tins for humid areas.

The less economically developed a market is, the greater degree of change a product may need for acceptance. One study found only 1 in 10 products could be marketed in developing countries without modification of some sort. Of the modifications made, nearly 25 per cent were mandatory; the other modifications were made to accommodate variations in cultures.

GOING INTERNATIONAL 15.6

New products in the auto industry

Toyota Prius - 2005 European Car of the Year
Issued 11/2004

Toyota launched its hybrid car, the Toyota Prius, in 2001 and sold 15 556 models in the first year. In 2005 it is expected to sell more than 100 000. The Prius cuts fuel consumption by combining an electric motor with a gas engine. It is not only cheaper to run but also environmentally friendly as compared to other autos.

Now Toyota is moving its hybrid technology to its main product lines. First it is being incorporated in Lexus models (RX SUVs); the Camry is next in line, which is America's best-selling car. Honda has also started using the technology in its Civics and Accord models. The American auto industry is, however, far behind. In the age of high gas/oil prices, it is expected that hybrid autos will capture 20 per cent of the US car market. This will allow Toyota and Honda to achieve economies of scale, and means that customers will not have to pay any extra for the new technology. Both companies are focusing on power and luxury to attract more customers: the Toyota Highlander SUV features 270 horsepower and a better economy than a normal compact sedan.

Ford is the only American auto-maker to launch a hybrid SUV, the Ford Escape; but, in applying the technology as a strategy, it is far behind. Land Rover, now a Ford brand, is next in line for the hybrid technology.

Source: Business Week, 'How Hybrids are Going Mainstream', 1 November 2004, p. 37.

Product Life Cycle and Adaptation

Even between markets with few cultural differences, substantial adaptation could be necessary if the product is in a different stage of its life cycle in each market. Product life cycle and the marketing mix are interrelated; a product in a mature stage of its life cycle in one market can have unwanted and/or unknown attributes in a market where the product is perceived as new and thus in its introductory stage. Marketing history is replete with examples of mature products in one market being introduced in another and failing (see Exhibit 15.2).

Exhibit 15.2 Life cycle for products in international markets

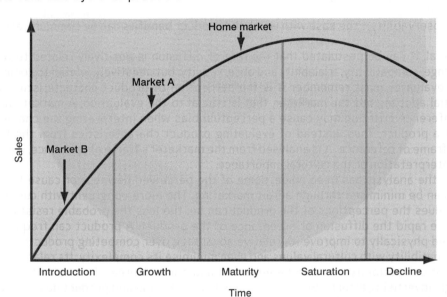

Certainly an important approach in analysing products for foreign markets is determining the stage of the product's life cycle. All subsequent marketing plans must then include adaptations necessary to correspond to the stage of the product life cycle in the new market.

The success of these alternatives depends on the product and the fundamental need it fulfils, its characteristics, its perception within the culture and the associated costs of each programme. To know that foreign markets are different and that different product strategies may be needed is one thing; to know when adaptation of your product line and marketing programme is necessary is another and more complicated problem.

Screening Products for Adaptation

Evaluating a product for marketing in another country requires a systematic method of screening products to determine if there are cultural resistances to overcome and/or physical or mandatory changes necessary for product acceptance. Only when the psychological (or cultural) and physical dimensions of the product, as determined by the country market, are known can the decision for adaptation be made. Products can be screened on two different bases by using 'analysis of characteristics of innovations' to determine if there are cultural-perceptual reasons why a product will be better accepted if adapted, and/or 'analysis of product components' to determine if there are mandatory or physical reasons why a product must be adapted.

Summary

The growing globalisation of markets that gives rise to standardisation must be balanced with the continuing need to assess all markets for those differences that might require adaptation for successful acceptance. Each product must be viewed in light of how it is perceived by each culture with which it comes into contact, however, we should not mix brands with products. The bands can be global, but the product may still need some adaptations. What is acceptable and comfortable within one group may be radically new and resisted within others depending on the experiences and perceptions of each group. Understanding that an established product in one culture may be considered an innovation in another is critical in planning and developing consumer products for foreign markets. Analysing a product as an innovation and using the product component model may provide the marketer with important leads for adaptation.

In some cases, the marketer needs only to adapt the packaging, while in others product characteristics and features need to change to make it compatible for the foreign market. More and more consumers and societies/governments are becoming aware of environmental issues. Many countries/markets have put these responsibilities on the shoulders of companies that sell the products to ensure that their products and packaging are not causing environmental problems. The marketer thus has to check these rules and regulations when entering these markets.

Questions

1 Debate the issue of global versus adapted products for the international marketer.
2 What is the difference between a product and a brand? Explain with examples.
3 Discuss how different stages in the life cycle of a product can influence the standardisation/adaptation decision. Give three examples.
4 Discuss the different promotional/product strategies available to an international marketer.
5 Assume you are deciding to 'go international'; outline the steps you would take to help you decide on a product line.
6 Products can be adapted physically and culturally for foreign markets. Discuss.
7 What are the three major components of a product? Discuss their importance to product adaptation.
8 How can knowledge of the diffusion of innovations help a product manager plan international investments?
9 Discuss the characteristics of an innovation that can account for differential diffusion rates.
10 Give an example of how a foreign marketer can use knowledge of the characteristics of innovations in product adaptation decisions.
11 Discuss 'environmentally friendly' products and product development.

Further Reading

L. De Chernatony, C. Halliburton and R. Bernath, 'International Branding: Demand or Supply-driven Opportunity', *Harvard Business Review*, 1989, 12(2), pp. 9–21.

P.G.P. Walters, P. Whitla and H. Davies, 'Global strategy in the international advertising industry', *International Business Review*, 2008, 17(3), pp. 235–49.

T.-Y. Huang, J.-S. Hu and K.-C. Chen, 'The influence of market and product knowledge resource embeddedness on the international mergers of advertising agencies: The case-study approach' *International Business Review*, 2008, 17(5), pp. 587–99.

References

1   Rahul Jacob, 'The Big Rise: Middle Classes Explode Around the Globe Bringing New Markets and New Prosperity', *Fortune*, 30 May 1994, pp. 74–90; and 'Consumers Have Money to Burn', *Business Week*, 20 April 1998, pp. 30–1.

2   'Brazil's New Look: A Sounder Economy is Emerging', *Business Week*, 4 May 1998, pp. 22–6; and 'What to do about Asia', *Business Week*, 26 January 1998, pp. 48–50.

3   For an empirical study of the debate, see David M. Szymanski, Sundar G. Bharadwaj and Rajan P. Varadarajan, 'Standardization versus Adaptation of International Marketing Strategy: An Empirical Investigation', *Journal of Marketing*, October 1993, pp. 1–17.

4   For a balanced view, see S. Tamer Cavusgil, Shaoming Zou and G.M. Naidu, 'Product and Promotion Adaptation in Export Ventures: An Empirical Investigation', *Journal of International Business Studies*, Third Quarter 1993, pp. 479–506.

5   P. Magnusson, D.W. Baack, S. Zdravkovic, K.M. Staub and L.S. Amine, 'Meta-analysis of cultural differences: Another slice at the apple', *International Business Review*, 2008, 17(5), pp. 520–32.

6   An interesting comment on the increasing importance of consistency in product design for the European market is covered in 'Cross-Border Design', *Business Europe*, 9–15 January 1995, pp. 6–7; and Pervez Ghauri, 'Recent Trends in Global Business and the Asian Crisis: Cooperation vs Competition', *KELOLA*, *Journal of Gajah Mada University*, Indonesia, 1998, 18/VII, pp. 1–15.

7   L. Alvarez, 'Consumers in Europe Resist Gene-altered Food', *New York Times*, 11 February 2003. p. 43.

8   'Electrolux Targets Southeast Asia', *Dow Jones News Service*, 4 January 1995.

9   I. Chaney and J. Gamble, 'Retail store ownership influences on Chinese consumers', *International Business Review*, 2008, 17(2), pp. 170–83.

10 For a good reference book on new product development, see E.M. Rogers, *Diffusion of Innovations*, 5th edn (New York: Free Press, 2003).

11 G.M. Eckhardt and M.J. Houston, 'Cultural Paradoxes Reflected in Brand Meaning: McDonald's in Shanghai, China', *Journal of International Marketing*, 2001, 9(2), pp. 97–114.

Relationship marketing is not new, but it has become increasingly important in international marketing activities. The importance of relationships in China, *guanxi* (connections), has been reported by a number of scholars, where a business relationship often started with a social relationship. The development of a good relationship 'with a friend' was usually considered as a prerequisite for a business relationship. Due to recent decentralisation of economic decision making in China, relationships have become even more important.[21]

The characteristics that define the uniqueness of industrial products discussed above lead naturally to relationship marketing.[22] The long-term relationship with customers, which is at the core of relationship marketing, fits the characteristics inherent in industrial products and is a viable strategy for industrial goods marketing. The first and foremost characteristic of industrial goods markets is the motive of the buyer – to make a profit. Industrial products fit into a business or manufacturing process, and their contributions will be judged on how well they contribute to that process. In order for an industrial marketer to fulfil the needs of its customer, the marketer must understand those needs as they exist today and how they will change as the buyer strives to compete in global markets that call for long-term relationships.[23]

Relationship marketing ranges all the way from gathering information on customer needs to designing products and services, channelling products to the customer in a timely and convenient manner, and following up to make sure the customer is satisfied. For example, SKF, the bearing manufacturer, seeks strong customer relations with after-sales follow-through. The end of the transaction is not delivery; it continues as SKF makes sure the bearings are properly mounted and maintained. This helps customers reduce downtime, thus creating value in the relationship with SKF. SKF's marketing efforts encompass an array of activities to support long-term relationships that go beyond 'merely satisfying the next link in the distribution chain to meeting the more complex needs of the end user, whether those needs are technical, operational, or financial'.[24]

The industrial customer's needs in global markets are continuously changing, and suppliers' offerings must also continue to change. The need for the latest technology means that it is not a matter of selling the right product the first time but one of continuously changing the product to keep it right over time. The objective of relationship marketing is to make the relationship an important attribute of the transaction, thus differentiating oneself from competitors. It shifts the focus away from price to service and long-term benefits. The reward is loyal customers that translate into substantial profits.

IBM of Brazil stresses stronger ties with its customers by offering planning seminars that address corporate strategies, competition, quality and how to identify marketing opportunities. One of these seminars showed a food import/export firm how it could increase efficiency by decentralising its computer facilities to better serve its customers. The company's computers were centralised at headquarters while branches took orders manually and mailed them to the home office for processing and invoicing. It took several days before the customer's order was entered and added several days to delivery time. The seminar helped the company realise it could streamline its order processing by installing branch office terminals that were connected to computers at the food company's headquarters. A customer could then place an order and receive an invoice on the spot, shortening the delivery time by several days or weeks. Not all participants who attend the 30 different seminars offered annually become IBM customers, but it creates a continuing relationship among potential customers. 'So much so,' as one executive commented, 'that when a customer does need increased computer power, he will likely turn to us.'[25]

Promoting Industrial Products

The promotional problems encountered by foreign industrial marketers are little different from the problems faced by domestic marketers. Until recently there has been a paucity of specialised advertising media in many countries. In the last decade, however, specialised

GOING INTERNATIONAL 16.3

How Intel got inside

In microprocessors Intel has the kind of monopoly that any company would be proud to control. More than 85 per cent of all personal computers (PCs) rely on Intel technology. Intel's current and very challenging goal is to maintain its PC monopoly while dominating the market for the new high-performance chips that promise to put PCs on a par with high-end workstations. Many computer analysts think that Intel could eventually control more than 90 per cent of the desktop market, including workstations.

A future mobile internet device enabled with platform power management

By aggressively promoting the Pentium processor in the media, Intel bypassed its traditional customers – the computer manufacturers – and directly targeted PC users. This 'awareness campaign' for its processors has led the majority of PC buyers – especially business users – to specifically demand an Intel processor in their computers. In turn this has created an additional barrier for Intel's competitors: they not only have to deliver processors that are faster and cheaper than Intel's but, more importantly, they also have to convince consumers that their products are fully compatible with Intel's. Andy Grove, Intel's chairman and until recently CEO, says, 'It was an attitude change, a change we actually stimulated, but one whose impact we did not fully comprehend.'

However, as Intel's business model is essentially based around selling a continuous stream of faster microprocessors, its investment in production, R&D and marketing has reflected this at every stage. But growth in high-powered (read high-margin) Pentium II chips has slowed down, mainly as consumers have flocked to sub-thousand-dollar PCs. In this price-sensitive segment, Pentium's premium image doesn't stand for much. Customers look at the best price-performance.

Source: European Business Report, Spring 1Q, 1998, p. 31.

industrial media have been developed to provide the industrial marketer with a means of communicating with potential customers, especially in Western Europe and to some extent in Eastern Europe, the Commonwealth of Independent States (CIS) of the former USSR, and China. In addition to advertising in print media and reaching industrial customers through catalogues and direct mail, the trade show has become the primary vehicle for doing business in many foreign countries.

Industrial Trade Shows

One of the most powerful international promotional media is the trade show or **trade fair**. As part of their international promotion activities, the European Union, Germany and the US Department of Commerce and many other countries sponsor trade fairs in many cities around the world. Additionally, there are annual trade shows sponsored by local governments in most countries. African countries, for example, host more than 70 industry-specific trade shows.

Trade shows serve as the most important vehicles for selling products, reaching prospective customers, contacting and evaluating potential agents and distributors, and marketing in most countries. They have been at the centre of commerce in Europe for centuries and are

TRADE FAIR
exhibition where participants are able to show/sell their products and services. Also used to establish and maintain contacts

GOING INTERNATIONAL 16.5

Keys to success in the European entertainment market

© AP/Wide World Photos

Despite increased competition throughout the industry, Europe is still an attractive market for entertainment companies. This is partly due to more vacation days (the European Union standard is at least 20 days), higher disposable incomes and leisure developments encouraged by city and county planning authorities.

Europe has a long and extensive history of theme parks and attractions, which historically were family-owned, small-scale operations. Although many of these mum-and-dad parks and attractions have disappeared, Europe still boasts the oldest operating amusement park – in Bakken, Denmark.

Many family entertainment projects – such as Disneyland Paris, Port Aventura in Spain and LegoLand in Windsor, England – emerged within the last decade through various public and privately funded bodies.

Their success in Europe is often driven by weather considerations, the addition of rides and attractions, retail propositions linked to a park, and movie or intellectual property that enhance the overall brand.

Based on our work with many US entertainment companies, we have developed the 'Top 10 Predictors of Success' for an entertainment venture in Europe.

10 Do your homework. Make sure you are aware of past case studies, regional and national consumer tastes, preferences and traditions.

9 Get your relationship right with HQ. Strike a balance between the amount of autonomy or control your headquarters and European teams are given, and develop a reporting structure that enables all involved to share best marketing practices with colleagues across geographic boundaries.

8 Manage expectations within your company about when your European activities will start showing a profit (or, at least, break even).

7 'Glocalise' your concepts, striking a balance between how much of your US ideas should be brought to Europe, while still making them appeal to 'local' European tastes.

6 Set realistic payback periods.

5 Understand that the different business customs across these 25 distinct markets mean that you have at least 25 different customer tastes, and therefore need to consider how 'entertainment' is defined by and made relevant to such a disparate population.

4 There is no such thing as the 'United States of Europe'. Because of differing consumer tastes, the implementation of your marketing plans within each of the EU countries will vary significantly.

3 Use local experts wherever possible, to ensure you've been given an accurate, current picture of your target market trends and concerns.

2 Test your concepts and ideas with your target guests to learn what they like, their propensity to pay various entry fees, promotional tie-ins and other marketing activities.

1 Plan, plan, plan!

Source: Allyson L. Stewart-Allen, 'Marketing Perspective', *Marketing News*, 17 August 1998, p. 9.

while it is being created. The intangibility of services results in characteristics unique to a service: it is *inseparable* in that its creation cannot be separated from its consumption; it is *heterogeneous* in that it is individually produced and is thus virtually unique; it is *perishable* in that once created it cannot be stored but must be consumed simultaneously with its creation. Contrast these characteristics with a tangible product that can be produced in one location and consumed elsewhere, that can be standardised, whose quality assurance can be determined and maintained over time, and that can be produced and stored in anticipation of fluctuations in demand.[33]

Services can be classified as being either consumer or industrial in nature. Additionally, the same service can be marketed both as industrial and consumer, depending on the motive of, and use by, the purchaser. For example, travel agents and airlines sell industrial services to a business person and a consumer service to a tourist. Financial services, hotels, insurance, legal services and others all may be industrial or consumer services.

These fundamental characteristics explain why it is important that services be discussed separately from industrial and consumer goods and why their very nature affects the manner in which they are marketed internationally.

Entering International Markets

Client Followers and Market Seekers   Most Western service companies entered international markets to service their Western clients, business travellers and tourists. Banks, accounting and advertising firms were among the earlier companies to establish branches or acquire local affiliations abroad to serve their Western multinational clients. Hotels and car-rental agencies followed the business traveller and tourist to fill their needs.[34] Their primary purpose for marketing their services internationally was to service home-country clients. Once established, many of these **client followers**, as one researcher refers to them, expanded their client base to include local companies. As global markets grew, creating greater demand for business services, service companies became market seekers in that they actively sought customers for their services worldwide. One study of select types of service industries shows that the relative importance of client following or market seeking as a motive for entry into foreign markets varies by type of service.[35]

CLIENT FOLLOWERS companies that have followed their clients to other countries (become international) to service primary clients while they are abroad

---

GOING INTERNATIONAL 16.6

Vodafone's low-cost cell phone Gambit

The world's top mobile operator wants to pitch cheap sets to emerging markets. Can it compete with established brands like Nokia and Motorola? Hoping to push deeper into emerging markets, the world's largest mobile operator, Vodafone Group, is taking a page from the Nokia and Motorola songbook. On 21 May 2007 Vodafone executives announced in London that the company is rolling out its own line of ultra-low-cost handsets. To be built by a Chinese partner, the GSM-standard phones will carry the Vodafone brand name and sell for $25 to $45, depending on locale.

With its unexpected move, Vodafone becomes the first carrier to introduce its own phones intended specifically for customers in developing countries.

© P. Ghauri

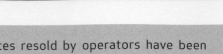

Until now most so-called 'private-label' devices resold by operators have been aimed at the high end of the market. 'These will be the lowest priced GSM products ever,' crowed Jens Schulte-Bockum, Vodafone's global director of terminals, at the event.

True enough, but Vodafone could have a tough time getting its new-fangled devices into the hands of consumers. For one thing, it faces stiff competition from the likes of Nokia, Motorola, and Sony Ericsson, all of which market their own inexpensive models and already have a big head start in markets such as Africa, South Asia, and Latin America.

Vodafone lacks brand awareness in markets such as India, so it's hoping that selling phones carrying its own moniker will bolster its image and visibility among first-time buyers. Despite a relatively late market entry, the company argues it can compete successfully against Nokia and others, selling 'double-digit millions' of the candy bar-shaped phones over the next three years. Still, observers praise Vodafone's low-cost handsets as a useful experiment. The move should help get the Vodafone name out to a new generation of customers.

Source: Business Week, 23 April 2007.

The most important motive for engaging in international business for most business service firms is to seek new markets. The notable exceptions are accounting and advertising firms whose motives are about equally divided between being client followers and market seekers.

Entry Modes   Because of the varied characteristics of business services, not all of the traditional methods of market entry discussed earlier are applicable to all types of services. Although most services have the inseparability of creation and consumption just discussed, there are those where these occurrences can be separated. Such services are those whose intrinsic value can be 'embodied in some tangible form (such as a blueprint or document) and thus can be produced in one country and exported to another'. Data processing and data analysis services are other examples. The analysis or processing is completed on a computer located in a Western country and the output (the service) is transmitted via satellite to a distant customer. Some banking services could be exported from one country to another on a limited basis through the use of ATMs (automatic teller machines). Architecture and engineering consulting services are exportable when the consultant travels to the client's site and later returns home to write and submit a report or a blueprint. In addition to exporting as an entry mode, these services also use franchising, direct investment (joint ventures and wholly owned subsidiaries) and licensing.

Most other services – car rentals, airline services, entertainment, hotels and tourism, to name a few – are inseparable and require production and consumption to occur almost simultaneously and, thus, exporting is not a viable entry method for them. The vast majority of services enter foreign markets by licensing, franchising and/or direct investment.

Market Environment for Business Services

Service firms face most of the same environmental constraints and problems confronting merchandise traders. Protectionism, control of transborder data flows, competition and the protection of trademarks, processes and patents are possibly the most important problems confronting the MNC in today's international services market.

GOING INTERNATIONAL 16.7

A tale of globalisation and its malcontents

In Moscow on 21 May 2008, for the first time two English teams faced each other in the final of the Champions League, a football competition that pits 32 of the best teams across Europe against each other. Manchester United prevailed over Chelsea, as the rest of the continent looked on.

© P. Ghauri

This was no one-off fluke but the latest indicator of the growing dominance of England's Premier League, once a poor cousin of Spain's La Liga, Italy's Serie A and Germany's Bundesliga. Each of its big four clubs – Arsenal, Chelsea, Liverpool and Manchester United – has reached at least one Champions League final in the past four years.

This primacy owes little to home-grown talent. Twelve of the 22 players who started the game in Moscow were foreign. Roughly half of those fielded in an average Premier League weekend are neither British nor Irish. The most celebrated star (Manchester United's Cristiano Ronaldo) is Portuguese. England's national team failed to qualify for the 2008 European championships.

Foreign investors have poured in (Liverpool and Manchester United are owned by Americans, Chelsea by a Russian). England's big four clubs are among the world's ten richest, according to Deloitte, an accounting firm. This allows the clubs to hire the best players, which in turn draws crowds and increases revenues.

In most industries such a virtuous circle would be a cause for celebration. But Sepp Blatter, the president of FIFA, football's governing body, cites English dominance of the Champions League as proof of the need to restrict how many foreigners a team may field. Michel Platini, the head of UEFA, the European wing of FIFA, concurs. Some old-style, hoof-it English managers claim that import restrictions would somehow help the coaching of young British talent.

● Should there be a restriction on how many foreigners can play in each team?

Source: The Economist, 22 May 2008, p. 47.

Protectionism   The most serious threat to the continued expansion of international services trade is **protectionism**. The growth of international services has been so rapid during the past decade that it has drawn the attention of domestic companies and governments. As a result, direct and indirect trade barriers have been imposed to restrict foreign companies from domestic markets. Every reason, from the protection of infant industries to national security, has been used to justify some of the restrictive practices. The General Agreement on Trade in Services (GATS), part of the Uruguay round package, provides for most-favoured-nation treatment, national treatment, market access, transparency and the free flow of payments and transfers.

Until the GATT and WTO agreements there were few international rules of fair play governing trade in services. Service companies faced a complex group of national regulations that impeded the movement of people and technology from country to country. The industrialised nations want their banks, insurance companies, construction firms and other service providers to be allowed to move people, capital and technology around the globe unimpeded.

PROTECTIONISM
when governments do not allow freedom of activity for foreign companies, to protect their own companies

Summary

Industrial goods marketing requires close attention to the exact needs of customers. Basic differences across various markets are less than for consumer goods but the motives behind purchases differ enough to require a special approach. Global competition has risen to the point that industrial goods marketers must pay close attention to the level of economic and technological development for each market to determine the buyer's assessment of quality. Companies that adapt their products to these needs are the ones that should be the most effective in the marketplace. Industrial markets are lucrative and continue to grow as more countries strive for at least a semblance of industrial self-sufficiency. The derived nature of demand for industrial products encourages these companies to have close relationships with their customers. Relationship marketing is therefore becoming important in this sector.

One of the fastest-growing areas of international trade is business services. This segment of marketing involves all countries at every level of development; even the least-developed countries are seeking computer technology and sophisticated data banks to aid them in advancing their economies. Their rapid growth and profit profile make them targets for protectionism and piracy. The increasing competition in the form of outsourcing of service jobs is resulting in some job losses in the service sector in developed countries. More qualified and sensitive jobs, such as R&D and design, are kept at home.

Questions

1 What are the differences between consumer and industrial goods, and what are the implications for international marketing? Discuss.

2 'The adequacy of a product must be considered in relation to the general environment within which it will be operated rather than solely on the basis of technical efficiency.' Discuss the implications of this statement.

3 What role do service, replacement parts and standards play in competition in foreign marketing? Illustrate.

4 Discuss the part industrial trade fairs play in international marketing of industrial goods.

5 Describe the reasons an MNC might seek ISO 9000 certification.

6 What ISO 9000 legal requirements are imposed on products sold in the EC? Discuss.

7 Discuss how the characteristics that define the uniqueness of industrial products lead naturally to relationship marketing. Give some examples.

8 Select several countries, each at a different stage of economic development, and illustrate how the stage affects the usage of relationship marketing.

Further Reading

J. Sheth and A. Parvatiyar, 'The Evolution of Relationship Marketing', *International Business Review*, 1995, 4(4), pp. 471–81.

P.G.P. Waltersa, P. Whitla and H. Davies, 'Global strategy next term in the international advertising industry', *International Business Review*, 2008, 17(3), pp. 235–49.

F. Contractor, S.K. Kundu and C.C. Hu, 'A Three Stage Theory of International Expansion: The Link between Multinationality and Performance in the Service Sector', *Journal of International Business Studies*, 2003, 34, pp. 5–19.

References

1 For a discussion on networks in industrial marketing see e.g. Pervez Ghauri (ed.), *Advances in International Marketing: From Mass Marketing to Relationships and Networks* (Greenwich, NY: JAI Press, 1999).
2 Hans Gemünden, Thomas Ritter and Achim Walter (eds), *Relationships and Networks in International Markets* (Oxford: Pergamon, 1997).
3 Frederick Webster, *Industrial Marketing Strategy*, 3rd edn (New York: Wiley, 1991).
4 Karin Venetis, 'Service Quality and Customer Loyalty in Professional Business Service', PhD dissertation, Maastricht University, 1997.
5 John Naisbitt, *Mega Trends Asia* (New York: Simon & Schuster, 1996).
6 Philippe Lasserre and Helmut Schütte, *Strategies for Asia Pacific* (London: Macmillan, 1995).
7 Gregory Ingram and Christine Kessides, 'Infrastructure for Development', *Finance and Development*, September 1994, pp. 18–21.
8 'The Big Emerging Markets', *Business America*, March 1994, pp. 4–6.
9 Kyung-Il Ghymn, Paul Johnson and Weijiong Zhang, 'Chinese Import Managers' Purchasing Behaviour', *Journal of Asian Business*, vol. 9, no. 3, Summer 1993, pp. 35–45.
10 J. Carbone, 'Who Will Survive?' *Purchasing*, 15 May 2003, pp. 33–42.
11 Tom Reilly, 'The Harmonization of Standards in the European Union and the Impact on US Business', *Business Horizons*, March–April 1995, pp. 28–34.
12 Neil Morgan and Nigel Piercy, 'Interactions Between Marketing and Quality at the SBU Level: Influences and Outcomes', *Journal of the Academy of Marketing Science*, vol. 26, no. 3, 1998, pp. 190–208.
13 Robert W. Peach (ed.), *The ISO 9000 Handbook*, 2nd edn (Fairfax, VA: CEEM Information Services, 1994).
14 'Quality: ISO 9000 Certification Standardization', *Business China*, 30 May 1994, p. 4.
15 T. Witkowski and M. Wolfinbearger, 'Comparative Service Quality: German and American Ratings of Five Different Service Settings', *Journal of Business Research*, 2002, November, pp. 875–81.
16 M. Terziovski, D. Power and A.S. Sohal, 'The Longitudinal Effects of the ISO 9000 Certification Process on Business Performance', *European Journal of Operations Research*, May 2003, pp. 580–95.
17 Jagdish Sheth and Atul Parvatiyar, 'The Evolution of Relationship Marketing', *International Business Review*, vol. 4, no. 4, 1995, pp. 397–418.
18 R.M. Morgan and S.D. Hunt, 'The Commitment–Trust Theory of Relationship Marketing', *Journal of Marketing*, vol. 58, July 1994, pp. 20–38.
19 J.N. Sheth and R. Sisodia, 'Improving the Marketing Productivity', in *Encyclopaedia of Marketing for the Year 2000* (Chicago, IL: American Marketing Association – NTC, 1995).
20 R. Salle, B. Cova and C. Pardo, 'Portfolio of Supplier–Customer Relationships', in A.G. Woodside (ed.), *Advances in Business Marketing and Purchasing*, vol. 9, 2000, pp. 419–42.

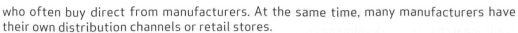

who often buy direct from manufacturers. At the same time, many manufacturers have their own distribution channels or retail stores.

Distribution in Japan has long been considered the most effective non-tariff barrier to the Japanese market.[5] The distribution system is different enough from its United States or European counterparts that it should be carefully studied by anyone contemplating entry. The Japanese system has four distinguishing features: (1) a structure dominated by many small wholesalers dealing with many small retailers; (2) channel control by manufacturers; (3) a business philosophy shaped by a unique culture; and (4) laws that protect the foundation of the system – the small retailer.[6] A comparison of the US, Japan and Germany, the biggest market in Europe, is presented in Exhibit 17.1.

High Density of Middlemen There is a density of middlemen, retailers and wholesalers in the Japanese market unparalleled in any Western industrialised country. The traditional structure serves consumers who make small, frequent purchases at small, conveniently located stores. For contrast, Exhibit 17.2 shows a short distribution channel from France.

Exhibit 17.1 Retail structure in three countries

	Retail outlets (000s)		
	Germany	Japan	United States
Food stores			
Supermarkets	9.0	15.0	43.7
Hypermarkets	2.3	1.5	3.1
Discounters	15.4	1.0	29.1
Independent grocers	34.2	62.0	9.7
Bakers	47.2	74.7	2.8
Butchers	44.3	16.4	8.0
Fishmongers	27.1	27.0	1.6
Greengrocers	16.1	27.7	3.3
Non-food stores			
Booksellers	25.6	37.0	12.7
Chemists	39.4	83.3	47.4
Department stores	1.2	0.3	13.5
Electronics, computers	30.6	61.9	30.3
Home furnishings	11.7	38.7	28.2
Sporting goods	8.3	19.3	23.2
Toy shops	3.6	12.1	18.0

Source: Euromonitor, 2003.

Exhibit 17.2 Distribution channel production and marketing of fruit and vegetables in France

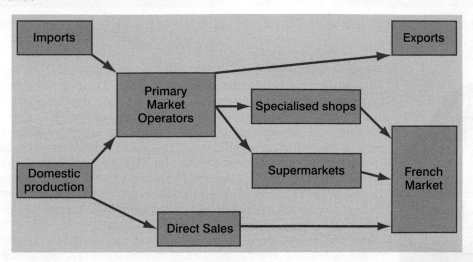

In Japan small stores (95.1 per cent of all retail food stores) account for 57.7 per cent of retail foods sales, whereas in the United States small stores (69.8 per cent of all retail food stores) generate 19.2 per cent of food sales. A disproportionate percentage of non-food sales are made in small stores in Japan as well. In the United States small stores (81.6 per cent of all stores) sell 32.9 per cent of non-food items; in Japan small stores (94.1 per cent of all stores) sell 50.4 per cent.[7]

Channel Control   In Japan, manufacturers depend on wholesalers for a multitude of services to other members of the distribution network. Financing, physical distribution, warehousing, inventory, promotion and payment collection are provided to other channel members by wholesalers. The system works because wholesalers and all other middlemen downstream are tied to manufacturers by a set of practices and incentives designed to ensure strong marketing support for their products and to exclude rival competitors from the channel.[8]

Business Philosophy   Coupled with the close economic ties and dependency created by trade customs and the long structure of Japanese distribution channels is a unique business philosophy that emphasises loyalty, harmony and friendship. The value system supports long-term dealer/supplier relationships that are difficult to change as long as each party perceives economic advantage. The traditional partner, the insider, generally has the advantage.

A general lack of price competition, the provision of costly services and other inefficiencies render the cost of Japanese consumer goods among the highest in the world.

Large-scale Retail Store Law   Competition from large retail stores has been almost totally controlled by *Daitenho* – the large-scale retail store law. Designed to protect small retailers from large intruders into their markets, the law requires that any store larger than 500 square metres (5382 square feet) must have approval from the prefectural government to be 'built, expanded, stay open later in the evening, or change the days of the month they must remain closed'.[9]

Agreements between the European Union, the United States and Japan have had a profound impact on the Japanese distribution system, leading to deregulation of retailing and by strengthening rules on monopoly business practices.[10] The retailing law has been relaxed to permit new outlets as large as 1000 square metres without prior permission. Limits on store hours and business days per year have also been lifted.[11] Officially relaxing laws and regulations on retailing is but one of the important changes signalling the beginning of profound changes in how the Japanese shop.[12]

GOING INTERNATIONAL 17.1

Mitsukoshi department store, established 1611 – but will it be there in 2016?

Japanese department stores have a long history in Japanese retailing. Mitsukoshi department store, the epitome of Japanese retailing, began as a dry goods store in 1611. To visit a Japanese department store is to get a glimpse of Japanese life. In the basements and sub-basements, food abounds with everything from crunchy Japanese pickles to delicate French pastry and soft-coloured, seasonally changing forms of Japanese candies. Besides the traditional floors for women's and men's clothing and furniture, most stores have a floor devoted to kimonos and related accessories, and another floor dedicated to children's needs and wants. On the roof there may be miniature open-air amusement parks for children.

But wait, there's more. Department stores are not merely content to dazzle with variety, delight with imaginative displays and accept large amounts of yen for clothes and vegetables. They also seek to serve up a bit of culture. Somewhere between the floors of clothing and the roof, it is likely that you will find a banqueting hall, an art gallery, an exhibition hall and one or two floors of restaurants serving everything from *doria* (creamy rice with cheese) to *tempura*. Department stores aim to be 'total lifestyle enterprises', says one manager. 'We try to be all-inclusive, with art, culture, shopping and fashion. We stress the philosophy of *i-shoku-ju*, the three big factors in life: what you wear, what you eat and how you live.'

Japanese retailing is dominated by two kinds of store, giant department stores like Mitsukoshi and small neighbourhood shops, both kept alive by a complex distribution system that translates into high prices for the Japanese consumer. In exchange for high prices, the Japanese consumer gets variety, services and, what may be unique to Japanese department stores, cultural enlightenment.

But there are winds of change. Sales for department stores have been down. The Japanese like the amenities of department stores but they are beginning to take notice of the wave of 'new' discount stores that are challenging the traditional retail system by offering quality products at sharply reduced prices. Aoyama Trading Company, which opened a discount men's suit store in the heart of Ginza, where Tokyo's most prestigious department stores are located, may be the future. The owner says he can sell suits for two-thirds the department store price by purchasing directly from manufacturers. Another omen may be Toys 'R' Us, which has opened 16 discount toy stores in Japan. Department store response has been to discount toy prices, for the first time, by as much as 30 per cent.

● As one discounter after another 'cherry picks' item after item to discount, can department stores continue to be 'total lifestyle enterprises'? Will there be a Mitsukoshi, as we know it today, in 2016?

Sources: 'A World in Themselves', *Look Japan*, January 1994, pp. 40–2; 'From Men's Suits to Sake, Discounting Booms in Japan', *Advertising Age International*, 21 March 1994, pp. 1–4; F. Crawford, 'Business Without Borders', *Chain Store Age*, December 2001, pp. 86–96.

Trends: from Traditional to Modern Channel Structures

Today, few countries are so sufficiently isolated that they are unaffected by global economic and political changes. These currents of change are altering all levels of economic fabric, including the distribution structure. Traditional channel structures are giving way to new forms, new alliances and new processes – some more slowly than others, but all changing. Pressures for change in a country come from within and without. Multinational marketers are seeking ways to profitably tap market segments that are served by costly, traditional distribution systems. Direct marketing, door-to-door selling, hypermarkets, discount houses, shopping malls, catalogue selling and selling through the Internet are being introduced in an attempt to provide efficient distribution channels.[13]

Exhibit 17.3 Retail structure in selected countries

Country	All retailers (000)	People served per retailer	Internet users (000)
United States	702	395	223 000
Canada	112	276	28 000
Argentina	296	127	3813
Germany	410	200	42 500
Poland	390	99	16 000
Israel	53	119	2000
South Africa	93	482	5100
China	21 188	61	253 000
Japan	1202	106	88 110
Australia	93	208	11 240

Source: Euromonitor, World Bank 2003 and World Fact Book 2009.

In anticipation of a single European market, national and international retailing networks are developing throughout Europe. An example is Sainsbury's, the UK supermarket giant, which has entered an alliance with Esselunga of Italy (supermarkets), Docks de France (hypermarkets, supermarkets and discount stores) and Belgium's Delhaize (supermarkets). The alliance provides the opportunity for the four to pool their experience and buying power and prepare to expand into other European markets.[14] Ahold (Albert Heijn) of the Netherlands is expanding globally from the United States to Asia. More than 60 per cent of its revenue is coming from abroad. While European retailers see a unified Europe as an opportunity for pan-European expansion, foreign retailers are attracted by the high margins and prices characterised as 'among the most expensive anywhere in the world'. Costco, the US-based warehouse retailer, saw the high gross margins British supermarkets command, 7 to 8 per cent compared with 2.5 to 3 per cent in the United States, as an opportunity. Costco prices will be 10 to 20 per cent cheaper than rival local retailers. The impact of these and other trends is to change traditional distribution and marketing systems, leading to greater efficiency in distribution. Competition will translate those efficiencies into lower consumer prices. Exhibit 17.3 gives you an idea of the retail structures found in selected countries.

In India one of the most promising new retail centres, the vast majority of the 600 or so malls currently under construction have been designed locally and there is widespread industry concern that many will be poorly located, badly laid out and redundant before they even open. With property prices already crippling in India's main commercial cities, a lack of suitable retail sites may genuinely hamper its burgeoning consumer explosion.

The place	The time	The sell
Dubai Mall	August 2008, Dubai, UAE	Dubai does retail the only way its knows how, with French department store Galeries Lafayette as one anchor, a huge aquarium and much, much more
Forum Istanbul	Late 2008, Istanbul, Turkey	This massive project is the latest to join the plethora of malls opening in the Turkish capital and will combine shopping with houses and offices
Liverpool One	Phase 1, May, Liverpool, UK	Five-district open streets mixed use development entwined within the existing city centre
Mall of Arabia	2010, Dubai, UAE	Part of the City of Arabia mega-tourism and leisure project, Mall of Arabia will have over 1000 stores and will be the grand-daddy of them all in the region
Milano Santa Giulia	Phased opening, completion 2010, Milan, Italy	Massive mixed-use scheme with master plan by Foster Milan, Italy + Partners, with an upscale shopping district to rival nearby Milan at its heart, surrounded by housing and offices
Parklake Plaza	2011, Bucharest, Romania	Five-level mall close to the city centre – the biggest of the plethora of retail projects under construction in the Romanian capital
Puerto Venecia	Phased opening, completion 2009, Zaragoza, Spain	Combining sports, leisure, big-box retail and a fashion mall around a 10 000 m^2 artificial lake, the scheme is designed as a major out-of-town destination
Somerset Central	2009, Singapore	An eight-storey fashion mall located at the gateway to Singapore's main shopping streets
Westfield London	October 2008, London, UK	Stunning mall in White City, just to the west of London's West End, featuring luxury zones, restaurants and over 270 stores
Meadowlands Xanadu	Mid-2009, New Jersey, USA	A troubled history has dogged mixed-use scheme Xanadu, based on the mall of the same name outside Madrid, complete with indoor ski slope. Original developer Mills went bust and the project is now run by Colony Capital

Source: CNBC European Business, July/ August 2008, p. 51–2.

Alternative Middleman Choices

A marketer's options range from assuming the entire distribution activity (by establishing its own subsidiaries and marketing directly to the end user) to depending on intermediaries for distribution of the product. Channel selection must be given considerable thought since, once initiated, it is difficult to change, and if it proves inappropriate, future growth of market share may be affected.

Exhibit 17.6 shows some of the possible channel-of-distribution alternatives. The arrows show those to whom the producer and each of the middlemen may sell. In the home country, the seller must have an organisation (generally the international marketing division of a company) to deal with channel members needed to move goods between countries. In the foreign market, the seller must supervise the channels that supply the product to the end user.

Once the marketer has clarified company objectives and policies, the next step is the selection of specific intermediaries needed to develop a channel. External middlemen are differentiated on whether or not they take title to the goods. Agent middlemen represent the principal rather than themselves, and merchant middlemen take title to the goods and buy and sell on their own account. The distinction between agent and merchant middlemen is important because a manufacturer's control of the distribution process is affected by who has title to the goods in the channel.

- **Agent middlemen** work on commission and arrange for sales in the foreign country but do not take title to the merchandise. By using agents, the manufacturer assumes trading risk but maintains the right to establish policy guidelines and prices, and to require its agents to provide sales records and customer information.
- **Merchant middlemen** actually take title to manufacturers' goods and assume the trading risks, so they tend to be less controllable than agent middlemen. Merchant middlemen provide a variety of import and export wholesaling functions involved in purchasing for their own account and selling in other countries. Because merchant middlemen are primarily concerned with sales and profit margins on their merchandise, they are

Exhibit 17.6 International channel-of-distribution alternatives

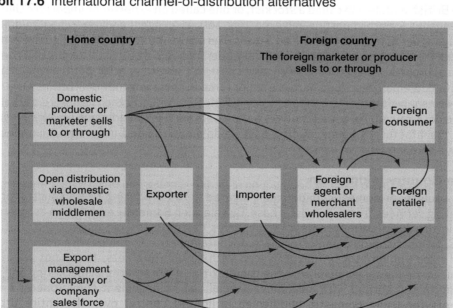

FOREIGN-COUNTRY MIDDLEMEN
middlemen in foreign markets

MANUFACTURERS' REPRESEN-TATIVES
represent the producing company in another country

FOREIGN BROKERS
agents who deal largely in commodities and food products, typically part of small firms operating in one or a few countries

MANAGING AGENT
conducts business within a foreign nation under exclusive contract to the parent company

DEALER
anyone who has a continuing relationship with a supplier in buying and selling goods

Using **foreign-country middlemen** moves the manufacturer closer to the market and involves the company more closely with problems of language, physical distribution, communications and financing. Foreign middlemen may be agents or merchants; they may be associated with the parent company to varying degrees; or they may be temporarily hired for special purposes. Some of the more important foreign-country middlemen are manufacturers' representatives and foreign distributors.

Manufacturers' Representatives   Manufacturers' representatives are agent middlemen who take responsibility for a producer's goods in a city, regional market area, entire country or several adjacent countries. When responsible for an entire country, the middleman is often called a 'sole agent'. The well-chosen, well-motivated, well-controlled manufacturers' representative can provide excellent market coverage for manufacturers in certain circumstances. The manufacturers' representative is widely used in distribution of industrial goods overseas and is an excellent representative for any type of manufactured consumer goods.

Foreign **manufacturers' representatives** have a variety of titles including sales agent, resident sales agent, exclusive agent, commission agent and indent agent. They take no credit, exchange or market risk but deal strictly as field sales representatives. They do not arrange for shipping or for handling and usually do not take physical possession. Manufacturers who desire the type of control and intensive market coverage their own sales force would afford, but who cannot field one, may find the manufacturers' representative a satisfactory choice.

Distributors   A foreign distributor is a merchant middleman. This intermediary often has exclusive sales rights in a specific country and works in close cooperation with the manufacturer. The distributor has a relatively high degree of dependence on the supplier companies, and arrangements are likely to be on a long-term, continuous basis. Working through distributors permits the manufacturer a reasonable degree of control over prices, promotional effort, inventory, servicing and other distribution functions.

Foreign-country Brokers   Like the export broker discussed earlier, brokers are agents who deal largely in commodities and food products. The **foreign brokers** are typically part of small brokerage firms operating in one country or in a few contiguous countries. Their strength is in having good continuing relationships with customers and providing speedy market coverage at a low cost.

Managing Agents   A managing agent conducts business within a foreign nation under an exclusive contract arrangement with the parent company. The **managing agent** in some cases invests in the operation and in most instances operates under a contract with the parent company. Compensation is usually on the basis of cost plus a specified percentage of the profits of the managed company.

Dealers   Generally speaking, anyone who has a continuing relationship with a supplier in buying and selling goods is considered a dealer. More specifically, dealers are middlemen selling industrial goods or durable consumer goods direct to customers; dealers are the last step in the channel of distribution. **Dealers** have continuing, close working relationships with their suppliers and exclusive selling rights for their producer's products within a given geographic area. Finally, they derive a large portion of their sales volume from the products of a single supplier firm. Usually a dealer is an independent merchant middleman, but sometimes the supplier company has an equity in its dealers.

Some of the best examples of dealer operations are found in the farm equipment, earth-moving and automotive industries. These categories include Massey Ferguson, with a vast, worldwide network of dealers; Caterpillar Tractor Company, with dealers in every major city of the world; and the various car companies.

Import Jobbers, Wholesalers and Retailers   Import jobbers purchase goods directly from the manufacturer and sell to wholesalers and retailers and to industrial customers. Large and small **wholesalers and retailers** engage in direct importing for their own outlets and for redistribution to smaller middlemen. The combination retailer-wholesaler is more important in foreign countries than in Western countries. It is not uncommon to find large retailers wholesaling goods to local shops and dealers. Exhibit 17.9 summarises the characteristics of foreign-country middlemen.

> **WHOLESALERS AND RETAILERS**
> facilitate the exchange of goods between manufacturer and consumer

Exhibit 17.9 Characteristics of foreign-country middlemen

Type of duty	Agent broker	Manufacturers' representative	Managing agent	Merchant distributor	Dealer	Import jobber	Wholesaler and retailer
Take title	No	No	No	Yes	Yes	Yes	Yes
Take possession	No	Seldom	Seldom	Yes	Yes	Yes	Yes
Continuing relationship	No	Often	With buyer, not seller	Yes	Yes	No	Usually not
Share of foreign output	Small	All or part for one area	n.a.	All, for certain countries	Assignment area	Small	Very small
Degree of control by principal	Low	Fair	None	High	High	Low	Nil
Price authority	Nil	Nil	Nil	Partial	Partial	Full	Full
Represent buyer or seller	Either	Seller	Buyer	Seller	Seller	Self	Self
Number of principals	Many	Few	Many	Small	Few major	Many	Many
Arrange shipping	No	No	No	No	No	No	No
Type of goods	Commodity and food	Manufactured goods	All types manufactured goods	Manufactured goods	Manufactured goods	Manufactured goods	Manufactured consumer goods
Breadth of line	Broad	Allied lines	Broad	Narrow to broad	Narrow	Narrow to broad	Narrow to broad
Handle competitive lines	Yes	No	Yes	No	No	Yes	Yes
Extent of promotion and selling effort	Nil	Fair	Nil	Fair	Good	Nil	Nil usually
Extend credit to principal	No	No	No	Sometimes	No	No	No
Market information	Nil	Good	Nil	Fair	Good	Nil	Nil

Note: n.a. = not available.

first considered, relate to perishability or bulk of the product, complexity of sale, sales service required and value of the product.

Channel commanders must be aware that channel patterns change; they cannot assume that once a channel has been developed to fit the character of both company and market no more need be done. The United Kingdom, for example, has epitomised distribution through speciality-type middlemen, distributors, wholesalers and retailers; in fact, all middlemen have traditionally worked within narrow product speciality areas. In recent years, however, there has been a trend towards broader lines, conglomerate merchandising and mass marketing.

Continuity

Channels of distribution often pose longevity problems. Most agent middlemen firms tend to be small institutions. When one individual retires or moves out of a line of business, the company may find it has lost its distribution in that area. Wholesalers, and especially retailers, are not noted for their continuity in business either. Most middlemen have little loyalty to their vendors. They handle brands in good times when the line is making money, but quickly reject such products within a season or a year if they fail to produce during that period. Distributors and dealers are probably the most loyal middlemen, but even with them manufacturers must attempt to build brand loyalty downstream in a channel lest middlemen shift allegiance to other companies or other inducements.

Locating, Selecting and Motivating Channel Members

The actual process of building channels for international distribution is seldom easy and many companies have been stopped in their efforts to develop international markets by their inability to construct a satisfactory system of channels.

Despite the chaotic condition of international distribution channels, international marketers can follow a logical procedure in developing channels. After general policy guides are established, marketers need to develop criteria for the selection of specific middlemen. Construction of the middleman network includes seeking out potential middlemen, selecting those who fit the company's requirements and establishing working relationships with them.

In international marketing the channel-building process is hardly routine. The closer the company wants to get to the consumer in its channel contact, the larger the sales force required. If a company is content with finding an exclusive importer or selling agent for a given country, channel building may not be too difficult; but if it goes down to the level of subwholesaler or retailer it is taking on a tremendous task and must have an internal staff capable of supporting such an effort.

Locating Middlemen

The search for prospective middlemen should begin with study of the market and determination of criteria for evaluating middlemen servicing that market. The company's broad policy guidelines should be followed, but expect expediency to override policy at times. The checklist of criteria differs according to the type of middlemen being used and the nature of their relationship with the company. Basically, such lists are built around four subject areas: (1) productivity or volume; (2) financial strength; (3) managerial stability and capability; and (4) the nature and reputation of the business. Emphasis is usually placed on either the actual or potential productivity of the middleman.

Screening

The screening and selection process itself should follow this sequence: (1) a letter including product information and distributor requirements in the native language to each prospective middleman; (2) a follow-up to the best respondents for more specific information concerning lines handled, territory covered, size of firm, number of sales

people and other background information; (3) check of credit and references from other clients and customers of the prospective middleman; and (4) if possible, a personal check of the most promising firms.

Selecting Middlemen

Finding prospective middlemen is less a problem than determining which of them can perform satisfactorily. Most prospects are hampered by low volume or low potential volume, many are underfinanced, and some simply cannot be trusted. In many cases, when a manufacturer is not well known abroad, the reputation of the middleman becomes the reputation of the manufacturer, so a poor choice at this point can be devastating.

The Agreement   Once a potential middleman has been found and evaluated, there remains the task of detailing the arrangements with that middleman. So far the company has been in a buying position, now it must shift into a selling and negotiating position to convince the middleman to handle the goods and accept a distribution agreement that is workable for the company. Agreements must spell out the specific responsibilities of the manufacturer and the middleman, including an annual sales minimum. The sales minimum serves as a basis for evaluation of the distributor and failure to meet sales minimums may give the exporter the right of termination.

Some experienced exporters recommend that initial contracts be signed for one year only. If the first year's performance is satisfactory, they should be reviewed for renewal for a longer period. This permits easier termination and, more important, after a year of working together in the market, a more workable arrangement can generally be reached.

Motivating Middlemen

Once middlemen are selected, a promotional programme must be started to maintain high-level interest in the manufacturer's products. A larger proportion of the advertising budget must be devoted to channel communications than in the head office because there are so many small middlemen to be contacted. Consumer advertising is of no avail unless the goods are actually available. On all levels, there is a clear correlation between the middleman's motivation and sales volume. The hundreds of motivational techniques that can be employed to maintain middleman interest and support for the product may be grouped into five categories: financial rewards, psychological rewards, communications, company support and corporate rapport.

Obviously, margins or commissions must be competitive and set to meet the needs of the middleman, and may vary according to the volume of sales and the level of services offered. Without a combination of adequate margin and adequate volume, a middleman cannot afford to give much attention to a product.

Being human, middlemen and their sales people respond to psychological rewards and recognition for the jobs they are doing. A trip to the parent company's home or regional office is a great honour. Publicity in company media and local newspapers also builds esteem and involvement among foreign middlemen.

Terminating Middlemen

When middlemen do not perform up to standards or when market situations change, requiring a company to restructure its distribution, it may be necessary to terminate relationships with certain middlemen or certain types of middlemen. In Western markets, it is usually a simple action regardless of the type of middleman – agent or merchant, they are simply dismissed. However, in other parts of the world, the middleman typically has some legal protection that makes it difficult to terminate relationships. Some companies give all middlemen contracts for one year, or for another specified period, to

avoid such problems. But as many experienced international marketers know, the best rule is to avoid the need to terminate distributors by screening all prospective middlemen carefully.

Controlling Middlemen

The extreme length of channels typically used in international distribution makes control of middlemen particularly difficult. Some companies solve this problem by establishing their own distribution systems; others issue franchises or exclusive distributorships in an effort to maintain control through the first stages of the channels.

Some manufacturers have lost control through 'secondary wholesaling' – when rebuffed discounters have secured a product through an unauthorised outlet. A manufacturer may then find some of the toughest competition from its own products that have been diverted through other countries or manufactured by subsidiaries and exported or bootlegged into markets the parent would prefer to reserve. Such action can directly conflict with exclusive arrangements made with distributors in other countries and may undermine the entire distribution system by harming relationships between manufacturers and their channels.[28]

Summary

From the foregoing discussion, it is evident that the international marketer has a broad range of alternatives for developing an economical, efficient, high-volume international distribution system. To the uninitiated, however, the variety may be overwhelming.

Careful analysis of the functions performed suggests more similarity than difference between international and domestic distribution systems; in both cases there are three primary alternatives of using agent middlemen, merchant middlemen or a company's own sales and distribution system. In many instances, all three types of middleman are employed on the international scene, and channel structure may vary from nation to nation or from continent to continent. The neophyte company in international marketing can gain strength from the knowledge that information and advice are available relative to the structuring of international distribution systems and that many well-developed and capable middleman firms exist for the international distribution of goods. Within the past decade, international middlemen have become more numerous, more reliable, more sophisticated and more readily available to marketers in all countries. Such growth and development offer an ever-wider range of possibilities for entering foreign markets, but the international business person should remember that it is just as easy for competitors.

Questions

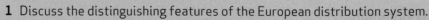

1 Discuss the distinguishing features of the European distribution system.
2 Discuss the ways Japanese manufacturers control the distribution process from manufacturer to retailer.
3 Discuss how the globalisation of markets, especially in the European Union, affects retail distribution.
4 In what ways and to what extent do the functions of domestic middlemen differ from those of their foreign counterparts?

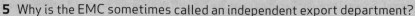

5 Why is the EMC sometimes called an independent export department?

6 Discuss how physical distribution relates to channel policy and how they affect one another.

7 Explain how and why distribution channels are affected as they are when the stage of development of an economy improves.

8 In what circumstances is the use of an EMC logical?

9 In what circumstances are trading companies likely to be used?

10 How is distribution-channel structure affected by increasing emphasis on the government as a customer and by the existence of state trading agencies?

11 Review the key variable that affects the marketer's choice of distribution channels.

12 Account, as best you can, for the differences in channel patterns that might be encountered in a highly developed country and an emerging country.

13 One of the first things companies discover about international channel-of-distribution patterns is that in most countries it is nearly impossible to gain adequate market coverage through a simple channel-of-distribution plan. Discuss.

14 Discuss the factors influencing marketing via the Internet.

Further Reading

A. Nicholas, 'Retailers and International Markets', *International Marketing Review*, 1990, 7(4), pp. 75–85.

P.N. Ghauri, U. Elg and R.R. Sinkovics, 'Foreign Direct Investment – Location Attractiveness for Retailing Firms in the European Union', in *European Union and the Race for Foreign Direct Investment in Europe*, Pervez N. Ghauri and Lars Oxelheim (eds), 2004, Oxford: Pergamon, pp. 407–28.

P.Y.K. Chau, M. Cole, A.P. Messey, M. Montoya-Weiss and R. O'Keefe, 'Cultural Differences in Online Behaviour of Consumers', *Communication of the ACM*, 2002, 45(1), pp. 138–43.

References

1 J. Evans, A. Treadgold and F.T. Movondo, 'Psychic Distance and the Performance of International Retailers: A Suggested Theoretical Framework', *International Marketing Review*, 2000, 17(4/5), pp. 297–309.

2 D. Ford, 'Distribution, Internationalisation and Networks', *International Marketing Review*, 2002, 19(2/3), pp. 225–35.

3 P. Ellis, 'Are International Trade Intermediaries Catalysts in Economic Development?', *Journal of International Marketing*, 2003, 112(12), pp. 73–96.

4 For a report on research on a nation's level of economic development and marketing channels, see Janen E. Olsen and Kent L. Granzin, *Journal of Global Marketing*, 7(3), 1994, pp. 7–39.

5 Constantine Katsikeas, Ali Al-Khalifa and Dave Crick, 'Manufacturers' Understanding of their Overseas Distributors: The Relevance of Export Involvement', *International Business Review*, 6(2), 1997, pp. 147–64.

6 A comprehensive review of the changing character of the Japanese distribution system is presented in John Fahy and Fuyuki Taguchi, 'Reassessing the Japanese Distribution System', *Sloan Management Review*, Winter 1995, pp. 49–61.

7 Arieh Goldman, 'Japan's Distribution System: Institutional Structure, Internal Political Economy, and Modernization', *Journal of Retailing*, Summer 1991, pp. 156–61.

them shipped to Japan for a price below that of the camera purchased in Japan. In addition to the higher prices for products at home, the rising value of the yen makes these price differentials even wider. When the New York price for Panasonic cordless telephones was €54.10 ($59.95), they cost €137.20 ($152) in Tokyo, and when the Sony Walkman was €80.30 ($89), it was €149.14 ($165.23) in Tokyo.

GOING INTERNATIONAL 18.1

Driving a Golf through the grey market

© iStockphoto.com/ isgaby

Estimates of the grey market's current share of car sales range from 3 per cent to 10 per cent, depending on the country. Assuming a conservative 5 per cent, the total only in Europe could hit 600 000 vehicles' worth in just one year, which would total €10.8 billion. The biggest source of grey market cars is Italy, where more than 10 per cent of the cars sold, roughly 185 000, end up in other countries. Re-importers also handle cars from the Netherlands and even from countries outside the European Union, such as Canada. The major destination is Germany, where about 330 000 grey market cars are sold annually. The grey market has benefited consumers while giving fits to traditional dealers and car makers.

Competition from the grey market is forcing dealers to negotiate lower prices, while producers have cancelled or delayed planned price increases. Because most of the re-importers are legitimate, the car manufacturers' only hope of stopping them is to block renegade dealers from selling to the grey market. In 1994, for example, Peugeot asked the European Commission to ban sales to re-importers, but was not successful.

Car makers can withdraw a dealer's franchise, as Peugeot did when it pulled its dealer in Italy. But it is almost impossible to spot and stop these side deals. Golf is a typical example: VW ships Golfs from its plant in Wolfsburg, Germany, to a VW distributor in Italy, pricing it low to compete locally. The distributor sells the car to a franchised VW dealer in, let's say, Florence. An independent re-importer buys the car from the Italian dealer and ships it back to Germany. A German consumer then buys the car from the re-importer for some €3000–3500 less than it would cost at a German VW dealer.

Source: 'Carmakers Think Monetary Union is the Answer', *Business Week*, 20 November 1995, p. 21.

Foreign companies doing business in Japan generally follow the same pattern of high prices for the products they sell in Japan, thus creating an opportunity for parallel markets in their products. Eastman Kodak prices its film higher in Japan than in other parts of Asia. Coca-Cola imported from the United States sells for 27 per cent less through discounters than Coke's own made-in-Japan product.[5]

The possibility of a parallel market occurs whenever price differences are greater than the cost of transportation between two markets. In Europe, because of different taxes and competitive price structures, prices for the same product vary between countries. When this occurs, it is not unusual for companies to find themselves competing in one country with their own product imported from another country at lower prices. Presumably such price differentials will cease to exist once and a full monetary union is achieved, stabilising prices in the EU countries.[6]

Perfume and designer brands such as Gucci and Cartier are especially prone to grey markets. To maintain the image of quality and exclusivity, prices for such products traditionally include high profit margins at each level of distribution, differential prices among markets and limited quantities, as well as distribution restricted to upmarket retailers. In the United States, wholesale prices for exclusive brands of fragrance are often 25 per cent more than wholesale prices in other countries. These are the ideal conditions for a lucrative grey market for unauthorised dealers in other countries who buy more than they need at wholesale prices lower than US wholesalers pay. They then sell the excess at a profit to unauthorised US retailers, but at a price lower than the retailer would have to pay to an authorised US distributor.

GOING INTERNATIONAL 18.2

How do Levi's 501s get to international markets?

Levi Strauss sells in international markets – how else would 501 jeans get to market? The answer is via the grey market, or 'diverters'. Diverters are enterprising people who legally buy 501s at retail prices, usually during sales, and then resell them to foreign buyers. It is estimated that Levi Strauss sells millions of dollars of Levi's abroad at discount prices – all authorised sales. US retail prices for Levi's 501s are $30 to $40 a pair; in Germany, they are sold to authorised wholesalers for about $40, and authorised retailers sell them at about $80. The difference of $40 or so makes it economically possible for a diverter to buy 501s in the United States and sell them to unauthorised dealers who then sell them for $60 to $70, undercutting authorised German retailers. Similar practices happen around the world, but how do diverters work?

Here is an example of what is repeated in city after city all over the United States. 'They come into a store in groups and buy every pair of Levi's 501 jeans they can,' says one store manager. He has seen two or three vans full of people come to the store when there is a sale and buy the six-pair-a-day limit, returning day after day until the sale is over. In another retail chain store, where a similar thing was happening, a month-long storewide sale was stopped, at the behest of Levi's, after only two weeks. The Levi's are then channelled to a diverter, who exports them to unauthorised buyers throughout the world. Many eventually end up in discount stores and are sold at discounted prices relative to those distributed through approved channels. This is but one way diverters acquire merchandise. Another is for wholesalers to buy quantities in excess of their needs and then divert the excess to foreign buyers.

These practices are feasible because the retail prices in the United States are often more competitive than in other countries where, historically, price competition is not as fierce. For example, Levi's 501s sell for $73 in Britain versus $45 in the United States. Some, but not all, of the price differences can be attributed to price escalation – that is, tariffs, shipping and other costs associated with exporting – but that portion of the difference attributable to higher margins creates an opportunity for profitable diverting.

In an attempt to stop discount stores not in the manufacturer's official distribution channel from selling 'unauthorised Levi's', Tesco, a UK supermarket chain, was sued by Levi-Strauss & Company. After a four-year court battle, Levi's won when it was ruled that the supermarket has been selling Levi's illegally. However, Tesco, Costco, Wal-Mart and

GOING INTERNATIONAL 18.3

BMW in warning on pricing pressures

© P. Ghauri

BMW warned of increasing pricing pressure in the premium end of the auto market as the world's largest luxury carmaker surprised the markets with a smaller than expected loss. Norbert Reithofer, BMW's chief executive, said rival premium carmakers were offering heavy incentives to car buyers in an effort to rapidly reduce their large piles of unsold cars.

'Some rivals try to push their cars to the market with high incentives,' Mr Reithofer said, without naming the companies. 'This shows that the worldwide car market has not started to recover yet.' Analysts have said that a number of premium carmakers were slow to put the brakes on production after global demand started to collapse late last year. They singled out BMW's rival Daimler in particular, which burned more than a €1bn in cash in the first quarter after its inventories weighed heavily on its financials.

Daimler said it had reduced its inventory of unsold cars by the end of March 2009 and it aimed to return to normal levels. But analysts suspected BMW was itself fuelling the price war with its leasing policy. 'Current leasing rates still suggest the company is selling at subsidised rates,' Arndt Ellinghorst, analyst at Credit Suisse, said.

Friedrich Eichiner, BMW's chief financial officer, conceded the group might have to join the incentive battle in the market, which had had an impact on its earnings in the first quarter. He said he expected the price pressure to abate during the year. Analysts have pressed BMW and Daimler – which already collaborate on hybrid engine technologies and small purchasing projects – to work closer together. They have argued that both carmakers lack the necessary scale to compete in a rapidly shrinking premium car market.

Source: Financial Times, 7 May 2009.

Factors Influencing International Pricing

People travelling abroad are often surprised to find goods that are relatively inexpensive in their home country priced outrageously higher in other countries. It is also possible that goods priced reasonably abroad may be priced enormously high in the home market. Beginning with the import tariff, each time a product changes hands an additional cost is incurred. First, the product passes through the hands of an importer, then to the company with primary responsibility for sales and service, then to a secondary or even a tertiary local distributor, and finally to the retailer and the consumer. The factors influencing pricing in international markets include the objective of the firm in a particular market, price escalation, competition, target customer segment and pricing control (see Exhibit 18.3).

Pricing Objectives

In general, price decisions are viewed two ways: pricing as an active instrument of accomplishing marketing objectives or pricing as a static element in a business decision. If the former view is followed, the company uses price to achieve a specific objective, whether a targeted return on profits, a targeted market share or some other specific goal. The

Exhibit 18.3 Factors influencing international pricing

company that follows the second approach probably exports only excess inventory, places a low priority on foreign business and views its export sales as passive contributions to sales volume. Profit is by far the most important pricing objective. Pricing objectives should be consistent with the marketing objectives of the firm in a particular market as well as the overall strategy of the firm. Essentially, objectives are defined in terms of profit, market share or positioning.

The more control a company has over the final selling price of a product, the better it is able to achieve its marketing goals. However, it is not always possible to control end prices, and in this case, companies may resort to 'mill net pricing', that is, the price received at the plant.

Price Escalation

Excess profits do exist in some international markets, but generally the cause of the disproportionate difference in price between the exporting country and the importing country, here termed *price escalation*, is the added costs incurred as a result of exporting products from one country to another. Specifically, the term relates to situations where ultimate prices are raised by shipping costs, insurance, packing, tariffs, longer channels of distribution, larger middlemen margins, special taxes, administrative costs and exchange-rate fluctuations (see Exhibit 18.4). The majority of these costs arise as a direct result of moving goods across borders from one country to another and combine to escalate the final price to a level considerably higher than in the domestic market.

Taxes, Tariffs and Administrative Costs   'Nothing is surer than death and taxes' has a particularly familiar ring to the ears of the international trader because taxes include tariffs, and tariffs are one of the most pervasive features of international trading. Taxes and tariffs affect the ultimate consumer price for a product and, in most instances, the consumer bears the burden of both. Sometimes, however, the consumer benefits when manufacturers selling goods in foreign countries reduce their net return to gain access to a foreign market. Absorbed or passed on, taxes and tariffs must be considered by the international business person.

A tariff, or duty, is a special form of taxation and, like other forms of taxes, may be levied for the purpose of protecting a market or for increasing government revenue. A tariff is a fee charged when goods are brought into a country from another country. The level of tariff is typically expressed as the rate of duty and may be levied as specific, *ad valorem*, or a combination. A *specific* duty is a flat charge per physical unit imported, such as 15 cents per bushel of rye. *Ad valorem* duties are levied as a percentage of the value of the goods imported, such as 20 per cent of the value of imported watches. *Combination* tariffs include both a specific and an *ad valorem* charge, such as €1 per camera plus 10 per cent of its value.

pricing. To remain price competitive when the dollar is strong (i.e. when it takes more units of the foreign currency to buy a dollar), companies must find ways to offset the higher price caused by currency values. By comparing the price of a relatively standardised product, it is possible to gain an insight into the under- or over-valuation of currencies (see Exhibit 18.6).

Middleman Channel length and marketing patterns vary widely. In some countries, channels are longer and middleman margins higher than is customary. The diversity of channels used to reach markets and the lack of standardised middleman mark-ups leave many producers unaware of the ultimate price of a product.

Exhibit 18.6 The hamburger standard

	Big Mac prices in dollars*	Implied PPP† of the dollar	Under(−)/over(+) valuation against the dollar, %
United States‡	3.57	–	–
Argentina	3.02	3.22	−15
Australia	3.37	1.22	−6
Brazil	4.02	2.25	+13
Britain	3.69	1.56§	+3
Canada	3.35	1.09	−6
Chile	3.19	490	−11
China	1.83	3.50	−49
Denmark	5.53	8.26	+55
Egypt	2.33	3.64	−35
Euro Area**	4.62	1.08††	+29
Hong Kong	1.72	3.73	−52
Hungary	3.62	201	+1
Indonesia	2.05	5854	−43
Japan	3.46	89.6	−3
Malaysia	1.88	1.90	−47
Mexico	2.39	9.24	−33
New Zealand	3.08	1.37	−14
Norway	6.15	11.20	+72
Peru	2.66	2.26	−25
Philippines	2.05	27.8	−42

Exhibit 18.6 (The hamburger standard, continued)

	Big Mac prices in dollars*	Implied PPP[†] of the dollar	Under(−)/over(+) valuation against the dollar, %
Poland	2.41	2.13	−33
Russia	2.04	18.8	−43
Saudi Arabia	2.93	3.08	−18
Singapore	2.88	1.18	−19
South Africa	2.17	5.03	−39
South Korea	2.59	952	−28
Sweden	4.93	10.9	+38
Switzerland	5.98	1.82	+68
Taiwan	2.26	21.0	−37
Thailand	1.89	18.1	−47
Turkey	3.65	1.58	+2
UAE	2.72	2.80	−24

*At current exchanges rates.
[†]Purchasing-power parity; local price divided by price in the United States.
[‡]Average of New York, Chicago, Atlanta, San Francisco.
[§]Dollars per pound.
[**]Weighted average of prices in euro area.
[††]Dollars per euro.

Sources: McDonald's; *The Economist*, 18 July 2009, p. 78.

Besides channel diversity, the fully integrated marketer operating abroad faces various unanticipated costs because marketing and distribution channel infrastructures are underdeveloped in many countries. The marketer can also incur added expenses for warehousing and handling of small shipments, and may have to bear increased financing costs when dealing with underfinanced middlemen. Because no convenient source of data on middleman costs is available, the international marketer must rely on experience and marketing research to ascertain middleman costs.

Transportation Exporting also incurs increased transportation costs when moving goods from one country to another. If the goods go over water, there are additional costs for insurance, packing and handling not generally added to locally produced goods. Such costs add yet another burden because import tariffs in many countries are based on the landed cost that includes transportation, insurance and shipping charges. These costs add to the inflation of the final price. The next section details how a reasonable price in the home market may more than double in the foreign market.

Exhibit 18.7 illustrates some of the effects these factors may have on the end price of a consumer item. Because costs and tariffs vary so widely from country to country, a hypothetical but realistic example is used. It assumes (1) that a constant net price is received

essence, a tax-free enclave and not considered part of the country as far as import regulations are concerned. When an item leaves an FTZ and is officially imported into the host country of the FTZ, all duties and regulations are imposed.[10]

By shipping unassembled goods to an FTZ in an importing country, a marketer can lower costs in a variety of ways.

1 Tariffs may be lower because duties are typically assessed at a lower rate for unassembled versus assembled goods.
2 If labour costs are lower in the importing country, substantial savings may be realised in the final product cost.
3 Ocean transportation rates are affected by weight and volume; thus, unassembled goods may qualify for lower freight rates.
4 If local content, such as packaging or component parts, can be used in the final assembly, there may be a further reduction of tariffs.

All in all, an FTZ is an important method for controlling price escalation. Incidentally, all the advantages offered by an FTZ for an exporter are also advantages for an importer. These zones are used in many countries in the West as well as in the emerging markets. Over 100 FTZs in the United States are used by US importers to help lower their costs of imported goods.[11]

GOING INTERNATIONAL 18.4

Merkel ponders Atlantic free-trade zone

© iStockphoto.com/
MarkGabrenya

Spurred by concern about China's growing economic might, Germany is considering a plan for a free-trade zone between Europe and the US. A senior aide to Angela Merkel said the chancellor was 'interested' in promoting the idea as long as such a zone did not create 'a fortress' but rather 'a tool' to encourage free trade globally, 'which she is persuaded is a condition of Germany's future prosperity'.

The US, Canada and the European Union complained to the World Trade Organisation about China's tariffs on car parts, raising the prospect of Beijing facing its first WTO dispute. The three said they had lost patience with Beijing's refusal to open the $19bn (€15bn, £10bn)-a-year market.

News that the free-trade zone, last pursued by Sir Leon Brittan, when European trade commissioner in 1998, is being debated in the German chancellery testifies to the rapprochement between Washington and Berlin since Ms Merkel's election last November.

This convergence of views was underlined this week when Wen Jiabao, Chinese premier, was politely chided by Ms Merkel for China's poor human rights record and recent restrictions on foreign news agencies, during an official visit to Berlin.

As German perceptions of China have grown more American, Washington's approach has also shifted. Speaking before his first trip to Beijing, Hank Paulson, US Treasury Secretary, outlined a more balanced policy, mixing traditional US criticism with praise for China's reforms.

● Do you think that a FTA between the EU and the US is a good idea? Why/Why not?

Source: Financial Times, 16 September 2008.

Competition

The nature of market structure in particular is an important determinant of price. It refers to the number of competing firms, their size and relative position. In the case of an oligopoly structure, the entering firm would have little freedom to choose a price. Depending on the income levels, a certain market can take only a certain level of pricing. The prices have thus to be set at the level of the competing products. A company can also use competitors' prices as a landmark for positioning its products as compared to competitors. For example, if it wants to position its product as being of higher quality than its competitors, it has to price it accordingly. On the other hand, if a company decides to compete with its competitors on price, it has to set a competitive price. When entering a market and using competitive pricing, a company needs also to check on the cost structure of its competitors. The price is just one of the elements of the marketing mix and has thus to be matched with other elements of it. When a higher price is charged, the company should be able to convince the market that it has a better product, thereby justifying its higher price.

Target Customer

Marketers have to evaluate and understand a particular segment or target customer group in the market that they are entering. Knowledge of **demand elasticity** and price is essential, as is knowledge of how customers would react in the case of price change. Demand for a product is *elastic* if demand can be considerably increased by lowering the price. If a decrease in price would have little effect on demand, it will be considered *inelastic*. Other than the buying behaviour, the ability of customers to buy, prices of substitute and competing products, and the nature of non-price competition are of the utmost importance. In the case of undifferentiated products, the competition is more on pricing, but with differentiated products, market share of a company can even be enhanced through higher prices. Brand names and an image of high quality are two of the factors that characterise differentiated products that can be sold at premium prices.

DEMAND ELASTICITY
when demand for a product changes due to minor changes in the price

GOING INTERNATIONAL 18.5

How are foreign-trade zones used?

There are more than 100 foreign-trade zones (FTZs) in the United States and FTZs exist in many other countries as well. Companies use them to postpone the payment of tariffs on products while they are in the FTZ. Here are some examples of how FTZs are used in the United States.

- A Japanese firm assembles motorcycles, jet skis and three-wheel all-terrain vehicles for import as well as for export to Canada, Latin America and Europe.
- A US manufacturer of window blinds and miniblinds imports and stores fabric from Holland in an FTZ, thereby postponing a 17 per cent tariff until the fabric leaves the FTZ.
- A manufacturer of hair dryers stores its product in an FTZ, which it uses as its main distribution centre for products manufactured in Asia.
- A European-based medical supply company manufactures kidney dialysis machines and sterile tubing using raw materials from Germany and US labour. It then exports 30 per cent of its products to Scandinavian countries.

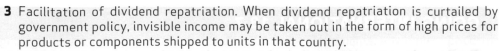

3 Facilitation of dividend repatriation. When dividend repatriation is curtailed by government policy, invisible income may be taken out in the form of high prices for products or components shipped to units in that country.

4 To show more or less profit in crucial times; for example, in the case of new emission, government rules, to please shareholders or to show the good performance of new/ old management.

The tax and financial manipulation possibilities of transfer pricing have not been over-looked by government authorities. Transfer pricing can be used to hide subsidiary profits and to escape foreign market taxes. Transfer pricing is managed in such a way that profit is taken in the country with the lowest tax rate. For example, a foreign manufacturer makes a Blue-ray player for €45 ($50) and sells it to its European subsidiary for €135 ($150). The European subsidiary sells it to a retailer for €180 ($200), but it spends €45 ($50) on advertising and shipping so it shows no profit and pays no taxes. Meanwhile, the parent company makes a €90 ($100) gross margin on each unit and pays a lower tax rate in the home country. If the tax rate was lower in the country where the subsidiary resides, the profit would be taken there and no profit taken in the home country.[13]

The overall objectives of the transfer pricing system include: (1) maximising profits for the corporation as a whole, (2) facilitating parent-company control, and (3) offering man-agement at all levels, both in the product divisions and in the international divisions, an adequate basis for maintaining, developing and receiving credit for their own profitability.

An intracorporate pricing system should employ sound accounting techniques and be defensible to the tax authorities of the countries involved. All of these factors argue against a single uniform price or even a uniform pricing system for all international operations.

Four arrangements for pricing goods for intracompany transfer are:

1 sales at the local manufacturing cost plus a standard mark-up
2 sales at the cost of the most efficient producer in the company plus a standard markup
3 sales at negotiated prices
4 arm's-length sales using the same prices as quoted to independent customers.

Of the four, the arm's-length transfer is most acceptable to tax authorities and most likely to be acceptable to foreign divisions, but the appropriate basis for intracompany trans-fers depends on the nature of the subsidiaries and market conditions.

Dumping

A logical outgrowth of a market policy in international business is goods priced competi-tively at widely differing prices in various markets. Marginal (variable) cost pricing, as dis-cussed above, is one way prices can be reduced to stay within a competitive price range. The market and economic logic of such pricing policies can hardly be disputed, but the practices are often classified as dumping and are subject to severe penalties and fines (see Exhibit 18.8). **Dumping** is defined differently by various economists. One approach classifies international shipments as dumped if the products are sold below their cost of production. The other approach characterises dumping as selling goods in a foreign market below the price of the same goods in the home market. Even rate cutting on cargo shipping has been called dumping.

In the 1960s and 1970s dumping was hardly an issue because world markets were strong, but since the 1980s dumping has become a major issue for a large number of indus-tries. Excess production capacity relative to home-country demand caused many compa-nies to price their goods on a marginal-cost basis, figuring that any contribution above variable cost was beneficial to company profits. In a classic case of dumping, prices are

DUMPING
when a product is sold for a lesser price than its actual cost

Exhibit 18.8 Anti-dumping: number of investigations initiated

Source: WTO, May 2009.

maintained in the home-country market and reduced in foreign markets. For example, the European Union charged that differences in prices between Japan and EU countries ranged from 4.8 to 86 per cent. To correct for this dumping activity, a special import duty of 33.4 per cent was imposed on Japanese computer printers.

Assembly in the importing country is one way companies attempt to lower prices and avoid dumping charges. However, these screwdriver plants, as they are often called, are subject to dumping charges if the price differentials reflect more than the cost savings that result from assembly in the importing country. The increased concern and enforcement in the European Union reflects the changing attitudes among all countries towards dumping. The EU has had anti-dumping legislation from its inception and the Department of Trade of the EU has imposed duties on a variety of products.

Countertrade as a Pricing Tool

The challenges of **countertrade** must be viewed from the same perspective as all other variations in international trade. Marketers must be aware of which markets will be likely to require countertrades just as they must be aware of social customs and legal requirements. Assessing this factor along with all other market factors will enhance a marketer's competitive position.

Ben and Jerry's Homemade Ice Cream, Inc., a well-known US ice cream vendor, is manufacturing and selling ice cream in Russia. With the roubles it earns, it is buying Russian walnuts, honey and *matryoshky* (Russian nesting dolls) to sell in the United States. This was the only means of getting its profit out of Russia because there was a shortage of hard currency in Russia, making it difficult to convert roubles to dollars. PepsiCo sold Pepsi to Russians in exchange for the exclusive rights to sell Stolichnaya vodka in the United States. In neither transaction did cash change hands; these were barter deals, a type of countertrade. Although cash may be the preferred method of payment, countertrades are becoming an important part of trade with Eastern Europe, China and, to a varying degree, some Latin American and African nations.[14] Today, an international company must include in its market-pricing toolkit some understanding of countertrading.

Types of Countertrade

Countertrade includes four distinct transactions: barter, compensation deals, counterpurchase and buy-back.[15]

COUNTERTRADE
when products are exchanged for other products instead of cash

trade organisations utilise the marketing organisations and expertise of Western companies to market their goods for them.

To upgrade manufacturing capabilities. By entering compensation arrangements under which foreign (usually Western) firms provide plant and equipment and buy back resultant products, the trade organisations of less developed countries can enlist Western technical cooperation in upgrading industrial facilities.

To maintain prices of export goods. Countertrade can be used as a means to dispose of goods at prices that the market would not bear under cash-for-goods terms. Although the Western seller absorbs the added cost by inflating the price of the original sale, the nominal price of the counter-purchased goods is maintained, and the seller need not concede what the value of the goods would be in the world supply-and-demand market. Conversely, if the world price for a commodity is artificially high, such as the price for crude oil, a country can barter its oil for Western goods (e.g. weapons) so that the real 'price' the Western partner pays is below the world price.

To force reinvestment of proceeds from weapon deals. Many Arab countries require that a portion of proceeds from weapons purchases be reinvested in facilities designated by the buyer – everything from pipelines to hotels and sugar mills.

● Do you think these are good reasons to impose counter trade?

Sources: Leo G.B. Welt, 'Countertrade? Better Than No Trade', *Export Today*, Spring 1985, p. 54; and Anne Marie Squeo and Daniel Pearl, 'The Big Sell: How a Gulf Sheikdom Landed its Sweet Deal with Lockheed Martin', *Wall Street Journal*, 20 April 2000.

BARTER HOUSES
international trading companies able to introduce merchandise to outlets and geographic areas previously untapped

Barter houses specialise in trading goods acquired through barter arrangements and are the primary outside source of aid for companies beset by the uncertainty of a counter-trade. While barter houses, most of which are found in Europe and Asia, can find a market for bartered goods, it requires time, which puts a financial strain on a company because capital is tied up longer than in normal transactions. Seeking loans to tide it over until sales are completed usually solves this problem.

There are many examples of companies losing sales to competitors who were willing to enter into countertrade agreements. A Western oilfield equipment manufacturer claims it submitted the lowest dollar bid in an Egyptian offer but lost the sale to a bidder who offered a counter-purchase arrangement. Incidentally, the successful company was Japanese, with a sizeable established trading company to dispose of the Egyptian goods received in the counter-purchase arrangement.

Proactive Countertrade Strategy

Some authorities suggest that companies should have a defined countertrade strategy as part of their marketing strategy rather than be caught unprepared when confronted with a countertrade proposition. Currently most companies have a reactive strategy, that is, they use countertrade when they believe it is the only way to make a sale. Even when these companies include countertrade as a permanent feature of their operations, they use it to react to a sales demand rather than using countertrade as an aggressive marketing tool for expansion.[21]

Successful countertrade transactions require that the marketer (1) accurately establishes the market value of the goods being offered and (2) disposes of the bartered goods once they are received. Most countertrades judged unsuccessful result from not properly resolving one or both of these factors.

In short, unsuccessful countertrades are generally the result of inadequate planning and preparation. One experienced countertrader suggests answering the following questions

 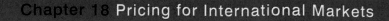

before entering into a countertrade agreement: (1) Is there a ready market for the goods bartered? (2) Is the quality of the goods offered consistent and acceptable? (3) Is an expert needed to handle the negotiations? (4) Is the contract price sufficient to cover the cost of barter and net the desired revenue?

Summary

Pricing is one of the most complicated decision areas encountered by international marketers. Rather than deal with one set of market conditions, one group of competitors, one set of cost factors and one set of government regulations, international marketers must take all these factors into account, not only for each country in which they are operating, but often for each market within a country. The continuing growth of the less developed country markets, coupled with their lack of investment capital, has increased the importance of countertrades for most marketers, making it an important tool to include in pricing policy.

Market prices at the consumer level are much more difficult to control in international than in domestic marketing, but the international marketer must still approach the pricing task on a basis of objectives and policy, leaving enough flexibility for tactical price movements. Pricing in the international marketplace requires a combination of intimate knowledge of market costs and regulations, an awareness of possible countertrade deals, infinite patience for detail and a shrewd sense of market strategy.

Questions

1 Discuss the causes of and solutions for parallel imports and their effect on price.
2 Why is it so difficult to control consumer prices when selling overseas?
3 What are the causes of price escalation? Do they differ for exports and goods produced and sold in a foreign country?
4 Define the following: parallel imports, skimming, price escalation, dumping, transfer pricing and cartel.
5 Price escalation is a major pricing problem for the international marketer. How can this problem be counteracted? Discuss.
6 Changing currency values have an impact on pricing strategies. Discuss.
7 'Regardless of the strategic factors involved and the company's orientation to market pricing, every price must be set with cost considerations in mind.' Discuss.
8 'Price fixing by business is not generally viewed as an acceptable practice (at least in the domestic market); but when governments enter the field of price administration, they presume to do it for the general welfare, to lessen the effects of destructive competition.' Discuss.
9 Do value added taxes discriminate against imported goods?
10 Explain specific tariffs, *ad valorem* tariffs and combination tariffs.
11 Suggest an approach a marketer may follow in adjusting prices to accommodate exchange-rate fluctuations.
12 Why has dumping become such an issue in recent years?
13 Discuss the various ways in which governments set prices. Why do they engage in such activities?
14 Discuss the alternative objectives possible in setting transfer prices.

15 Why do governments scrutinise transfer pricing arrangements so carefully?
16 Why are costs so difficult to assess in marketing internationally?
17 Discuss why countertrading is on the increase.
18 Discuss the major problems facing a company that is countertrading.
19 If a country you are trading with has a shortage of hard currency, how should you prepare to negotiate price?
20 Of the four types of countertrade discussed in the text, which is the most beneficial to the seller? Explain.
21 Why should a knowledge of countertrades be part of an international marketer's pricing toolkit? Discuss.

Further Reading

S.T. Cavusgil, 'Unravelling the Mystique of Export Pricing', *Business Horizon*, 1988, 31(3), pp. 54–63.

R. Veale and P. Quester, 'Do consumer expectations match experience? Predicting the influence of price and country of origin on perceptions of product quality', *International Business Review*, 2009, 18(2), pp. 134–44.

N. Tzokas, S. Hart, P. Argouslidis and M. Saren, 'Strategic pricing in export markets: empirical evidence from the UK', *International Business Review*, 2000, 9(1), pp. 95–117.

References

1 For a comprehensive review of pricing and the integration of Europe, see Wolfgang Gaul and Ulrich Luz, 'Pricing in International Marketing and Western European Economic Integration', *Management International Review*, vol. 34, no. 2, 1994, pp. 101–24.
2 S. Tamer Cavusgil, 'Unravelling the Mystiques of Export Pricing', in Sidney J. Levy *et al.* (eds), *Marketing Manager's Handbook* (New York: Dartnell, 1994), pp. 1357–74; and 'The Debate on Export Subsidies', *European Business Report*, Spring IQ, 1998, p. 58.
3 For a complete and thorough discussion of parallel markets, see Robert E. Weigand, 'Parallel Import Channels – Options for Preserving Territorial Integrity', *Columbia Journal of World Business*, Spring 1991, pp. 53–60.
4 S.T. Cavusgil, K. Chan and C. Zhang, 'Strategic Orientations in Export Pricing: A Clustering Approach to Create Firm Taxonomies', *Journal of International Marketing*, 2003, 11(1), pp. 47–72.
5 R.A. Kustin, 'Marketing Mix Standardization: A Cross-cultural Study of Four Countries', *International Business Review*, 13(5), pp. 637–49.
6 'Cross-border Pricing: Is the Price Right?', *Business Europe*, 6–12 February 1995, pp. 6–7; and 'Showroom Tactics: New Car Prices', *The European*, 2–8 February 1998, p. 22.
7 For a comprehensive review of pricing in foreign markets, see James K. Weekly, 'Pricing in Foreign Markets: Pitfalls and Opportunities', *Industrial Marketing Management*, May 1992, pp. 173–9.
8 See, for example, Joseph Neu, 'Profiting from Leasing Abroad', *International Business*, April 1995, pp. 56–8.
9 B. Seyoum 'Trade liberalization and patterns of strategic adjustment in the US textiles and clothing industry, *International Business Review*, 2007, 16(1), pp. 109–35.
10 'Special Section: FTZs', *Global Trade and Transportation*, September 1994, pp. 24–7.
11 D. Scott Freeman, 'Foreign Trade Zones: An Underutilized US Asset', *Trade and Culture*, September–October 1994, pp. 94–5.

12 P. Verburg, 'Diamond Cartels Are Forever', *Canadian Business*, 10 July 2000, p. 135.

13 L.W. Siegel, 'Critics Believe DeBeers Manipulates the Market to Keep Diamonds High', *All Things Considered* (NPR), 11 November 2001.

14 Most countertrade is found in countries with shortages of foreign exchange, which is often given as the reason why countertrades are mandated by these countries. An interesting study, however, casts some doubt on this thesis and suggests instead that countertrades may be a reasonable way for countries to minimise transaction costs. For an insightful report on this research, see Jean-Francois Hennart and Erin Anderson, 'Countertrade and the Minimization of Transaction Costs: An Empirical Examination', *The Journal of Law, Economics, and Organization*, vol. 9, no. 2, 1993, pp. 290–313.

15 A variety of terms are used to describe the transactions the authors classify as countertrades. Switch trading, parallel trades, offset trades and clearing agreements are other terms used to describe countertrade, but they are only variations of the four types mentioned here. In order not to further confuse the issue but to help standardise terminology, the authors have used the terms developed by *Business International*.

16 D. West, 'Countertrade', *Business Credit*, April 2002, p. 48.

17 M.R. Snyder, 'Doing Business in Russia Again?', *Moscow Times*, 9 January 2002.

18 A report on risk sharing in countertrade is found in Erwin Amann and Dalia Marin, 'Risk-sharing in International Trade: An Analysis of Countertrade', *The Journal of Industrial Economics*, March 1994, pp. 63–77.

19 D. Hew, 'Time for Asia to Cash in on Countertrade', *Business Times*, Singapore, 4 September 2002.

20 See, for example, the study by Aspy P. Palia and Heon Deok Yoon, 'Countertrade Practices in Korea', *Industrial Marketing Management*, July 1994, pp. 205–14, which examines the kinds of countertrade practices most appropriate in Korea.

21 B. Meyer, 'The Original Meaning of Trade Meets the Future in Barter', *World Trade*, January 2000, p. 46.

A review of some of the global trends that can impact international advertising is followed by a discussion of global versus modified advertising. A survey of problems and challenges confronting international advertisers – including basic creative strategy, media planning and selection, sales promotions and the communications process – concludes the chapter.

International Advertising

Intense competition for world markets and the increasing sophistication of foreign consumers have led to a need for more sophisticated advertising strategies. Increased costs, problems of coordinating advertising programmes in multiple countries, and a desire for a common worldwide company or product image have caused companies to seek greater control and efficiency without sacrificing **local responsiveness**. In the quest for more effective and responsive promotion programmes, the policies covering centralised or decentralised authority, use of single or multiple foreign or domestic agencies, appropriation and allocation procedures, copy, media and research are being examined.

One of the most widely debated policy areas pertains to the degree of specialised advertising necessary from country to country.[3] One view sees advertising customised for each country or region because every country is seen as posing a special problem. Executives with this viewpoint argue that the only way to achieve adequate and relevant advertising is to develop separate campaigns for each country. At the other extreme are those who suggest that advertising should be standardised for all markets of the world and who overlook regional differences altogether.[4]

Debate on the merits of standardisation compared to modification of international advertising has been going on for decades. Theodore Levitt's article 'The Globalisation of Markets' caused many companies to examine their international strategies and to adopt a global marketing strategy.[5] Levitt postulated the existence and growth of the global consumer with similar needs and wants, and advocated that international marketers should operate as if the world were one large market, ignoring superficial regional and national differences. In our opinion, although we do have some global products and brands, we need to adapt our marketing approach and tactics according to cultural differences and segments. Even in the EU, a truly integrated market, the buying behaviour for global products, such as Sony TVs or Philips vacuum cleaners, is different.

Another example is Gillette, which sells 800 products in more than 200 countries. It has a consistent worldwide image as a masculine, sports-oriented company, but its products have no such consistent image. Its razors, blades, toiletries and cosmetics are known by many names. Trac II blades in the United States are more widely known worldwide as G-II, and Atra blades are called Contour in Europe and Asia. Silkience hair conditioner is known as Soyance in France, Sientel in Italy and Silkience in Germany. Whether or not a global brand name could have been chosen for Gillette's many existing products is speculative. However, Gillette's current corporate philosophy of globalisation provides for an umbrella statement, 'Gillette, the Best a Man Can Get', in all advertisements for men's toiletries products in the hope of providing some common image.

It would be difficult for Gillette or Unilever to standardise their products and brand names across different markets, since each brand is established in its market. Yet, with such a diversity of brand names it is easy to imagine the problem of coordination and control, and the potential competitive disadvantage against a company with global brand recognition.

As discussed earlier, there is a fundamental difference between a multidomestic marketing strategy and a global marketing strategy. One is based on the premise that all markets are culturally different and a company must adapt marketing programmes to accommodate the differences, whereas the other assumes similarities as well as differences, and standardises where there are similarities but adapts where culturally required. Further, it may be possible to standardise some parts of the marketing mix and not others. Also, the same standardised products may be marketed globally but, because of

GOING INTERNATIONAL 19.1

Economists assume that people know what they want. Advertisers assume that they do not. Who is right?

Companies such as Coca-Cola, Kodak and McDonald's believe that the huge sums they spend on advertising are an investment in their valuable brands. They are not the only ones, however, who pay close attention to advertising. To economists – the official sponsors of rational decision making – the motives and methods of advertisers raise doubts about a fundamental claim: that people are good at making decisions for themselves.

In the economist's view of the world there is little need for firms to spend so much money cajoling consumers into buying their wares. Of course, people need good information to make good choices and it is often too costly or time-consuming to collect it themselves. So advertising a product's features, its price or even its existence can provide genuine value. But many ads seem to convey no such 'hard' information. Moreover, most advertising firms place a huge emphasis on creativity and human psychology when designing campaigns.

Economists need to explain, therefore, why a rational consumer would be persuaded by an ad that offers nothing but an enticing image or a good laugh. If consumers are rational, they should ignore such obvious gimmicks. If producers are rational, they should not waste money on ads that consumers will ignore.

Pizza Hut gets a slice of the action on a Russian rocket
AP/WideWorld Photos

This explanation was first developed by Phillip Nelson in a classic paper written in 1974. He argued that a great deal of seemingly wasteful advertisement is in fact intended to send a 'signal' to consumers – that even though a product's quality is hard to verify in advance, it really is one of the best on the market. From this perspective, it does not matter what an advertisement says – so long as consumers can see the firm spending big sums on advertising.

On the whole, economists find Nelson's account convincing. But they believe that he had only half the story: companies need pricing as well as advertising to convey quality to consumers. However, they have not been able to agree how prices and advertising should be related.

Part of the problem is that it is extremely difficult to measure the amount firms spend on advertising 'hard' information about a product's price, say, or how it works, as opposed to their spending on 'signal' advertising of the touchy-feely sort. Moreover, some kinds of product – those whose quality can be verified only through experience – should have more 'signal' advertising. But what is quality? And can an economist tell how easily it can be verified? In fact, two economists recently conducted a different kind of study, which suggests that the 'signalling' theory may be wrong. Sridhar Moorthy and Scott Hawkins ran an experiment in which people read foreign-language magazines with ads for unfamiliar brands in several product categories: cookware, overcoats, nasal spray and yoghurt. The ads were real, but the magazines were altered to change the frequency with which they appeared.

Although they did not understand the ads' content, the subjects associated a high frequency of advertising with high quality. However, a control group saw each ad only once, with a message attached telling them how often it appeared in other magazines. Even though the control group could remember the frequency of the ads, they did not assume – as their peers had done – that more ads meant higher quality. This suggests that people do indeed associate more ads with higher quality, but not because they have

Colgate-Palmolive announced it was decentralising its advertising; marketing in future would be tailored specifically to local markets and countries. An industry analyst reported that 'There will be little, if any, global advertising.' This appeared to be a reversal for Colgate, one of the first companies to embrace worldwide standardised advertising.[6] The apparent reversal in policy represents what is happening in many companies that initially took extreme positions on standardising their marketing efforts. Companies have discovered that the idea of complete global standardisation is more myth than reality.

As discussed earlier, markets are constantly changing and are in the process of becoming more alike, but the world is still far from being a homogeneous market with common needs and wants for all products. Myriad obstacles to strict standardisation remain. Nevertheless, the lack of commonality among markets should not deter a marketer from being guided by a global strategy, that is, a marketing philosophy that directs products and advertising towards a worldwide rather than a local or regional market, seeking standardisation where possible and modifying where necessary. To achieve global advertising huge sums are being spent on a worldwide basis. Top companies spend billions on advertising.

GOING INTERNATIONAL 19.2

Companies target female customers

Cereal product targeted primarily at women: Kellogg's Special K Fruit & Nut clusters

Never mind the fight to get people to open their wallets in the recession – some companies are taking a different tack, and trying to get customers to open their purses instead. In America, where female consumers make more than 80 per cent of discretionary purchases, companies have started tailoring their products and messages to appeal to women, in an effort to boost their sales.

Frito-Lay, a snack-food company owned by PepsiCo, has launched an advertising campaign called 'Only In A Woman's World' to convince women that crisps and popcorn are not just for male, beer-guzzling sport fans. OfficeMax, America's second-largest office-supplies company, has redesigned its notebooks and file-holders to appeal to women and has run advertisements that encourage women to make their cubicles more colourful. For the first time, McDonald's was a sponsor of New York Fashion Week in February, promoting a new line of hot drinks to trendsetting women.

Aside from their greater purchasing clout, women are valuable customers for three reasons. First, they are loyal, says Marti Barletta, author of *Marketing to Women*, and more likely to continue to buy a brand if they like it. Second, women are more likely than men to spread information about products they like through word of mouth and social-networking sites. Third, most of the lay-offs so far in America have been in male-dominated fields, like manufacturing and construction. This means women may bring home a greater share of household income in the months ahead and have even more buying power.

But marketing to women may not work for every company. In particular, for firms (such as some carmakers) with brands that are regarded as strongly male, 'gender bending', or trying to attract the opposite sex, could enhance short-term sales but cause a longer-term decline. Jill Avery of the Simmons School of Management in Boston

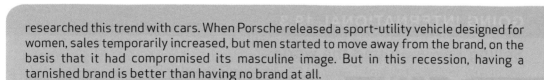

researched this trend with cars. When Porsche released a sport-utility vehicle designed for women, sales temporarily increased, but men started to move away from the brand, on the basis that it had compromised its masculine image. But in this recession, having a tarnished brand is better than having no brand at all.

● Do you think targeting female customers for such products will hurt the companies in the long run?

Source: compiled from *The Economist*, 12 March 2009.

Pan-European Advertising

The attraction of a single European market has enticed many companies to standardise as much of their promotional effort as possible. As media coverage across Europe expands, it will become more common for markets to be exposed to multiple advertising messages and brand names of the same product. To avoid the confusion that results when a market is exposed to these, as well as for reasons of efficiency, companies will strive for harmony in brand names, advertising and promotions across Europe.

Mars, the confectionery company, traditionally used several brand names for the same product but recently has achieved uniformity by replacing them with a single name. A chocolate bar sold in some parts of Europe under the brand name Raider was changed to Twix, the name used in the United States and the United Kingdom.

Along with changes in behaviour patterns, legal restrictions are gradually being eliminated, and viable market segments across country markets are emerging. While Europe will never be a single homogeneous market for every product, it does not mean that companies should shun the idea of developing European-wide promotional programmes especially for global, European brands and for corporate image. A pan-European promotional strategy would mean identifying a market segment across all European countries and designing a promotional concept appealing to market segment similarities.

International Market Segmentation and Promotional Strategy

Rather than approach a **promotional strategy** decision as having to be either standardised or adapted, a company should first identify market segments. Market segments can be defined within country boundaries or across countries. Global market segmentation involves identifying homogeneous market segments across groups of countries.

Procter & Gamble is an example of a company that identified mass-market segments across the world and designed brand and advertising concepts that apply to all. The company's shampoo positioning strategy, 'Pro-V vitamin formula strengthens the hair and makes it shine', was developed for the Taiwan market, and then launched successfully in several other countries with only minor adaptation for hair types and languages. L'Oréal's I'm worth it' brand position also works well worldwide. Unilever's fabric softener's teddy bear brand concept has worked well across borders, even though the 'Snuggle' brand name changes in some countries; it is Kuschelweich in Germany, Coccolino in Italy and Mimosin in France.[7]

Other companies have identified niche segments too small for country-specific development but, when taken in aggregate, they have become profitable markets. The luxury-brand luggage Vuitton is an example of a product designed for a niche segment. It is marketed as an exclusive, high-priced, glamorous product worldwide to relatively small segments in most countries.

While there are those who continue to argue the merits of standardisation versus adaptation, most will agree that identifiable market segments for specific products exist across country markets, especially in some types of product, and that companies should approach promotional planning from a global perspective, standardise where feasible and adapt where necessary.

PROMOTIONAL STRATEGY
systematic planning to promote a product

Taxi Media, which has about 10 000 drivers on its books, says the market, which is worth about £17 million in the UK, was flat in 2002, and would grow slightly in 2003. Of the 16 000 licensed cabs in London, 10 per cent carry advertisements. Compared to other outdoor media, taxi ads can be relatively cheap – £3000 to £5000 for a full livery per taxi for 12 months, of which £1000 will go to the driver. An outdoor poster in London can cost more than double that, depending on the location, for only a few weeks. Buses and taxis also cover areas often denied to other outdoor media. They are seen in every tourist spot as well as the royal parks, residential areas and the City of London.

● Is this an effective way to advertise? How do you react to this as a customer?

Source: adapted from Emiko Terazono. 'Do Ask Me, Guv', *Financial Times Creative Business*, 12 August 2003, p. 6.

Nestlé came up with a way to dramatically improve the quality of life for any parent and baby on the road.

It provides rest-stop structures along the road where parents can feed and change their babies. Sparkling clean Le Relais Bébés are located along main travel routes. Sixty-four hostesses at these rest stops welcome 120 000 baby visits and dispense 600 000 samples of baby food each year. There are free disposable nappies, a changing table and highchairs for the babies to sit in during meals. A strong tie between Nestlé and French mothers developed as a result of Le Relais Bébé. The most recent market research survey showed an approval rating of 94 per cent and Nestlé's share of the market has climbed to more than 43 per cent – close to a 24 share-point rise in under seven years.

As is true in advertising, the success of a promotion may depend on local adaptation. Major constraints are imposed by local laws, which may not permit premiums or free gifts to be given. Some countries' laws control the amount of discount given at retail, others require permits for all sales promotions and in at least one country no competitor is permitted to spend more on a sales promotion than any other company selling the product. Effective sales promotions can enhance the advertising and personal selling efforts and, in some instances, may be effective substitutes when environmental constraints prevent full utilisation of advertising.

International Advertising and the Communications Process

Promotional activities (advertising, personal selling, sales promotions and public relations) are basically a communications process. All the attendant problems of developing an effective promotional strategy in domestic marketing plus all the cultural problems discussed earlier must be overcome to have a successful international promotional programme. A major consideration for foreign marketers is to ascertain that all constraints (cultural diversity, media limitations, legal problems, and so forth) are controlled so the right message is communicated to and received by prospective consumers. International communications may fail for a variety of reasons: a message may not get through because of media inadequacy, the message may be received by the intended audience but not be understood because of different cultural interpretations or the message may reach the intended audience and be understood but have no effect because the marketer did not correctly assess the needs and wants of the target market.[15]

The effectiveness of promotional strategy can be jeopardised by so many factors that a marketer must be certain no influences are overlooked. Those international executives who understand the communications process are better equipped to manage the diversity they face in developing an international promotional programme.[16]

In the communications process, each of the seven identifiable segments can ultimately affect the accuracy of the process. As illustrated in Exhibit 19.5 the process consists of:

1 an information source – an international marketing executive with a product message to communicate

2 encoding – the message from the source converted into effective symbolism for transmission to a receiver

3 a message channel – the sales force and/or advertising media that conveys the encoded message to the intended receiver

4 decoding – the interpretation by the receiver of the symbolism transmitted from the information source

5 receiver – consumer action by those who receive the message and are the target for the thought transmitted

6 feedback – information about the effectiveness of the message, which flows from the receiver (the intended target) back to the information source for evaluation of the effectiveness of the process, and to complete the process, and

7 noise – uncontrollable and unpredictable influences such as competitive activities and confusion detracting from the process and affecting any or all of the other six steps.

Exhibit 19.5 The international communication process

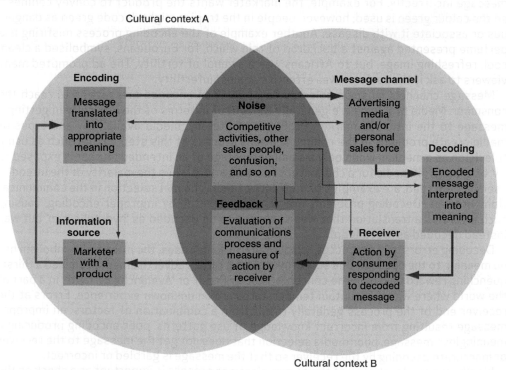

four-foot model of the Red Bull can. The cars carried fridges stocked with more than 250 cans of Red Bull, to be distributed to 'those in need of energy': shift workers, truck drivers, university students, executives, clubbers and athletes. Red Bull also sponsors a number of 'extreme' sports, backed by TV and press advertisements, and allied itself with those who push boundaries. Today, it has a 65 per cent share of the US energy drink market. The company keeps tight control on how it markets itself to clubs and bars. In the US, its representatives scout out hot spots – the bars and clubs frequented by trendsetters. They then offer them branded refrigerators and offer free goods along with their first order.

Red Bull is not alone in using buzz marketing. Among others are the following.

- **Piaggio:** During its Vespa campaign, Piaggio had models drive around Los Angeles on Vespa scooters and chat up customers in cafés and bars. If asked about the Vespa, they would casually mention its various qualities and drop the names of celebrities who had recently purchased one. If anyone showed interest, the model would give them details of the nearest Vespa dealer.
- **Ford:** Ford identified 120 people in six core markets as trendsetters (for example, local DJs). Each was given a Focus to drive for six months as well as promotional material to distribute to anyone who expressed interest.
- **Hasbro:** Hasbro enlisted 'cool' pre-teenage boys to play its POX game, then sent them back to school to tell their jealous friends. They were given $30 and copies of the games to give out.

Buzz is useful in many contexts but is particularly effective for products that generate conversation – in other words, products with which consumers are emotionally involved. It can be a perfect tool to create an underground campaign, yet it can backfire badly if it appears contrived, turning off precisely those consumers it wishes to attract.

- Do you think guerrilla marketing is a successful way to market products like Red Bull or computer games? Which products are most suitable for this type of marketing?

Source: adapted from Nirmalya Kumar and Sophie Linguri, 'Buzz, Chat and Branding Give Red Bull Wings', *Financial Times Summer School*, 8 August 2003, p. 13.

The Advertising Agency

Just as manufacturing firms have become international, US, Japanese and European advertising agencies are expanding internationally to provide sophisticated agency assistance worldwide. Local agencies have also expanded as the demand for advertising services by MNCs has developed. Thus, the international marketer has a variety of alternatives available. In most commercially significant countries, an advertiser has the opportunity to employ (1) a local domestic agency, (2) its company-owned agency or (3) one of the multinational advertising agencies with local branches.

ADVERTISING CAMPAIGN
designed and implemented for a particular product/ purpose over a fixed period

A local domestic agency may provide a company with the best cultural interpretation in situations where local modification is sought, but the level of sophistication can be weak. Another drawback of local agencies is the difficulty of coordinating a worldwide campaign. One drawback of the company-owned agency is the possible loss of local input when it is located outside the area and has little contact within the host country. The best compromise is the multinational agency with local branches because it has the sophistication of a major agency with local representation. Further, the multinational agency with local branches is better able to provide a coordinated worldwide **advertising campaign**. This has become especially important for firms doing business in Europe. With the interest in

global or standardised advertising, many agencies have expanded to provide worldwide representation. Many companies with a global orientation employ one or perhaps two agencies to represent them worldwide.

Compensation arrangements for advertising agencies throughout the world are based on 15 per cent commissions. However, agency commission patterns throughout the world are not as consistent as they are in Europe or the United States; in some countries, agency commissions vary from medium to medium. Services provided by advertising agencies also vary greatly but few foreign agencies offer the full services found in Western agencies.

International Control of Advertising

European Union officials are establishing directives to provide controls on advertising as cable and satellite broadcasting expands. Deception in advertising is a major issue because most member countries have different interpretations of what constitutes a **misleading advertisement**. Demands for regulation of advertising aimed at young consumers is a trend appearing in both industrialised and developing countries.

Decency and the blatant use of sex in advertisements are also receiving public attention. One of the problems in controlling decency and sex in ads is the cultural variations around the world. An ad perfectly acceptable to a Westerner may be very offensive to someone from the United States or, for that matter, a Spaniard. Standards for appropriate behaviour as depicted in advertisements vary from culture to culture. Regardless of these variations, there is growing concern about decency, sex and ads that demean women and men.

The difficulty that business has with self-regulation and restrictive laws is that sex can be powerful in some types of advertisement. European advertisements for Häagen-Dazs, a premium ice cream, and LapPower, a Swedish laptop computer company, received criticism for their ads as being too sexy. The Häagen-Dazs ad shows a couple, in various states of undress, in an embrace feeding ice cream to one another. Some British editorial writers and radio commentators were outraged. One commented that 'the ad was the most blatant and inappropriate use of sex as a sales aid'. The ad for LapPower personal computers that the Stockholm Business Council on Ethics condemned featured the co-owner of the company with an 'inviting smile and provocative demeanour displayed'. (She was bending over a LapPower computer in a low-cut dress.)

The bottom line for both these companies was increased sales. In the United Kingdom, sales soared after the 'Dedicated to Pleasure' ads appeared, and in Sweden the co-owner stated that 'Sales are increasing daily'. Whether laws are passed or the industry polices itself, there is an international concern about advertising and its effect on people's behaviour.

The advertising industry is sufficiently concerned with the negative attitudes of consumers and governments and with the poor practices of some advertisers that the International Advertising Association and other national and international industry groups have developed a variety of self-regulating codes. Sponsors of these codes feel that unless the advertisers themselves come up with an effective framework for control, governments will intervene. This threat of government intervention has spurred interest groups in Europe to develop codes to ensure that the majority of ads conform to standards set for 'honesty, truth and decency'. In those countries where the credibility of advertising is questioned and in those where the consumerism movement exists, the creativity of the advertiser is challenged.

In many countries, there is a feeling that advertising, and especially TV advertising, is too powerful and persuades consumers to buy what they do not need. South Korea, for example, has threatened to ban advertising of bottled water because the commercials may arouse public mistrust of tap water.[18]

MISLEADING ADVERTISEMENT
gives incorrect message/ impression of a product/company

GOING INTERNATIONAL 19.10

Bond trading

Daniel Craig as James Bond wearing an OMEGA watch.
Copyright OMEGA 2008

Advertisers pump £50 million into 007

James Bond's outing in Quantum of Solace is backed by a £50m advertising campaign from the companies whose products will appear in the movie. The Bond franchise has long been a favourite with brands, but 007 – now Daniel Craig– has become more choosey about who he does business with.

Sony Pictures has cut the number of product placements after 2002's *Die Another Day* had so many critics dubbed it Buy Another Day.

The companies lined up for Quantum are Ford, Heineken, Omega, Smirnoff, Sony and Virgin Atlantic. The metallic gold Ford driven by Kurylenko became generally available in November and the Sony Ericsson C902 Cyber-shot mobile phone was launched when the picture was released.

Smirnoff has the longest history with Bond. The Diageo-owned brand appeared in the 1962's *Dr No*, although the secret agent did have a brief fling with rival Finlandia.

● Is product placing in films and TV dramas ethical? Is it effective?

Source: Sunday Times, 17 August 2008.

Summary

Global advertisers face unique legal, language, media and production limitations in every market that must be considered when designing a promotional mix. As the world and its markets become more sophisticated, there is greater emphasis on international market-ing strategy. The current debate among marketers is the effectiveness of standardised versus modified advertising for culturally varied markets. And, as competition increases and markets expand, greater emphasis is being placed on global brands and/or image recognition.

The most logical conclusion seems to be that, when buying motives and company objectives are the same for various countries, the advertising orientation can be the same. When they vary from nation to nation, the advertising effort will have to reflect these variations. In any case, variety in media availability, coverage and effectiveness will have to be taken into consideration in the advertiser's plans. If common appeals are used, they may have to be presented by a radio broadcast in one country, by cinema in another, and by television in a third.

A skilled advertising practitioner must be sensitive to the environment and alert to new facts about the market. It is also essential for success in international advertising endeavours to pay close attention to the communications process and the steps involved.

Questions

1 'Perhaps advertising is the side of international marketing with the greatest similarities from country to country throughout the world. Paradoxically, despite its many similarities, it may also be credited with the greatest number of unique problems in international marketing.' Discuss.

2 Discuss the difference between advertising strategy when a company follows a multidomestic strategy rather than a global market strategy.

3 With satellite TV able to reach many countries, discuss how a company can use it and deal effectively with different languages, different cultures and different legal systems.

4 Outline some of the major problems confronting an international advertiser.

5 Defend either side of the proposition that advertising can be standardised for all countries.

6 Review the basic areas of advertising regulation.

7 How can advertisers overcome the problem of low literacy in their markets?

8 What special media problems confront the international advertiser?

9 Discuss the reason for pattern advertising.

10 Will the ability to broadcast advertisements over TV satellites increase or decrease the need for standardisation of advertisements? What are the problems associated with satellite broadcasting? Comment.

11 'Foreign newspapers cannot be considered homogeneous advertising entities.' Elaborate.

12 What is sales promotion and how is it used in international marketing?

13 Show how the communications process can help an international marketer avoid problems in international advertising.

14 Take each of the steps of the communications process and give an example of how cultural differences can affect the final message received.

15 Discuss the problems created when the communications process is initiated in one cultural context and ends in another.

Further Reading

P. Gabrielsson, M. Gabrielsson and H. Gabrielsson, 'International advertising campaigns in fast-moving consumer goods companies originating from a SMOPEC country', *International Business Review*, 2008, 17(6), pp. 714–28.

P. Walters, P. Whitla and H. Davies, 'Global strategy in the international advertising industry', *International Business Review*, 2008, 17(3), pp. 235–49.

S. Brown, 'O Customer, Where Art Thou?', *Business Horizon*, 2004, 47(4), pp. 61–70.

References

1 Laurent Gallissor, 'The Cultural Significance of Advertising: A General Framework of the Cultural Analysis of the Advertising Industry in Europe', *International Sociology*, March 1994, pp. 13–28.

2 Jean-Claude Usunier, *Marketing Across Cultures* (Hemel Hempstead: Prentice Hall, 1996).

3 F.S.L. Cheung and W.-F. Leung, 'International expansion of transnational advertising agencies in China: An assessment of the stages theory approach', *International Business Review*, 2007, 16(2), pp. 251–68.

4 Michel Laroche, V.H. Kirpalani, Frank Pons and Lianxi Zhou, 'A Model of Advertising Standardization in Multinational Corporations', *Journal of International Business Studies*, 2001, 32(2), pp. 249–66.

5 Theodore Levitt, 'The Globalization of Markets', *Harvard Business Review*, May–June 1983, pp. 92–102.

6 'How Colgate-Palmolive Crafts Ad Strategies in Eastern Europe', *Crossborder Monitor*, 2 March 1994, p. 8.

7 Carl Arthur Solberg, 'The Perennial Issue of Adaptation or Standardization of International Marketing Communication: Organisational Contingencies and Performance', *Journal of International Marketing*, 2002, 10(3), pp. 1–21.

8 'Pepsi Spots Banned in Asia', *Advertising Age International*, 21 March 1994, pp. 1–2.

9 D.K. Boojihawon, P. Dimitratos and S. Young, 'Characteristics and influences of multinational subsidiary entrepreneurial culture: The case of the advertising sector', *International Business Review*, 2007, 16(5), pp. 549–72.

10 N.S. Hong and C.Y. Poon, *Business Restructuring in Hong Kong* (Oxford: Oxford University Press, 2004).

11 L.S Amine, 'Country-of-origin, animosity and consumer response: Marketing implications of anti-Americanism and Francophobia', *International Business Review*, 2008, 17(4), pp. 402–22.

12 Swee Hoon Ang, 'Advertising Strategy and Advertising: Comparing USA and Australia', *The Journal of Marketing Communications*, 2002, 8(3), pp. 179–88.

13 S. Samee, I. Jeong, J.H. Pae and S. Tai, 'Advertising Standardization in Multinational Corporations: The Subsidiary Perspective', *Journal of Business Research*, 2003, 56(8), pp. 613–26.

14 C.A. Solberg, 'The Perennial Issue of Adaptation or Standardization of International Marketing Communication: Organisational Contingencies and Performance', *Journal of International Marketing*, 2002, 10(3), pp. 1–21.

15 A.S. Hoon, 'Advertising Strategy and Effective Advertising: Comparing the USA and Australia', *The Journal of Marketing Communications*, 2002, 8(3), pp. 179–88.

16 R.A. Kustin, 'Marketing Mix Standardization: A Cross-Cultural Study of Four Countries', *International Business Review*, 2004, 13(5), pp. 637–49.

17 Sudhir H. Kale, 'How National Culture, Organizational Culture and Personality Impact Buyer–Seller Interactions', in Pervez Ghauri and Jean-Claude Usunier (eds), *International Business Negotiations* (Oxford: Pergamon, 1996).

18 Marieke de Mooij, *Consumer Behaviour and Culture: Consequences for Global Marketing and Advertising* (Thousand Oaks: Sage, 2004).

Chapter 20
Personal Selling and Negotiations

Chapter Outline

Chapter Learning Objectives

What you should learn from Chapter 20

- Understand the importance of relationships in international selling
- Understand the nuances of cross-cultural communication and its impact on sales negotiations
- Understand the attributes of international sales personnel and how to manage a multicultural sales force
- How to handle the problems unique to selecting and training foreign sales staff
- Comprehend the impact of globalisation on future personnel selection
- Understand the importance of skill in a foreign language while negotiating internationally
- How to identify the factors influencing cross-cultural negotiation
- How to handle international sales negotiation

RELATIONSHIP-CENTRED
when the sales person aims to build an ongoing relationship with the customer

DEAL-CENTRED
when a sales person is solely concerned to complete the particular transaction

PERSONAL SELLING
when a product is sold through personal methods (e.g. sales people)

There are four ways of achieving marketing communication: advertising, sales promotions, personal selling and public relations. Cultural differences as well as the type of product have a major impact on how an optimal mix is found among the above-mentioned four ways to achieve the objectives of a company. People who want to take into account cultural differences have to be **relationship-centred** rather than purely **deal-centred**.[1]

The sales person provides a company's most direct contact with the customer and, in the eyes of most customers, the sales person *is* the company. As the presenter of the company's offerings and gatherer of customer information, the sales person is the final link in the culmination of a company's marketing and sales effort.

The tasks of building, training, compensating and motivating an international marketing group generate unique problems at every stage of management and development. This chapter discusses the importance of communications and negotiations in building marketing relationships with international customers.

Selling in International Markets

Increased global competition coupled with the dynamic and complex nature of international business increases the need for closer ties with both customers and suppliers. Selling in international marketing, built on effective communications between the seller and buyer, focuses on building long-term relationship rather than treating each sale as a onetime event.[2] This approach is becoming increasingly important for successful international marketers, especially in industrial buyer–seller interactions.[3] In **personal selling**, persuasive arguments are presented directly in a face-to-face relationship between sellers and potential buyers. To be effective, sales people must be certain that their communication and negotiation skills are properly adapted to a cross-cultural setting.

In many countries a low status is associated with selling. It is associated with the negative connotation of taking money from people rather than usefully bringing products and services to them. Seller status can also be associated with a particular group of people, e.g. Chinese, Dutch or Lebanese. In this perception, the seller's role is to convince and show the buyer the worth of the product on offer. In marketing, however, one of the seller's roles is to recognise the customer's needs and make them known to his or her company. The style of selling is often related to national culture, but it also depends on the personality of the sales person and the type of industry. Selling styles can also depend on which types of result or achievement are sought – for example, whether it is to win a new customer or maintaining an old relationship. According to Usunier, when preparing arguments, a sales

Exhibit 20.1 Selling orientations

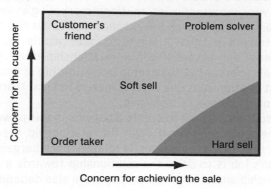

Source: Jean-Claud Usunier, *Marketing Across Cultures* (Hemel Hempstead: Prentice Hall, 1996), p.464.

person has two main concerns: one is for the customers and their needs, the other is for achieving the sales.[4] This is illustrated in Exhibit 20.1.

If we separate the seller's role from that of the negotiator, the role of the sales person is mainly persuasion. There are, however, differences between persuasion and rather insistent and annoying behaviour. The main issue here is to understand what arguments will be best and quickest to persuade a particular customer.

In addition to the above factors, the two main components of personal selling are content and style. Content refers to the substantive aspects of the interaction for which the buyer and the seller come together. It includes suggesting, offering and negotiating. Style refers to the rituals, format, mannerisms and ground rules that the buyer and the seller follow in their encounter. A satisfactory interaction between the buyer and the seller is contingent upon buyer–seller compatibility with respect to both the content and the style of communication. The level of this compatibility is determined by cultural and personality factors.[5] The effectiveness of personal selling in international marketing is influenced by a number of factors, such as the nature of the sales person–customer relationship, the behaviour of the sales person, the resources of the sales person and the nature of the customer's buying task, as illustrated by Exhibit 20.2.

Exhibit 20.2 Factors influencing the effectiveness of personal selling

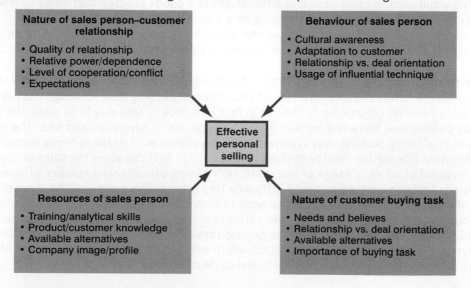

The Nature of the Sales Person–Customer Relationship   The sales person–customer relationship is very important in international marketing as keeping a sales force in a foreign market means that the company is concerned about the continuity in the relationship with its customers and that it wants to meet people face to face rather than through printed material and advertising. The relationship development thus becomes very important. The sales person has to develop a relationship of trust and friendship with its customers. In most relationships one party is more dominant than the other; this is also true in the sales person–customer relationship.

Here the sales person should seek to create a balance in this power/dependence situation. Depending on the above and the nature of the relationship, the parties perceive it as cooperative or conflicting. This issue is directly related to the bargaining power of the parties. The sales person's job is to drive the relationship towards a cooperative one. The nature of this relationship and willingness to cooperate also depends on what the parties expect from each other in the future. The more they anticipate a future beneficial interaction, the more the relationship is improved.

Behaviour of the Sales Person   The behaviour of the sales person in international marketing interaction is highly dependent on his or her awareness of the local culture, values and norms. Due to this, companies normally use a local sales force. Whether the sales person is an **expatriate** or a local, the sales message, approach and behaviour to the customer should be adapted in terms of language, level of argument and local norms. A relationship orientation instead of a one-shot deal orientation is essential in interaction with customers. In fact, this is often the main reason behind having a sales force. Sales people should also use the influential techniques mentioned earlier and in the negotiation section of this chapter. One should be aware that these techniques can be different in different markets, depending on culture, type of product and company.

EXPATRIATE
employee of the company/ organisation sent to another country to work

Resources of the Sales Person   The sales person to be used in international marketing needs to be trained not only for a particular market/culture but also for general skills such as analytical techniques and negotiation. These skills are essential for international marketing activities and for developing relationships with customers. The sales force should be fully aware of the company's products and customers' needs, and how these two could be matched. A holistic view of the company's capabilities and resources is essential for representing the company fully and efficiently. The sales person should have full knowledge of the market and customer segmentation, not only of existing customers. Having a full picture of all available alternatives is a good resource that helps customer relationships. The image and positioning of a company in a particular market is of the utmost importance and is good baggage for the sales person. There should be some consistency in the company image and the message a sales person is taking to customers.

Nature of Customer's Buying Task   Another important factor, external to the sales person, is the nature and characteristic of the customer's buying task. Although it is beyond the sales person's control, he or she can in fact influence it. One way is to make the customer believe that there is a perfect match between his or her needs and what the sales person is offering. Another way is to work with the customer in defining those needs. The relationship orientation from both sides is thus crucial, as it can allow the sales person to get involved at an early stage of the customer's buying process. The number of alternatives available to customers would influence this aspect. The more options a customer has, the harder the sales person has to work to convince the customer. The importance of the buying task in the customer's organisation is also valuable information a sales person should have. The more important the buying task, the earlier the customer should be directed towards relationship orientation, which will lead to an earlier involvement of the sales organisation in the customer's internal decision making.

GOING INTERNATIONAL 20.1

Are international assignments glamorous?

'Glamorous' is probably not the adjective the following executives would use.

'The problem as I see it with the company's talk about international managers is that they were just paying lip-service to it. When I applied for the posting to Malaysia they gave me all this stuff about the assignment being a really good career move and how I'd gain this valuable international experience and so on. And don't get me wrong, we really enjoyed the posting. We loved the people and the culture and the lifestyle and when it came to returning home, we weren't really all that keen ... The problem was that while I had been away, the company had undergone a wholesale restructuring ... This meant that when I got back, my job had effectively been eliminated.'

© iStockphoto.com/
sjlocke

'We have been in the United States for 11 months and I reckon it will be another six to 12 months before my wife and the kids are really settled here. I'm still learning new stuff every day at work and it has taken a long time to get used to American ways of doing things ... I mean if the company said, "Oh, we want you to move to South Africa in a year's time," I would really dig my heels in because it was initially very disruptive for my wife when she first came here.'

And 'glamorous' would not be on the tip of these expatriate spouses' tongues either.

'I found I haven't adapted to Spanish hours. I find it a continual problem because the 2–5 pm siesta closure is really awkward. I always find myself where I have to remind myself that from 2–5 I have a blank period that I can't do anything ... We started adjusting to the eating schedule. Whether we like it or not, we eat a lot later.'

'Well, we went down to Club Med for a vacation and the French were all topless and my eight-year-old son didn't say anything, but my seven-year-old daughter now refuses to wear a top. I will not let her get away with it back in the US.'

'We've been really fortunate we haven't had to use health care services here ... The thought of going to, needing to go to a doctor is scary because for me it would have to be someone English speaking or I wouldn't, you know, feel comfortable.'

● Given these kinds of problems, do you think that international sales positions being offered are as attractive as they look? Will such a position help your career?

Sources: Nick Forster, 'The Myth of the "International Manager"', *International Journal of Resource Management*, February 2000, 11(1), pp. 126–42; and Mary C. Gilly, Lisa Penaloza and Kenneth M. Kambara, 'The Role of Consumption in Expatriate Adjustment and Satisfaction', Working Paper, Graduate School of Management, University of California, Irvine, 2004.

The International Selling Sequence

Knowing the customer in international sales means more than understanding the customer's product needs. It includes knowing the customer's culture. A cosmopolitan sales person will become more adept at cross-cultural selling if given a thorough grounding in the sequence that should be followed. Exhibit 20.3 presents a flowchart of international selling transactions. This step-by-step approach can be utilised for salesforce planning and training.[6]

Exhibit 20.3 The international selling sequence

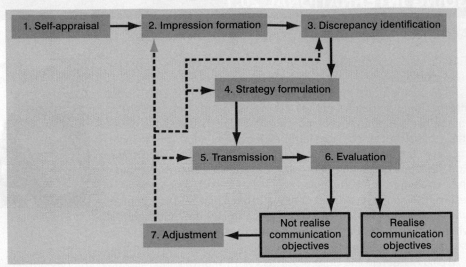

Source: Sudhir Kalé, 'How National Culture, Organizational Culture and Personality Impact Buyer–Seller Interactions', Pervez Ghauri and Jean-Claud Usunier, *International Business Negotiations* (Oxford: Pergamon, 1996), p. 35.

The selling sequence starts with a self-appraisal, which is quite similar to the self-reference criteria (SRC) discussed in earlier chapters. The aim of self-appraisal is to develop a frame of reference whereby one's own communication preferences with regard to content and style could be understood. Dimensions of SRC (that is, an unconscious reference to one's own cultural values, experience and knowledge) serve as a basis for self-awareness (see Chapter 1).

Impression formation involves understanding the buyer's cultural position. Typically, national culture and **organisational culture** can be assessed even before the seller meets with the buyer. Hofstede provides scores and ranks for 50 countries on the basis of positions on the four dimensions of national culture.[7] The organisational culture of most large and medium-sized companies can be gleaned from their press releases, annual reports and from popular literature. A trained sales person can assess a buyer's temperament with a fair degree of accuracy in a relatively short period of interaction. An accurate impression of the buyer in terms of national culture, organisational culture and temperament lays the foundation for relationship building, which is so critical to successful selling.

In the third step, the seller goes through the mental exercise of 'discrepancy identification'. This involves comparing the buyer's estimated position on the various dimensions of culture with one's own. This alerts the seller to potential problem areas in communication arising out of differences in temperament and cultural conditioning.

Strategy formulation involves minimising the impact of problem areas identified in the earlier step. For instance, if the buyer is a feeler, and the seller is a thinker, the seller needs to modify his persuasion style. While his preferred persuasion style is logical and impersonal, this may not fit well with the buyer. The appropriate style in this instance would be to appeal to the buyer's feelings and emotions, and to point out the people-benefits behind the seller's offering. Similar adjustments need to be made on other dimensions as well where discrepancies exist between the seller and the buyer.

Transmission involves implementation of the communication/persuasion strategy. During the course of transmission, the seller should be sensitive to the verbal and non-verbal feedback received from the buyer. If the seller has correctly identified the seller's mindset based on temperament and culture, the strategy should be on target and the feedback received from the buyer will be encouraging.

ORGANISATIONAL CULTURE
values and norms of working in an organisation

Assessing the effect of the communication strategy constitutes the 'evaluation' phase. If the seller's communication objectives are realised then the encounter has been successful. If not, the seller goes through the 'adjustment' process where buyer impressions, discrepancies and strategy are re-evaluated and the transmission is modified. At the evaluation and adjustment phase, the seller always has the choice of cutting short the encounter, and trying again at some time in the future. Regardless of the outcome, every encounter adds to the seller's repertoire of experiences, skills, strategies and alternative transmission approaches.

Understanding the Nuances of Cross-cultural Communications

Communications and the art of persuasion, knowledge of the customer and product, the ability to close a sale and after-sale service are all necessary for successful selling. These are the attributes sought when hiring an experienced person and those taught to new employees. Since culture impacts on the international sales effort just as it does on international advertising and promotion, the marketer must be certain that all international sales personnel have an understanding of the influence of culture on communications. After all, selling is communication and, unless the sales person understands the overtones of cross-cultural communications, the sales process could be thwarted.

Effective communication requires an understanding of the nuances of the spoken language as well as the silent language.[8] Perhaps more important than language nuances are the meanings of different **silent languages** spoken by people from different cultures. They may think they are understanding one another when, in fact, they are misinterpreting one another. For example:

> A Briton visits a Saudi official to convince him to expedite permits for equipment being brought into the country. The Saudi offers the Briton coffee, which is politely refused (he had been drinking coffee all morning at the hotel while planning the visit). The latter sits down and crosses his legs, exposing the sole of his shoe. He passes the documents to the Saudi with his left hand, enquires after the Saudi's wife and emphasises the urgency of getting the needed permits.

In less than three minutes, the Briton unwittingly offended the Saudi five times. He refused his host's hospitality, showed disrespect, used an 'unclean' hand, implied a familial familiarity and displayed impatience with his host. He had no intention of offending his host and probably was not aware of the rudeness of his behaviour. The Saudi might forgive his British guest for being ignorant of local custom, but the forgiven sales person is in a weakened position.

Knowing your customer in international sales means more than knowing your customer's product needs; it includes knowing your customer's culture. One international consultant suggests five rules of thumb for successful selling abroad.

1 **Be prepared** and do your homework. Learn about the host's culture, values, geography, religion and political structure. In short, do as complete a cultural analysis as possible to avoid cultural mistakes.
2 **Slow down**. Westerners are slaves to the clock. Time is money to a Westerner but, in many countries, emphasis on time implies unfriendliness, arrogance and untrustworthiness.
3 **Develop relationships** and trust before getting down to business. In many countries, business is not done until a feeling of trust has developed.
4 **Learn the language,** its nuances and the idiom, and/or get a good interpreter. There are just too many ways for miscommunication to occur.
5 **Respect the culture**. Manners are important. You are the guest, so respect what your host considers important.[9]

SILENT LANGUAGES
communication without the use of language or words

In international sales and purchase transactions, the responsibilities need to be clearly defined. For example, who is responsible for freight and insurance and from which point (ex-factory, on board, etc.) to which point are crucial issues and, if ignored, can lead to serious problems. What are the penalties for delays, and how is responsibility for delays to be determined, for example, in the case of strike, accident or fire? What if the goods do not correspond to the agreed sample or specifications? What if the payment is not made on time? Although a number of middlemen, such as clearing agents, are available to handle these issues, the sales person is solely responsible for negotiating these terms. The price or terms might be different with different responsibilities.

LOCAL NATIONALS
employees of a company that are local to the market

THIRD-COUNTRY NATIONALS
expatriates from the business's own country working for a foreign company in a third country

Recruitment of an International Sales Force

The number of marketing management personnel from the home country assigned to foreign countries varies according to the size of the operation and the availability of qualified locals. Increasingly, the number of home-country nationals (expatriates) assigned to foreign posts is smaller as the pool of trained, experienced locals grows.

The largest personnel requirement abroad for most companies is the sales force, drawn from three sources: expatriates, **local nationals** and **third-country nationals**. A company's staffing pattern may include all three types in any single foreign operation, depending on qualifications, availability and a company's needs.

GOING INTERNATIONAL 20.2

Cross-cultural selling

Golf course negotiations are common in many different business cultures
© Macduff Everton/CORBIS

Some stereotypes of selling styles are often associated with different markets. Here are some examples.

In Asian countries, where arrogance and showing of extreme confidence are not appreciated, sales people should make modest, rational, down-to-earth points. They should avoid trying to win arguments with the customers, who could suffer from a 'loss of face' and react negatively. In Japan, one is expected to play golf with one's customers.

In Italy, in contrast, lack of self-confidence would be perceived as a clear sign of lack of personal credibility and reliability; thus one needs to argue strongly in order to be taken seriously.

In Switzerland, you have to speak precisely and your words will be taken quite literally.

In the United Kingdom, it is advisable to use the *soft sell* approach. Do not be pushy, instead try to 'chat' and convince.

In Germany, you should use the *hard sell* approach by being persistent. Make visits, offer trials and be very visible.

Blending company sales objectives and the personal objectives of sales people is a task worthy of the most skilled manager. The Western manager must be constantly aware that many of the techniques used to motivate Western personnel and their responses to these techniques are based on Western cultural premises and may not work in other countries.

Expatriates   The number of companies relying on expatriate personnel is declining as the volume of world trade increases and as more companies use locals to fill marketing positions. However, when products are highly technical, or when selling requires an extensive background of information and applications, an expatriate sales force remains the best choice. The expatriate sales person may have the advantages of greater technical training, better knowledge of the company and its product line and proven dependability and effectiveness. And, because they are not locals, expatriates sometimes add to the prestige of the product line in the eyes of local customers.

Local Nationals   The historical preference for expatriate managers and sales people from the home country is giving way to a preference for locals. At the sales level, the picture is clearly biased in favour of the locals because they transcend both cultural and legal barriers. More knowledgeable about a country's business structure than an expatriate would be, local sales people are better able to lead a company through the maze of unfamiliar distribution systems. Furthermore, there is now a pool of qualified local personnel available that costs less to maintain than a staff of expatriates. In Asia many locals will have earned Master's or MBA degrees in Europe or the United States; thus you get the cultural knowledge of the local meshed with an understanding of Western business management. Although expatriates' salaries may be no more than those of their national counterparts, the total cost of keeping comparable groups of expatriates in a country can be considerably higher because of special cost-of-living benefits, moving expenses, taxes and other costs associated with keeping an expatriate abroad.

Third-country Nationals   The internationalisation of business has created a pool of third-country nationals (TCNs), expatriates from their own countries working for a foreign company in a third country. The TCNs are a group whose nationality has little to do with where they work or for whom. An example would be a German working in Malaysia for a US company. Historically, there have been a few expatriates or TCNs who have spent the majority of their careers abroad, but now a truly 'global executive' has begun to emerge. The recently appointed chairman of a division of a major Dutch company is a Norwegian who gained that post after stints in the United States, where he was the US subsidiary's chairman, and in Brazil, where he held the position of general manager. At one time, Burroughs Corporation's Italian subsidiary was run by a Frenchman, the Swiss subsidiary by a Dane, the German subsidiary by an Englishman, the French subsidiary by a Swiss, the Venezuelan subsidiary by an Argentinean, and the Danish subsidiary by a Dutchman. The CEO of Up John-Pharmacia, an American–Swedish pharmaceutical multinational with its head office in Michigan, was a Pakistani.

  Development of TCN executives reflects not only a growing internationalisation of business but also acknowledges that personal skills and motivations are not the exclusive property of one nation.[10] TCNs are often sought because they speak several languages and know an industry or foreign country well. More and more companies are realising that talent flows to opportunity regardless of nationality.

Host Country Restrictions   The host governments' attitudes towards foreign workers complicate flexibility in selecting expatriate nationals or local nationals. Concern about foreign corporate domination, local unemployment and other issues cause some countries to restrict the number of non-nationals allowed to work within the country.

Selecting an International Sales Force

People operating in the home country need only the attributes of effective sales persons, whereas a transnational manager can require skills and attitudes that would challenge a

diplomat. Personnel requirements for various positions vary considerably, but despite the range of differences, some basic requisites leading to effective performance should be considered because effective executives and sales people, regardless of the foreign country in which they are operating, share certain characteristics. Special personal characteristics, skills and orientations are demanded for international operations.

Maturity is a prime requisite for expatriate and third-country personnel. Sales personnel working abroad must typically work more independently than their domestic counterparts. The company must have confidence in their ability to make decisions and commitments without constant recourse to the home office, or they cannot be individually effective.

The marketer who expects to be effective in the international marketplace needs to have a positive outlook on an international assignment. People who do not like what they are doing and where they are doing it stand little chance of success. Failures are usually the result of overselling the assignment, showing the bright side of the picture, and not warning about the bleak side.

Successful adaptation in international affairs is based on a combination of attitude and effort. A careful study of the customs of the market country should be initiated before the marketer arrives, and should continue as long as there are facets of the culture that are not clear. One useful approach is to listen to the advice of national and foreign business people operating in that country. Cultural empathy is clearly a part of basic orientation because it is unlikely that anyone can be effective if antagonistic or confused about the environment.

The personal characteristics, skills and orientation that identify the potentially effective sales person have been labelled in many different ways. Each person studying the field has a preferred list of characteristics, yet rising above all the characteristics there is an intangible something that some have referred to as a 'sixth sense'. This implies that, regardless of individual attributes, there is a certain blend of personal characteristics,

GOING INTERNATIONAL 20.3

How important are those meetings?

© Charles Gupton/
CORBIS

Selling in East Asia: guanxi in action

You are the newly-hired marketing manager of Glorious Paints, a Singapore manufacturer of marine paints. It is a fast-growing company headed by three young, Western-educated directors.

Last year the marketing director led Glorious Paints to its first overseas sale, selling a large quantity of paint to Australia and New Zealand. Director Tan achieved this success by first sending information to potential distributors along with covering letters requesting appointments.

After receiving replies, Tan met with the interested candidate firms at their offices to negotiate a distribution agreement with the company best qualified to handle that market area. This process took about four months and today sales volume already exceeds expectations. Following that success you were hired to expand exports to other Pacific Rim markets. The director called you into his office to discuss market research showing that Taiwan is a very promising market with high demand and little local competition. So you were instructed to set up distribution there using the approach that had worked in Australia/ New Zealand.

By searching a number of databases you came up with the names and contact information of a number of Taiwanese importers, agents, representatives and wholesalers involved in the paint business. Next you sent off brochures and product information to these prospects, enclosing a covering letter requesting an appointment to discuss possible representation.

To your surprise, six weeks went by without a single response. At a strategy session Mr Tan pointed out that many Taiwanese are not comfortable corresponding in English, so you fired off a second mailing, this time in Chinese. But after another two months not a single prospective distributor has answered your request for an appointment. Mr Tan is upset with your lack of progress in this attractive market. He has called an urgent meeting for this afternoon and expects you to come up with a solution. As you sit stirring your tea the questions revolve in your head like the spoon in the teacup. 'What have I done wrong? This strategy worked fine with the Aussies. Why not with the Taiwanese? What do we do now?'

Source: © Copenhagen Business School Press, 2002. With thanks to the author, Richard R. Gesteland, Global Management LLC: 2002, and CBS Press (www.cbspress.dk/).

skills and orientation that is hard to pinpoint and that may differ from individual to individual, but that produces the most effective overseas personnel.

Training and Motivation

The nature of a training programme depends largely on whether expatriate or local personnel are being trained as sales people. Training for the expatriates focuses on the customs and the special foreign sales problems that will be encountered, whereas local personnel require greater emphasis on the company, its products, technical information and selling methods. In training either type of personnel, the sales training activity is burdened with problems stemming from long-established behaviour and attitudes.

Continual training may be more important in foreign markets than in domestic ones because of the lack of routine contact with the parent company and its marketing personnel. One aspect of training is frequently overlooked: home-office personnel dealing with international marketing operations need training designed to make them responsive to the needs of the foreign operations. In most companies, the requisite sensitivities are expected to be developed by osmosis in the process of dealing with foreign affairs; a few companies send home-office personnel abroad periodically to increase their awareness of the problems of the foreign operations.[11]

One company found its sales people were losing respect and had low motivation because they did not have girls to pour tea for customers in the Japanese branch offices. The company learned that, when male personnel served tea, they felt they lost face; tea girls were authorised for all branches.

A common complaint among international sales people is that their head office does not understand them. They often feel left alone or deserted. Their morale can be boosted through realistic sales targets, giving them full support and making them feel that head office is fully behind them. Their achievements should be properly rewarded in accordance with their career goals. *Job stability* – sales people often have an uneasy feeling that while they are on the road other people at the office are getting all the benefits with regard to promotions and job stability. They may also be afraid about what will happen if they do not meet their target. Sales people worried about these issues cannot be very effective; it is therefore very important to select sales people with care, train them, and then support them with confidence and backing.

GOING INTERNATIONAL 20.4

Personal selling tips, from Brussels to Bangkok

A YOTEL room

The best training programmes are much more than just a list of tips. But a quick read-through of such tips provides a glimpse of the cultural variation facing sales representatives around the globe.

Belgium: Be able to identify the decision makers. In Flanders (Dutch-speaking region) group decisions are common, but in Wallonia (French-speaking region) the highest-level execs have the final say.

China: Expect to continue negotiations after a deal is inked. To Chinese, signing a contract is just the beginning of the business relationship; therefore, they expect both sides to continue working together to fix problems that arise.

Colombia: Business counterparts want to get to know you personally and form a strong friendship with you. Be sure not to change reps in midstream, because a switch often puts an end to negotiations.

Germany: Be prepared with data and empirical evidence that supports your sales proposition. German business people are unimpressed by flashy advertising and brochures, so keep them serious and detailed, with unexaggerated information.

India: Make sure your schedule remains flexible. Indians are more casual about time and punctuality. Because of India's rigid hierarchy, decisions are made only by the highest-level boss.

Mexico: When planning a meeting, breakfast and lunch are preferable. Take your time and cultivate relationships with business contacts. Those relationships are generally considered more important than professional experience.

Peru: Peruvians relate to individuals and not corporate entities. Establish personal rapport and don't switch your representative in the middle of negotiations.

Russia: Your first meeting will be just a formality. Your Russian counterparts will take this time to judge your credibility, so it's best to be warm and approachable.

Scotland: Scottish people tend to be soft-spoken and private. It takes time to build relationships, but business counterparts seem friendlier after bonds are established. (By the way, Scotch is a drink, not a nationality – it's Scottish.)

South Korea: Status is important. Make sure your business card clearly indicates your title. Don't send a rep to meet with a Korean executive of higher status – it could be viewed as disrespectful.

Thailand: The Thai culture emphasises non-conflict, so don't make assertive demands when making sales pitches.

Source: Sales and Marketing Management publishes these tips regularly in its magazine and on its website (www.salesandmarketing.com).

Cross-cultural Negotiations

The keystone of effective marketing and buyer–seller interactions is effective negotiation. Poorly conducted negotiations can leave the seller and the buyer frustrated, and do more to destroy effective relationships than anything else. Negotiation should be handled in such a way that a long-term relationship between buyer and seller is ensured.[12]

The basic elements of business negotiations are the same in every country; they relate to the product, its price and terms, services associated with the product and, finally, friendship between vendors and customers. Selling is often thought of as a

routine exchange with established prices and distribution networks from which there is little deviation. But, particularly in international sales, the selling transaction is almost always a negotiated exchange. Price, delivery dates, quality of goods or services, volume of goods sold, financing, exchange rate risk, shipping mode, insurance, and so on, are all set by bargaining or negotiations. Such negotiations should not be conducted in a typical 'win-lose' situation but as a shared benefit that will ensure a long-term relationship.[13]

Simply stated, to negotiate is to confer, bargain or discuss with a view to reaching an agreement. It is a sequential rather than simultaneous give-and-take discussion resulting in a mutually beneficial understanding. Most authorities on negotiating include three stages in the negotiating process: (1) pre-negotiation stage; (2) negotiation stage; and (3) post-negotiation stage. In the pre-negotiation stage, parties attempt to understand each other's needs and offers, which is done through informal meetings and arrangements. The negotiation stage refers to face-to-face negotiations, and the post-negotiation stage refers to the stage when parties have agreed to most of the issues and are to agree on contract language and format, and signing of the contract, how it leads to more business and relationship development.

In addition to these stages, the process of international business negotiation has two more dimensions: (1) strategic factors and (2) cultural factors (see Exhibit 20.4).

Cultural factors play an important role in each and every stage of the international negotiation process. Cultural factors include time, pattern of communication and emphasis on personal relationships. While 'time is money' in Western cultures, it has no such value attached to it in Asia, Latin America and Africa. Knowing whether the other party is looking for a collective solution or an individual benefit is very important. According to Hofstede's studies, we can place different countries on different scales of individual and collective behaviour.[14] Different cultures have different patterns of communication as regards direct versus indirect and explicit versus implicit communication. Some languages are traditionally vague, others exaggerate, which makes communication difficult for those from outside who are not familiar with the language. Finally, different cultures give different importance to personal relations in negotiations. In the West, the negotiators are more concerned with the issue at hand, irrespective of who is representing the other side.

Pre-negotiation Stage

Before entering an international negotiation process, the two parties should know which type of decision-making procedure is going to be followed by the other party and which type of strategy should be used to match it. How should a party present its offer and capabilities? The formal versus informal and argumentative versus informative presentation style is very distinct in many countries. If not prepared, negotiators can make serious blunders. In negotiations people refer to different types of strategy, such as tough, soft

Exhibit 20.4 The process of international sales negotiations

negotiators coming from the other side can make all decisions? Who in their team or head office is in fact the decision maker?

5 Patience is an asset in international business negotiations. In many cultures, Asian, Middle Eastern and even in Eastern Europe, things take their time. Negotiators from these cultures are not to be hurried; they really need to feel the negotiation process before they are ready to make a decision. In such cases it is not useful to push them to make a decision.

GOING INTERNATIONAL 20.6

Russia: opportunities and rules of engagement

© iStockphoto.com/ Mikbis

Russia is the world's biggest country – it crosses 11 time zones and has 150 million inhabitants. Although it remains difficult to crack, the Russian market holds attraction for foreign investors, not least because of its high potential and abundance of raw materials. At present, more than 900 North American and more than 700 German companies are registered in Moscow. As purchasing power is recovering from the 1998 crisis that wiped out people's savings, sales are rising for everything from beer to hair colouring. In 2001 sales of Carlsberg's popular Baltika beer soared 60 per cent and L'Oréal's sales jumped 52 per cent.

Hypermarkets are gaining a hold in the retailing arena as Russian consumers, who do not have mortgages and loans to pay off due to underdeveloped banking systems, spend most of their income on food and other household products. Economic growth fostered by FDI has created a new social class in Moscow and St Petersburg: *Novye Bysinessmeny*, the new business people.

On the downside, the cost of living has risen considerably in recent years, making Moscow the most expensive city in the world after Tokyo and London. Rising inflation has meant that ordinary people can afford less now than before. The chaos and corruption of Russia's labyrinthine bureaucracy has had a serious effect on business life, while crime has reached alarming proportions in some parts of the country. However, those who are prepared to brave the difficulties and take advantage of the opportunities that Russia offers may find the following advice from the *Financial Times* useful.

- During business negotiations in Russia, the relaxed and humorous Western way of communicating is not really appropriate. Negotiations are a serious matter and should be treated accordingly. The first encounter is usually calm and formal. However, subsequent meetings can be lively and spirited – occasional emotional outbursts are not uncommon.
- Personal relationships are very important, and in many cases the success of the venture depends on them rather than on official petitions or applications. Russian negotiators generally do not expect help from bureaucracy.
- Most Russians are suspicious of public authorities and red tape, and will be mistrustful of any changes to contracts. If you have to make changes to meet laws or regulations, you will have to offer a good explanation.
- The dress code in Russia is rather formal and conservative. When you are introduced to a business partner, use your family name and your title, not your first name. Later on, during the conversation, you can switch to the Russian style of combining your own and your father's first name, although the *Novye Bysinessmeny* usually address each other by their first names.

- It is a good idea to bring a supply of business cards showing your title and academic qualifications.
- Business meetings usually take place in restaurants. Invitations to private houses are rare, but if invited you should not refuse such an opportunity.
- Russians drink a lot of vodka. Be careful to take part in a toast, which is an important ritual. The host has the honour of performing the first toast. Think about an honest toast in reply and use it to create a positive feeling and move the business along.
- Russian business partners are rather slow, but once you have won their sympathy, you will have formed a long-lasting relationship.
- Negotiation can be difficult outside big cities because the use of foreign languages is not as widespread there. Do not expect your business partner to speak English. Interpreters play an important role when doing business in Russia; it is worth spending some time to find a good one.
- Negotiations can be protracted, starting up to an hour late. They are often interrupted and sometimes two or more talks are held at the same time, which can distract your business partner. However, your partner will take all the time they need to consider the information – Russians believe you can never gather enough information about a prospective deal.
- Enterprises operating in Russia commonly encounter fiscal obscurities, problematic legal issues and difficulties in dealing with public authorities. New laws and regulations have only added to the complications. Some licences – especially for export – are hard to obtain. Make sure you have trustworthy professionals such as lawyers and accountants on your side.

Sources: adapted from Sergey Frank, 'A Market Emerging From a Country in Turmoil', *Financial Times*, 19 February 2001, p. 7; and 'To Russia, With Love: It's the Multinationals' New Darling', *Business Week*, 16 September 2002, pp. 20–1.

Post-negotiation Stage

In the post-negotiation stage the contract is drawn up. Experience shows that writing the contract and its language and formulations can be a negotiation process in itself as meanings and values differ between the two parties. If not properly handled, this stage can lead to renewed face-to-face negotiations. The best way to avoid this is to make sure that both parties thoroughly understand what they have agreed on before leaving each negotiation session.

Summary

An effective international sales force constitutes one of the international marketer's greatest concerns. The company sales force represents the major alternative method of organising a company for foreign distribution and, as such, is on the front line of a marketing organisation.

The role of marketers in both domestic and foreign markets is changing rapidly, along with the composition of international managerial teams and sales forces. These last two have many unique requirements that are being filled by expatriates, locals, third-country nationals, or a combination of the three. In recent years, the pattern of development has been to place more emphasis on local personnel operating in their own countries.

The importance of negotiations is more evident in international as compared to domestic marketing. The sales force needs to be trained in cross-cultural communication and negotiation for successful marketing performance. For successful negotiations in an international context, you have to understand the other party and its priorities. The impact of culture on the decision-making process of the parties involved is of utmost importance and should be fully understood in order to handle the negotiations efficiently. Moreover, you need to adapt your communication pattern to one that is easily understandable by the other party.

Questions

1 What are the factors that influence the effectiveness of personal selling in international marketing? Explain.
2 Define the following: expatriate, third-country national, non-verbal feedback, cultural empathy.
3 Why might it be difficult to adhere to set job criteria in selecting foreign personnel? What compensating actions might be necessary?
4 Under what circumstances should expatriate sales people be utilised?
5 Discuss the problems that might be encountered in having an expatriate sales person supervising foreign sales people.
6 'It is costly to maintain an international sales force.' Comment.
7 Adaptability and maturity are traits needed by all sales people. Why should they be singled out as especially important for international sales people?
8 Discuss the stages in cross-cultural negotiations. How can you effectively manage an international negotiation process? Discuss.
9 Why is sound negotiation the key to effective relationship marketing? Discuss.

Further Reading

P.N. Ghauri and T. Fang, 'Negotiating with the Chinese: A socio-cultural analysis', *Journal of World Business*, 2001, 36(3), pp. 303–25.

P.N. Ghauri, 'Guidelines for International Business Negotiations', *International Marketing Review*, 1986, 3(3), pp. 72–82.

S. Kale, 'How National Culture, Organisational Culture and Personality Impact Buyer-Seller Interaction', in P. Ghauri and J.-C. Usunier, *International Business Negotiations*, 2nd edn (Oxford: Elsevier, 2004).

G.S. Insch and J.D. Daniel, 'Causes and Consequences of Declining Early Departure from Foreign Assignments', *Business Horizon*, 2003, 45(6), pp. 39–48.

References

1   L.S. Amine, Country-of-origin, animosity and consumer response: Marketing implications of anti-Americanism and Francophobia, *International Business Review*, 2008, 17(4), pp. 402–22.

2   R.B. Money, M.C. Gilly and J.L. Graham, 'National Culture and Referral Behaviour in the Purchase of Industrial Services in the United States and Japan', *Journal of Marketing*, 1998, 62(4), pp. 76–87.

3   Harald Biong and Fred Selnes, 'Relational Selling Behavior and Skills in Long-Term Industrial Buyer–Seller Relationships', *International Business Review*, 1995, 4(4), pp. 483–98.

4   Jean-Claude Usunier, *Marketing Across Cultures* (Hemel Hempstead: Prentice–Hall, 1996).

5   Jagdish Sheth, 'Cross-cultural Influences on the Buyer–Seller Interaction/Negotiation Process', *Asia Pacific Journal of Management*, 1983, 1(1), pp. 46–55.

6   This section is based on Sudhir Kalé, 'How National Culture, Organizational Culture and Personality Impact Buyer–Seller Interactions', in Pervez Ghauri and Jean-Claude Usunier, *International Business Negotiations* (Oxford: Pergamon, 1996), pp. 21–37.

7   Geert Hofstede, 'National Cultures in Four Dimensions: A Research-based Theory of Cultural Differences Among Nations', *International Studies of Management and Organization*, 1983, xii(1–2), pp. 46–74.

8   See, for example, 'Nonverbal Negotiation in China: Cycling in Beijing', *Negotiation Journal*, January 1995, pp. 11–18.

9   This section draws on Lennie Copeland, 'The Art of International Selling', *Business America*, 25 June 1984, pp. 2–7; and Roger E. Axtell, *The Do's and Taboos of International Trade* (New York: Wiley, 1994).

10 D. Rouzies, M. Segalla and B.A. Weitz, 'Cultural Impact on European Staffing Decisions in Sales Management', *International Journal of Research in Marketing*, 2003, 20(1), pp. 67–85.

11 For a comprehensive review of the difference between human resource management in Europe and the United States, see Chris Brewster, 'Towards a "European Model of Human Resource Management"', *Journal of International Business Studies*, First Quarter 1995, pp. 1–21.

12 This section draws on Pervez Ghauri and Jean-Claude Usunier (eds), *International Business Negotiations*, 2nd edn (Oxford: Elsevier, 2004).

13 S.C. Schneider and J.-L. Barsoux, *Managing Across Cultures*, 2nd edn (Harlow, UK: Pearson, 2003).

14 Geert Hofstede, 'National Cultures in Four Dimensions: A Research-based Theory of Cultural Differences Among Nations', *International Studies of Management and Organization*, 1983, xii(1–2), pp. 46–74.

15 A. Rugman and R. Rodgetts, 'The End of Global Strategy', *European Management Journal*, 19(4), pp. 333–43.

16 See, for example, Lennie Copeland and Lewis Griggs, *Going International* (New York: Plume, 1985); John L. Graham and Yoshihiro Sano, *Smart Bargaining: Doing Business with the Japanese*, rev. edn (New York: Harper, 1990); and Pervez Ghauri and Jean-Claude Usunier, *International Business Negotiations* (Oxford: Elsevier, 2004).

17 T. Fang, V. Worm and R.L. Tung, 'Changing success and failure factors in business negotiations with the PRC', *International Business Review*, 2008, 17(2), pp. 159–69.

Part 6
Supplementary
Resources

The Country Notebook: a Guide
for Developing a Marketing Plan

Case Studies

The Country Notebook: a Guide for Developing a Marketing Plan

The Country Notebook Outline

A number of books and articles have described strategic marketing planning at corporate or business unit level.[1] Here we are mainly concerned about a marketing plan for a foreign market or a marketing plan for a particular product in one particular market. The guidelines provided here can be used for different markets; however, depending on the market and the product, the emphasis on different parts of the framework may change.[2]

The first stage in the planning process is a preliminary country analysis. The marketer needs basic information to: (1) evaluate a country market's potential, (2) identify problems that would eliminate a country from further consideration, (3) identify aspects of the country's environment that need further study, (4) evaluate the components of the marketing mix for possible adaptation and (5) develop a strategic marketing plan. One further use of the information collected in the preliminary analysis is as a basis for a country notebook.

Many companies, large and small, have a country notebook for each country in which they do business. The country notebook contains information a marketer should be aware of when making decisions involving a specific country market. As new information is collected, the country notebook is continually updated by the country or product manager. Whenever a marketing decision is made involving a country, the country notebook is the first database consulted. New product introductions, changes in advertising programmes, and other marketing programme decisions begin with the country notebook. It also serves as a quick introduction for new personnel assuming responsibility for a country market.[3]

This section presents four separate sets of guidelines for collection and analysis of market data and preparation of a country notebook: (1) guideline for cultural analysis; (2) guideline for economic analysis; (3) guideline for market audit and competitive analysis; (4) guideline for a preliminary marketing plan. These guidelines suggest the kinds of information a marketer can gather to enhance planning.

The points in each of the sets of guidelines are general. They are designed to provide direction to areas to explore for relevant data. In each set, specific points must be adapted to reflect a company's products. The decision as to the appropriateness of specific data and the depth of coverage depends on company objectives, product characteristics, and the country market. Some points in the guidelines are unimportant for some countries and/or some products and should be ignored. Preceding chapters of this book provide specific content suggestions for the topics in each guideline.

Cultural Analysis

The data suggested in the cultural analysis include information that helps the marketer make market planning decisions. However, its application extends beyond product/market analysis to an important source of information for someone interested in understanding business customs and other important cultural features of the country.

The information in this analysis must be more than a collection of facts. Whoever is responsible for the preparation of this material should attempt to interpret the meaning of cultural information. That is, how does the information help in understanding the effect on the market? For example, the fact that almost all the populations of Italy and Ireland are Catholic is an interesting statistic but not nearly as useful as understanding the effect of Catholicism on values, beliefs and other aspects of market/consumer behaviour. Even though both countries are predominantly Catholic, the influence of their individual and unique interpretation and practice of Catholicism can result in important differences in market behaviour.

Guidelines
I Introduction.
  Include short profiles of the company, the product to be exported, and the country with which you wish to trade.
II Brief discussion of the country's relevant history.
III Geographical setting.
  A Location.
  B Climate.
  C Topography.
IV Social institutions.
  A Family.
    1 The nuclear family.
    2 The extended family.
    3 Female/male roles (are they changing or static?).
  B Education.
    1 The role of education in society.
    2 Literacy rates.
  C Political system.
    1 Political structure.
    2 Stability of government.

3 Special taxes.

4 Role of local government.

D Legal system.

  1 Organisation of the judiciary system.

  2 Code, common, socialist or Islamic-law country?

  3 Participation in patents, trademarks and other conventions.

E Social organisations.

  1 Group behaviour.

  2 Social classes.

  3 Race, ethnicity and subcultures.

F Business customs and practices.

V Religion and aesthetics.

A Religion and other belief systems.

  1 Which religions are prominent?

  2 Membership of each religion.

B Aesthetics.

  1 Visual arts (fine arts, plastics, graphics, public colours, etc.).

  2 Importance given to aesthetics.

VI Living conditions.

A Diet and nutrition.

  1 Typical meals.

B Housing.

  1 Types of housing available.

  2 Do most people own or rent?

  3 Do most people live in one-family dwellings or with other families?

C Clothing.

  1 National dress.

  2 Types of clothing worn at work.

D Recreation, sports, and other leisure activities.

E Social security.

F Healthcare.

VII Language.

A Official language(s).

B Spoken versus written language(s).

VIII Executive summary.

After completing all of the other sections, prepare a two-page (maximum length) summary of the major points and place it at the front of the report. The purpose of an executive summary is to give the reader a brief glimpse of the critical points of your report. Those aspects of the culture a reader should know in order to do business in the country but would not be expected to know or would find different based on his or her SRC should be included in this summary.

IX Sources of information.

X Appendices.

Economic Analysis

The reader may find the data collected for the economic analysis guidelines are more straightforward than for the cultural analysis guidelines. There are two broad categories of information in these guidelines: general economic data that serve as a basis for an evaluation of the economic soundness of a country and information on channels of distribution and media availability. As mentioned earlier, these guidelines focus only on broad categories of data and must be adapted to particular company/product needs.

Guidelines

I Introduction.

II Population.

A Total.

  1 Growth rates.

B Distribution of population.

  1 Age.

  2 Sex.

  3 Geographic areas (urban, suburban and rural density and concentration).

  4 Ethnic groups.

III Economic statistics and activity.

A Gross national product (GNP or GDP).

  1 Total.

  2 Rate of growth (real GNP or GDP).

B Personal income per capita.

C Average family income.

D Distribution of wealth.

  1 Income classes.

  2 Proportion of the population in each class.

  3 Is the distribution distorted?

E Minerals and resources.

F Surface transportation.

  1 Modes.

  2 Availability.

G Communication systems.

  1 Types.

  2 Availability.

H Working conditions.

  1 Employer–employee relations.

  2 Employee participation.

  3 Salaries and benefits.

I Principal industries.

  1 What proportion of the GNP does each industry contribute?

  2 Ratio of private to publicly owned industries.

J Foreign investment.

  1 Opportunities?

  2 Which industries?

3 Personal selling.
4 Other promotional methods.
D Distribution: from origin to destination.
 1 Port selection.
  a Origin port.
  b Destination port.
 2 Mode selection: advantages/disadvantages of each mode.
  a Railroads.
  b Air carriers.
  c Ocean carriers.
  d Motor carriers.
 3 Packing.
  a Marking and labelling regulations.
  b Containerisation.
 4 Documentation required.
 5 Insurance claims.
 6 Freight forwarder.
  If your company does not have a transportation or traffic management department, then consider using a freight forwarder. There are distinct advantages and disadvantages to hiring one.
E Channels of distribution (micro analysis).
 This section presents details about the specific types of distribution in your marketing plan.
 1 Retailers.
  a Type and number of retail stores.
  b Retail mark-ups for products in each type of retail store.
  c Methods of operation for each type (cash/credit).
  d Scale of operation for each type (small/large).
 2 Wholesale middlemen.
  a Type and number of wholesale middlemen.
  b Mark-up for class of products by each type.
  c Methods of operation for each type (cash/credit).
  d Scale of operation (small/large).
 3 Import/export agents.
 4 Warehousing.
  a Type.
  b Location.
F Price determination.
 1 Cost of the shipment of goods.
 2 Transportation costs.
 3 Handling expenses.
 4 Insurance costs.

5 Customs duties.
6 Import taxes and value added tax.
7 Wholesale and retail mark-ups and discounts.
8 Company's gross margins.
9 Retail price.
G Terms of sale.
 1 Ex works, fob, fas, c&f, cif.
H Methods of payment.
 1 Cash in advance.
 2 Letters of credit.
II Pro forma financial statements and budgets.
 A Marketing budget.
  1 Selling expense.
  2 Advertising/promotion expense.
  3 Distribution expense.
  4 Product cost.
  5 Other costs.
 B Pro forma annual profit and loss statement (first year and fifth year).
III Resource requirements.
 A Finances.
 B Personnel.
 C Production capacity.
IV Executive summary.
 After completing the research for this report, prepare a summary (two pages maximum) of the major points of your successful marketing plan and place it at the front of the report.
V Sources of information.
VI Appendices.
 The intricacies of international operations and the complexity of the environment within which the international marketer must operate create an extraordinary demand for information. When operating in foreign markets, the need for thorough information as a substitute for uninformed opinion is equally as important as it is in domestic marketing. This information should be systematically collected and analysed before it is presented as a base for decision making.[4]

Summary

Market-oriented firms build strategic market plans around company objectives, markets and the competitive environment. Planning for marketing can be complicated even for one country, but when a company is doing business internationally the problems are multiplied. Company objectives may vary from market to market, from product to product and from time to time; the structure of international markets also

changes periodically and from country to country, and the competitive, governmental and economic parameters affecting market planning are in a constant state of flux. These variations require international marketing executives to be specially flexible and creative in their approach to strategic marketing planning.

References

1 See, for example, David Aaker, *Strategic Marketing Management*, 8th edn (New York: Wiley, 2007).

2 For going into a new market see, for example, Franklin Root, *Entry Strategies for International Markets* (Washington, DC: Heath and Company, 1994).

3 Tamer Cavusgil, Pervez Ghauri and Milind Aganwal, *Doing Business in Emerging Markets: Entry and Negotiation Strategies* (Thousand Oaks: Sage, 2002).

4 Pervez Ghauri and Kjell Grønhaug, *Research Methods in Business Studies: A Practical Guide* (Hemel Hempstead: FTPrentice Hall, 2005).

level that makes it harder and harder to grow, just due to the law of large numbers.'

To duplicate the staggering returns of its first decade, Starbucks has no choice but to export its concept aggressively. Indeed, some analysts give Starbucks only two years at most before it saturates the US market. The chain now operates 1200 international outlets, from Beijing to Bristol. That leaves plenty of room to grow. Indeed, about 400 of its planned 1200 new stores this year will be built overseas, representing a 35 per cent increase in its foreign base. Starbucks expects to double the number of its stores worldwide, to 10 000 in three years. During the past 12 months, the chain has opened stores in Vienna, Zurich, Madrid, Berlin, and even in far-off Jakarta. Athens comes next. And within the next year, Starbucks plans to move into Mexico and Puerto Rico. But global expansion poses huge risks for Starbucks. For one thing, it makes less money on each overseas store because most of them are operated with local partners. While that makes it easier to start up on foreign turf, it reduces the company's share of the profits to only 20–50 per cent.

Unpredictable Market

Moreover, Starbucks must cope with some predictable challenges of becoming a mature company in the United States. After riding the wave of successful baby boomers through the 1990s, the company faces an ominously hostile reception from its future consumers, the twenty- or thirty-somethings of Generation X. Not only are the activists among them turned off by the power and image of the well-known brand, but many others say that Starbucks' latte-sipping sophisticates and piped-in Kenny G music are a real turn-off. They don't feel wanted in a place that sells designer coffee at $3 a cup.

Even the thirst of loyalists for high-price coffee can't be taken for granted. Starbucks' growth over the past decade coincided with a remarkable surge in the economy. Consumer spending has continued strong in the downturn, but if that changes, those $3 lattes might be an easy place for people on a budget to cut back. Starbucks executives insist that won't happen, pointing out that even in the weeks following the terrorist attacks, same-store comparisons stayed positive while those of other retailers skidded.

Starbucks also faces slumping morale and employee burnout among its store managers and its once-cheery army of baristas. Stock options for part-timers in the restaurant business was a Starbucks innovation that once commanded awe and respect from its employees. But now, though employees are still paid better than comparable workers elsewhere – about $7 per hour – many regard the job as just another fast-food gig. Dissatisfaction over odd hours and low pay is affecting the quality of the normally sterling service and even the coffee itself, say some customers and employees. Frustrated store managers among the company's roughly 470 California stores sued Starbucks in 2001 for allegedly refusing to pay legally mandated overtime. Starbucks settled the suite for $18 million

this past April, shaving $0.03 per share off an otherwise strong second quarter. However, the heart of the complaint – feeling over-worked and underappreciated – doesn't seem to be going away.

To be sure, Starbucks has a lot going for it as it confronts the challenge of maintaining its growth. Nearly free of debt, it fuels expansion with internal cash flow. And Starbucks can maintain a tight grip on its image because stores are company-owned: there are no franchisees to get sloppy about running things. By relying on mystique and word-of-mouth, whether here or overseas, the company saves a bundle on marketing costs. Starbucks spends just $30 million annually on advertising, or roughly 1 per cent of revenues, usually just for new flavours of coffee drinks in the summer and product launches, such as its new instore web service. Most consumer companies its size shell out upwards of $300 million per year. Moreover, unlike a McDonald's or a Gap Inc., two other retailers that rapidly grew in the United States, Starbucks has no nationwide competitor.

Starbucks also has a well-seasoned management team. Schultz, 49, stepped down as chief executive in 2000 to become chairman and chief global strategist. Orin Smith, 60, the company's number-cruncher, is now CEO and in charge of day-to-day operations. The head of North American operations is Howard Behar, 57, a retailing expert who returned last September, two years after retiring. The management trio is known as H2O, for Howard, Howard, and Orin.

Schultz remains the heart and soul of the operation. Raised in a Brooklyn public housing project, he found his way to Starbucks, a tiny chain of Seattle coffee shops, as a marketing executive in the early 1980s. The name came about when the original owners looked to Seattle history for inspiration and chose the moniker of an old mining camp: Starbo. Further refinement led to Starbucks, after the first mate in the novel *Moby-Dick*, which they felt evoked the seafaring romance of the early coffee traders (hence the mermaid logo). Schultz got the idea for the modern Starbucks format while visiting a Milan coffee bar. He bought out his bosses in 1987 and began expanding. Today, Schultz has a net worth of about $700 million, including $400 million of company stock.

Starbucks has come light-years from those humble beginnings, but Schultz and his team still think there's room to grow in the United States – even in communities where the chain already has dozens of stores. Clustering stores increases total revenue and market share, Smith argues, even when individual stores poach on each other's sales. The strategy works, he says, because of Starbucks' size. It is large enough to absorb losses at existing stores as new ones open up, and soon overall sales grow beyond what they would have with just one store. Meanwhile, it's cheaper to deliver to and manage stores located close together. And by clustering, Starbucks can quickly dominate a local market.

The company is still capable of designing and opening a store in 16 weeks or less and recouping the initial investment in three years. The stores may be oases of tranquillity, but management's expansion tactics are something else. Take what critics call its 'predatory real estate'

strategy – paying more than market-rate rents to keep competitors out of a location. David C. Schomer, owner of Espresso Vivace in Seattle's hip Capitol Hill neighbourhood, says Starbucks approached his landlord and offered to pay nearly double the rate to put a coffee shop in the same building.

The landlord stuck with Schomer, who says: 'It's a little disconcerting to know that someone is willing to pay twice the going rate.' Another time, Starbucks and Tully's Coffee Corp., a Seattle-based coffee chain, were competing for a space in the city. Starbucks got the lease but vacated the premises before the term was up. Still, rather than let Tully's get the space, Starbucks decided to pay the rent on the empty store so its competitor could not move in. Schultz makes no apologies for the hardball tactics, 'The real estate business in America is a very, very tough game,' he says. 'It's not for the faint of heart.'

Still, the company's strategy could backfire. Not only will neighbourhood activists and local businesses increasingly resent the tactics, but customers could also grow annoyed over having fewer choices. Moreover, analysts contend that Starbucks can maintain about 15 per cent square-footage growth in the United States – equivalent to 550 new stores – for only about two more years. After that, it will have to depend on overseas growth to maintain annual 20 per cent revenue growth.

Beyond Coffee

Starbucks was hoping to make up much of that growth with more sales of food and other non-coffee items, but has stumbled somewhat. In the late 1990s Schultz thought that offering $8 sandwiches, desserts, and CDs in his stores and selling packaged coffee in supermarkets would significantly boost sales. The speciality business now accounts for about 16 per cent of sales, but growth has been less than expected. A healthy 19 per cent this year, it's still far below the 38 per cent growth rate of fiscal 2000. That suggests that while coffee can command high prices in a slump, food – at least at Starbucks – cannot. One of Behar's most important goals is to improve that record. For instance, the company now has a test programme of serving hot breakfasts in 20 Seattle stores and may move to expand supermarket sales of whole beans.

What's more important for the bottom line, though, is that Starbucks has proven to be highly innovative in the way it sells its main course: coffee. In 800 locations it has installed automatic espresso machines to speed up service. And in November, it began offering prepaid Starbucks cards, priced from $5 to $500, which clerks swipe through a reader to deduct a sale. That, says the company, cuts transaction times in half. Starbucks has sold $70 million-worth of the cards.

In early August Starbucks launched Starbucks Express, its boldest experiment yet, which blends java, web technology, and faster service. At about 60 stores in the Denver area, customers can pre-order and prepay for beverages and pastries via phone or on the Starbucks Express website. They just make the call or click the mouse before arriving at the store, and their beverage will be waiting – with their name printed on the cup. The company will decide in January on a national launch.

Starbucks is bent on even more fundamental store changes. On 21 August it announced expansion of a high-speed wireless Internet service to about 1200 Starbucks locations in North America and Europe. Partners in the project – which Starbucks calls the world's largest Wi-Fi network – include Mobile International, a wireless subsidiary of Deutsche Telekom, and Hewlett-Packard. Customers sit in a store and check email, surf the web, or download multimedia presentations without looking for connections or tripping over cords. They start with 24 hours of free wireless broadband before choosing from a variety of monthly subscription plans.

Starbucks' executives hope such innovations will help surmount their toughest challenge in the home market: attracting the next generation of customers. Younger coffee drinkers already feel uncomfortable in the stores. The company knows that because it once had a group of twenty-somethings hypnotised for a market study. When their defences were down, out came the bad news: 'They either can't afford to buy coffee at Starbucks, or the only peers they see are those working behind the counter,' says Mark Barden, who conducted the research for the Hal Riney & Partners ad agency (now part of Publicis Worldwide) in San Francisco. One of the recurring themes the hypnosis brought out was a sense that 'people like me aren't welcome here except to serve the yuppies,' he says. Then there are those who just find the whole Starbucks scene a bit pretentious. Katie Kelleher, 22, a Chicago paralegal, is put off by Starbucks' Italian terminology of *grande* and *venti* for coffee sizes. She goes to Dunkin' Donuts, saying: 'Small, medium and large is fine for me.'

Happy Staff

As it expands, Starbucks faces another big risk: that of becoming a far less special place for its employees. For a company modelled around enthusiastic service, that could have dire consequences for both image and sales. During its growth spurt of the mid- to late 1990s, Starbucks had the lowest employee turnover rate of any restaurant or fast-food company, thanks largely to its then unheard-of policy of giving health insurance and modest stock options to part-timers making barely more than minimum wage.

Such perks are no longer enough to keep all the workers happy. Starbucks' pay doesn't come close to matching the workload it requires, complain some staff. Says Carrie Shay, a former store manager in West Hollywood, California: 'If I were making a decent living, I'd still be there.' Shay, one of the plaintiffs in the suit against the company, says she earned $32 000 a year to run a store with 10 to 15 part-time employees. She hired employees, managed their schedules, and monitored the store's weekly profit-and-loss statement. But she was also expected to put in significant time behind the counter and had to sign an affidavit pledging to work up to 20 hours of overtime a week without extra pay – a requirement the company has dropped since the settlement.

Case 1.3 Halliburton 'Over-billing' Controversy

The Pentagon audit confirms what we've known for months: Halliburton has been gouging taxpayers, and the White House has been letting them get away with it.[1]

– Henry Waxman, Democrat elected from State of California, US

No company is busier in Iraq than Halliburton. And no company in Iraq is as busy battling to clear its name.[2]

– James Cox, journalist, *USA Today*

The Allegations

On 20 March 2003 the US-led coalition forces attacked Iraq in pursuance of 'Operation Iraqi Freedom.'[3] The war ended in two months. For all the various requirements of the pre-war and post-war period, the US government declared that it had awarded no-bid contracts[4] to Halliburton Company.[5] Analysts and media reports questioned the US government's decision to award contracts to Halliburton. They said that the company had a tainted past and was infamous for its unethical business practices. The major opposition came from the Democrats (the leading opposition party of the Republican government in the US). They alleged that the contracts had been awarded to Halliburton mainly because of the ties that the Vice President Dick Cheney[6] had with the company.

However, Kellogg Brown & Root (KBR), the engineering and construction subsidiary of Halliburton that was supposed to carry out the military contracts denied these allegations. KBR said that it had bagged the contract because of its excellent track record and expertise. The company commented, 'KBR was selected for this award based on the fact that KBR is the only contractor that could commence implementing the complex contingency plan on extremely short notice.'[7] Dave Lesar, the CEO of Halliburton, said, 'We are proud of our record and of our employees who serve the military. We receive contracts to make omelets and build infrastructure because of our unique skill sets.'[8]

In August 2003 the Department of Defense (DoD) of the US complained that the food that was cooked and served to the US troops in Iraq was done so in extremely unhygienic conditions. A report[9] mentioned that the food was cooked with 'rotting meats and vegetables' and with 'blood all over the floor', and was served in 'dirty pans', 'dirty grills', and 'dirty salad bars'. Moreover, the DoD also charged KBR with over billing of oil that it imported to Iraq. The DoD said that KBR had overcharged to the tune of $61 million. The auditors with DoD alleged that the company charged $1.09 per gallon more for gasoline. Following this, there were allegations that KBR had overcharged for food as well. The company was put under scrutiny for overbilling.

Meanwhile, KBR denied all the allegations and said that the company was doing a good job under the extremely difficult situation of war. It alleged that it was being targeted for political reasons as the presidential elections were due in November

2004. A few analysts agreed with the company's argument and said that since the charges against the company had not been proved, criticism of the company was not justified. A journalist wrote, 'The difference between a potential overcharge and an actual overcharge is a big one, of course. It's the difference between a suspicion and a proven fact.'[10]

Background Note

Founded in 1919, Halliburton was one of the world's largest providers of oil field services. The company was involved in providing oil and gas services to business, industries and government agencies throughout the world. Catering to the energy customers worldwide, Halliburton operated through its two main subsidiaries – KBR and Halliburton Energy Services.

Although a successful company, Halliburton had been dogged by controversy since the late 1980s. In 1995 the company was charged with doing business with Libya in spite of the US ban.[11] It was charged with exporting six pulse neutron generators to Libya between 1987 and 1989. These devices, apart from being oil and gas well survey tools, could be used to detonate nuclear weapons. This fact made the allegation against Halliburton more serious than just violation of trade practices. The controversy continued for a few years and eventually, in 1995, the company pleaded guilty to criminal charges that it had violated the ban. Subsequently, it was asked to pay a fine of $3.81 million.

Halliburton was also criticised for its trade with Azerbaijan and Burma. The US Government had imposed a ban on trade with Azerbaijan as it believed that the country indulged in 'ethnic cleansing'[12] of Armenians. Halliburton had an oil pipeline project in Burma. In 2001 the company had to face the wrath of its shareholders for having a project in Burma as the Burmese army was blamed for killing thousands of pro-democracy protesters to remain in power. The country's military had been widely condemned as one of the world's most brutal violators of human rights. However, justifying the company's project in Burma, Cheney commented, 'The problem is that the Lord didn't see fit to always put oil and gas resources where there are democratic governments.'[13]

Media reports commented that Halliburton had a strong political network (refer to Exhibit 1 for Halliburton's political connections). Cheney served Halliburton as CEO of the company between 1995 and 2000. Analysts opined that at the time of joining the organisation, Cheney did not have much business experience of running a company. However, his stint as Secretary of Defense (1988–1993)[14] helped him perform his role effectively. During his tenure Halliburton grew to become the leading oil services company in the US. Cheney brought with him a new direction for the company. During Cheney's tenure Halliburton got contracts worth $2.3 billion as against only $1.2 billion during the previous five years between 1990 and 1995.

Exhibit 1 Halliburton's political connections

Halliburton Company is known for its political connections. One reason for the company having a strong political network is its expenditure on political parties, especially Republicans. These expenditures became higher after 1995 when Dick Cheney became the CEO. The company had a Political Action Committee (PAC), which contributed donations to the federal candidates. Halliburton also made soft money contributions since 1995. In November 2002, the soft money payment was banned in the US. The cumulative contribution made by the company between 1995 and 2002 is given in Table 1.

Table 1 Halliburton PAC and soft contribution

PAC		Soft	
Democrats	Republicans	Democrats	Republicans
$44 500	$710 002	$0	$432 375

Source: Alternative Annual Report on Halliburton, http://users2.ev1.net/, April 2004.

In addition to the contribution to specific political candidates, Halliburton had spent $2.6 million on lobbying public officials since 1998, employing well-connected lobbyists with extensive histories in the US Defense Department (see Table 2).

Table 2 Halliburton total expenditures on politicians

Election cycle	Lobbying expenditure	PAC & soft contribution	Total
1995–96	–	$218 000	$218 000
1997–98	$540 000	$354 175	$894 175
1999–00	$1 200 000	$376 952	$1 576 952
2001–02	$600 000	$163 250	$763 250
2003	$300 000	$75 500	$375 500

Source: Alternative Annual Report on Halliburton, http://users2.ev1.net/, April 2004.

With Cheney's efforts, the number of subsidiaries situated in offshore tax havens grew to 44, whereas it was only nine before his tenure. This meant that the company received an $85 million tax refund in 1999, whereas it had paid $302 million in 1998. Analysts said that these changes were the result of Cheney's personal network with different countries from his time as the Secretary of Defense. By the early 2000s Halliburton and its subsidiaries employed more than 100 000 people in 120 countries serving almost 7000 customers.

The Accounting Scandal

Though Halliburton's operations expanded significantly during Cheney's tenure, it did not always result in improved financial performance. One of the major changes that Halliburton witnessed during this period was that the company started receiving contracts of fixed prices rather than

on the more usual cost-plus[15] basis. The fixed-price contract did not guarantee any profit margin to the company in the event of cost overruns or unforeseen cost increases. All that Halliburton could do was to try to persuade its clients to pay for at least a part of the increased cost. The amount involved in those persuasions was referred to as 'disputed claims'. Prior to 1998 Halliburton did not include disputed claims as revenues and such claims were recognised as revenues only after settling with the clients as it depended entirely on the negotiation ability of the company whether it could get the customers to pay for those extra costs incurred or not. Since the fourth quarter of 1998 the company included a portion of disputed claims as revenues.

Analysts also commented on the timing of the change in accounting practices. They pointed out that Halliburton faced a tough time in 1998 as lower oil prices had affected its business adversely. The problem was aggravated by the acquisition of

Dresser for $5.4 billion. Analysts said that the company reported $175 million of pre-tax operating profits, more than half of which ($89 million) resulted from the change in the accounting policy. They said that since the bottom line of the company was under pressure, without the accounting practice change, the company would have fallen short of its revenue estimates and this would have affected its share price negatively. They alleged that this prompted Halliburton and its auditor Arthur Andersen[16] to change the company's accounting policy.

Analysts also pointed out the accounting technicality involved in the Halliburton case. They referred to paragraph 81 of the American Institute of Certified Public Accountants Statement of Position 81–1 (also known as SOP 81–1), which said that the recognition of amounts of additional contract revenue was appropriate only when it was probable that the claim would result in additional contract revenues and if the amount could be reliably estimated. Paul Brown, chairman of the accounting department at the Stern School of Business at New York University opined, 'In general, companies are not supposed to book sales unless they are certain that they will be paid – and how much they will be paid.'[17] However, Halliburton argued that it had applied the percentage of completion method[18] and had not violated any accounting norms. The company also added that it included disputed claims as revenues only when there was some probability of it receiving the contract money.

Responding to these allegations, Halliburton said that it had not disclosed the change because it was too small to matter. The company said that it had earned $14.5 billion revenues for the financial year 1998, hence the inclusion of $89 million was not at all significant. The company stood by its accounting practice, whereas SEC continued its investigation for any possible malpractice in the financial reporting.

The Contract

In March 2003 the US Government waged a war with Iraq. For all required logistic support, it gave a 'no-bid contract' to Halliburton months before the actual war started (refer to Exhibit 2 for the details of the contracts awarded to Halliburton). The DoD asked the company to get military bases into the Kuwaiti desert ready for possible invasion. About 1800 employees of Halliburton began working in Kuwait and within a few weeks they had erected camps that were capable of supporting 80 000 soldiers. This contract was secretly awarded to Halliburton and was not made public until the war started.

In March 2003 the US Government also awarded another contract to Halliburton to extinguish oil-well fires. This contract was to be carried out by Halliburton's subsidiary KBR. The company was supposed to extinguish oil-well fires, capping oil-well blowouts, as well as respond to any oil spills. When this information was made public, the government was criticised vehemently by many analysts and observers. They complained that the contract was given to a company that had a history of doing business with terrorist regimes and was being investigated by the SEC. They also raised their voice against the manner in which the contract had been awarded. As it was a no-bid contract, many analysts alleged that Halliburton was awarded the contract because of Cheney's financial interests in the company.

Exhibit 2 Contracts awarded to Halliburton

Contract awarded by	Job	Value of the contract	Company's fee
US Army Corps of Engineers Task Force Restore Iraqi Oil	Assess and repair Iraq's oil infrastructure, restore production	Anticipated value: $1.9 billion	2% of the total value, performance bonus up to 5%
US Army Corps of Engineers Task Force Restore Iraqi Oil II	Repair oil infrastructure in southern Iraq and restore production	Maximum value: $1.2 billion	0% of the total value, performance bonus up to 3%
US Army material Command's Logistics Civil Augmentation Program (LOGCAP)	Build and maintain base camps, supply food, water, laundry, sanitation, recreation, transport and other services	Maximum value: $4 billion	1% of the total value performance bonus up to 2%
US Army Corps of Engineers Transatlantic Program Center	Design and build facilities for US Central Command (CENTCOM) in area stretching from Horn of Africa to Central Asia	Maximum value: $1.5 billion	Undisclosed

Source: US Army Corps of Engineers, US Army Material Command, Halliburton.

Responding to these allegations, Cheney said that after his retirement from the company in 2000, he had no financial interests in Halliburton. But a media report[19] mentioned that Cheney was still receiving $1 million every year as a part of his retirement compensation of $20 million. Another report[20] stated that the package of $20 million was approved by the company on 20 July 2000, just five days before he was announced as the vice-presidential candidate. The report also stated that Cheney's compensation for the eight months of 2000 in which he served as the CEO of Halliburton was $4.3 million in deferred compensation and bonuses and $806 332 in salary.

Halliburton claimed that it had got the contract because of its competency as it was the only contractor that could do the work required at extremely short notice. Dave Lesar, the CEO of Halliburton, commented, 'We get government contracts because of what we know, not who we know.'[21]

By 14 April 2003 the US Government had declared that the major fighting in Iraq was over, following the capture of Tikrit, the birthplace of Saddam Hussein. However, the troops encountered resistance from Iraqi fighters in small towns and cities. A formal declaration regarding the end of war by the US came a fortnight later on 1 May 2003.

After the war the US forces had the major task of rebuilding Iraq. There was an immediate need for oil as many oil wells had been destroyed in Iraq. The country had no electricity to power its refineries. The Iraqis did not even have the required fuel to make food. The US forces suspected that if oil was not made available in Iraq soon, the problem may lead to a civil war. The US government aptly expanded the scope of the contract earlier given to Halliburton and asked it to start exporting gasoline to Iraq. All the contracts were awarded on a cost-plus basis.

The Controversy

In August 2003 the DoD charged Halliburton with serving mediocre-quality food to the US army in extremely unhygienic conditions for which it charged $28 per day per soldier. Reportedly the soldiers could have had their food in the best hotels of Iraq for this sum. Moreover, the company was also alleged to have falsely charged $186 million for meals that were never delivered. According to reports, the company did not keep records of how many soldiers were having their meals at a time. Analysts felt that this was done in order to make the estimate of the food bill impossible to calculate.

Halliburton, however, denied these charges and said that it was possible that there was some overestimation. The company said that in wartime, exact estimation of number of soldiers that would come for lunch/dinner was not possible as soldiers went on leave or troops were shifted to other locations frequently without the knowledge of the company. The company also said that it did not keep records of the number of meals because the commanders did not want the soldiers to 'sign in' for meals due to security reasons. They also did not want the troops to wait in a queue to have food. The company, however, agreed to pay

back $27.4 million, but underlined that 'this is not any sort of admission of wrongdoing.'[22] Later, the company also suspended $141 million of its food bill. The company said that it would receive the payment from the government only when the controversy about over-billing was resolved.

By the end of 2003 the allegations of over-billing against Halliburton increased significantly. Waxman was one of the first people to charge the company with over-billing. According to him, the company charged the US Government $1.59 per gallon (excluding own commission), whereas the average wholesale rate of gasoline in the Middle East countries during the same period was about 71 cents a gallon. This meant that the company was charging almost 90 cents per gallon for transportation. According to Waxman, the reasonable transportation cost was the maximum of 25 cents. He commented, 'When we checked with independent experts to see if this fee was reasonable, they were stunned.'[23] The US DoD audit suggested an even higher amount of over-billing. It reported that Halliburton had overcharged the army by $1.09 per gallon for 57 million gallons of gasoline delivered to the Iraqis, taking the total amount of over billing to about $61 million.

Halliburton claimed that the US army initially wanted all the fuel to come from Kuwait, and it was only because of the recommendation of the company that Turkey was considered as the second option. According to the company, this suggestion saved millions of dollars of the US taxpayers' money as by December 2003, the company was buying two-thirds of its oil requirement from Turkey and only one-third from Kuwait. The company added that the army did not accept the idea of using only Turkey for bringing in fuel as it considered it risky to supply oil to Iraq from such a distant place. It also added that the army wanted the supply of oil from both the north (Turkey) and south (Kuwait) so that even if one route was closed, Iraq's oil supply was not stopped completely. Randy Harl, the president and CEO of KBR, said, 'KBR delivered fuel to Iraq at the best value, the best price and the best terms.'[24]

Halliburton received a major blow in January 2004 when it was reported that two of its employees accepted bribes of $6 million to award the contract to a subcontractor of Kuwait. However, the company took quick action by sacking these employees immediately. The company released a statement: 'We do not tolerate this kind of behavior by anyone at any level in any Halliburton company.'[25]

In another report[26] released in February 2004, two ex-employees of Halliburton were reported to have met Waxman and told him that the company had routinely over-charged the US Government. They alleged that Halliburton had wasted millions of dollars of the US taxpayers. They also gave many examples of wasteful spending by the company, including:

- abandoning of trucks worth $85 000 because of flat tyres and minor problems
- lodging 100 workers at a five-star hotel in Kuwait for a total of $10 000 a day while the US DoD wanted them to stay in tents, like soldiers, at $139 a night

- paying $100 to have a 15-pound bag of laundry cleaned in Kuwait whereas it cost only $28 in Iraq
- paying $1.5 to buy a can of soda, about 24 times higher than the contract price
- purchasing special towels for soldiers at $7.50 a piece when ordinary ones would have cost one-third of the price.

The ex-employees said that Halliburton did not mind paying high prices because the motto of the company was, 'Don't worry about price. It's cost plus.'

On 22 February 2004 the DoD announced that it had opened a criminal investigation against Halliburton for allegations regarding overpricing of fuel delivered in Iraq. The investigation was focused on KBR. On 16 March 2004 the DoD decided to withhold $300 million (about 15 per cent of the total bill) of the food bill until it received the new cost estimates from Halliburton. Responding to this, the company said that if did not receive the payment from the DoD, it would be forced to withhold the payments to its subcontractors.

By June 2004 analysts started saying that Halliburton was so mired in the over-billing controversy that it should no longer be allowed to carry on the work in Iraq. Moreover, its presence in Iraq had reportedly angered Iraqi contractors. A report said, 'Qualified Iraqi businesses are hungry to take over the work that Halliburton has been doing unsatisfactorily, and at a fraction of the cost. The Iraqi people deserve to be the first bidders on contracts to rebuild their country rather than being prohibited from bidding as is currently the case.'[27]

Halliburton, however, claimed that it had performed its work successfully while fighting against all odds. It also said that seven of its employees had been killed in the war. However, the company denied that the allegations levelled against it would have any substantial impact on its domestic and global business. Surprisingly, in spite of the controversy Halliburton's stock price has witnessed a steady increase since early 2003.

Further Reading

Peter Waldman, 'Pipeline Project in Burma Puts Cheney in the Spotlight', www.burmaformula.org, 27 October 2000.

Alex Berenson and Lowell Bergman, 'Under Cheney, Halliburton Altered Policy on Accounting', *The New York Times*, 22 May 2002.

Press release, 'Halliburton Reports SEC Investigation of Accounting Practice', www.halliburton.com, 28 May 2002.

'Halliburton Falls on SEC Probe', http://money.cnn.com, 29 May 2002.

Jane Bussey, 'Judicial Watch Sues Cheney', Halliburton, http://www.dfw.com, 10 July 2002.

Press release, 'Halliburton Responds to News of Judicial Watch Lawsuit', www.halliburton.com, 10 July 2002.

Anne Rittman, 'A Halliburton Primer', Washingtonpost.com, 11 July 2002.

Dana Milbank, For Cheney, Tarnish From Halliburton http://www.truthout.org, 16 July 2002.

'Vice President Denies Wrongdoing in Connection with Halliburton, which is Under SEC Investigation', money.cnn.com, 7 August 2002.

David Teather, 'Halliburton Staff Sacked "for Taking Bribes"', *Guardian*, 24 January 2003.

Press release, 'KBR implements plan for extinguishing oil well fires in Iraq', www.halliburton.com, 24 March 2003.

Jason Leopold, 'Halliburton and the Dictators: The Bloody History of Cheney's Firm', http://www.ccmep.org, 16 April 2003.

Sue Pleming, 'Iraq: Halliburton Accused of Overbilling', Reuters, www.corpwatch.org, 15 October 2003.

'Halliburton Accused of Iraq Overbilling', http://money.cnn.com, 16 October 2003.

Douglas Jehl, 'Halliburton Overcharges Government in Iraq', *New York Times*, 12 December 2003.

'Halliburton: $61m Overcharge?', http://www.cbsnews.com/, 12 December 2003.

'Halliburton Disputes are a Feature of its Government Contracts', http://www.spacewar.com, 13 December 2003.

'Contractor Served Troops Dirty Food in Dirty Kitchens', www.taipeitimes.com, 14 December 2003.

Paul Krugman, 'Profiteering and Patriotism', *New York Times*, 17 December 2003.

'Halliburton Denies Price Gouging Charges; Oil Services Firm says it Saved Taxpayers Millions', *MSNBC News Services*, 18 December 2003.

Jim Wolf, 'Democrats Press Rumsfeld for Halliburton Records', *Reuters*, 20 December 2003.

'Report: Feds Accuse Halliburton In Iraq Fuel Contract', The Street.Com, 20 December 2003.

Stephen Glain, 'Waxman hits Halliburton fuel contract', *The Boston Globe*, 16 January 2004.

'Halliburton Admits $6 Million Kickbacks', http://news.bbc.co.uk, 23 January 2004.

'Halliburton Pays for Possible Overcharge', http://money.cnn.com, 23 January 2004.

Lesley Stahl, 'Doing Business With The Enemy', *CBS*, 25 January 2004.

'More Halliburton Overcharges?', www.cbsnews. com, 2 February 2004.

Jackie Spinner, 'Halliburton to Return $27.4 million to Government', http://www.washingtonpost.com, 4 February 2004.

'Another Halliburton Probe', *Newsweek*, 4 February 2004.

John Kerry: 'Halliburton Investor', www.latefinal. com, 6 February 2004.

'Ex-Halliburton Employees Tell of Overbilling', www.reuters. com, 12 February 2004.

Andrew Limburg, 'Documenting the Halliburton/Cheney Crimes and Controversies, Part II', *Independent Media TV*, 14 February 2004.

John King, 'US Lifts Travel Ban to Libya', www.cnn.com, 27 February 2004.

'Piling on Halliburton', *Washington Post*, 3 March 2004.

James Cox, 'Halliburton CEO says Firm Saves Money for Pentagon', *USA Today*, 19 March 2004.

Press statement, 'KBR Continues to Work With Government to Resolve Billing Issues', www.halliburton.com, 17 May 2004.

Marian Wilkinson, 'Major Iraq Contract Falls Over', www. theage.com, 20 May 2004.

'*Time* Reports Cheney Hand in Contract', www.iht.com, 31 May 2004.

www.halliburton.com.

www.bigcharts.com.

www.hoovers.com.

http://biz.yahoo.com.

References

1   Douglas Jehl, 'Halliburton Overcharges Government in Iraq', *New York Times*, 12 December 2003.

2   James Cox, 'Halliburton CEO says Firm Saves Money for Pentagon', *USA Today*, 19 March 2004.

3   The US Government believed that Osama Bin Laden-led terrorist organisation, Al-Qaida, which was responsible for the September 11 2001 terrorist attacks on the World Trade Center in the US may obtain weapons of mass destruction (WMD) from Iraq. As Iraq was ruled by Saddam Hussein, who was openly hostile to the US, the US officials considered it a severe threat to the country's security, and felt the need for preemptive war against Iraq to prevent further damage from occurring in the US. In March 2003 the US declared war against Iraq (the second war, the first being in January 1991), called 'Operation Iraqi Freedom', aimed at freeing Iraq from the ruling Hussein government and gaining control over the WMD. The war ended in May 2003, following the capture of Tikrit, the birthplace of Hussein. Hussein was captured by the US army in December 2003.

4   A no-bid contract is a military or government contract that is made directly with a corporation, bypassing the standard process of bidding. These contracts can be finalised much more quickly than a typical contract. However, they are often viewed with suspicion when the company to which the contract has been issued has any ties with the administration in power at the time.

5   The Houston-based Halliburton Company provides products and services to the petroleum and energy industries to aid in the exploration, development and production of natural resources. Halliburton KBR, the company's engineering and construction division, designs, builds and provides additional services for the energy industry, governments and civil infrastructure.

6   Born on 30 January 1941 in Lincoln, Nebraska (US), Dick Cheney is the vice president of the US. He had been the CEO of Halliburton from 1995 to 2000.

7   Press release, 'KBR Implements Plan for Extinguishing Oil Well Fires in Iraq', www.halliburton.com, 24 March 2003.

8   'Piling on Halliburton', *The Washington Post*, 3 March 2004.

9   'Contractor Served Troops Dirty Food in Dirty Kitchens', www.taipeitimes.com, 14 December 2003.

10 'Anti-Bush Ad Overstates Case Against Halliburton', www.factcheck.org, 8 June 2004.

11 The US ban on commercial trade with Libya was imposed in 1986 when Libya allegedly bombed a German disco theatre killing two US soldiers and a Turkish woman and injuring 229 others. In early 2004 US lifted the ban after Libya acknowledged that it had secret weapons of mass destruction and agreed to dismantle them.

12 An act of either driving out or exterminating the people of the minority race in order to create an ethnically homogeneous state.

13 Peter Waldman, 'Pipeline Project in Burma puts Cheney in the Spotlight', www.burmaformula.org, 27 October 2000.

14 Cheney held the position of Secretary of Defense under George Bush Sr. During his tenure as Secretary of Defense, he was responsible for directing the US invasion of Panama and the first Gulf War. As Secretary of Defense, Cheney also conveniently changed the rules restricting private contractors doing work on the US military bases. He subsequently oversaw the awarding of billions of dollars in Department of Defense contracts to Halliburton, his future employer.

15 Cost-plus contracts are contracts wherein the bill amount is not decided beforehand. The bill amount is equal to whatever the expenses incurred on the contract plus a small profit margin for the contractor. Under this method, the contractor is assured to have a fixed margin even in the case of a sudden or unforeseen increment in the cost.

16 Arthur Andersen LLP was a US-based partnership firm engaged in auditing and consultancy. It came under fire in the Enron scandal in which it was convicted for obstructing justice in relation to the Enron scandal, which left the firm unable to perform audits for publicly traded US companies.

17 Alex Berenson and Lowell Bergman, 'Under Cheney, Halliburton Altered Policy on Accounting', *New York Times*, 22 May 2002.

18 A procedure for computing partial payments on a large contract wherein identifiable portions of the work may be satisfactorily completed, invoiced and paid before the entire project is completed and paid in full.

19 Mairesse Michelle, 'The Spoils of War', www.hermes-press.com.

20 'Halliburton Has Been Very, Very Good to Dick Cheney', www.democrats.org.

21 'Piling on Halliburton', *Washington Post*, 3 March 2004.

22 'Halliburton in Pentagon Payback', *BBC News*, 4 February 2004.

23 'Halliburton Accused of Iraq Over-billing', http://money.cnn.com, 16 October 2003.

24 'Halliburton Denies Price Gouging Charges, Oil Services Firm Says it Saved Taxpayers Millions', *MSNBC News Services*, 18 December 2003.

25 David Teather, 'Halliburton Staff Sacked for Taking Bribes', *Guardian*, 24 January 2004.

26 In another report Ex-Halliburton employees tell of over-billing, www.reuters.com, 12 February 2004.

27 Alternative annual report on Halliburton, http://users2.ev1.net/, April 2004.

This case was written by Avishek Suman, under the direction of Vivek Gupta, ICFAI Center for Management Research (ICMR). It is intended to be used as a basis for class discussion rather than to illustrate either effective or ineffective handling of a management situation. The case was compiled from published sources.

Part 2
Case Studies

Cases

Case 2.1 Cultural Norms: Fair & Lovely and Advertising

Fair & Lovely, a branded product of Hindustan Unilever Ltd (HUL – formerly called Hindustan Lever), is touted as a cosmetic that lightens skin colour. On its website (www.hul.co.in) the company called its product, 'the miracle worker', which is 'proven to deliver one to three shades of change'. While tanning is the rage in Western countries, skin-lightening treatments are popular in Asia.

According to industry sources, the top-selling skin lightening cream in India is Fair & Lovely from Hindustan Unilever, followed by CavinKare's Fairever brands. HUL's Fair & Lovely brand was the undisputed monarch of the market with a 90 per cent share until CavinKare Ltd (CKL) launched Fairever. In just two years, the Fairever brand gained an impressive 15 per cent market share. HUL's share of market for the Fair & Lovely line generates about $60 million annually. The product sells for about 23 rupees ($0.29) for a 25-gram tube of cream.

The rapid growth of CavinKare's Fairever (www.cavinkare.com) brand prompted HUL to increase its advertising effort and to launch a series of ads depicting a 'fairer girl gets the boy' theme. One advertisement featured a financially strapped father lamenting his fate, saying, 'If only I had a son', while his dark-skinned daughter looks on, helpless and demoralised because she can't bear the financial responsibility of her family. Fast-forward and Plain Jane has been transformed into a gorgeous light-skinned woman through the use of a 'fairness cream', Fair & Lovely. Now clad in a miniskirt, the woman is a successful flight attendant and can take her father to dine at a five-star hotel. She's happy and so is her father.

In another ad two attractive young women are sitting in a bedroom; one has a boyfriend and, consequently, is happy.

The darker-skinned woman, lacking a boyfriend, is not happy. Her friend's advice? Use a bar of soap to wash away the dark skin that's keeping men from flocking to her.

HUL's series of ads provoked CavinKare Ltd to counter with an ad that takes a dig at HUL's Fair & Lovely ad. CavinKare's ad has a father-daughter duo as the protagonists, with the father shown encouraging the daughter to be an achiever irrespective of her complexion. CavinKare maintained that the objective of its new commercial is not to take a dig at Fair & Lovely but to 'reinforce Fairever's positioning'.

'We have noticed attempts by Fair & Lovely to blur our positioning by changing its communication platform from "wanting to get married" to "achievement", the principal Fairever theme. Since we don't have the spending power to match HUL, a tactical way for us to respond is to reinforce our brand positioning and the commercial will be aired until the company's "objective" is achieved', a CavinKare official said.

Skin colour is a powerful theme in India as well as much of Asia where a lighter colour represents a higher status. While Americans and Europeans flock to tanning salons, many across Asia seek ways to have 'fair' complexions. Culturally, fair skin is associated with positive values that relate to class and beauty. One Indian lady commented that when she was growing up, her mother forbade her to go outdoors. She was not trying to keep her daughter out of trouble but was trying to keep her skin from getting dark.

Brahmins, the priestly caste at the top of the social hierarchy, are considered fair because they traditionally stayed inside, poring over books. The undercaste at the bottom of the ladder

Exhibit 1 What happened in India?

In May 2001 managing directors of McDonald's India – Vikram Bakshi of Delhi's Connaught Plaza Restaurants and Amit Jatia of Mumbai's Hardcastle Restaurants – said at a press conference, 'We are open to any kind of investigation by the authorities, from the state or central governments. We categorically state that the French fries and other vegetarian products that we serve in India do not contain any beef or animal extracts and flavouring of whatsoever kind.'

Bakshi said that the company had developed a special menu for Indian customers taking into consideration Indian culture and religious sentiments. McDonald's officials circulated official statements by McCain Foods India Pvt. Ltd. and Lamb Weston, suppliers of French fries to McDonald's India, stating that the fries were par-fried in pure vegetable oil without any beef tallow or any fat ingredient of animal origin.

People were however sceptical of the company's assurance because it had made similar false promises in the US as well. Their fears were realised when it was revealed that Lamb Weston's supplies had been rejected after they failed to meet standards set by McDonald's. McCain Foods was still in the process of growing the appropriate potatoes and needed another two years to begin supply. The French fries were being sourced from the US.

However, tests conducted on the French fries and the cooking medium by Brihanmumbai Municipal Corporation (BMC) and the Food and Drug Administration (FDA) confirmed the fries contained no animal fat.

Source: ICMR.

A McDonald's quality assurance manager testified in the case that the company was aware of the risk of serving dangerously hot coffee, but it had no plans to lower the temperature or to post a warning on the coffee cups about the possibility of severe burns. In 1994 the court declared McDonald's guilty of serving 'unreasonably dangerous' hot coffee. The court awarded punitive damages of $2.7 million dollars, which was later lowered to $480 000.

The company also had to settle multi-million-dollar lawsuits in many other cases, the majority of which were spearheaded by two London Greenpeace activists (Steel and Morris). The company was severely criticised for hiring detective agencies to break into the activist group. According to an analyst, 'The company had employed at least seven undercover agents to spy on Greenpeace. During some London Greenpeace meetings, about half the people in attendance were corporate spies. One spy broke into the London Greenpeace office, took photographs and stole documents. Another had a six-month affair with a member of London Greenpeace while informing on his activities.'

Steel and Morris were later found to have libelled McDonald's by a British court. However, the company was also found guilty of endangering the health of its customers and paying workers unreasonably low wages. The case, chronicled completely at www.mcspotlight.org, has become a classic example of a corporate giant's struggle to uphold its image amid allegations of unethical practices.

In the light of the company's chequered history of legal problems, the French fries controversy seemed run-of-the-mill. However, when McDonald's issued a conditional apology, the matter acquired serious undertones. This was because it was one of the very few instances where the company seemed to have publicly acknowledged any kind of wrongdoing.

The Beef Fries Controversy

With an overwhelming majority of the people in the West being non-vegetarian, products often contain hidden animal-based ingredients. Incidents of vegetarians finding non-vegetarian food items in their food abound throughout the world. Whether a person has chosen to be a vegetarian for religious, health, ethical or philosophical reasons, it is not easy to get vegetarian food in public restaurants. According to the manager of a Thai food café in the US, 'We have a lot of customers already. We don't need to have any vegetarian food.' Commenting on this dilemma, a US-based Hindu vegetarian said, 'We can't blame anybody. You have to find out for yourself. If you have any doubts, try to avoid it. Otherwise, you just have to close your eyes and try to eat.'

The French fries controversy began in 2000, when a Hindu Jain software engineer Hitesh Shah, working in the US, happened to read a news article, which mentioned that the French fries at McDonald's contained beef. Shah sent an email to the McDonald's customer service department, asking whether the French fries contained beef or not and, if they did, why this was not mentioned in the ingredient list. Shah soon got a reply from Megan Magee, the company's Home Office Customer Satisfaction Department.

The reply stated, 'Thank you for taking time to contact McDonald's with your questions regarding the ingredients in our French fries. For flavor enhancement, McDonald's French fry suppliers use a minuscule amount of beef flavoring as an ingredient in the raw product. The reason beef is not listed as an ingredient is because McDonald's voluntarily (restaurants are not required to list ingredients) follow the "Code of Federal Regulations" (required for packaged goods) for labeling its products. As such, like food labels you would read on packaged goods, the ingredients in "natural flavors" are not broken down. Again, we are sorry if this has caused any confusion.'

A popular Indian-American newspaper, *West India*, carried Shah's story. The news created widespread outrage among Hindus and vegetarians in the US. In May 2001 Harish Bharti, a US-based Indian attorney, filed the class-action lawsuit against McDonald's.

McDonald's immediately released a statement saying it never claimed the fries sold in the US were vegetarian. A spokesperson said that though the fries were cooked in pure vegetable oil, the company never explicitly stated that the fries were appropriate for vegetarians and customers were always told that the flavour came partly from beef. He added that it was up to the customer to ask about the flavour and its source. This enraged the vegetarian customers further. Bharti said, 'Not only did they deceive millions of people who may not want to have any beef extraction in their food for religious, ethical and health reasons, now McDonald's is suggesting that these people are at fault, that they are stupid. This adds insult to injury.'

Interestingly enough, McDonald's statement that it never claimed its French fries were vegetarian was proved completely wrong after Bharti found a 1993 letter sent by the company's corporate headquarters to a consumer in response to an enquiry about vegetarian menu items. The letter clearly bundled the fries along with garden salads, wholegrain cereals and English muffins as a completely vegetarian item.

The whole controversy rested on a decision McDonald's had taken in 1990 regarding the way French fries were prepared. Prior to 1990 the company made the fries using tallow.[3] However, to address the increasing customer concern about cholesterol control,[4] McDonald's declared that it would use only pure vegetable oil to make the fries in the future. However, after the decision to change from tallow to pure vegetable oil, the company realised that it could have difficulty in retaining customers who were accustomed to beef-flavoured fries.

According to Eric Scholsser, author of the best-selling book *Fast Food Nation: The Dark Side of the All-American Meal*,[5] 'For decades, McDonald's cooked its French fries in a mixture of about 7 per cent cottonseed oil and 93 per cent beef tallow. The mix gave the fries their unique flavour.' This unique flavour was lost when tallow was replaced by vegetable oil. To address this issue, McDonald's decided to add the 'natural flavour', i.e. the beef extract, which was added to the water while the potatoes were being partially cooked.

The 'beef fries' controversy attained greater dimensions in India as 85 per cent of the country's population was vegetarian. Non-vegetarian Indians also usually did not consume beef because Hindus consider cows to be holy and sacred. Eating beef is thus a sacrilege. A US-based Hindu plaintiff in one of the lawsuits said, 'I feel sick in the morning every day, like I want to vomit. Now it is always there in my mind that I have done this sin.'

Experts commented that the issue was not of adding beef extract to a supposedly vegetarian food item – it was more to do with the moral and ethical responsibility of a company to be honest about the products and services it offered. According to James Pizzirusso, founder of the Vegetarian Legal Action Network at George Washington University, 'Corporates need to pay attention to consumers who avoid certain food products for religious or health reasons, or because they have allergies. They say they are complying with the law in terms of disclosing their ingredients, but they should go beyond the law.'

Meanwhile, in June 2001 another class-action lawsuit was filed in the District Court in Travis County, Austin, Texas, on behalf of all Hindus in Texas, alleging that Hindu moral and religious principles had been violated by their unintentional consumption of French fries that were flavoured with beef. As public outrage intensified, McDonald's released a conditional apology on its website, admitting that the recipe for the fries used a 'a minuscule trace of beef flavoring, not tallow' (refer to Exhibit 2 for McDonald's response to the allegations).

McDonald's said that it issued an apology only to provide more details about its products to customers. A company spokesperson said, 'Customers responded to the news about the lawsuit. In the end, we are responding to those customers. We took a fresh look at how we could help customers get more information about natural flavors.'

Unsatisfied by the apology, Bharti said, 'Apology is good for the soul if it comes from the heart. It is not an unconditional apology. Why do they go around using words like "if there was any confusion" in their apology?' Further, news reports quoting company sources said that the apology did not mean McDonald's was admitting to claims that it misled million of customers by adding beef extract to its fries. Bharti said that the legal battle would continue and that McDonald's would have to issue an unconditional apology and pay a substantial amount of money. By this time, two more lawsuits had been filed in Illinois and New Jersey, taking the total number of cases to five.

The Aftermath

The courtroom battle had entered its 11th month when McDonald's announced that it would issue a new apology and pay $10 million to vegetarians and religious groups in a proposed settlement of all the lawsuits in March 2002. Around 60 per cent of this payment went to vegetarian organisations and the rest to various groups devoted to Hindus and Sikhs, children's nutrition and assistance, and kosher dietary practices.[6]

The company also decided to pay $4000 each to the 12 plaintiffs in the five lawsuits, and post a new and more detailed apology on the company website and in various other publications. McDonald's also decided to convene an advisory board to advise on vegetarian matters.

In April 2002 McDonald's planned to insert advertisements in newspapers apologising for its mistakes, 'We acknowledge that, upon our switch to vegetable oil in the early 1990s for the purpose of reducing cholesterol, mistakes were made in communicating to the public and customers about the ingredients in our French fries and hash browns. Those

Exhibit 2 McDonald's response to the allegations

It has always been McDonald's practice to share nutrition and ingredient information with our customers, including facts about our French fries. In the US, we consistently communicate this information through in-store posters, wallet-sized cards and various brochures, which offer a wide variety of dietary details.

McDonald's USA is always sensitive to customer concerns. Because it is our policy to communicate to customers, we regret if customers felt that the information we provided was not complete enough to meet their needs. If there was confusion, we apologise.

Meanwhile, here are the details of our French fry production in the US. A small amount of beef flavoring is added during potato processing – at the plant. After the potatoes are washed and steam-peeled, they are cut, blanched, dried, par-fried, and frozen. It is during the par-frying process at the plant that the natural flavoring is used. These fries are then shipped to our US restaurants. Our French fries are cooked in vegetable oil at our restaurants.

McDonald's 1990 switch to vegetable oil in the US as our standard cooking oil was made for nutritional reasons, to offer customers a cholesterol-free menu item. This nutrition announcement received national media coverage, widely broadcasting the facts about our switch and why we made it.

As a local business in 121 countries, our French fry process varies country-by-country to account for cultural or religious dietary considerations. For example, in predominantly Muslim countries – as in Southeast Asia, the Middle East and Africa – McDonald's strictly conforms to halal standards. This means no use of beef or pork flavorings or ingredients in our French fries. In India, where vegetarian concerns are paramount, no beef or pork flavorings are used in our vegetarian menu items.

Our 'McDonald's Nutrition Facts' brochure uses the term 'natural flavor' in the ingredient list for French fries. This description is in full compliance with and permitted by the US Food and Drug Administration (FDA).

Source: www.mcdonalds.com.

Exhibit 3 McDonald's: social responsibility statement

The McDonald's brand lives and grows where it counts the most – in the hearts of customers worldwide. We, in turn, hold our customers close to our heart, striving to do the right thing and giving back to the communities where we do business. At McDonald's, social responsibility is a part of our heritage and we are committed to building on it worldwide; some of our efforts to do so are described here.

Ronald McDonald House Charities – McDonald's supports one of the world's premier philanthropic organisations, Ronald McDonald House Charities (RMHC). RMHC provides comfort and care to children and their families by awarding grants to organisations through chapters in 31 countries and supporting more than 200 Ronald McDonald Houses in 19 countries.

Environmental Leadership – We take action around the world to develop innovative solutions to local environmental challenges. Ten years ago, we began a groundbreaking alliance with the Environmental Defense Fund (EDF) to reduce, reuse and recycle. Since then we eliminated 150 000 tons of packaging, purchased more than $3 billion of recycled products and recycled more than one million tons of corrugated cardboard in the US. We continue to set new waste reduction goals and are focusing on reducing energy usage in our restaurants. In Switzerland, we annually avoid 420 000 kilometers of trucking and, in turn, the use of 132 000 liters of diesel fuel by shipping restaurant supplies via rail. In Latin America, we have partnered with Conservation International to create and implement a sustainable agriculture program to protect the rainforests in Costa Rica and Panama. In Australia, we have committed to meet that country's Greenhouse Challenge to reduce greenhouse emissions.

Diversity – We believe a global team of talented, diverse employees, franchisees and suppliers is key to the company's ongoing success. We work to create and maintain an inclusive environment and expand the range of opportunities, thereby enabling all our people to reach their highest potential and generate the most value for McDonald's and the best experience for customers. McDonald's also provides opportunities for women and minorities to become franchisees and suppliers and offers a wide range of support to help them build their businesses. These efforts have paid off: Today, more than 30 per cent of McDonald's franchisees are women and minorities, and in 1999, we purchased about $3 billion worth of goods and services from women and minority suppliers.

Employment – Being a good corporate citizen begins with the way we treat our people. We are focused on developing people at every level, starting in our restaurants. We invest in training and development programs that encourage personal growth and higher levels of performance. These efforts help us attract and retain quality people and motivate superior performance.

Education – As one of the largest employers of youth, education is a key priority. So the company, our franchisees and RMHC proudly provide about $5 million in educational assistance through a variety of scholarship programs. We also honor teachers' dedication and commitment to education with the McDonald's Education Award.

Safety/quality – We are committed to ensuring safety and quality in every country where we do business. Accordingly, we set strict quality specifications for our products and work with suppliers worldwide to see that they are met. This includes ongoing testing in labs and on-site inspection of supplier facilities. Restaurant managers worldwide are extensively trained in safe handling and preparation of our food. Also, we continually review, modify and upgrade the equipment at PlayPlaces and Playlands to provide a safe play environment. Our quality control efforts also encompass animal welfare. Notably, we are working with a leading animal welfare expert in the US to implement an auditing process with our meat suppliers to ensure the safe and humane treatment of animals.

Source: www.mcdonalds.com.

mistakes included instances in which French fries and hash browns sold at US restaurants were improperly identified as vegetarian. We regret we did not provide these customers with complete information, and we sincerely apologise for any hardship that these miscommunications have caused among Hindus, vegetarians and others.'

Unhappy with the monetary compensation the company was offering, Bharti said, 'Wish I could do better in terms of money. But our focus was to change the fast-food industry, and this is a big victory for consumers in this country because we have brought this giant to this.'

Though $10 million was definitely a pittance for the $24 billion McDonald's, what remained to be seen was whether the case would set a precedent and make corporates throughout the world more aware and responsible towards their customers or not.

Questions

1 Analyse the various allegations levelled against McDonald's before the French fries controversy. Why do you think the company attracted so much hostility and criticism despite being the number one fast-food chain in the world?

2 Discuss the French fries controversy and critically comment on the company's stand that it had never claimed the fries were vegetarian. Do you think the company handled the controversy effectively? Give reasons to support your answer.

3 Discuss the steps taken by McDonald's to play down the French fries controversy, and critically comment on whether the company will be able to come out of this unscathed.

Further Reading

David Emery, 'Ratburger – Family Sues McDonald's After Allegedly Finding Rat's Head in Burger', www.urbanlegends.about.com, 4 April 2001.

Viji Sundaram, 'Where's the Beef? It's in Your French Fries', *India-West*, 9 April 2001.

'Lawsuit says McDonald's Uses Beef Fat in French Fries', www.seattleinsider.com, 2 May 2001.

Pais, J. Arthur, 'Harish Bharti Fears Dirty Tricks', www.rediff.com, 4 May 2001.

Nanda Harbaksh Singh, 'Hindu Zealots Throw Cow Dung at McDonald's', www.mcspotlight.org, 4 May 2001.

'Bharti's Beef With McDonald's', www.rediff.com, 4 May 2001.

Nirsha Perera, 'Bharti gets Clinching Evidence Against McDonald's', www.rediff.com, 5 May 2001.

'Indian Beef Protesters Raid McDonald's', www.europe.cnn.com, 5 May 2001.

'McDonald's India Denies Beef Flavouring', www.blonnet.com, 5 May 2001.

'No Beef Extract in French Fries, Claims McDonald's', www.rediff.com, 5 May 2001.

'Quit India, Sena tells McDonald's', www.hindu.com, 6 May 2001.

Arthur J. Pais, 'I've Been Violated for Over a Decade!' www.rediff.com, 6 May 2001.

Venugopal, Arun, 'Even the Pea Soup has Ham!', www.rediff.com, 9 May 2001.

Laurie Goodstein, 'For Hindus and Vegetarians, Surprise in McDonald's Fries', www.commondreams.org, May 2001.

Nirshan Perera, 'Will You Get Any McDonald's Money?' www.rediff.com, 1 June 2001.

Emma Brockes, 'Life After McLibel', www.mcspotlight.org, 7 June 2000.

Guha Suman Mozumder, 'Another Class Action Lawsuit Against McDonald's', *India Abroad*, June 2001.

Deborah Cohen, 'McDonald's Tries to Diffuse Meaty Fries Row', www.mcspotlight.org, 13 August 2001.

Vivian Chu, 'Big Mac Will Pay $10 million to Patrons if Offended', *Economic Times*, 9 March 2002.

'Big Mac Atones for Beef Fries With $10 million', *Business Line*, 9 March 2002.

Chidananda Rajghatta, 'McDonald's Apologises, to Pay $10 million to Veggies', *Times of India*, 9 March 2002.

'McFacts about the McDonald's Coffee Lawsuit', www.lawandhelp.com.

www.mcspotlight.org.

www.mcdonalds.com.

References

1. A class-action suit is a suit filed to protect the interests of groups of individuals who are affected or may be affected by a perceived fraud or misconduct of a similar nature. The number of people could be as few as under 10 to millions. Typically, class-action suits in the US drag on for years and very often parties settle out of court within the first year of filing.
2. Thinly sliced, finger-sized pieces of potato, deep fried and served with a sprinkling of salt.
3. Tallow refers to shortening made from beef fat.
4. Cholesterol is a soft, waxy substance found in the lipids (fats) in the bloodstream and in all body cells. It forms cell membranes, hormones and other needed tissues in the body. However, a very high level of cholesterol in the blood causes cardiovascular diseases and leads to heart attacks and strokes. Foods rich in saturated fats cause the cholesterol level to rise thereby increasing the chances of cardiovascular diseases.
5. The book provides a detailed account of the negative aspects associated with the products and operations of fast-food giants such as Burger King and McDonald's.
6. The term 'kosher' is used to describe foods or other animal products that are fit for consumption according to the religious rules of the Jewish community. By ensuring that the food is kosher, the Jews believe that they recognise the value of the life taken, while at the same time integrating religion into their dietary practices.

Source: © 2002, ICFAI Center for Management Research. All rights reserved. Reprinted with permission. www.icmindia.org.

This case was written by A. Mukund, ICFAI Center for Management Research (ICMR). It is intended to be used as a basis for class discussion rather than to illustrate either effective or ineffective handling of a management situation.

The case was compiled from published sources.

Case 2.3 Coke and Pepsi Learn to Compete in India

The Beverage Battlefield

In 2003 Jagdeep Kapoor, chairman of Samsika Marketing Consultants in Mumbai (formerly Bombay), commented that 'Coke lost a number of years over errors. But at last it seems to be getting its positioning right'. Similarly, Ronald McEachern, PepsiCo's Asia chief, asserted 'India is the beverage battlefield for 2003'.

The experience of the world's two giant soft drinks companies in India during the 1990s and the beginning of the new millennium was not a happy one, even though the governments had opened its doors wide to foreign companies. Both companies experienced a range of unexpected problems and difficult situations that led them to recognise that competing in India requires special knowledge, skills and local expertise. In many ways, Coke and Pepsi managers had to learn the hard way that 'what works here' does not always 'work there'. In spring 2003 Alex von Behr, the president of Coca-Cola India admitted ruefully, 'The environment in India is challenging, but we're learning how to crack it'.

The Indian Soft Drinks Industry

In India over 45 per cent of the soft drinks industry in 1993 consisted of small manufacturers. Their combined business was worth $3.2 million dollars. Leading producers included Parle Agro (hereafter 'Parle'), Pure Drinks, Modern Foods, and McDowells. They offered carbonated cola drinks, orange, and lemon-lime beverages. Coca-Cola Corporation (hereafter 'Coca-Cola') was only a distant memory to most Indians at that time. The company had been present in the Indian market from 1958 until its withdrawal in 1977, following a dispute with the government over its trade secrets. After decades in the market, Coca-Cola chose to leave India rather than cut its equity stake to 40 per cent and hand over its secret formula for the syrup.

Following Coca-Cola's departure, Parle became the market leader and established thriving export franchise businesses in Dubai, Kuwait, Saudi Arabia, and Oman in the Gulf, along with Sri Lanka. It set up production in Nepal and Bangladesh, and served distant markets in Tanzania, Britain, the Netherlands and the United States. Parle invested heavily in image advertising at home, establishing the dominance of its flagship brand, Thums Up.

Thums Up is a brand associated with a 'job well done' and personal success. These are persuasive messages for its target market of young people aged 15 to 24. Parle has been careful in the past not to call Thums Up a cola drink, so it has avoided direct comparison with Coke and Pepsi, the world's brand leaders.

The soft drinks market in India is composed of six product segments: cola, 'cloudy lemon', orange, 'soda' (carbonated water), mango and 'clear lemon', in order of importance. Cloudy lemon and clear lemon together make up the lemon-lime segment. Prior to the arrival of foreign producers in India, the fight for local dominance was between Parle's Thums Up and Pure Drinks' Campa Cola.

In 1988 the industry had experienced a dramatic shakeout following a government warning that BVO, an essential ingredient in locally produced soft drinks, was carcinogenic. Producers either had to resort to using a costly imported substitute, estergum, or they had to finance their own R&D in order to find a substitute ingredient. Many failed and quickly withdrew from the industry.

Competing with the segment of carbonated soft drinks is another beverage segment composed of non-carbonated fruit drinks. These are a growth industry because Indian consumers perceive fruit drinks to be natural, healthy, and tasty. The leading brand has traditionally been Parle's Frooti, a mango-flavoured drink, which was also exported to franchisees in the United States, Britain, Portugal, Spain and Mauritius.

Opening Up the Indian Market in 1991

In June 1991 India experienced an economic crisis of exceptional severity, triggered by the rise in imported oil prices following the first Gulf War (after Iraq's invasion of Kuwait). Foreign exchange reserves fell as non-resident Indians (NRIs) cut back on repatriation of their savings, imports were tightly controlled across all sectors and industrial production fell while inflation was rising. A new government took office in June 1991 led by Prime Minister Narasimha Rao. Inspired by Finance Minister Dr Manmohan Singh, the government introduced measures to stabilise the economy in

547

the short term and launched a fundamental restructuring programme to ensure medium-term growth. Results were dramatic. By 1994 inflation was halved, exchange reserves were greatly increased, exports were growing and foreign investors were looking at India, a leading Big Emerging Market, with new eyes.

The turnaround could not be overstated; one commentator said, 'India has been in economic depression for so long that everything except the snake-charmers, cows and the Taj Mahal has faded from the memory of the world'. For many years, the outside world had viewed the Indian Government as unfriendly to foreign investors. Outside investment had been allowed only in high-tech sectors and was almost entirely prohibited in consumer goods sectors. The 'principle of indigenous availability' had specified that if an item could be obtained anywhere else within the country, imports of similar items were forbidden. As a result of this policy, India became self-reliant in its defence industry, developing both nuclear and space programmes. In contrast, Indian consumers had little choice of products or brands, and no guarantees of quality or reliability.

Following liberalisation of the Indian economy in 1991 and introduction of the New Industrial Policy intended to dismantle complicated trade rules and regulations, foreign investment increased dramatically. Beneficiary industries included processed foods, software, engineering plastics, electronic equipment, power generation and petroleum generation. A commentator observed, 'In the 1970s and 1980s, it was almost antinational to advocate foreign investment. Today the Prime Minister and Finance Minister are wooing foreign investors.'

Foreign companies that had successfully pioneered entry into the Indian market many decades earlier, despite all the stringent rules, quickly increased their equity stakes under the new rules from 40 per cent to 51 per cent. These long-established companies included global giants such as Unilever, Procter & Gamble, Pfizer, Hoechst, BAT and Philips (of the Netherlands).

Coca-Cola and PepsiCo Enter the Indian Market

Despite its huge population, India had not been considered by foreign beverage producers to be an important market in the past. In addition to the deterrents imposed by the government through its austere trade policies, rules and regulations, local demand for carbonated drinks in India was very low, compared to countries at a similar stage of economic development. In 1989 the average Indian was buying only three bottles a year. This compared to per capita consumption rates of 11 bottles a year in Bangladesh and 13 in Pakistan, India's two neighbours.

PepsiCo

PepsiCo lodged a joint venture application to enter India in July 1986. It had selected two local partners, Voltas and Punjab Agro. This application was approved under the name 'Pepsi Foods Ltd' by the government of Rajiv Gandhi in September 1988. As expected, very stringent conditions were imposed on the venture. Sales of soft drink concentrate to local bottlers could not exceed 25 per cent of total sales for the new venture. This limit also included processing of fruits and vegetables by Pepsi Foods Ltd. Robert Beeby, CEO of Pepsi-Cola International, said at that time: 'We're willing to go so far with India because we wanted to make sure we get an early entry while the market is developing.'

In May 1990 the government mandated that Pepsi Food's products be promoted under the name 'Lehar Pepsi' ('lehar' meaning 'wave'). Foreign collaboration rules in force at the time prohibited use of foreign brand names on products intended for sale inside India. Other examples of this policy were Maruti Suzuki, Carrier Aircon, L&T Honeywell, Wilkinson's Wiltech, Modi-Champion, and Modi-Xerox.

In keeping with local tastes, Pepsi Foods launched Lehar 7UP in the clear lemon category, along with Lehar Pepsi. Marketing and distribution were focused in the north and west around the major cities of Delhi and Mumbai. An aggressive pricing policy on the one-litre bottles had a severe impact on the local producer, Pure Drinks. The market leader, Parle, pre-empted any further pricing moves by Pepsi Foods by introducing a new 250 ml bottle that sold for the same price as its 200 ml bottle.

Pepsi Foods struggled to fight off local competition from Pure Drinks' Campa Cola, Duke's lemonade and various brands of Parle. Aware of its difficulties, Pepsi Foods approached Parle in December 1991 to offer an alliance. Parle declined the offer, choosing to stand its ground and continuing to fight to preserve its number one position.

The fight for dominance intensified in 1993 with Pepsi Food's launch of two new brands, Slice and Teem, along with the introduction of fountain sales. At this time, market shares in the cola segment were 60 per cent for Parle (down from 70 per cent), 26 per cent for Pepsi Foods, and 10 per cent for Pure Drinks.

Coca-Cola

In May 1990, Coca-Cola attempted to re-enter India by means of a proposed joint venture with a local bottling company owned by the giant Indian conglomerate, Godreg. The government of Rajiv Gandhi turned down this application just as PepsiCo's application was being approved. Undeterred, Coca-Cola made its return to India by joining forces with Britannia Industries India Ltd, a local producer of snack foods. The new venture was called Britco Foods. In 1993 Coca-Cola filed an application to create a 100 per cent-owned soft drinks company, Coca-Cola India.

The arrival of Coca-Cola in the Indian soft drinks industry forced local small producers to consider extreme survival measures. The small Delhi-based company, Pure Drinks, tried to revamp its bottling alliance with Coca-Cola from earlier years, even offering to withdraw its own leading brand, Campa Cola, as an inducement to

Coca-Cola. Campa Cola's brand share at the time was 10 per cent. However, Coca-Cola had its sights set on a different partner, Parle.

Among local producers, it was believed at that time that Coca-Cola would not take market share away from local companies because the beverage market was itself growing consistently from year to year. Yet this belief did not stop individual local producers from trying to align themselves with the market leader. Thus, in July 1993 Parle offered to sell its leading brands including Thums Up, Limca, Citra, Gold Spot and Mazaa. It chose to retain ownership only of Frooti and a soda (carbonated water) called Bisleri.

As a result of Parle's offer, two new ventures were set up to bottle and market both companies' products. The marketing venture would provide advertising, media services, and promotional and sales support. Parle's chief, Ramesh Chauhan, was named chairman and Coca-Cola staffed the managing director's position. Parle held 49 per cent of the marketing venture but took an equal 50 per cent stake in the bottling venture.

Fast Forward to the New Millennium
Seasonal Sales Promotions – the 2000 Navrartri Campaign

In India the summer season for soft drink consumption lasts 70–75 days from mid-April to June. During this time over 50 per cent of the year's carbonated beverages are consumed across the country. The second-highest season for consumption lasts only 20–25 days during the cultural festival of Navrartri ('Nav' means nine and 'rarti' means night). This is a traditional Gujarati festival and it goes on for nine nights in the state of Gujarat, in the western part of India. Mumbai also has a significant Gujarati population that is considered part of the target market for this campaign.

As Sunil Kapoor, regional marketing manager for Coca-Cola India stated, 'As part of the "think local – act local" business plan, we have tried to involve the masses in Gujarat with "Thums Up Toofani Ramjhat": with 20 000 free passes issued, one per Thums Up bottle. ['Toofan' means a thunderstorm and 'ramjhat' means 'let's dance,' so together these words convey the idea of a 'fast dance.'] There are a number of [retail] on-site activities too, such as the "buy one – get one free" scheme and lucky draws where one can win a free trip to Goa.' (Goa is an independent Portuguese-speaking state on the west coast of India, that is famed for its beaches and tourist resorts.)

For its part, PepsiCo also participates in annual Navrarti celebrations through massive sponsorships in 'garba' competitions in selected venues in Gujarat. ('Garba' is the name of a dance, which is performed by women during the Navratri festival.) In 2000 Deepak Jolly, executive vice-president for PepsiCo India, commented: 'For the first time, Pepsi has tied up with the Gujarati TV channel, Zee Alpha, to telecast "Navrartri Utsav 2000 at Mumbai" on all nine nights. ['Utsav' means festival.] Then there is the mega offer for the people of Ahmedabad, Baroda, Surat, and Rajkot where every refill of a case of Pepsi 300 ml bottles will fetch one kilo of Basmati rice free.' (These are four cities located in the state of Gujarat. Basmati rice is considered to be a premium-quality rice. After the initial purchase of a 300 ml bottle, consumers can get refills at reduced rates at select stores.)

During the Navrartri festival, both companies are extremely generous with give-aways in their sales promotions. For example, in 2000 Pepsi Foods offered a free Kit-Kat with every 1.5 litre bottle and a packet of Polos (hard candies like 'Lifesavers') with each 500 ml bottle of Pepsi and Mirinda.

The 2002 Summer TV Campaign

In 2002 Pepsi Foods took the lead in the clear lime category with 7UP leading its category, followed by Coca-Cola's Sprite brand. On 7 March 2002 it launched a new summer campaign for 7UP. This date was chosen to coincide with the India–Zimbabwe one-day cricket series. The new campaign slogan was 'Keep It Cool' to emphasise the product attribute of refreshment.

A nationwide television advertising campaign was designed with the objectives of growing the category and building brand salience. The national campaign was to be reinforced with regionally adapted TV campaigns, outdoor activities, and retail promotions.

PepsiCo's ad spending for 7UP was not comparable to the level invested in its flagship brand Pepsi-Cola because the clear lime segment in 2002 was minuscule, accounting for just 4.5 per cent of the total carbonated soft drinks market. This was equal to about 250–270 million cases. The cloudy lemon segment is more than twice this size, with 10 per cent market share; carbonated orange drinks account for about 15 per cent.

7UP was being sold in 250 ml, 300 ml and 500 ml bottles, and in 200 ml bottles in southern states. The industry trend was pushing towards 200 ml bottles in order to increase frequency of purchase and volume of consumption. Pepsi Foods rolled out its Mirinda Lemon, Apple and Orange in 200 ml bottles in the Delhi market, following similar market launches in Punjab and Uttar Pradesh in the previous year.

In the past celebrity actors, Amitabh Bachchan and Govinda, who are famous male stars of the Indian movie industry, had endorsed Mirinda Lemon. This world-famous industry is referred to as 'Bollywood' (the Hollywood of India, based in Bombay).

Both Coca-Cola and PepsiCo routinely keep close track of the success of their seasonal advertising campaigns in India through use of marketing research agencies. Coca-Cola has used ORG-MARG, while Pepsi Foods has worked with IMRB. ORG-MARG uses its weekly 'Ad Track' to study spontaneous ad recall among 1000 male and female respondents aged 12–49 in 17 cities. IMRB's 'Perception Analyser System' surveys 15 to 30-year-olds in four cities. Responses are sought on measures of likeability of the ad and intention to buy.

549

strategy in June 2002. Despite this, Motorola continued to lose its market share, and analysts were sceptical about its continued dominance in the Chinese market.

Background

The history of US-based Motorola's presence in China dates back to the late 1980s, when Motorola established a representative office in Beijing in 1987. It exported telecommunications gear and semiconductors to China and employed around 600 people to market its products. With increasing competition and production costs, Motorola decided to shift some of its manufacturing activities to China. In 1992 Motorola established Motorola (China) Electronics Ltd and opened a manufacturing facility at Tianjin in north China.

Over the years, Motorola expanded its business in China to various segments, such as personal communication sector (PCS), global telecom solutions sector (GTSS), semiconductor products sector (SPS), commercial, government and industrial solutions sector (CGISS), broadcast communications sector (BCS) and integrated electronics systems sector (IESS).

In 1998 Motorola relocated its north Asia headquarters to Beijing from Hong Kong. By 2000, Motorola was the leader in the mobile handset industry, with around 31 per cent market share. In 2002, revenues from China were reported to be 47 billion yuan ($5.7 billion) – 13 per cent of Motorola's total global revenues – and it employed around 13 000 employees in its 18 R&D facilities and 26 sales offices across China. It was also one of the largest exporters from China – exporting goods worth $3.6 billion.

The Recipe for Success

Initially Motorola was wary about setting up manufacturing facilities in China and put up a makeshift plant in Tianjin to manufacture paging devices. However, by 2003, Motorola was regarded as the most successful foreign company in China. When asked to comment on the reasons for its success, Lai Bingrong, senior vice president of Motorola in China said, 'Understand Chinese culture, pay respect to Chinese conditions, do not be self-opinionated, do not always blame others.'[4] Initially Motorola adopted a four-point strategy in China, which was as follows:

1 investment/technology transfer
2 management localisation
3 local sourcing
4 joint ventures/co-operative projects.

Investments and Joint Ventures

Initially, Motorola set up a plant at a total cost of $120 million in the Tianjin economic and technology development area for manufacturing pagers, simple integrated circuits and cellular phones. In the next phase of its investment of around $400 million, the company built its second plant for manufacturing automotive electronics, advanced microprocessors, walkie-talkie systems and fabricated silicon wafers. In addition to its wholly owned manufacturing plants, between 1995

and 2002, Motorola entered into nine joint ventures with Chinese firms to expand its presence in the market and also increase its production capacity.

Through these joint ventures, Motorola produced pagers, smart cards and mobile handsets that were marketed in China. The joint ventures helped Motorola gain access to the Chinese market without establishing additional manufacturing plants. These joint ventures also resulted in savings for the company.

In line with its four-point strategy, Motorola invested in research and development centres in China. In 1999 Motorola established the Motorola China Research and Development Institute in Beijing. The company announced that its research centre would focus on technological development and innovation. Motorola's R&D institute conducted research in the areas of communication, software, and semiconductors. Motorola also established a production procedure lab, an analytical lab, and software and equipment labs for developing new technologies that would make China a high-technology manufacturing hub. By 2003 Motorola had established 18 research centres in China.

Motorola employed around 650 engineers for its research activities in China. The company also entered into research partnerships with Chinese universities and institutes. Motorola gave scholarships to students and faculties of around eight Chinese universities. It also donated computers, and offered opportunities to college students to work as interns in the company and get acquainted with high technologies.

Over the years, Motorola entered into agreements with two Chinese telephone service providers – China Unicom and China Mobile – for installing telecom networks across the country. It also provided GSM technology to the mobile service vendors Hubei Mobile Communications[5] and Eastern Communications Co. Ltd (popularly known as Eastcom).[6] It was reported that Motorola had won a number of contracts from Chinese mobile service providers to install telecom networks across China.

Management Localisation

The company realised that in order to increase its market share, it had to hire more Chinese employees. However, Motorola also realised that the Chinese managers were not familiar with Western management concepts and that the country lacked managerial talent. Though the Chinese were good at basics, they lacked practical application of theories. Thus, Motorola established the Motorola University in 1993 to train young Chinese people to take up global managerial positions. The mission of the university was 'to train and develop world-class staff for Motorola'. The university campus was situated near Beijing airport and had Western-style restaurants, conference rooms, pool tables and tennis courts.

Motorola University had a rigorous training programme known as China Accelerated Management Program (CAMP) for its Chinese employees. CAMP consisted of six weeks classroom learning and 14 months' on-the-job training, which included action learning, project management, coaching and rotation of employees through Motorola's worldwide facilities.

The training was imparted thrice a year and in each cycle the university trained around 15 people. The syllabus for CAMP included sections on market economy, value creation, business process design and benchmarking. In addition to these topics, they were trained in the areas of team building, situational leadership, and presentation style. Candidates had to go through a rigorous selection process to qualify for CAMP. Aspirants who wanted to join the program had to be nominated by their superiors. The employees underwent individual interviews and a test in the English language. After clearing these, they appeared for a 32-part structured interview where they had to answer questions like, 'Do you think you make decisions quickly?', and 'If a co-worker wanted to discuss a personal problem with you, what would you do?' Commenting on the selection procedure, one of the university staff said, 'The screening is meant to explore eight skill areas, including cognitive and administrative skills. It also surfaces "soft" characteristics such as motivation, a capacity for empathy, a talent for self-organisation.'[7]

In addition to CAMP, Motorola also provided in-house training to its employees. The engineering recruits were sent to its manufacturing plants in other countries like the US, Singapore and Hong Kong for on-the-job training in designing and other high-tech manufacturing procedures. It also initiated a career management programme called 'Cadres 2000'. Under this, Motorola selected around 20 top employees for a leadership training programme and posted them in Motorola manufacturing plants across the world.

Sourcing Locally

To the extent possible, Motorola sourced components from the local Chinese players. This reduced its cost and also complied with the government's requirement that MNCs working in China had to source a certain percentage of components from the local firms. Motorola provided training to the local suppliers to improve their standards by extending technological and managerial support. It also helped them to increase their productivity and quality levels, and even assisted them to enter global markets. Motorola also encouraged its foreign suppliers to set up plants in China. According to reports, by 2002, around 45 Motorola suppliers had set up manufacturing bases in China.

In order to inculcate a competitive spirit among its Chinese suppliers, Motorola conducted exhibitions, such as Teaming for Excellence, which allowed its suppliers to showcase their talent and components. By 2002 Motorola had 176 direct suppliers and 700 indirect suppliers, and the usage of local components increased from 58.85 per cent in 2000 to 65 per cent in 2001.

Building an Image

Motorola also focused on building its brand among the Chinese. It installed glow signs in busy market areas and placed advertisements in print and television to increase awareness among consumers about the company. It was reported that due to its extensive marketing the Chinese

associated Motorola with quality and did not mind paying a premium price for its products. The company also opened up Motorola exclusive showrooms in the upmarket areas such as Shanghai and Beijing, offering the latest mobile handset models.

Motorola also introduced a new retailing concept called *Motorola Towns*. These towns were based on the Nike Town in the US and aimed at providing a unique retailing experience to consumers. In Motorola Towns mobile handsets were displayed and consumers could walk in and use various technological gadgets without spending any money. According to company sources, the concept was not only about selling the company's products but it also allowed consumers to learn about the latest technological trends and connect them emotionally with the company. According to company sources, Motorola Towns would provide the company with feedback about its products. Motorola encouraged customers to express honest opinions about the sample products they had used and to suggest any additional features they would like to have.

Along with its marketing activities, Motorola concentrated on building its image as a good corporate citizen in China. Motorola associated itself with 'Project Hope' which was initiated by the China Youth Development Foundation. The project not only aimed at spreading primary education, but also offered financial assistance to school drop-outs in rural areas for completing their education. As part of its assistance to Project Hope, Motorola donated huge amounts and established *Motorola Hope Schools*. The company also donated teaching equipment and provided training for the schoolteachers.

According to Motorola sources, from 1994 it provided financial aid to more than 9000 children to complete their school education and constructed around 40 Motorola Hope Schools in about 25 provinces. It also established multi-media labs in the schools and trained more than 500 teachers to enhance the educational standards. To encourage children to read, it set up Hope Libraries in about 30 schools.

To strengthen Project Hope, Motorola undertook a Motorola Hope Tour in which the company's top executives visited underdeveloped areas in the country to learn about the local conditions. Motorola also organised programmes like 'Green China' to protect the environment in the country. Commenting on Motorola's role in the social responsibility area, former Motorola CEO Gary Tooker said, 'We seek a partnership with China for mutual development. Closely linked with this strategy is our promise to be a worthy corporate citizen of China, participating in and contributing to the building of a caring and responsible society.'[8]

Thanks to its focused strategy in the Chinese market, Motorola was the leader in the mobile handset market with a share of 31 per cent in 2000. However, with increasing competition Motorola started experiencing a decline in its market share and by 2002 this was down to 28 per cent.

Change in Recipe

With increasing competition and declining market share, Motorola announced a new five-year '2 + 3 + 3 strategy' in June 2002.

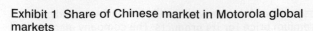

Exhibit 1 Share of Chinese market in Motorola global markets

Year	China's share in global revenues (in %)
1999	10
2000	12
2001	13
2002	14

Source: Motorola annual reports.

The new strategy was announced by Tim Chen who took over as president of Motorola China in 2002. This strategy was aimed at strengthening the company's position in China as it had become a strategically important market for Motorola. Analysts reported that while Motorola experienced declining sales in the other markets across the world, in China, its sales were on the rise. According to company sources, China's share in Motorola's global revenues was increasing over the years (refer to Exhibit 1).

Commenting on the new strategy Tim said that it was an extension of Motorola's earlier four-point strategy and added:

> The core of the new strategy is the same as that of the four-point strategy: win-win for Motorola and China. Based on the new strategy, Motorola will continue to be a good corporate citizen in China, to deeply root itself in China and to be integrated into the China society. Our final goal is to become a genuine Chinese company by establishing an unshakable partnership with China. The 2 + 3 + 3 strategy will ensure our continuous success in China.[9]

The new strategy focused on three broad goals for the company in the Chinese market. All the numbers in the new strategy – 2 + 3 + 3 – signified specific goals for the company. The new strategy was as follows:

- The number '2' referred to two goals: developing China into a worldwide manufacturing and R&D centre.
- The first '3' referred to three growth areas identified by the company – semiconductors, broadband and digital trunking systems (the mobile-communications systems used by police, taxi drivers, and delivery fleets).
- The second '3' symbolised three goals of Motorola to be achieved by 2006. These were to increase the value of its annual production to $10 billion, and its investments to $10 billion and to purchase $10 billion worth of components from Chinese markets.

However, analysts were divided on whether Motorola would be able to retain its market leadership position in China. While some felt that with its long-standing profile in the Chinese market, Motorola would be able to retain its position, others said that with the increasing local competition, it would be very difficult for it to do so.

Referring to Motorola's new strategy, *Business Week* wrote:

> A critical part of Motorola's strategy is to show Beijing its commitment to the Chinese economy. That's especially important given that local rivals are usually government-owned and have good guanxi, or connections, with local officials. Motorola, though, contends that it is as Chinese as any of its rivals, with more than 10 000 employees in the country – roughly the same number as Ningbo Bird.[10] And since Motorola isn't blind to Beijing's desire to boost China's science and technology prowess, it recently announced a $100 million expansion of an R&D center in the capital. Chinese officials appreciate the effort.[11]

Motorola was confident of its success in the Chinese market and to ensure this announced that it would collaborate with its competitors and sell cell phone chips to TCL and Eastcom.

The Road Ahead

Motorola experienced a slowdown in sales in China with the outbreak of severe acute respiratory syndrome (SARS)[12] in early 2003, which disrupted normal life in China for over a month. It was reported that weekly sales of mobile handsets (which constituted a major share of Motorola's revenues in China) in mainland China were down by 40 per cent in the last week of April, resulting in a drop in revenues for cellular companies. Motorola was forced to close down its Beijing office for a week as one of its employees was diagnosed with SARS.

Unlike other multinationals which deferred their investment plans in China, Motorola announced that it would go ahead with its plans to invest further. To show solidarity with the Chinese authorities, Zafirovski visited Beijing in May 2003, defying the travel ban on the country. Addressing reporters, he said, 'We are optimistic about China's economy and our commitment to China is not changed at all. This confidence is based on Motorola's deep-rooted investment in China and its close co-operation and partnership with the Chinese government and enterprise.'[13] Motorola also donated $1.4 million worth of communication equipment to fight SARS.

Meanwhile, Motorola announced a decline in its second quarter earnings for the year 2003 due to problems in its Asian operations. While the company blamed SARS for the decline in its earnings, analysts pointed out that increasing competition was the real reason. They said that during the period Motorola experienced a decline in its market share, the local players had increased share to 20 per cent.

For the same period, Motorola's sales declined by around 58 per cent. Commenting on Motorola's position in the Chinese market, Paul Sagawa, analyst, Sanford C. Bernstein, said, 'There are very aggressive Chinese handset manufacturers that are fighting for their lives and fighting for market share, and that's hitting Motorola smack-dab in

the forehead. Motorola is dealing with excess inventory, desperate competitors, and cut-throat pricing. That's why it's losing market share.'[14]

A major problem faced by Motorola in China was the piling-up of inventory. According to company sources, Motorola had an inventory of around 30 million handsets and it would take around six to nine months to dispose them. With increasing inventory, Motorola resorted to heavy discounting and price wars, which only compounded its woes. It was reported that the average selling price of Motorola handsets declined by 10 per cent in the second quarter of 2003.

In addition to the above problems, Motorola also faced exodus at senior managerial level. In September 2003 Chen resigned to join Microsoft. Analysts were quick to point out that it was a very big loss for the company, as Chen was popular with both Motorola partners and distributors and had also developed a very good rapport with the Chinese officials.

Analysts also pointed out that with the slowing-down of demand in the urban areas, mobile companies need to focus more on smaller cities and rural areas. However, for multinationals such as Motorola, which did not have strong distribution networks in the rural areas, it would be difficult to make inroads compared to the local players.

Further, the global slump in the semiconductor market after the dotcom burst was also hurting Motorola badly. Motorola invested heavily in the semiconductor chip plant at Tianjin during the dotcom boom. In 2003, Motorola announced that it would sell its chip plant to Shanghai-based Semiconductor Manufacturing International Corp. (SMIC). Analysts were of the opinion that this would streamline Motorola's operations in China and the company would be able to focus more on the mobile handset business. In October 2003 Motorola launched 21 new mobile handset models in China. Analysts were of the opinion that the success of these new models would decide the future of Motorola in China.

Questions

1 According to company sources, Motorola wanted to become more Chinese than the local Chinese companies. Explain the strategies adopted by Motorola to gain popularity with Chinese consumers. How far do you think these strategies helped Motorola become a successful company in China?

2 Though Motorola was successful in China, many analysts feel that with competition in the mobile handset market increasing, it would be difficult for the company to sustain its competitive position. Do you agree with the analysts? What according to you is the future of the mobile handset industry in China and where do you see Motorola in the changing scenario?

Further Reading

Pete Engardio, 'Motorola in China: A Great Leap Forward', *Business Week*, 17 May 1993.

Bernard Avishai, 'In China, It's the "Year of the Manager"', www.fastcompany.com, November 1995.

Karl Schoenberger, 'Motorola Bets Big on China', *Fortune*, 27 May 1996.

Bill Menezes, 'Pricing Hurts Motorola', www.wirelessweek.com, 13 July 1998.

Kuhl, Craig, 'Motorola Takes Chinese Staff Back to School', www.multichannel.com, 10 January 1999.

Dexter Roberts, 'China's Local Cell-Phone Boys Get Tough', *Business Week*, 20 September 1999.

Yu Donghui, 'How Did Motorola Succeed in China?', www.ultrachina.com, 2 June 2000.

'Motorola Continues Success in China Market With $55 Million GSM Business in Hubei', *Business Wire*, 11 June 2000.

Mei Fong, 'Motorola Lusts for China', *Forbes*, 13 July 2000.

He, Zhong, 'Chinese Mobile Phone Market', www.ultrachina.com, 18 August 2000.

'Motorola's Investment in China Amounts to 28.5 Billion Yuan', www.pfeng.peopledaily.com, 12 September 2000.

zonghui Yu, 'Why Motorola Invested Additional RMB16 Billion in China', www.ultrachina.com, 29 September 2000.

Allen T. Cheng, 'Who Will Win China's Phone Wars?', www.asiaweek.com, 1 December 2000.

'Motorola to Invest $10B in China by 2006', www.electronic-news.com, 11 July 2001.

Steven Fyffe, 'Chasing the Dragon – Motorola fires up its investment in China', www.ebasia.com, January 2002.

'Domestic Mobile Market in Shake-up', www.fpeng.peopledaily.com, 9 May 2002.

Borton, James, 'Motorola University Scores High Grades in China', www.atimes.com, 4 June 2002.

'Chinese Home Appliance Makers Turning to Cell Phones', www.fpeng.peopledaily.com, 5 June 2002.

'Motorola China Announces 5-Year Strategy', www.motorola.com, 6 June 2002.

'Motorola Marks 10th anniversary of investment in Tianjin', www.motorola.com, 11 September 2002.

'China Becomes World's Leading Mobile Phone Market!', www.fiducia-china.com, 2002.

Bruce Einhorn, Dexter Roberts and Roger O. Crockett, 'Winning in China', *Business Week*, 27 January 2003.

'The Local Touch', *The Economist*, 6 March 2003.

'SARS Case Shuts Down Motorola Offices in China', www.austing.bizjournals.com, 6 May 2003.

'Motorola China not for Turning', www.fpeng.peopledaily.com, 19 May 2003.

Caroline Daniel, 'Motorola Keeps an Eye on China Numbers', *Financial Times*, 28 July 2003.

'News Conference: The New Chairman of Motorola China', www.english.enorth.com.cn, 16 September 2003.

Bruce Einhorn, 'Motorola's China Challenge', *Business Week*, 23 September 2003.

'Motorola to Sell China Fab to SMIC', www.eetimes.com, 23 October 2003.

Rose, Barbara, 'Motorola to Sell China Chip Plant', www.chicagotribune.com, 24 October 2003.

'Motorola Sells $1B Chip Plant in China', www.bizjournals.com, 24 October 2003.

'Motorola Slims Semiconductor Unit in China', www.techweb.com, 27 October 2003.

www.ultrachina.com.

www.apspg.motorola.com.

www.motorola.com.

www.aberdeen.com.

References

1 'Motorola China not for Turning', www.english.peopledaily.com, 19 May 2003.

2 [Germany], Europe's largest manufacturer of automobiles, was the fourth largest automobile producer in the world. Volkswagen manufactured a variety of automobiles including cars, trucks and vans. The company's major car brands included Golf, Passat, Audi, Jetta, Lamborghini, Bentley and Beetle.

3 World's leading business magazine published in the US.

4 'How Motorola Succeeds in China', www.ultrachina.com, 6 June 2000.

5 Hubei Mobile Communications is a subsidiary of China Mobile – China's largest mobile communications operator. It provides mobile voice, data, IP phone, multimedia transmission and many other value-added services in Hubei Province (situated in central China).

6 Eastcom is the largest listed company in the mobile communication industry in China. The company provides integrated solutions in mobile telecommunications network, operation and maintenance of project network, value-added services of communication systems, upstream industry of mobile communications as well as optical industry.

7 Bernard Avishai, 'In China, It's the "Year of the Manager"', www.fastcompany.com, November 1995.

8 www.apspg.motorola.com.

9 'Motorola China Announces 5-Year Strategy', www.motorola.com, 6 June 2002.

10 Established in 1992, Ningbo Bird is engaged in development and manufacturing of electronic communication products. Its product range includes system equipments, handheld PCs, mobile phone accessories and pagers, etc.

11 Bruce Einhorn, Dexter Roberts and Roger O. Crockett. 'Winning in China', *Business Week*, 27 January 2003.

12 Severe acute respiratory syndrome (SARS) is a viral respiratory illness caused by a corona virus, called SARS-associated coronavirus (SARS-CoV). It first broke out in Asia in early 2003.

13 'Motorola China Not for Turning', www.english.peopledaily.com, 19 May 2003.

14 'Motorola Blames View on SARS: Street Sees China Price War', www.c114.net, 10 June 2003.

This case was written by K. Subhadra, under the direction of Sanjib Dutta, ICFAI Center for Management Research (ICMR). It is intended to be used as a basis for class discussion rather than to illustrate either effective or ineffective handling of a management situation. Reprinted with permission. www.icmrindia.org.

The case was compiled from published sources.

Case 3.2 Adidas: The Marketing Policy for the European Market

The sporting goods market, and more specifically the athletic shoes market, is enjoying a period of strong growth. Athletic shoes are associated with values of freedom, well-being and success, and can be found in the closets of all generations. The European athletic shoes market is up-market oriented, with a growing importance given to fashion and brands. The three market leaders, Nike, Adidas and Reebok, are developing increasingly sophisticated marketing strategies to attract consumers in search of the newest products.

In view of the growing worldwide craze for running, Adidas has decided to reinforce its marketing actions in order to increase its position on the running shoes market. Written in close collaboration with the marketing team of Adidas, this case study presents the Adidas corporation, the athletic shoes market, its competitive environment, and various segments of the running shoes market.

Presentation of the Company

The Adidas group is a global leader in the sporting goods industry and offers a broad portfolio of products. The group possesses three major brands: Adidas (footwear, apparel, accessories), Reebok (footwear, apparel and accessories) and Taylor Made (golf equipment). It employs more than 31 000 people and owns 150 subsidiaries across the world. The headquarters are located in Herzogenaurach, near Nuremberg (Germany). In 2007 the Adidas group registered total net sales of 10.3 billion euros (against 10.1 billion euros in 2006). In 2007 its net income reaches 555 million euros (496 million euros in 2006). The group is expecting an increase of its sales and profits for the next few years.

The European market represents about 42.4 per cent of the total sales of the Adidas group, followed by North America (28.4 per cent) and Asia (21.9 per cent). Over the past few years, the group has registered a strong sales increase in the European market, especially in France, Italy and the United Kingdom.

The Adidas group strives to be the global leader in the sporting goods industry with sports brands built on a passion for sports and a sporting lifestyle. The values of the company can be defined as follows:

1 The Adidas group is consumer focused and therefore continuously improves the quality, look, feel and image of products and organisational structures in order to match and exceed consumer expectations and to provide them with the highest value.
2 The group intends to be an innovation and design leader who seeks to help athletes of all skill levels achieve peak performance with every product it brings to market.
3 It considers itself as a global organisation that is socially and environmentally responsible, creative and financially rewarding for both employees and shareholders.
4 The company is committed to continuously strengthening its brands and products to improve its competitive position.
5 Its dedicated to consistently delivering outstanding financial results.

The classical Adidas brand is the major brand of the group, representing 69.1 per cent of the total sales in 2007 (the Reebok brand accounts for 22.7 per cent of the total sales). The mission of the Adidas brand is 'to be the leading sports brand in the world'. Product and marketing initiatives at Adidas primarily focus on five global priorities, which are expected to generate over 80 per cent of the brand's top-line growth: running, football, basketball, training and Originals. The Adidas brand attitude 'impossible is nothing' drives all brand communication initiatives and helps strengthen the brand's bond with consumers.

One of the objectives of the company is to develop the running footwear sales. Isabelle Madec, Marketing Director of Adidas France, considers that:

the perceived value of running shoes relies, to some extent, on objective attributes (materials, resistance, comfort, etc.), but also on intangible dimensions. It is true that for the Adidas brand, these intangible dimensions are more related to sports such as football and tennis. In the sector of running, this can be considered as a handicap because we are not perceived as a 'running' brand.

The European Sporting Goods Market

The European sporting goods market has developed considerably over the past few years. Three main factors explain the European sporting goods market's growth: (1) the fitness trend, (2) young people's access to the market, and (3) the search for new identities to replace traditional values. With

Table 3 Top 10 athletic shoes manufacturers (in 2006)

Rank	Company	Net sales (in million US dollars)	Market share (%)	Net sales evolution/2005 (%)
1	Nike	9328	37.9	+8.1
2	Adidas group	5649	22.9	+5.3
3	Puma	1900	7.7	+14.7
4	New Balance	1550	6.3	+10.7
5	Asics	1162	4.7	+13.4
6	Vf Corp	605	2.5	+23.5
7	K-Swiss	482	2	−2.2
8	ASG*	481	2	0
9	Stride Ride	362	1.5	+17.5
10	Mizuno	312	1.3	+13
Top 20		23 518	95.5	+8.9
Others		1100	4.5	0
Total		24 618	100	+8.5

*ASG: American Sporting Goods: Ryka, Avia, Turntec, Nevados.

Source: SGI (Sporting Goods Intelligence).

of market share, followed by Puma with 7.7 per cent. Table 3 presents the main actors of the highly competitive athletic shoes market.

Running Shoes Manufacturers

Non-specialist brands (Nike, Adidas, Reebok, Puma) and specialist brands (Asics, New Balance, Mizuno) are present in the running footwear market.

- The American brand Nike, also leader of the running footwear market, has an excellent image, particularly thanks to its top-of-the-line products (whose selling prices are higher than 100 euros).
- Adidas relies on technical innovation as well as its sponsored athletes' performances. The brand is striving to become the best sports brand in the world. People who take part in sport as well as athletes perceive the brand to be legitimate and authentic, with a credible track record. Adidas claims to be a 'genuine' sports brand.
- The Reebok brand is very active on down-market segments.

- The German brand Puma relies on its rather lifestyle-centred brand image and its innovation skills, particularly as far as design and colours are concerned.
- Thanks to its positioning as a running specialist, the Japanese brand Asics is now considered the market's leading brand by runners (third in the running footwear market).
- The American brand New Balance benefits from a strong technical brand image, also favoured by female customers.
- The Japanese brand Mizuno is trying to strengthen its specialist image by developing the technical features of its products.

Over the past few years Adidas has focused its efforts on high-level athletes. The brand now intends to broaden its target, while still addressing people who practise sport (runners). As a matter of fact, Adidas does not need to position itself as a leisure brand. In this highly competitive market, Adidas knows that success means winning over those people who practise sports. Therefore, its marketing activities will mainly try to reach active runners.

Questions

1 Define a marketing strategy for the Adidas brand for the European running shoes market, including market segmentation, target definition, and product positioning.

2 Elaborate the marketing mix (product, price, distribution and communication policies) for the Adidas brand in the European running shoes market.

Further Reading

Adidas (2009), *Internal Documents*.

Hertrich, S. and Mayrhofer, U. (eds) (2008), *Cas en marketing*, Cormelles-le-Royal, Editions Management & Société, Coll. Etudes de cas.

Hertrich, S., Mayrhofer, U. and Roederer, C. (2005), *Adidas : The Athletic Shoes Market*, Paris, Centrale de Cas et de Médias Pédagogiques.

Mayrhofer, U. (2004), *Marketing International*, Paris, Economica.

Mayrhofer, U. (2006), *Marketing*, 2nd edn, Paris, Editions Bréal, Coll. Lexifac.

Ohl, F. and Tribou, G. (2004), *Les marchés du Sport. Consommateurs et distributeurs*, Paris, Armand Colin.

Sportlab (2000), *Etude Exploratoire: Course sur Route*.

http://www.adidas.com

http://www.adidas-group.com

http://www.sginews.com

http://www.sport-guide.com

This case study was written by Sylvie Hertrich, Ecole de Management Strasbourg – Université de Strasbourg, and Ulrike Mayrhofer, IAE de Lyon – Université Jean Moulin Lyon 3 and Groupe ESC Rouen. The authors would like to thank Mrs Isabelle MADEC, Marketing Director of Adidas France, for her precious contribution.

Sylvie Hertrich and Ulrike Mayrhofer have developed a rich expertise in the field of marketing case studies: they have written twenty case studies in collaboration with companies like Adidas, Audi (Volkswagen), Club Méditerranée, Eurodisney (Disneyland Resort Paris), Hilton, Parc Astérix (Compagnie des Alpes). These case studies have been published at the Centrale de Cas et de Médias Pédagogiques, CCMP, Paris (http://www.ccmp.fr). The authors have received eight times the Golden Pen of the Chamber of Commerce and Industry in Paris. This prestigious award distinguishes authors whose case studies are extensively used by European business schools and universities.

Co. OHG based in Essen, Germany. Karl Albrecht took over the lead for the southern part of Germany and established the Aldi Süd GmbH & Co. OHG based in Mülheim, Germany. Today, both companies operate independently, except in strategic decisions such as price promotions and purchasing conditions, where they consult each other.[2] During all market entries in foreign countries, the company followed the initial territorial agreement from 1961. So Theo Albrecht focused his expansion on the north eastern, western and southwestern countries in Europe. Karl Albrecht concentrated on the southern and southeastern regions. Additionally, Karl was responsible for the market entries in the anglophone countries such as Australia, Ireland, United Kingdom and the USA.

In 2007 Aldi operated more than 8500 stores in 15 countries and generated sales revenues of about €47 billion worldwide. Further statistics show that about 52 per cent of the worldwide sales can be assigned to Germany, 31 per cent were generated in other European markets and 17 per cent were achieved outside Europe.

Lidl's History

In 1973, eleven years after the Albrecht brothers opened their first Aldi stores, Dieter Schwarz established the grocery discount retailer Lidl in Ludwigshafen, Germany. Similarly to Karl and Theo Albrecht, Schwarz had worked in a small family-owned retail business before he launched his own discount retailer business. Today, the Lidl Stiftung GmbH & Co. KG is a part of the 'Unternehmens- gruppe Schwarz', a group of the three independent companies Lidl, Kaufland and Mega Cent.

At first sight, it seems that Dieter Schwarz has successfully copied Aldi's business model for his own grocery discount stores. However, a closer look reveals that Lidl follows a so-called 'soft' discount strategy where the product assortment in the stores is enlarged to almost 3000 items and customers are offered branded products as well as store brands. Statistics show that Lidl's soft discount concept has been expanded successfully: in 2007 Lidl operated about 7900 stores in 21 countries and generated sales of about €36 billion on a worldwide level. Forty per cent of the sales were achieved in Germany and 60 per cent in European markets. Exhibit 3 presents a comparison of Aldi's and Lidl's key operating figures.

Nevertheless, today Lidl is still number two behind its rival Aldi with regard to sales volume and number of stores in Germany and on a worldwide level. However, on a European level, the company has already taken the lead with regard to the number of stores: Lidl operates about 7900 stores whereas Aldi operates 7200 stores only.

International Expansion of Aldi and Lidl

Aldi realised early that international expansion could be a key lever in enhancing the company's growth. In 1967 the management decided to enter Austria by acquiring the local grocery retailer, Hofer. Then, from 1976 to 2006, Aldi

Exhibit 3 Comparison of Aldi's and Lidl's key operating figures

	Aldi	Lidl
Founding year	1962	1973
Business model	Hard discount	Soft discount
Sales volume (€ bn) in 2007	47.1	35.9
– thereof Germany	24.3 (52%)	14.3 (40%)
– thereof European foreign markets	14.7 (31%)	21.6 (60%)
– thereof non-European foreign markets	8.1 (17%)	0.0 (0%)
Number of stores in 2007	8541	7879
– thereof Germany	4228 (49%)	2902 (37%)
– thereof European foreign markets	2963 (35%)	4977 (63%)
– thereof non-European foreign markets	1350 (16%)	0 (0%)
Number of foreign markets in 2007	14	21
– thereof European foreign markets	12 (86%)	21 (100%)
– thereof non-European foreign markets	2 (14%)	0 (0%)

Exhibit 4 Aldi's and Lidl's market presence and number of stores in 2007

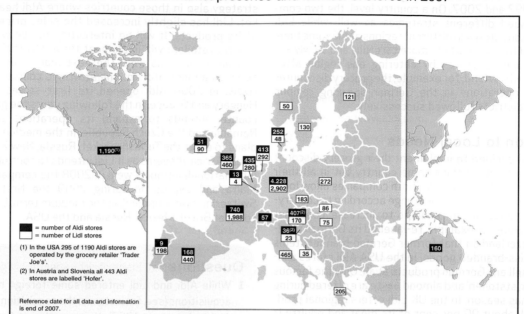

= number of Aldi stores
= number of Lidl stores

(1) In the USA 295 of 1190 Aldi stores are operated by the grocery retailer 'Trader Joe's'.

(2) In Austria and Slovenia all 443 Aldi stores are labelled 'Hofer'.

Reference date for all data and information is end of 2007.

entered another 13 foreign markets. However, the expansion plans were not limited to Europe only – ten years after the market entry in Austria, Aldi began to make gains in the US market and, in 2000, the grocery discounter extended its operations into Australia.

Unlike Aldi, Lidl limited its expansion plans to the German market first. Thereafter, in the period from 1989 to 2007, the company entered 21 foreign markets and impressed experts with its astonishing rate of internationalisation. Additionally, Lidl seized the opportunity to expand into a number of developing European markets and developed markets, where no competitor had been present previously. While Aldi – in most cases – preferred to wait for a retail sector to mature, Lidl has been far more adventurous and began its Eastern European expansion with the market entry into Poland in 2002. Exhibit 4 illustrates the international market presence of Aldi and Lidl as well as the number of stores in each country.

Lidl's rapid expansion into Poland seems to have paid off: in 2007 the company achieved sales of about €759 million and was ranked among the top three grocery discounters in the country. With this well-established position, Lidl has a clear advantage over its rival Aldi who entered the Polish market in 2008 and still has to build up consumer trust and market share.

Some of Aldi's and Lidl's market entries were a result of simple trial and error: often the grocery retailers declined support from market research companies or management consultants and judged the attractiveness of a foreign market on the basis of their own manager's gut feeling. In 2008 Lidl were forced to realise the defects of this strategy: after four years of unsatisfactory sales, the company retreated from the Norwegian market and sold its 50 stores

to the local competitor Rema. Norway's unique geographic structure and the distribution of its population were key factors that led to Lidl's failure. The thinly spread population density in Norway required Lidl to build up several central warehouses in order to ensure smooth supplies for each discount store in the country. Consequently, logistics became more expensive and the additional costs threatened the profitability of Lidl's stores. Werner Evertsen, head of Lidl Norway, explained that the stores were closed because they offered no further development potential, and he indicated that the store location was a key issue, which should have been checked more carefully: 'It can simply be a case of wrong location or too low population density. Of course, we want to be where the population is.' In addition to these mistakes, Lidl Norway had to cope with a high level of fluctuation among its top managers. One of the country managers left the company 20 months after he signed his employment contract. The frequent change in Lidl's top management and the resulting uncertainty among the employees also affected the long-term strategic planning of the company in a negative way.

Differences in the International Timing Strategies of Aldi and Lidl

Aldi's internationalisation pattern is characterised by phases of 'action' and 'recovery'. In the past the company entered one or more markets within a short period of time and then paused its market entry activities for about ten years. Since 2000 Aldi has accelerated the internationalisation process and has entered about one new market per year. Lidl, in contrast, acts much faster: although the company started its internationalisation quite

Part 4
Case Studies

Cases

Case 4.1 Wal-Mart's German Misadventure

'Don't look now:' low prices all year round!
With thanks to Walmart

I don't think that Wal-Mart did their homework as well as they should have. Germany is Europe's most price-sensitive market. Wal-Mart underestimated the competition, the culture, the legislative environment.

— Steve Gotham, retail analyst,
Verdict Retail Consulting, October 2002[1]

We screwed up in Germany. Our biggest mistake was putting our name up before we had the service and low prices. People were disappointed.

— John Menzer, head of Wal-Mart International
December 2001[2]

German Blues

For the world's largest retailing company, Wal-Mart, Inc., the German market was proving difficult to crack. By 2003, even after five years of having entered Germany, Wal-Mart was making losses. Though Wal-Mart did not reveal these figures, analysts estimated losses of around $200–300 million per annum in Germany over the five-year period.

According to analysts, the main reason for Wal-Mart's losses was its failure to understand German culture and the shopping habits

Exhibit 3 A note on the retailing industry in Germany

As the world's third largest economy, Germany has attracted the attention of retailers from around the world such as Marks & Spencers and Toys 'R' Us for several decades. With a GNP of €2 trillion and a population of around 80 million, Germany was rated as one of the biggest retail markets in Europe. In 2002 Germany accounted for 15 per cent of Europe's €2 trillion retail market. The West German retail industry saw tremendous growth rates till the early 1990s. However, after the unification of Germany in 1990, the Germany economy went through a tough phase of restructuring, which had an impact on the retailing industry too. The difference between the levels of economic prosperity in West and East Germany pulled down the average growth rates in the German retail industry. By the late 1990s the German retail industry was growing slowly.

The German retail market was oligopolistic with a few players dominating the industry. In the early 2000s the top 10 players accounted for 84 per cent of sales and the top five players in the market garnered around 63 per cent of market share. German consumers reportedly attached more importance to value and price than customer service. According to analysts, the German market was one of the most price-sensitive markets in Europe.

Until the late 1990s discount stores concentrated only on food and other grocery items, but in the late 1990s, the trend changed and the discount stores moved to non-food items also. For instance, the discount store Aldi emerged as the largest seller of personal computers under its own brand name.

In the early 2000s, with the slowdown in the economy, the German retail industry experienced the lowest profit levels of all the developed countries. The profit margin in grocery retailing was just 1.1 per cent in 2002, and in the food segment it was only 0.5 per cent. Another important feature of the German retailing industry was the domination of family-owned enterprises. Most of the retailing enterprises were not listed on stock exchanges.

The German retailing industry is highly regulated. Analysts believe that the regulatory environment in Germany hindered the development of retailing in the county. There were many legislations relating to the competition and corporate strategies of retailers. The German government also pursues protectionist policies to support small and medium-scale German retailers. Some of the legislation which affects the retail industry in Germany significantly are summarised below.

- A retailer can operate for a maximum of 80 hours/week. The store working hours are the shortest in Europe. Retailers are not allowed to work on Sundays and holidays. Because of this regulation Wal-Mart was not able to operate its 24/7 convenience stores in Germany.
- Retailers are not allowed to sell below cost for an extended period of time.

However, a merchant can discount goods for a limited period of time.

As regards German consumers, for cultural reasons they were less friendly and less outgoing compared with American and British consumers. In line with this, in Germany the number of employees per store was low compared to the US and other developed markets.

In order to increase consumer spending, the German government undertook major tax reforms in 2001. This was expected to boost retail sales in the country. However, though government tax reforms boosted consumer spending, it did not benefit the retail industry as expenditure took place in the housing, tourism and communications sectors.

During 2003, too, the German retailing industry was expected to have slow growth because of the macroeconomic conditions. The increasing unemployment affected the food retailing sector in the country.

Source: adapted from various newspaper articles and websites.

were accustomed to centralised distribution, in Germany suppliers were not comfortable with the centralised distribution system that Wal-Mart adopted. As in the US, Wal-Mart in Germany wanted to rely on inputs from suppliers in order to decide on product assortments. However, in Germany, Wal-Mart's relationship with its suppliers was not mature enough to make this possible. Thus, Wal-Mart ended up trying to sell goods which its customers did not want but which suppliers wanted to push.

Wal-Mart also had a number of inventory problems. Initially Wal-Mart had only one stockroom which stocked all merchandise. The company found it difficult to hire employees for its stockroom due to the low wages it was offering. The shortage of workers delayed the movement of goods, leading to excessive stockpiling.

Another operational problem Wal-Mart faced was employee unrest. It was accused of paying low wages and not providing good working conditions. Wal-Mart did not understand the German work culture. As in its US operations, it discouraged employees from forming unions. After acquiring Interspar and Wertkauf, Wal-Mart prohibited members of the work councils of the erstwhile separate companies from meeting each other. The company also rarely consulted the elected representatives of its employees.

Wal-Mart ran into trouble with German unions when it announced employee lay-offs and store closures in 2002 in order to reduce its personnel costs.[8] In addition, it refused to accept the centralised wage-bargaining process[9] in the German retail industry. Because of this, the trade unions organised a walk-out from Wal-Mart stores which led to bad publicity for the company. Wal-Mart employees also went on a two-day strike in July 2002, demanding the negotiation of wage contracts with the company (see Exhibit 4).

Problems in the External Environment

Wal-Mart faced several problems on the legal front as well. It was accused of breaching various German laws. The company was accused of having violated Section (IV) (2) of the 'Act Against Restraints of Competition' (Gesetz gegen Wettbewerbsbeschrankungen or GWB) and Section 335a of the 'Commercial Act' (Handelsgesetzbuch or HGB). Section (IV) (2) of GWB forbids companies 'with superior market power in relation to small and medium-sized competitors' from lowering their prices and engaging in price wars with small companies. Such large companies were allowed to lower prices only after providing justification for the lower prices.

Wal-Mart had lowered the prices of some commodities, namely sugar, milk and margarine, in May 2000. The new prices were reportedly lower than the cost price at which Wal-Mart had bought them. In making this move, Wal-Mart was alleged to have violated Section (IV) (2). In response to Wal-Mart's move, the German retailers Aldi and Lidl also lowered their prices. As the price war continued, the German Federal Cartel Office (FCO) launched an investigation in September 2000. It ordered the retailers to stop selling the commodities below cost price as it would hurt small and medium-size retailers and lead to unfair competition.

In response to the FCO order, Wal-Mart took the case to the Appeals Court in Düsseldorf. The Appeals Court ruled in favor of Wal-Mart, stating that Section (IV) (2) prohibited big players from selling at lower prices, and Wal-Mart could not be considered as a big player in Germany as it did not have a considerable market share nor market capitalisation. However, the FCO took the case further up to the Supreme Court to argue against the verdict of the Appeals Court. In November 2002, the German Supreme Court gave its verdict, declaring that Wal-Mart's selling goods at prices below cost price would result in unfair competition against small and medium-size retailers, and that Wal-Mart should abandon its pricing strategies.[10]

Wal-Mart was also hauled up for violating the Commercial Act's Section 335a by not publishing financial data such as balance sheet and profit and loss account statements on its operations in Germany. The trade unions alleged that they were not given access to accounts of the company. In order to gain access to financial information, the trade unions filed a suit against Wal-Mart in the state court. In its verdict the court ruled that Wal-Mart should publish the required financial information; it also fined Wal-Mart senior executives for not providing the required financial information. Wal-Mart sources said that since the company was a limited partnership, it was not mandatory for it to publish financial information under German laws. However, according to the trade unions, under the altered German commercial code, even limited partnership firms were required to publish their financial accounts. In November 2002 Wal-Mart filed a suit in the German Supreme Court against the verdict of the state court, asking it to delay the state court's decision until the European Court of Justice came out with its decision on disclosure provisions by foreign companies.[11]

Cultural Mismatch

Apart from operational and regulatory problems, Wal-Mart also faced cultural problems in Germany. It found it difficult to integrate the two companies (Wertkauf and Interspar) that it had acquired. The companies had completely different work cultures; while Interspar had decentralised operations with independent regional units, Wertkauf was highly centralised with the head office making all decisions. Additionally, Wal-Mart found it difficult to integrate the two companies' cultures with its own.

Employee morale in Wal-Mart Germany was also reported to have been badly affected by the changes in internal rules and regulations effected by Wal-Mart. The earlier managements of both Interspar and Wertkauf had given their executives liberal expense accounts. But after Wal-Mart's acquisition of the firms, the executives' expense accounts were reduced. For instance, during business trips, they were required to share rooms – which came as a culture shock to the Germans.

Wal-Mart also faced a language problem in Germany. When Wal-Mart entered Germany, the top management who came from the US did not show any inclination to learn German. Within a few weeks, English became the official language of the company in Germany. This resulted in serious communication problems for the German employees. Making English the official language affected employee morale, with employees starting to feel like outsiders and getting increasingly frustrated. The German public also found it difficult to pronounce Wal-Mart's name correctly. They pronounced it as Vawl-Mart.

In Germany Wal-Mart's world-famous customer service methods fell flat. For example, Wal-Mart's famous Ten-Foot Rule[12] was not implemented in Germany, as German customers did not like strangers interfering with their shopping. Commenting on this, Tiarks said, 'You can't beat those things into your people. They have to be genuine, or the customer sees right through them.' For the same reason, Wal-Mart also did away with the idea of greeters at

Exhibit 4 Profiles of German retailers

ALDI: The history of Aldi dates back to the 1940s. In 1946 Theo Abrecht and Karl Abrecht inherited convenience stores from their parents. In 1960 Albrecht Discount Stores began to be called 'Aldi', and there were 300 such stores. In 1961 a hard discount format was formulated by Theo and Karl Abrecht. This combined ultra-low prices and high product quality with a very limited product assortment of around 600–700 products with a no-frills shopping experience. In 1962 the company was spilt into two independent operations – Aldi Nord (Aldi North) and Aldi Süd (Aldi South). Aldi's northern operations were headed by Theo Abrecht and its southern operations were headed by Karl Abrecht, who operated independently, coordinating major decisions such as suppliers and pricing. The company continued to be known as the Aldi group. By 2002 the Aldi group had around 3741 stores in Germany and had around 2643 stores internationally. It had a presence in Australia, the United Kingdom, the United States, France, Denmark, Belgium, Luxembourg, Netherlands, Ireland, Spain and Austria.

METRO AG: Metro AG was formed in 1996 after the merger of Metro Cash & Carry (established in 1964), Kaufhof Holding AG (established in 1879) and Asko Deutsche Kaufhaus AG (established in 1880). With the merger, the Metro AG group became world's third biggest supermarket group, with around 2300 sales outlets, and a distribution network in around 26 countries in the world covering not only European countries but also countries such as China, Turkey, Eastern Europe and Morocco. The Metro group divided its business into five segments: Cash & Carry, under the brand names Metro, Makro and Spar (since March 2002); Real (800 hypermarkets) and Extra (supermarkets) in the food sector; Mediamarkt and Saturn, selling electronic goods; Praktiker, selling home improvement products; and Galeria and Kaufhof, general stores offering consumer goods. More than 40 per cent of Metro AG's turnover was generated from its international stores. For 2002 Metro AG reported sales of €51.5 billion, compared to 2001 sales of €49.5 billion.

EDEKA GROUP: The history of the Edeka group dates back to the late 1890s. The Edeka group was the brainchild of Friedrich William Raiffeisen and Hermann Schulze Delizsch. Their idea was to set up a purchase association where goods were made available to buyers at low prices. In October 1907 the Edeka Foundation was formed with 23 purchase associations. In the same year a central procurement office called Edeka Center AG was established. Over the years, the group was able to maintain low prices because of its strong relations with its suppliers. Edeka procured goods from regional wholesalers. The Edeka group was made up of a number of independent retailers and co-operative societies. Edeka's product range included organic fruits, vegetables, dairy products and cereals. The food products were marketed under the brand name Bio Wertkost. The group's brands also included Rio Grande and Mibell. The group also had a presence in pharmacy retailing, food processing and wine operations, publishing and banking services.

Source: compiled from various newspapers and company websites.

German stores. In the US Wal-Mart used to employ greeters at all its stores to welcome customers as they entered. However, in Germany, the company found that customers did not appreciate this idea at all. Apart from this, the German consumers realised that they were the ones who would be paying more because of 'the guy standing at the door' – which is why they did not appreciate it. Wal-Mart in Germany could not offer loyalty cards[13] as they were banned in Germany.

Future Prospects

Even five years after entering the German market, Wal-Mart had not made a significant impact in the German retail industry. Wal-Mart reported losses over all the four years up to 2002 in its German operations

(see Exhibit 5). It was reported that between 1999 and 2002 Wal-Mart's sales declined by 5 per cent on average.

Exhibit 5 Sales and operating profit in Germany

Year	Sales ($ million)	Operating profit/(loss) ($ million)
1999	2815	(192)
2000	2468	(181)
2001	2506	(164)
2002	2420	(108)

Source: adapted from www.mventures.com.

Case 4.2 Handl Tyrol: Market Selection and Coverage Decisions of a Medium-Sized Austrian Enterprise

This case was written by Claudia Kl[...] versität Wien, Austria, and Rudolf R[...] Manchester, UK. The authors gratefully [...] support of Sonja Elmaver, marketing m[...]

Company Background

Handl Tyrol was established as a family business in the province of Tyrol, Austria, in 1902. The company focuses on the production and marketing of high-quality smoked and air-dried meat and sausage specialties from Tyrol. Handl Tyrol has three business locations: the Pians production facility, Schönwies service centre and Christanell GmbH in Naturns/South Tyrol, Italy (a wholly owned subsidiary since 1993); all of which have been certified under the International Food Standard (IFS, Version 04) and the higher-level British Retail Consortium Technical Standard (BRC 2002). Both of these certification procedures use the most stringent standards in the European food production industry, with a special focus on the areas of food safety, hygiene and the specific traceability of all goods throughout the entire processing chain. The long-term success of the company has been realised by means of a growth strategy in the form of equity interests and acquisition efforts as well as intensive innovation activities. Austria is Handl Tyrol's home market, and since 1978 the company has worked this entire market through selected food retailers and the restaurant and catering industry, as well as the company's own sales outlets in highly frequented tourist areas and larger cities.

Handl Tyrol's Growth Objectives

Handl Tyrol's strategic objectives are twofold:

1 to become the home market champion by dominating in those areas where the company excels (quality leadership, relationship to tradition)

2 to become a European champion, that is, Handl Tyrol strives for European market and brand leadership in its market segment.

Handl's Internationalisation and Expansion Strategy

Restricting Factors

As Handl Tyrol is a company which produces smoked bacon and ham products backed by a long-standing Alpine tradition, the connection between the product and its origins has to be maintained. This implies that the company has to confine production activities to the area in and around Tyrol when entering new markets. In the case of product adaptations, it is necessary to consider the Tyrolean lifestyle and culture in accordance with the company's slogan ('Der echte Nordtiroler', roughly: 'genuine northern Tyrolean products') and to ensure that the unique taste of Handl Tyrol products remains unchanged. Expansion activities have to be financed by the company's own cash flow in order to ensure the company's continued financial health.

Marketing Focus

Handl Tyrol pursues a distinctive niche strategy. The company strives to develop slowly but steadily as a hidden champion and to raise its position to the level of European market leadership. The company primarily concentrates on retail trade advertising and participation in relevant trade fairs (e.g. ANUGA in Cologne – international trade in food and semi-luxury goods – INTERMEAT in Düsseldorf and CIBUS in Parma). Hence, Handl Tyrol follows a push strategy. In 2003 and 2004 the company also increased its image advertising efforts on television and in print media. The consumer group targeted by Handl Tyrol's premium range comprises quality-conscious people who enjoy food and belong to the middle- and upper-income brackets. In Austria Handl Tyrol has reached a level of an unassisted brand recall of over 60 per cent. In 2004 the company entered into a sales alliance with the Spanish market leader Esteban Espuna. This alliance has the strategic advantage of providing customers with a competent source of typical air-dried and smoked specialities.

Country Selection Criteria

Handl's approach regarding the selection and servicing of foreign markets is based on a set of analytic country selection criteria. These have been applied in former expansion strategies, such as when entering Germany, Spain, etc. The selection of countries encompasses a preliminary strategic decision with due attention to the following business criteria: structure and development

Increasing costs also pushed up losses for the company. Wal-Mart sources indicated that personnel costs accounted for around 17 per cent of sales; these high costs prompted Wal-Mart to freeze new recruitment. Commenting on the operations in Germany, Wal-Mart CEO Scott said, 'We just walked in and said, "We're going to lower prices, we're going to add people to the stores, we're going to remodel the stores because inherently that's correct," and it wasn't. We didn't have the infrastructure to support the kind of things we were doing.'[14]

Though Wal-Mart claimed that sales were picking up, analysts felt otherwise, and said that Wal-Mart in Germany had failed on its customer service promise. Independent studies conducted by some newspapers indicated that Wal-Mart was rated seventh out of the 10 major retailers in Germany in terms of overall customer satisfaction (see Exhibit 6).

Wal-Mart announced that it would not be looking for further acquisitions in Germany and would concentrate on stabilising its business in the country. Commenting on the company's plans, Dave Ferguson, head of European operations, said, 'What we first have to achieve is that the existing stores are operating optimally.'

To revive its fortunes in Germany, Wal-Mart announced that it would be focusing on bringing down its capital costs. It announced that instead of opening Wal-Mart supercenters, the company would focus on opening smaller stores in Germany. Only time will tell whether Wal-Mart will become a significant player in the German retail market.

Exhibit 6 Customer satisfaction ratings of German retailers

Retailer name	Rank
Aldi Group	1
Globus	2
Kaufland	3
Lidl	4
Norma	5
Marktkauf	6
Wal-Mart	7
Metro	8
Penny	9
Real	10

Source: www.hicbusiness.org.

Questions

1 Wal-Mart started its global operations in the early 1990s when it opened its first international store in Mexico. Analyse the reasons for Wal-Mart's decision to go global.

2 When Wal-Mart announced that it would be entering the German market, analysts were surprised. Usually, the cultural affinity between the US and the UK led American companies to target the UK first, before launching on to the European continent. Do you think Wal-Mart's decision to enter the German market was correct? Justify your opinion.

3 Even after five years of doing business in Germany, Wal-Mart had failed to make an impact on the German market and had been incurring losses year after year. Analyse the reasons for Wal-Mart's problems in the German market. Do you think the company will be able to improve its performance in Germany?

Further Reading

Wendy Zellener, 'Wal-Mart's Newest Accent is German', *Business Week*, 18 December 1997.

Mike Troy, 'Wal-Mart Germany's New President Faces Culture, Customer Challenges', *Discount Store News*, 9 February 1998.

John Schmid, 'In Europe, Wal-Mart Pursues a Big Dream', *International Herald Tribune*, 2 October 1998.

'Wal-Mart Acquires Interspar Hypermarkets', www.prnewswire.com, 9 December 1998.

Mike Troy, 'Wal-Mart Germany Beefs Up', *Discount Store News*, 4 January 1999.

Jeremy Kahn, 'Wal-Mart Goes Shopping in Europe', *Fortune*, 7 June 1999.

Heidi Dawley, 'Watch out Europe: Here Comes Wal-Mart', *Business Week*, 28 June 1999.

'Wal-Mart in Germany is Not Doing Well', www.union-network.org, 7 March 2000.

'Wal-Mart Makes Bigger than Expected Losses in Germany', www.union-network.org, 10 March 2000.

'The Wal-Mart Effect', *Business Europe*, 17 May 2000.

'Wal-Mart's Low Prices too Low for Germany's Retail Regulators', www.enquirer.com, 9 September 2000.

'Germany: Stop Bullying Wal-Mart', *Business Week*, 25 September 2000.

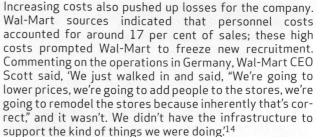

David Marino, 'Wal-Mart Steps up German Invasion', www.fool.com, 26 March 2001.

'Wal-Mart Continues to Lose Money in Germany – Responds through Escalating Price War', www.union-network.org, 29 March 2001.

'Operations Evolve to Offset Doldrums in Deutschland', *DSN Retailing Today*, 5 June 2001.

Wendy Zellner, Katharine A. Schmidt, Moon Ihlwan and Heidi Dawley, 'How Well Does Wal-Mart Travel?', *Business Week*, 3 September 2001.

Daniel Rubin, 'Grumpy German Shoppers Distrust the Wal-Mart Style', www.gaccwa.org, 30 September 2001.

'The First "Real" Wal-Mart is a flop?', www.unionnetwork.org, 12 February 2002.

Isabelle de Pommereau, 'Wal-Mart lesson: Smiling service won't win Germans', www.csmonitor.com, 17 October 2002.

www.walmartstores.com.

www.planetretail.net.

www.forbes.com.

www.hicbusiness.org.

www.mventures.com.

www.wilmercutler.com

References

1 Pommereau, Isabelle de, 'Wal-Mart Lesson: Smiling Service Won't Win Germans', www.csmonitor.com, 17 October 2002.

2 Rubin, Daniel, 'Grumpy German Shoppers Distrust the Wal-Mart Style', www.gaccwa.org, 30 December 2001.

3 EDLP was a pricing strategy adopted by Wal-Mart to ensure lowest prices among all retail chains on its products.

4 K-mart is a leading US retailer.

5 Target is one of the leading discount retail chains in the US.

6 Jeremy Khan, 'Wal-Mart Goes Shopping in Europe', *Fortune*, 7 June 1999.

7 'Operations Evolve to Offset Doldrums in Deutschland', *DSN Retailing Today*, 5 June 2001.

8 It was reported that Wal-Mart had the highest employee costs among German retailers. The high costs were

attributed to heavy recruiting by Wal-Mart anticipating huge business and its misreading of the German retailing environment. For instance, Wal-Mart had to lay off employees who were taken on as greeters as the German public did not take to the idea, and it also had to cut down the number of employees in many stores due to low sales.

9 In a centralised wage bargaining process, the wages across all companies in a particular industry are decided according to the average productivity in the industry.

10 The German Supreme Court felt that Wal-Mart pricing margarine below cost was legal as it was done for only a brief period. However, the court was against Wal-Mart's pricing of sugar and milk below cost prices.

11 Many European firms had filed cases against Germany's alterations to its commercial code which required the firms to publish financial information. The European Court of Justice's decision was still awaited.

12 As per the Ten-Foot Rule of the company, whenever an employee comes within 10 feet of a customer, the employee should look up to the customer, greet him and ask him if he needs any help.

13 Loyalty cards were offered by supermarkets and big retail chains to select loyal customers. The businesses offered special prices for the customers possessing loyalty cards. However, in 2002, many customer groups accused companies of using loyalty cards to track down the purchasing patterns of the customers and started opposing such schemes.

14 Zellner, Wendy, 'How Well Does Wal-Mart Travel?', *Business Week*, 3 September 2001.

This case was written by K. Subhadra, under the direction of Sanjib Dutta, ICFAI Center for Management Research (ICMR). It is intended to be used as a basis for class discussion rather than to illustrate either effective or ineffective handling of a management situation. The case was compiled from published sources.

---

of the company's international market presence, balance, risk diversification, preliminary decisions as to regional development paths and country portfolios. In addition, the company takes into account country-specific economic data such as per capita income, GDP, rate of inflation, per capita consumption of pork, level of internal supply of pork, price level, competition (number of providers, competitors' revenues), presence of Austrian companies in the food industry (experience), import conditions, distribution, risk, meat consumption, geographical location (distance from Austria), business contacts, living and consumption habits, frequency of tourism and retail trade structures.

Market Penetration in Germany, Italy and the Rest of Europe (Except Eastern Europe)

On the basis of its market leadership in Austria since the early 1990s, Handl Tyrol has been working the German and Italian markets more intensively since 2000. The products are listed at approximately 80 per cent of the retail trade chains in Germany. The company operates on the German market through its own distribution network, consisting of three internal employees as well as a dozen retail trade agencies. The competitive situation is becoming increasingly difficult. In addition to meat and sausage producers in general, the producers of the South Tyrolean smoked bacon brand ggA are also penetrating the market and creating fierce price competition. Handl's marketing mix is being expanded as revenues increase, with the main focus being on retail trade-related advertising. Sales activities in Germany are characterised by a major discrepancy between the north and the south due to the south's geographical proximity to the Tyrol, as well as similar consumption habits in those regions.

In Italy Handl Tyrol's distribution network (consisting of the company's own employees) is continuously expanded as sales activities are steadily increasing. The company's main competitors in Italy are the producers of the South Tyrolean smoked bacon brand ggA as well as salami producers. Sales activities in Italy focus on Handl Tyrol's premium real northern Tyrolean cured sausage and smoked bacon, mainly at the deli counter.

The company works the rest of the European market via its own sales force and various importers, focusing on Luxembourg, Denmark, Belgium, the Netherlands, Finland, France, Switzerland and England.

In general, Handl Tyrol's entire 'Alpine range' is offered in these countries, with the strongest differentiation by Handl Tyrol's genuine northern Tyrolean products.

Market Coverage in Eastern Europe

Incremental approach

Since 2002 exports have deliberately been expanded to Eastern European countries due to the high potential of Austrian specialities in these markets. For strategic reasons such as the proximity to the home market, existing relationships with international retail trade

groups, consumer preferences and e[...] ness, Handl Tyrol decided to extend [...] Eastern Europe in a two-step proces[...] Handl Tyrol genuine northern Tyrolean [...] to the Czech Republic, Hungary, Slo[...] Poland. Other Eastern European c[...] covered in later expansion stages.

With increasing incomes, the resi[...] European countries that are currently [...] also have higher expectations of fo[...] also prepared to pay more for them. In [...] are many domestic producers whose [...] reached Western standards. Aside f[...] national suppliers of similar meat an[...] these producers are Handl Tyrol's mos[...] itors. The company is therefore makin[...] its name as a high-quality supplier [...] specialties. With this clear positionin[...] differentiation from competing sup[...] offers consumers use-specific range [...] brand transfer can be created, especi[...] service goods.

The Eastern European markets are [...] importers. As revenues grow and co[...] further, the company plans to expand i[...] its own employees.

The retailing landscape in these m[...] ised by vast differences. In Hungary, n[...] national groups such as Metro, Teng[...] (Billa/Penny), Spar and Auchan are rep[...] to several Hungarian retail chains. In S[...] Rewe (Billa), Kaufland, Carrefour and [...] scene. In Poland, Makro, Auchan, Tes[...] represented on the market. The inte[...] not yet expanded to Slovenia due to [...] market, meaning that domestic sup[...] cially strong presence there.

Each month Handl Tyrol exports 2[...] meat products to the Czech Republ[...] include international retail chains suc[...] Billa. In Hungary, Handl Tyrol is now li[...] including Auchan – and in numerous sm[...] various branches. A contract has als[...] partner in Slovenia.

The product portfolio in these mar[...] Handl Tyrol's genuine northern Tyrol[...] tioning and differentiation makes it p[...] hold in the market with an ext[...] specialities. The products are adapt[...] they are distinguished in the languag[...] the market requires, Handl Tyrol has [...] ity to design products specifically for[...]

Communication activities focus he[...] Eastern Europe. In addition to typica[...] also performs public relations work. I[...] pany also plans to increase its par[...] trade fairs. Sales literature is transla[...] of each country.

Case 4.3 IKEA: Entering Russia

With thanks to IKEA

In Russia all possible things turn out to be impossible, and all impossible is possible.

Lennart Dahlgren, IKEA country manager, Russia

When Swedish furniture retailer IKEA's country manager arrived in Russia to set up the first store, the country was in a state of deep shock. It was 17 August 1998, the day the Russian monetary policy finally collapsed. Almost all foreign companies were leaving the country, but IKEA stayed and this may turn out as a very favourable strategic move from a long-term perspective. The decision to stay in Russia in 1998 was, however, taken almost entirely by one man, IKEA's founder Ingvar Kamprad. During one of his visits to Russia, he shared his vision of how IKEA Russia would develop in the coming years: 'IKEA becomes the main supplier of home furniture to the normal Russian families and our sales in Russia will exceed those in our old home country Sweden'. To make this vision come true, he stood in opposition to the whole management group when the decision to enter the country was taken.

The fact that IKEA's owner saw Russia as a long-term investment also enabled the management to apply a long-term view that may become a competitive advantage in the years to come. As a Russian manager commented: 'We have been on the market here for three and a half years now, and we can note the tendency, and if the tendency grows as quickly as it has done during this time, the market will be unlimited for a

company like [...] are now intere[...]

Transferring[...] and Values[...]

IKEA is a leadi[...] 200 stores in 3[...] articles and h[...] the IKEA gro[...] Kamprad in Sm[...] people are re[...] innovative, an[...] Today, the IKE[...] tion and the [...] Ingvar Kampra[...] nishing produ[...] much lower th[...] solutions that[...] is a prominent[...] its ambitious [...] Russia since [...] Moscow, only [...] stores have [...] December 200[...] and one in Ka[...] are controlled[...]

IKEA is cha[...] vision to crea[...] set of explicit[...] ing role in the[...] foundation of [...] which is an exp[...] the distributi[...] resource idea[...] affect the st[...] development [...] value of cost-[...] flat-package [...] sourcing, defi[...] does a half an [...] design, choice[...] plicity is refle[...] and routines [...] forward relat[...] well as in the[...] vision and valu[...] a new market.[...]

It was the [...] to establish b[...] sion that few [...] needs of the [...] at reasonable [...] the Russian m[...] in Moscow wa[...] was carried o[...]

representative commented: 'If we had done such a research, it should have shown that the consumption level is too low, the individual income level is too low, there are no traditions of retailing, which result in the fact that consumers generally don't go to the chains to shop.'

In each market IKEA enters it must recreate its company culture from scratch. In Moscow that included the replication of the store design and layout in accordance with the latest version of the existing store and an extensive cultural education that was carried out by the team of experienced IKEA people. It involved introducing the newly employed co-workers to IKEA routines and cultural traditions as well as helping them to develop the necessary competences (e.g. teamwork, leadership, skill diversity, etc.) and the IKEA management style. It has its roots in Swedish leadership style and gives responsibility to each co-worker and emphasises 'learning by doing'. In the Russian case, the store played an additional role by becoming the training site for new employees who later got involved in new projects or formed teams for the newly opened stores – a sort of cultural incubator. The extensive in-store training gave some very positive results. According to a store manager, the second store in Moscow could operate well from the first minute it opened because the whole staff was trained in the first store working with corresponding jobs: 'Here they just started and then they went on like this! No downturn, no nothing, no reaction, they just knew what to do!'

The role of IKEA's experienced management staff has also been indispensable in Russia. A main task is to train and prepare the local people who will be ready to lead further the expansion process. As a manager has commented about his management group: 'My main task is really to make this group more Russian and to export people for the upcoming expansion.' The demand for knowledgeable Russian staff is indeed very big with two stores just opened in St Petersburg (12 December 2003) and Kazan (22 March 2004). Development of experienced staff is impossible without extensive training.

As a whole, there is thus a strong emphasis on the vital role of training at IKEA Russia, at an overall management level as well as the store level. The local staff on the store level with a primarily academic education and a prioritisation of abstract knowledge is faced with the necessity to translate it into concrete sales figures. This includes both cultural training and education in IKEA values and different levels of professional on-the-job training.

Developing and Positioning the Retail Proposition in Russia

Market information was thus not regarded as necessary for selecting the Russian market. According to a manager, IKEA knew that a lot of people live in Moscow so that at least one store should succeed. A survey giving that information was considered as unnecessary. Furthermore it was considered less important to develop specific strategies for the market in advance. Instead, entry was based on the view that there is a need to live and learn about the new market before setting the strategies. Within IKEA, setting up a new business was described as very little theory and

very much practice. However, once the decision was made to enter the Russian market IKEA specialists were sent to Russia to make investigations, but data about the Russian market was often uncertain and difficult to assess. For example, one initial conclusion was that the IKEA store should be situated near a Metro station since there were hardly any cars in Moscow. Five years later, however, traffic jams were among Moscow's biggest problems. The country manager argued that instead of information about the market it is better to acquire market knowledge and the best way to get that knowledge is to live and learn in the market.

IKEA introduces more or less the same product range in all new countries – irrespective of what is considered popular by local customers. In Russia IKEA's Scandinavian furniture design is in some contrast to the historically preferred dark wood, massive, lacquered, expensive furniture. In order to support this strategy, IKEA most often identifies the potential needs that are similar across markets: 'We have the IKEA range and we have the market knowledge and the people needs, which are pretty much the same needs in Moscow and in Malmö.' Another IKEA approach was to create needs that could be satisfied within the range, and to inspire customers with numerous new solutions based on the existing range. The theme 'Living with small spaces' was one such solution used in Russia. The storage solutions are among those most popular in Russia since the average apartments are small and often house several families. Cheap and nice looking accessories for the home also became very popular with Russian customers and accounted for a big part of the stores' turnover.

IKEA's basic strategy – neither to adjust the style of the products to the local needs nor follow the competitors' product development – was central to preserving the IKEA concept and image: 'The range is supposed to be IKEA unique and typical IKEA.' All range products are divided into four major categories or styles: Scandinavian, Country, Modern and Young Swede, which are clearly distinguished in all business areas across the store. One of the reasons why IKEA was successful with its standard product ranges in Russia was the fact that several of these IKEA ranges emphasise the modern style, which is very different from the traditional Russian style but is attractive and new for the Russian customers since it symbolises change.

An important part of the market approach was to identify the needs that are not fully recognised and to teach customers what IKEA is about. IKEA's retail proposition is based to a large extent on its Swedish roots and history, which is, in turn, very different from Russian traditions. Therefore, learning as much as possible about the local culture and customer needs was considered essential. For example, IKEA practised home visits to customers in order to talk to people, see how they lived and used their homes and to identify potential needs and wants not fully realised by customers themselves. Understanding the local family conditions and furnishing traditions then provided a basis for an effective introduction and marketing of the IKEA concept. As exemplified by a store manager, the main priority in Russia is the normal living costs; then comes the car and TV and afterwards maybe a trip

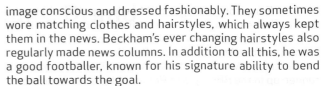

Beckham also had a £2 million per year deal with Pepsi to promote the cola drink. The company also conducted several contests, wherein participants could win a session with Beckham. Beckham was also part of an 11-member team that featured in Pepsi's advertisements before the World Cup 2002, where the players fought with Sumo wrestlers to win drinks of Pepsi. He was also featured in other television ads with some of his team-mates.

Marks & Spencer also brought out a range of products branded the DB07 range which were quite popular. The range for boys, which comprised T-shirts and other garments, had his initials in lettering style that was similar to what he used on his body tattoos. Beckham was also said to have had a hand in designing the range and none of the products went to the store without his approval.

Beckham also promoted Police Sunglasses; however, he was replaced by George Clooney in early 2003. Beckham initially endorsed the glasses in the UK and Japan, while Clooney was the global face. He also had a £1 million plus royalties deal with RAGE software, a maker of computer games. The company entered into a three-year contract with Beckham to develop various games that featured a character in his likeness. His pictures were also used on the packaging. Beckham was said to have played an important role in contributing to the development of the games' software. After RAGE started using Beckham to endorse its products, the revenues increased by £4.2 million.

Beckham's popularity was not restricted to Europe alone. In fact he was far more popular than any other soccer player in the Far East, especially Japan. Beckham endorsed a number of products in Japan. He and his wife Victoria modelled for a chain of beauty clinics in Tokyo called TBC and for confectioner Meiji Seika Kaisha. He shot a television advertisement for Meiji chocolates and his face also featured on the packing of the company's chocolates. The company revealed that the chocolate sales had doubled in the week after the ads featuring Beckham were first aired. In 2002 the same company had also generated a lot of publicity by building a chocolate statue of Beckham. Fans in Japan, who were rather traditional and family-oriented, seemed to like the fact that he gave a lot of importance to his wife and family. Most of them admired him for that.

Beckham's Appeal as a Brand

'We use David as a lifestyle icon. He does not appear in our advertising dressed in football kit, he is always appearing in his own casual clothing,' said Michael Caldwell, Director of Corporate Communication at Vodafone.[10] Beckham's appeal as a brand endorser went much beyond his abilities as a football player.

Beckham was a style icon. His rise from a working-class background to become the richest footballer made him seem approachable and real, and at the same time created an image of exclusivity and luxury. He had a special ability to reach out to the public. Good looking and photogenic, he was the natural choice of advertisers wanting to make an impact on the market. His wife Victoria also played an important role in designing the Beckham brand. The couple were always

image conscious and dressed fashionably. They sometimes wore matching clothes and hairstyles, which always kept them in the news. Beckham's ever changing hairstyles also regularly made news columns. In addition to all this, he was a good footballer, known for his signature ability to bend the ball towards the goal.

Beckham also had the clean-cut image of a family man which endeared him to the public, as well as advertisers wanting to portray that image. He did not smoke, drank very little and showed his commitment to his family. This image was especially effective in Asian countries where people gave importance to familial ties. In Japan, Beckham almost acquired the status of a demigod and set instant fashion trends with his changing hairstyles. His fans there called him Beckhamu-sama (the Honourable Mr Beckham), using an honorific to show admiration and respect. 'A lot of people think that my life is more glamorous than it actually is. I enjoy spending time with my family,' Beckham told a newspaper in China when he was on a promotional tour to the country in 2003.[11] The couple were also media savvy and made an effort to maintain positive public relations.

The couple were looked on as fashion icons and whatever they wore or did immediately became a trend. Even their sons were part of the fashion game and set trends in the market for children's products. Beckham had a unique ability to create news. For instance, when he injured his foot before the World Cup in 2002, there was a complete frenzy among the public. Even the Prime Minister of England, Tony Blair, was said to have remarked in a cabinet meeting that 'Nothing is more important to England's arrangements for the World Cup than the state of David Beckham's foot.'[12] During that time, phone-in shows on radio and television were inundated with talk of orthopedics. The tabloid *Sun* went to the extent of putting a picture of Beckham's injured foot on its front cover, asking people to touch it and make it better.

Real Madrid's Gain

The transfer of Beckham from Manchester United to Real Madrid gave rise to speculation about the effect it would have on the two clubs concerned. Manchester United was the best known club in Europe. It was estimated that the club had over 53 million fans worldwide. A number of products and services, such as financial planning, insurance, bed linen, jewellery, wallpaper, mortgages, a magazine and a television channel, were offered under the Manchester United brand. The presence of the club was even greater in the Asian region, where it was estimated that it had over 17 million fans. It also had stores to sell club-related merchandise in some Asian countries.

Real Madrid, which traditionally had had better players than Manchester United and had been nine times champion of the European club championship (to Manchester United's twice), was a better football club, but not as successful as Manchester United commercially. Real Madrid had conducted marketing research in the East Asian countries, which formed a crucial market, to test how it could increase its appeal to them. The club studied the appeal of individual players and found that there were very few people who could compete with Beckham's popularity in the region.

It was found that he had the charisma to attract even those people who had no traditional interest in the game. Associating with Beckham would extend the market for the club's merchandise considerably.

Real Madrid was also a competitive club, and had ambitions to overtake all its competitors, both on and off the pitch. When Florentino Perez, a construction mogul, became the club's president in 2000, he signed three of the world's best players, Ronaldo (Brazil), Zinedine Zidane (France) and Luis Figo (Portugal), in three successive seasons. Real Madrid had a lot to gain by signing Beckham. However, their need for him was mostly on the commercial front as the club already had at least four world-class players who were thought to be better than Beckham.

One of the important reasons why the move to Real Madrid was advantageous for Beckham was the fact that the various endorsement and sponsorship deals that he had at an individual level fitted in neatly with the deals of the club. At Manchester United there were clashes between the club's sponsorship interests and those of Beckham. For instance, Beckham was sponsored by German shoemaker Adidas, whereas the club was sponsored by rival Nike. On the other hand, Real Madrid's strip was made by Adidas, so the interests of the club and Beckham matched. One of Real Madrid's sponsors was Pepsi, which was also the personal sponsor of Beckham, so there was no conflicting move. Vodafone also found the move more beneficial than it would have if Beckham had been sold to AC Milan of Italy, as the team was sponsored by Telecom Italia, a rival, whereas Real Madrid worked with Siemens, a partner of Vodafone.

It was also thought to be an effective marketing move on the part of Real Madrid as the club had very low recognition and support in Asian countries where Manchester United was definitely more popular. The likely outcome of the transfer was that most of the fans of Beckham in Asian countries, who were a considerable number, would now support Real Madrid, thus increasing the club's reach. In terms of comparison, analysts estimated that almost 5 million of the 17 million fans of Manchester United in Asia would shift loyalties to Real Madrid. This was because, in Asia, the general trend was to root for an individual player, by contrast with Europe, where people were loyal to clubs. 'Many fans in Asia watch a team because of the individual star players. When those players are transferred quite often they will swap allegiances to a club and they will follow the player,' said Samantha McCollum, consultant at FutureBrand.[13] Therefore, the reason behind Real Madrid's offer was not just Beckham's football skills but his immense marketability.

Michael Sterling, a sports analyst at Field Fisher Waterhouse in London, estimated that Beckham would generate between £6 million and £10 million per year for the club – largely because he would open both the British and Asian markets for them. 'Real Madrid will rival Man U as a brand now. He's a sponsor's dream: a fashion icon, associated with success, a family man. Because of Beckham, football is no longer just about football, but about character and personality,' he said.[14]

Real Madrid offered Beckham compensation of £4.2 million a year. However, he was expected to turn in 50 per cent of his total endorsements to the club. He even had fans who did not know a single thing about football. It was profitable for the club to pay that amount to him because, according to sports marketing firm Apex, it was estimated that shirt sales alone would recover that amount in four years.

Analysts felt that it would not harm Manchester United to sell Beckham, who was its star player, because the club was already big enough to survive without having to depend on any one player. The major part of Manchester United's revenues came from ticket sales and media rights which were unlikely to be affected by Beckham's transfer. Merchandising, in which Beckham made a significant impact, comprised only 7 per cent of the club's revenues. However, there were rumours that Vodafone, which sponsored the shirts for Manchester United, would probably not want to renew the sponsorship when the contract expired in 2004, as a majority of the Manchester United shirts it sold were replicas of Beckham's shirts, and with Beckham no longer playing for the club, the shirt sales would fall significantly. In England a club was always bigger than any individual player, and observers felt that Manchester United probably did not like the fact that Beckham began to rival it in popularity. Analysts also felt that it was a good move on the part of Manchester United to sell Beckham at the peak of his career, when he fetched the best price.

The sale was not without its critics, however. There were a number of people who opposed the club's decision to sell Beckham. The sale of Beckham headed the list of bulletin board topics on a number of websites and discussion forums and was widely discussed in the media. On www.sina.com, one of the largest websites in China, fans criticised the sale severely. 'I'll never watch United again,' declared one fan.[15] Some fans were also worried that Beckham would not always be selected in a club that was already packed with some of the most talented players in the world, and they resented this.

There have also been people who criticised the amount spent by Real Madrid on purchasing Beckham. 'There are many better ways of spending money that has been earned with great sacrifices other than hiring Mr Beckham,' said Silvio Berlusconi, the Italian premier, who was also president of AC Milan.[16] Another important factor which took the gloss off the deal was that the demand for soccer and soccer stars was at an all time low at the time when the transfer deal was in negotiation. Because of the growth of pay channels on cable television, the viewing figures for matches had plummeted. A number of players were also being laid off by clubs, who were themselves facing bankruptcy, especially in Britain. In this situation, the amount paid for Beckham seemed unjustified.

Exhibit 1 Breakdown of Beckham's transfer fee

- £5.25 million on completion of Beckham's transfer
- £12 million in instalments over next four years
- £7 million based on Real's performances in Champions League (£875 000 every year they qualify, £875 000 every year they reach the quarter finals).

Source: news.bbc.co.uk.

Case 4.5 Luxottica: Internationalisation and Expansion

Luxottica goes direct: from eyeglass design and manufacturing to world leading distribution

Antonio Majocchi

Luxottica, an Italian firm listed on the New York and Milan Stock Exchanges, is today the global leader in the fashion and luxury eyewear industry. As a designer, manufacturer, and distributor for prescription frames and sunglasses, the firm owns such well-known brands as Ray-Ban, Oakley Arnette, Persol, Revo, and Vogue and holds the licence for brands such as Bulgari, Burberry, Chanel, Dolce & Gabbana, Polo Ralph Lauren, Prada, Tiffany & Co., and Versace. Luxottica's strength lies not only in the brand portfolio but also, among other things, in its large, international and well distributed wholesale and retail network. In 2007 Luxottica managed a wholesale distribution network covering more than 100 countries and including corporate-owned retail chains in the world's 44 largest eyewear markets.

How did a firm that in the early sixties was a small spectacle workshop placed in a remote place called Agordo in the North-eastern part of Italy became a world leader? Key to Luxottica's success was an internationalisation strategy that combined worldwide acquisitions of retail chains and strong brand development. The process of internationalisation of the firm dates back to 1971, when Leonardo Del Vecchio, the founder and owner of the firm, participated in a fair in Milan and contacted importers from Europe and the United States. This was the starting point for both soaring exports and a series of joint ventures and partnerships with local distributors in a number of European and North American countries. The eighties saw a development of a new growth strategy for distribution. Transition from an export-led strategy to a direct strategy was pursued either by acquiring local wholesale distributors or by directly setting up distribution channels where necessary. This shift was driven by Luxottica's early recognition of a sharp change in the consumers' perception of glasses. Thanks to high-profile advertising, the use of well-known sport and music celebrities and movie stars as testimonial, eyewear products began to be considered by consumers as something more than necessity and not just a medical product to correct sight defects or a device to protect eyes from sunlight. This trend was particularly

Table 1 Luxottica's key facts, numbers and brands

Key facts	Key numbers and house brands (2007)
● 1961 Company set up as a manufacturer of optical frames	● Sales = €4 966 054 000 ($6 805 977 000)

● 1990 Listing on the New York Stock Exchange	● Net sales by geographical area
	  – US 61%
	  – Asia Pacific 12%
	  – Rest of the world 27%,

● 1995 Acquisition of LensCrafters	● Net profit €492 204 ($674 566)
● 1999 Acquisition of Ray-Ban	● Work force 61 903 (7791 in Italy)
● 2000 Listing on the Italian Stock Exchange	● Retail outlets: (over 6400 worldwide)

● 2001–2007 Acquisition of different sunglass retailers and optical store chain operators in the US and Asia Pacific
● 2007 Acquisition of Oakley, the sports eyewear company
	● Key house brands
	  – Ray-Ban
	  – Oakley
	  – Vogue,
	  – Persol
	  – Arnette
	  – REVO

evident for sunglasses, once a typical season product but now no longer just a summer purchase. Consumers started buying different pairs of sunglasses for different attire or occasions – parties or shopping, skiing or sailing – so the average consumer has gone from owning one pair to owning many. Not only did this trend result in quickly raising demand, but it completely transformed the overall business, driving it towards industry patterns typical of the fashion industry with short replacement cycles, strong brand recognition and heavy dependence on the sales from fashion trends.

Luxottica capitalised on this trend by signing licence agreements with a large number of fashion and designer labels and entering into a long-term equity agreement with Giorgio Armani. Moreover, in 1999 the Group concluded the acquisition of the trendy Ray-Ban sunglasses business from the Bausch & Lomb group. Its cult status and the brand's worldwide fame leads back to Hollywood stars like Audrey Hepburn who wore Ray-Ban glasses in *Breakfast at Tiffany's* or Peter Fonda in *Easy Rider*, John Belushi in *The Blues Brothers* and Tom Cruise in *Top Gun*, giving to the group worldwide recognition and adding glamour to its international reputation.

Being part of the fashion industry does, however, mean also that direct relationships with consumers are of crucial importance, themselves allowing firms to direct customers towards their products and using customers as a source of valuable information in a fast-changing market. Luxottica, spotting this trend, decided to invest heavily in distribution channels. At the beginning of the 1990s the firm was already the world market leader with an international market share estimated at almost 9 per cent and with a large share in the US reaching about 20 per cent of the market. However, in view of the volatile nature of the market caused by changing consumer attitudes, the stated goal of the firm was to gain exclusive access to distribution channels. In order to reach this objective, a campaign of international acquisitions began in 1995, a campaign that has not yet finished. The year 1995 signalled the beginning of a new development in the firm's strategy, with the acquisition of US Shoe Corporation, a company owner of three different retail chains in the fashion business among which the brand LensCrafters is active in the eyewear segment. Since then, Luxottica has invested heavily in retail chains, pursuing a strategy of forward vertical integration that has transformed the firm from a mainly manufacturing one into an integrated company with important distribution activities. LensCrafters at the time of the acquisition held a market share of almost 7 per cent, allowing Luxottica to gain a strong foothold in the US and adding hundreds of shops to its distribution channels. Subsequently, Luxottica Group strengthened its position of global leadership by acquiring Sunglass Hut International. The acquisition in 2001 adds a total of 1733 Sunglass Hut locations to the Luxottica's existing chains and increases its presence not only in North America but also in Europe, Australia and Asia.

The growth in the distribution network realised through acquisitions and franchising agreements is reported in Table 2.

Recently, the Group entered the Chinese market with different acquisitions (see Table 3) but also with direct investments in order to open entirely new stores such as the LensCrafters' flagship store placed at the Oriental Plaza mall in Beijing, one of the city's most important shopping centres. As a result, the Group became the leading operator of premium optical stores in China, with a total of 276 locations in two regions of the Mainland China (Beijing and the Guangdong province) as well as in Hong Kong. Most recently, Luxottica signed a franchising agreement with an Indian partner in order to enter in the high-potential Indian retail market with the opening of over 100 Sunglass Hut stores. With this agreement Luxottica has filled one of the few holes still missing in its worldwide direct retail networks, developing a full range of retail brands covering not only the main geographical areas but also the different segments in the medium and higher range of the market.

Thanks to this new commercial strategy, Luxottica has developed a worldwide network based on short commercialisation channels, thus gaining direct control of the market outlets. The strategy has allowed the firms not only to raise economic margins, avoiding the cost of intermediation, but also to have full control of every aspect of the selling activities, which means monitoring the consumers' evolution and raising their level of satisfaction.

The positive effects of this strategy are reflected in the economic data reported in Figure 1, which depicts the evolution of net sales and profits (net and operating) from the acquisition of LensCrafters until the present. The data show the impressive sales growth that has been sustained throughout the period. Average growth of sales has been 15 per cent with only one year of negative growth in the year 2002 when the economic downturn, following the attack on the Twin Towers, affected the turnover of the firm. The data on net profit and operating profit (net sales less operating costs) show also that the aggressive acquisition campaign has not harmed profitability.

This conclusion is even clearer if one looks at margins in terms of net profit and operating profit (net sales less operating costs). Figure 2 shows that margins have slightly decreased in the 2002–2005 period following the economic crisis that affected the US market – the main market for Luxottica – but also following the massive investments the firms realised in this period to develop its own distribution networks. In spite of these investments Luxottica succeeds in maintaining operating profitability at a ratio that was always above 12.8 per cent with net profitability higher than 8 per cent. With a network of global and local distribution chains already in place covering all the main markets of the world and a brand portfolio of highly valuable brand names in its pocket, Luxottica seems to have a significant edge versus its competitors across the board. The company is now well prepared to gather the fruits of the high and consistent investments strategy in distribution channels realised through the years.

Table 2 Luxottica main acquisitions in the retail sector and franchising agreements 1995–2007

Year	Acquisition	Description
1995	Acquisition of US Shoe Corporation	US Shoe was the owner of the retail chain LensCrafters and also owned a retail chain of shoes and one of women fashion. These two retail chains have been subsequently sold by Luxottica.
2001	Sunglass Hut International	Leading sunglass retail chain operating with 1733 locations in North America, Europe, Australia and Asia.
2003	OPSM Group ('OPSM')	OPSM is the leading optical retailer in Australia, with 481 stores and three brands: OPSM, Laubman & Pank and Budget Eyewear. It is also the market leader in New Zealand, with 34 stores, and has expanded into Asia, where it has 80 stores in Hong Kong, 12 in Singapore and 12 in Malaysia. The total number of OPSM stores, at the time of the acquisition, was 619.
2004	Cole National	Cole National is the second largest player in the sector in the US, owner of retail brands such as Pearle Vision with a network of wholly owned stores and in franchising (197 locations in the US, Canada, Puerto Rico and the Virgin Islands). It is the operator of in-store optical departments with retail brands such as Pearle Vision, Sears Optical, Target Optical and BJ's Optical.
2005	Xueliang Optical	The leading premium optical chain in Beijing, China.
2005	Ming Long Optical	The largest premium optical chain in the province of Guangdong, China.
2006	Acquisition of Modern Sight Optics	A leader in China in the premium optical segment with 28 stores in Shanghai.
2006	Franchising agreement with Azal Group	A five-year franchising agreement with a retail group. According to the agreement Luxottica will open 50 new stores in the Middle East under the Sunglass Hut brand.
2006	Modern Sight Optics D.O.C Optics	A leading premium optical chain that operates a total of 28 stores in Shanghai, China. An optical retail business with approximately 100 stores located primarily in the Midwest United States.
2007	Oakley, Inc.	Worldwide specialist in sport performance optics and owner of ILORI, the retail brands (Oakley Stores and Vaults, Sunglass Icon, The Optical Shop of Aspen and Oliver Peoples).
2007	South African retail chains	Two prominent speciality sun chains in South Africa, for a total of 65 stores.
	Franchising agreement with DLF Group	DLF Group the country's largest real estate developer based in New Delhi. According to the agreement over 100 Sunglass Hut stores will be opened at select high-end malls and other premium retail locations across India.

Source: Luxottica.com.

Table 3 Group's retail chain worldwide. Brands, number and stores and geographical distribution

Geographical areas	Retail brand	Number of stores			
		2005	2006	2007	% 2007
North America	LensCrafters	893	902	951	
	Pearle (*)	837	840	880	
	Sears Optical	960	941	886	
	Target Optical	246	264	296	
	BJ's Optical (**)	143	153	156	
	Sunglass Hut	1557	1502	1600	
	Sunglass Icon			143	
	ILORI			6	
	TOTAL in North America	4636	4602	4918	76.8
Asia-Pacific	OPSM	314	314	322	
	Laubman & Pank	123	127	135	
	Budget Eyewear	75	86	94	
	Sunglass Hut	182	224	219	
	Bright Eyes			140	
	TOTAL Asia-Pacific	694	751	910	14.2
China	LensCrafters and others (**)	276	274	249	
	Sunglass Hut			6	
	TOTAL China	276	274	255	4.0
Europe	Sunglass Hut	110	92	87	1.4
South Africa	Sunglass Hut			68	1.1
Middle East	Sunglass Hut			23	0.4
Global	The Optical Shop of Aspen			21	
	Oliver Peoples			6	
	Oakley stores and Vaults			119	
	TOTAL Global			146	2.3
Total store		5716	5719	6407	100

(*) of which 403 in *franchising*. (**) = Xuelian Optical, Ming Long Optical, The optical shop, the Modern Sight.
Source: Luxottica Annual report, 2007, 2006, 2005. As at 31 December 2007.

Case 4.6 FedEx vs. UPS – Competing with Contrasting Strategies in China

I don't know that I agree that there's a sort of Chinese way and an American way. I think there is clearly more of an entrepreneurial and establishment way ... and China at the moment is a country that is very entrepreneurial in nature. We are more consonant with the new China.[1]

– Frederick W. Smith, Chairman and CEO, FedEx Corporation.

UPS expects continued strong and robust growth in China. We take a long-term approach to any expansion and believe the opportunity in China is great enough to overcome any business cycle.[2]

– Jim Kelly, Chairman and CEO, UPS.

Introduction

The US-based FedEx Corporation (FedEx),[3] one of the world's largest logistics solutions providers, announced a money-back guarantee scheme in September 2002 for its customers in China. Under the scheme, FedEx offered full refund of customers' money in case of late delivery of shipments. By introducing this scheme, FedEx became the first international logistics company to offer money-back guarantee in China.

Analysts were quick to comment that this measure was taken by FedEx to counterattack the move announced by its global competitor, the US-based United Parcel Service (UPS).[4] UPS had opened two representative offices in the Chinese cities – Shenzhen and Qingdao in early September 2002. UPS had also announced its plans to open four more offices, in Xiamen, Dongguan, Hangzhou and Tianjin by early 2003.

For a long time, FedEx and UPS had been arch-rivals in China, competing with each other for more market share in the Chinese logistics market (Refer Exhibit I). According to the analysts, FedEx had adopted an aggressive approach to increase its market share in China. The company invested heavily in procuring air routes and in deploying its own aircrafts within and

outside China for shipping goods. FedEx had also developed a vast distribution network with pickup outlets across China. Until 2001 the company used global advertising campaigns to advertise in China.

By contrast, UPS followed a more conservative and cautious approach while making inroads into the Chinese market. The company made efforts to position itself as a local company, rather than building an image of a global player. Instead of investing on building its own logistics infrastructure, the company decided to depend on leased facilities. Despite acquiring rights to fly its own plane in 2000, UPS was mostly dependent on its joint-venture relationships to ship goods within and outside China. Analysts felt that UPS' advertising was old-fashioned, even compared with the prevalent standards in China.

Until the late 1990s UPS followed a cautious approach, making limited investment in China compared to that of FedEx. However, with improving business prospects in China following its entry into the World Trade Organization (WTO) in 2001, the company started pursuing the Chinese market aggressively. This helped it in increasing its market presence in China.

Establishing Presence in China

According to the Chinese legal regulations, foreign logistics management companies including FedEx and UPS could do business in China only through a partnership or joint venture with a local company (refer Exhibit I). Foreign companies were not allowed to run businesses independently in China. Further, they were required to handle only international express cargo business (they were not permitted to carry out cargo-handling business within Chinese cities).

FedEx – Developing the Services Network

FedEx commenced its operations in April 1973 in Memphis, US. In 1984 FedEx entered China after acquiring Gelco Express International, a UK-based courier company which had operations in Europe and Asia Pacific. During the first decade of its operations in China, FedEx focused on establishing the required infrastructure and distribution network to provide reliable express freight and documentation services.

Rather than targeting leading Chinese companies, FedEx focused on those multinational companies which had Chinese operations and were already FedEx's customers in the US or elsewhere. FedEx also targeted those Chinese entrepreneurs who were expanding their business and whom the company believed would readily adopt FedEx's fast and accurate delivery techniques.

To compete effectively with the established local competitors in China, FedEx in its initial years invested heavily on building its own distribution network. In 1989 FedEx invested $880 million to acquire Flying Tiger Line Inc.

Exhibit 1 A Snapshot of the logistics industry in China (2002)

There are about 1500 licensed international freight-forwarding operators in China. Of these, 450 are Sino-foreign joint ventures, primarily involved in the management of international freight at the international level. Inland transportation is handled by Chinese freight forwarders – mainly single-truck operations subcontracted by international freight forwarders to move goods from warehouses to ports. Foreign logistics companies face a number of hurdles for conducting business in China. An overview of such hurdles and the future scenario is given below.

Entry barriers

Foreign logistics companies intending to do business in China can enter only through joint ventures with local Chinese companies.

Legal regulations

Foreign companies cannot:

- Distribute products other than those they manufacture in China
- Own and manage distribution networks, wholesale outlets or warehouses
- Conduct customs brokerage and clearance, ground transportation, warehousing and related services outside a transport joint venture.
- Hold a majority stake in a joint venture, with limitations on where and how fast joint ventures can expand.

Expected changes over the next decade

The Chinese government promised to make significant improvements to the regulations in the next decade, following the commitments made to the WTO. The promised improvements include the following:

- Foreign companies will be allowed to distribute imported products, besides those made in China.
- China has agreed to phase out all restrictions on distribution services within three years. Restrictions on all services auxiliary to distribution will be phased out in three to four years. These include express delivery services, vehicle rental and leasing, freight forwarding, storage and warehousing. Foreigners engaged in these businesses will be able to set up their wholly owned subsidiaries.
- In the most sensitive and protected sectors – chemicals, oil and petroleum – China will provide distribution rights to foreigners within five years.

Source: adapted from the article, 'FedEx has ideas for China,' written by David L Cunningham Jr. in *Nation (Thailand),* dated 15 October 2002.

(Tiger).[5] The acquisition helped FedEx to get ready access to Tiger's Asian routes, including a high-traffic route between Japan and China.

By 1995 FedEx had started freight operations in China. The company appointed EAS International Transportation Limited (EAS) as a global service participant for China to ship the goods and packages within China. EAS acted as the carrier of the goods and packages of FedEx within China through its network spread across 34 major commercial cities covering nearly 50 per cent of the Chinese population. By mid 1995 FedEx invested another $67.5 million to acquire Evergreen International Airlines,[6] the only cargo carrier with flying rights into China. This allowed FedEx to get a ready access to an all-cargo route to serve Chinese customers directly.

Following the receipt of the permit from the Civil Aviation Administration of China (CAAC) in January 1996, FedEx earned the distinction of being the only US-based all-cargo carrier with aviation rights to China. Having secured the aviation rights in China and several other Asian countries, FedEx introduced the 'hub and spoke system'[7] in Asia. FedEx had

already launched the Asia Pacific hub at Subic Bay, Philippines in September 1995 in order to expand its operations in other Asian countries. This enabled the company to launch an organised distribution system in Asia, called the FedEx AsiaOne network through which 13 major commercial and financial cities in Asia (spokes) were connected. This network enabled FedEx to provide an overnight delivery of goods shipped within the Asian countries. The Asian shipments could be further routed to the FedEx's global network through the Asia Pacific hub.

In March 1996 FedEx launched its first scheduled air service in China using its own aircraft in and out of China with bi-weekly flights to Beijing and Shanghai. In September 1996 the two cities were integrated into the FedEx AsiaOne network. These enabled the customers in Shanghai and Beijing to ship and receive packages between China and the US and the rest of Asia.

In April 1998 FedEx launched the Express Distribution Centers (EDCs) in Beijing and Hong Kong by entering into an agreement with U-Freight Holdings Limited.[8] The EDCs, which were company to develop a very good rapport with the Chinese customers and encouraged those who patronised other companies to shift to UPS. For instance, an advertising executive from a Chinese company shifted his account from a government-owned mail service company to UPS when a UPS executive approached him and explained the utility (both in terms of convenience as well as cost) of using UPS's services for their business operations.

The Investments Made

Since its entry into China, FedEx had invested heavily on building its services network in China, adopting a long-term approach. Wilson Chung, general manager of FedEx China said, 'China is one of the most important markets for FedEx. We are dedicated to continually investing in this market.'[17] However, the company faced a major setback with the South East Asian currency crisis during 1997–8. Following significant currency devaluations in the Southeast Asian countries, FedEx reported its first quarterly loss (quarter ending February 1998) on international operations since 1996. This was largely attributable to the high investments made in its extensive air network in Asia, coupled with declining cargo volume and revenues from troubled Asian countries. Joseph M. Pyne (Vice-President – Marketing) of UPS, was quick to comment: 'Because of the investment (FedEx) made, they're almost stuck in that market. That's the plan they have to live with. We're looking at the market and moving with it in China.'[18]

In contrast to the FedEx approach, UPS decided to make investments according to the market conditions in China. Up until 1997 UPS had invested significantly less compared to FedEx in China. UPS had stepped up its operations as the demand increased, sacrificing some market share in its limited risk strategy. Lacking its own air service, UPS was unable to offer customers in China the range of logistical services that FedEx could offer. The management of UPS always felt that, if business prospects in China improved later, the company could fly its own aircraft in and out of China. The company's low investment strategy in China saved it from any major losses from the South East Asian currency crisis. As the freight volumes reduced in China, UPS simply reduced the space it leased on other companies' planes.

FedEx felt that its high-investment strategy had helped in gaining more market share in China. According to Air Cargo Management Group, a Seattle-based consultancy, by mid-1998 FedEx had captured 13 per cent of the express market in China, excluding Hong Kong, while UPS had less than a 5 per cent share. Alan B. Graf, FedEx's chief financial officer commented: 'We knew it was risky when we built so much capacity, but we're staying. And that has just got to have a long-term payoff.'[19]

Logistics Industry in China – Improving Prospects

China was viewed as the logistics industry's most important emerging market. According to an industry analyst at Merge Global Incorporated,[20] an Arlington, US-based research company, China's air-cargo market was the world's fifth largest and its emerging express market was valued at $400 million in 1998. According to studies conducted during the late 1990s, China's demand for time-definite express freight was projected to grow by 20 per cent per year till 2002 – much faster compared to the global air-freight market.

By 2000 competition in the logistics industry in China had intensified. Both FedEx and UPS were facing competition from MNCs like DHL, and China's state-owned enterprises like China Post. Following the decision of the Chinese government to enter into the World Trade Organization in 2001, the competition in the industry intensified further. With the removal of a number of rules and regulations which had protected China's government-owned logistics companies, the business prospects for multinational logistics companies improved significantly.

With the improved business prospects, UPS decided to follow a more aggressive approach to expand its market presence in China. The company lobbied intensively in the US to secure a right to operate its own flight directly into China. The company also decided to invest significantly in infrastructural facilities in the new millennium.

In November 2000 the US Department of Transportation (DOT) granted UPS air rights to operate direct flights from the US to China. UPS was allowed six flights between US and China in a week. In December 2000, following DOT's decision to designate UPS as the fourth US air-carrier to service China market, FedEx appealed to US DOT to allow it one more flight per week to China.

Rising Competition

Analysts felt that granting of air rights to UPS would further intensify the competition in China and enable major US freight service carriers to access the Chinese market by offering low-cost and better service. Although FedEx had not questioned DOT's decision to permit six flights to UPS, the company objected to the awarding of three flights to United Airlines and Northwest Airlines, its other competitors in China. FedEx called DOT's decision 'fundamentally unfair' under the pretext that its contribution to the export growth in the US was significantly high when compared with that of Northwest Airlines or United Airlines.

In March 2001 UPS announced the launch of six weekly flights between China and the US using Boeing 747 aircraft, directly servicing Beijing and Shanghai. Four weekly flights were to start from Ontario International airport, California and the other two at Newark, New Jersey. On 1 April 2001 the first flight landed in China. Commenting on the event, Jim Kelly, Chairman and CEO of UPS said, 'This is the first time ever that a US cargo carrier will fly directly from the US to China. We believe this designation is a sign of the growing importance of global trade and UPS place in the new global marketplace. With these new flights, UPS will offer the broadest portfolio of services to customers shipping to and from China.'[21] The launch of the service turned out to be a successful move by UPS as its business in the US-China region grew by an estimated 40 per cent soon after the launch.

Reacting to this move by UPS, FedEx announced an additional flight to its existing fleet of 11 aircraft. In April 2001 FedEx also launched the Shanghai Express Freighter service. The newly launched flight service enabled FedEx to improve its services in the express segment between eastern China and the US by reducing the shipment time by three to four hours. FedEx also stated its plans to inaugurate new infrastructure facilities in four Chinese states – Nanjing, Hangzhou, Dongguan and Ningbo.

UPS further intensified its promotion activities following the launch of its direct flight to China. In May 2001 UPS launched an advertising campaign developed by reputed advertising agency, McCann-Erickson.[22] In the campaign titled 'Brown Survey', a lady was asked to identify what immediately came into her mind when a series of colours were flashed at her. When the colour brown flashed up, she instantly related it to reliability, and then to UPS. The campaign focused on creating a unique brand identity for UPS, as UPS was traditionally recognised by its fleet of brown trucks, which offered reliable service to the customers, through its customer-friendly employees and courier persons.

In an attempt to sell B2B e-commerce solutions to the cost-conscious Chinese businesses, UPS launched the 'Customer Automation Program' in June 2001. Under this programme, UPS offered to computerise the business units of its customers by providing the required PCs and software and by linking them to the UPS shipping systems free of cost. The customers could print their own shipping labels. By doing this, UPS enabled its customers to understand the cost benefits of purchasing UPS B2B e-commerce solutions.

To further promote its business and compete effectively with UPS, FedEx implemented further innovative ideas. For instance in mid-2001, in association with OMD, FedEx began to sponsor popular TV shows in China. The first to be sponsored was a popular television game show, *Who Wants to be a Millionaire*,[23] aired on Asia Television (ATV). The purpose of choosing the game show for sponsorship was to associate FedEx with speed and accuracy – the two key ingredients emphasised in the game show. The effort paid off for FedEx, as within three months of sponsoring the show, its top-of-mind recall[24] increased by 42 per cent among viewers in China. Encouraged by this success, FedEx sponsored another game show on ATV, *The Vault*. This interactive game show was used to display FedEx brand as a backdrop through an attractive FedEx motion TV billboard. This initiative was successful as FedEx's brand awareness increased and the company was able to position its services for its speed and accuracy.

In October 2001 FedEx introduced a unique service in China. The company inaugurated a massive 6080-square-metre FedEx-DTW Express Center at Shanghai Pudong International Airport. The integrated warehouse management system[25] at the centre comprised a sorting and distribution system which employed state-of-the-art wireless technology to enhance productivity and provide accurate information. The system could handle 6000 to 12 000 packages per hour. Analysts concluded that FedEx launched this system to cope up with the increasing volumes of goods and packages following China's entry into the WTO in 2001.

To counter FedEx's move, in December 2001 UPS launched two new services – UPS Signature Tracking TM and UPS Worldwide Express Plus TM. The signature tracking service provided proof of delivery of the package of the recipient (his signature) within minutes of its delivery.[26] This service was targeted primarily at business customers who needed to furnish proof of delivery to effect other business transactions. The UPS Worldwide Express plus TM enabled shipping of packages or documents from China to any major US city next day by 8 am or to other non-metropolitan cities in the US, 13 European countries and Canada by 8:30 am.

The Rivalry Intensifies

The rivalry between FedEx and UPS to grab more market share of the Chinese logistics market further intensified in 2002. In April 2002 UPS launched a new intra-Asia hub at Philippines. The new hub along with two other hubs of UPS located in Singapore, Hong Kong and Taipei comprised the worldwide network of hubs of UPS. This move enabled UPS to significantly enhance its operational capacity in China, as well as enabling it to increase its ability to serve Chinese customers by offering quicker and more reliable service.

In May 2002, following the launch of an intra-Pacific air hub in Philippines, which complemented the other hub facilities in Taiwan, Singapore, and Hong Kong, UPS launched an advertising campaign titled 'Asia', showcasing UPS as an integrated logistics solutions provider. This campaign, like the previous ad campaign, stressed the reliability of a UPS service. It also gave a glimpse of the advanced technology employed at UPS including the WAP-enabled, package-tracking technology.

In September 2002 FedEx planned to further improve its services in Southern China and the Pearl River Delta region by upgrading the aircraft serving Shenzhen from a DC-10 to an MD-11. This move also increased the freight capacity by 30 tons.

In order to understand the needs of the Chinese customers in smaller cities better and to offer these customers express delivery service of higher quality, in September 2002 UPS opened two offices in Chinese cities – Shenzhen and Qingdao. UPS followed this by opening an office in the southern Chinese city of Xiamen in October 2002, in an effort to further penetrate the local Chinese market. Another significant factor of this launch was that all the employees of the office were hired locally.

Status in 2003

By 2003 the competition between FedEx and UPS was at its peak. Both the companies had been aggressively pursuing the Chinese market by regularly announcing new and better services, agreements and tie-ups. Both the companies continuously revised their strategies in answer to the moves announced by their competitor.

In January 2003 FedEx announced an agreement with Kodak to offer self-delivery

Exhibit 4 Tetra Pak – customers around the world

Tetra Pak's packaging solutions have been used by a diverse group of food manufacturers (particularly liquid food) around the world. Some of the customers include companies like Coca-Cola, Tropicana Foods and Beverages, Britannia, Parle Agro Products, Paramalat (Italy) and Unilever. Following are some of the instances where Tetra Pak packaging systems were chosen by beverage manufacturers to differentiate their products and project them as contemporary products (lightweight, easy to use, hygienic, with longer shelf life).

South Africa: Ceres Fruit Juices, Africa's leading fruit juice manufacturer held a 55 per cent share of the domestic fruit juice (which have a longer shelf life) market. The company's flagship brand 'Ceres' which was positioned as the best quality fruit juice available in the market, had won the Gold Award from American Tasting Institute for its quality and taste in 1999, 2000 and 2001. It also received the ISO 9001 certification. Ceres was exclusively packed in Tetra Brik Aseptic (TBA) cartons, TBA 200 ml slim and TBA 1000 ml slim with ReCap. Other brands like Liqui-Fruit and Fruitee were also packaged in Tetra Brik Aseptic cartons.

US: Imagine Foods Inc, California manufactured and marketed its 'functional beverages'[21] product 'Power Dream' energy drink that contained soya protein. The company had reformulated the product with a new flavour. To market this, the company designed new graphics to print on the packaging. The graphics on the drink's Tetra Prisma Aseptic package included pictures of mountain biking, running, skydiving and downhill skiing. After the reformulation and introduction of new packaging in 2002, the company's sales had tripled since the products introduction in 1998.

Saudi Arabia: In 2002 Al Safi-Danone Co. Ltd, a leading beverage manufacturer in the country, launched a range of dairy products: full-cream milk, low-fat milk, full-cream Laban (a traditional drink made of cultured milk with a slightly salty taste) and low-fat Laban. These drinks were launched in Tetra Top Mini GrandTab 250 ml cartons and Tetra Top packs to achieve market differentiation and project the on-the-go and 'fresh' image. The company claimed that the market response to the product was very positive.

Lebanon: Liban Lait, a dairy in Lebanon, sold the Aryan drink (a popular drink in Middle East/Eastern Mediterranean made up of fermented milk, water and salt) under the Candia brand. The company packaged the drink in Tetra Prisma Aseptic cartons as it wanted the product to have a longer shelf life than the traditional chilled Aryan. The company also chose Tetra Prisma Aseptic because it wanted to target the product at a younger and modern consumer base.

Taiwan: Uni-President Enterprises Corporation, Taiwan's leading beverage manufacturer, launched two brands 'His Café' and 'Her Café' in 2002. The company wanted to introduce the brand in the premium segment with premium packaging. For this purpose, the company chose the Tetra Prisma Aseptic 250 ml carton. 'His Café' packaging was given a gold metallic design and 'Her Café' package was given a silver metallic design. The cartons were fitted with a Pull Tab opening and a telescopic straw.

Poland: Spídzielnia Mleczarska Mlekovita, a polish dairy, launched the 'Mlekovita' brand of feta cheese in 2002. The company used the Tetra Brik Aseptic 250 ml and 200 ml cartons to package the brand, which was targeted at young women with above average income and education.

Source: adapted from 'New Products from Tetra Pak Internationally' at www.tetrapak.com.

Apart from designing innovative packages, Tetra Pak also developed a variety of drinking straws. The company designed, produced and marketed straws to suit different kinds of packages and products. In order to make the straws look appealing, Tetra Pak manufactured them in many designs: straight, u-shaped, twisted and striped. As in the case of packaging, Tetra Pak designed straws that were hygienic and that appealed to customers.

One such innovation was the development of telescopic straws in early 2000. Tetra Pak developed the telescopic straws in association with BioGaia, a Swedish biotech major. These type of straws had a small tube fitted inside them. This tube was filled with 'supplementary, health boosting ingredients' known as neutraceuticals. The neutraceuticals were placed in the straw to separate them from the liquid until consumption.

Telescopic straws were commercialised with the launch of the 'LifeTop' range of straws. LifeTop straws contained a blue inner straw filled with Lactobacillus Reuteri (Reuteri), a bacterium which released lactic acid. According to

Exhibit 5 Tetra Pak – marketing initiatives

Part of Tetra Pak's success throughout the world can be attributed to its marketing efforts. Tetra Pak marketed itself through various modes such as corporate campaigns, product-level campaigns and business area-level campaigns. It also used campaigns that increased consumer awareness of the company's efforts to protect the environment. Since the company was present in many countries, it designed country-specific TV and print media campaigns. Tetra Pak advertisements emphasised various aspects of its packaging technology, like hygiene, safety, convenience and ease of use.

For over three decades Tetra Pak conveyed the benefits of its packaging technology for customers through the catch line 'More than the package'. When Tetra Pak acquired Alfa Laval, a US-based manufacturer of equipment for food provision, environmental care, pharmaceutical and light chemical industries (in the early 1990s), the company needed to communicate to the food industry that it had broadened its portfolio to include the full range of processing equipment for food. This requirement was met well by the old motto. However, in early 2003 Tetra Pak replaced the old catchline with a new one, 'Protects what's good'. The change was in tune with the company's global repositioning strategy for its packaging products. As part of this strategy, it wanted to communicate the benefits of its products not only to the food-processing companies but to all participants in the value chain (comprising suppliers, corporate customers and retail customers).

Source: compiled from www.tetrapak.com and other sources.

research conducted by the company, Reuteri helped reduce the risk of stomach disorders, improved nutrient absorption, and enhanced the body's immune and defence system. LifeTop straws released these probiotics[13] in the beverage when it was consumed through these straws.[14]

Commenting on the usefulness of the new product, Jacquelyn Paul, Global General Manager, COE, Nutritionals, Tetra Pak, said, 'Tetra Pak wants to provide innovative solutions to its clients. With a great product like LifeTop straw, Tetra Pak and BioGaia can drive both consumer satisfaction and a health conscious product at the same time.'[15]

The LifeTop straws were wrapped individually and attached to beverage cartons. Each straw was sealed in an aluminum sachet coated with polyethylene terepthlate and polyethylene, which acted as a barrier against moisture and prevented oxidation. This extended the shelf life of the bacteria from a few weeks to many months. The straw could be attached to all kinds of packages, thus allowing existing beverage packages to be used. The straw also allowed manufacturers to supply probiotics with any kind of beverage without having to compromise on its taste and ingredients. Moreover, the straw eliminated the concerns of food product manufacturers for providing a controlled dosage of probiotics, accurate blending and damage due to exposure to heat.

Commenting on the benefits of LifeTop to beverage manufacturers, Jonathan Middlemiss, Managing Director, Farm Produce Marketing Ltd. (FPM, a UK-based dairy products manufacturer and marketer),[16] said, 'The great advantage of this is that it enables us to add an extra health dimension to our product without having to reformulate it. Like many really good ideas, this is really very simple with a droplet of Reuteri attached to the inside of the telescopic straw that is only activated when used by the consumer.'[17]

In late 2001, Tetra Pak launched the 'EaZip' opening feature. In EaZip, the upper section of the straw cover could be torn along a tear point that was indicated by a red stripe.

This EaZip mechanism was described as much more hygienic than the straws then available because it allowed the straw to be removed from its protective cover without requiring the customer to touch the end that came in contact with the product. Some of the first companies to use the EaZip straw system were Lego (for its soft drinks) and Coca-Cola (for its fruit drink 'Five Alive').

During the same period, to make the distribution and handling of the straws more efficient and cost-effective, the company introduced a new product called the Apogee box. The new distribution box was compact since its width was exactly the same as the length of the straw. This way the straws were tightly packed and protected from damage. In traditional packing methods, the straws were loosely packed with the product cartons and were therefore prone to damage during transportation. Due to the compactness of the Apogee box, many boxes could be stored on a pallet, leading to efficient handling and cost savings during transportation and storage in production plants.

Innovating into the Future – Exploring New Areas

Having established its supremacy in packaging for milk, milk products and juices, Tetra Pak decided to venture into other food sectors like canned food (dry food like dehydrated potatoes and wet food like vegetables). In December 2002 the company began offering packaging solutions for dry fruits, cereal, sugar, confectionary and pet food. During the same year, the Siro Group, a Spanish biscuit and confectionary maker, launched chocolate-flavoured biscuits packaged in Tetra Rex packages.

Dori, a dry fruits company from Brazil, launched dry fruits (like cashew nuts and peanuts), sugar-coated candy, and fruit jellies (gumdrops) in 250 ml Tetra Rex cartons. The company said that it chose Tetra Rex packaging because 'it looks novel, is easy to open,

Exhibit 6 Tetra Pak – environment conservation initiatives

One of Tetra Pak's key business objectives was to lead the environmental protection initiatives related to the food processing and packaging industry. During the 1980s Tetra Pak began developing its environmental management system. The company's environmental managers working at production plants and market companies (those divisions of Tetra Pak which carried out only marketing activities) developed and implemented an environmental policy. Tetra Pak published its first environmental report in 2000. Some of the initiatives that the company took are described below:

- **Purchasing paperboards from well-managed forests.** Tetra Pak purchased paperboards from sustainable forests, that is, those forests that were managed according to recognised principles for maintaining a sustainable yield of timber and non-timber products, and ensuring biodiversity and a desirable socioeconomic impact.
- **Continuous improvements in manufacturing.** The company used only certified environmental management systems in its manufacturing operations. It also gave attention to energy reduction, waste management and hazardous substance reduction.
- **Tackling the environmental impact of transportation.** Tetra Pak developed a process for rating the performance of its transport suppliers on the basis of their compliance with the company's environmental management policy.
- **Employee awareness and commitment.** The company launched a programme called 'EcoDrive' (in September 2001) to raise the environmental awareness of consumers and the commitment of its employees to the conservation of the environment.
- **Recycling initiative.** Tetra Pak recycled its products. The company's recycled material was used as an energy source in paper mills, as raw material and an energy source in cement factories, and as raw material for different products like bags, pallets, etc.
- **Environment as part of customer services.** The company provided support to recycle the waste generated at the customer's own site. The company also provided information to customers about the environmental profile of its packages.
- **Supporting education programmes.** The company supported environmental education programs for schoolchildren around the world. Through the 'Cultura Ambiental em Escolas' programme in Brazil, over 3 million school children were educated about the environment.

Source: adapted from 'Tetra Pak makes Promising Progress Towards Environmental Leadership', www.tetrapak.com

and is recyclable'. In early 2003, Bonduelle, a leading processed vegetables manufacturer (based in Europe), chose Tetra Pak's Tetra Recart for launching its premium range of vegetable products in Italy. Bonduelle was reportedly impressed by the fact that Tetra Pak's products could pack wet and shelf-stable foods of any size and offered a shelf life of up to 24 months. Nestlé, the Swiss-based foods major, also reported that Tetra Recart packaging had played a major role in its Friskies range of pet food achieving a market share of 10 per cent in Italy in 2002.

In early 2003, Tetra Pak introduced another new straw concept in the market in the form of the 'Sensory' straw. The sensory straw was different from traditional straws as its opening end (top end) had four small holes punched on the sides with the top being closed. This mechanism enabled the liquid to flow in four different directions at the same time in the mouth. Research carried out by Tetra Pak on children aged between 7 and 12 (in Australia), revealed that the response to the new concept was very positive. Commenting on this, a Tetra Pak spokesperson said, 'Children and young

teenagers in the age group 8 to 14 are particularly sensitive to this change and really appreciate this new way of drinking. In fact, during tests, as many as 72 per cent preferred the Sensory Straw compared to the traditional one.'[18]

Initially launched in the shape of a u-straw, sensory straws (which were packaged in a transparent cover) could be attached to any existing package. Tetra Pak stated that the new straws could be manufactured by the existing straw applicators without making any technical modifications to the machines. Analysts pointed out that for consumers (mainly kids) the straws provided 'excitement and interactivity' and for beverage marketers it created a point of differentiation at a very low cost. Aimed at juice, nectar and flavoured milk drinkers, the sensory straw was first commercially launched in Australia through Paramalt, a beverage manufacturer. Tetra Pak reportedly planned to launch this straw in other markets once it was found to be commercially successful.

In 2003 Tetra Pak celebrated its 50 years in the packaging industry, providing innovative and revolutionary

Exhibit 7   Tetra Pak – competition profile

The global packaging industry has been termed a rather 'complex' industry due to the diverse nature of technologies and materials used for packaging, and the presence of a target market that spans the entire globe. The packaging industry can be divided into sectors such as liquid packaging, paper sacks, plastic packages, glass containers, etc. Most packaging companies concentrate on providing services to one established sector.

During the 1990s the packaging industry went through a phase of consolidation. The liquid packaging sector emerged as one of the most consolidated segments by the end of the century. Most of the leading companies consolidated, leaving room for new players for entry. The international market for liquid food packaging was dominated by Tetra Pak, SIG Combibloc (based in Germany) and Elopak (based in Norway), while many small and medium-sized packaging companies dominated local/regional markets across the world. Tetra Pak was the undisputed leader due to its innovative and useful products. The company advertised the benefits of its products directly to consumers and also initiated several recycling programmes to protect the environment. These two factors contributed greatly to its success.

SIG Combibolc was the second largest liquid-food packaging company and the world's second largest supplier of aseptic beverage cartons. The company had operations in Western Europe, Eastern Europe, North America, Latin America, Asia, China and Great Britain. In 2002 the company reported consolidated sales of €939 million. Established in 1957 by Fred, one of the largest privately owned industrial groups in Norway, Elopak was third largest liquid packaging manufacturer in the world. The company had brands like Pure Lak, Pak Lok and D Pak. Elopak was present in over 100 markets in Europe, Africa Asia, Australia and the Pacific. In 2001 Elopak reported consolidated sales of 4.2 billion NOK (Norwegnian Krone, Norway's currency).[22]

Source: Compiled from various sources.

packaging solutions to food manufacturers and marketers. Analysts expected the company to remain the leading player in the liquid food packaging business in the future (refer to Exhibit 7 for a note on Tetra Pak's competitors). According to company sources, Tetra Pak would continue to strive to reshape the food industry by researching new technologies in functional food packaging and intelligent packaging (use of radiofrequency identification) (refer to Exhibit 8 for a look at different Tetra Pak offerings).

Talking of Tetra Pak's commitment towards the development of innovating packaging solutions for its customers,

Aaron L. Broody, President and CEO, Packaging, Brody Incorporation, a strategic integrated media and communications service provider based in the US, said, 'Tetra Pak had thought outside the box for half a century. The food world stands to benefit from the company's continued commitment to delighting consumers through innovation in integrated packaging systems.'[19] Analysts observed that 'the surge of innovations in the opening systems, new packaging designs, ever-improving decorating techniques have ensured that they (Tetra Pak) will be around for another 50 years.'[20]

Exhibit 8   Tetra Pak – various packaging solutions offered

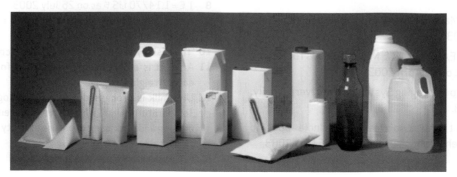

Source: www.tetrapak.com.

Table 1 The history of Levi Strauss group

1873	Levi Strauss & Co. created the world's first blue jeans.
1890	The lot number '501' was assigned to Levi's® 'waist overalls' (blue jeans).
1935	Introduction of 'Lady Levi's®', the company's first jeans for women.
1986	Launch of Dockers®, which became the fastest growing new brand in apparel history, bridging the gap between jeans and suits. The brand changed what office workers wear to work in the United States.
2000	The *Time* magazine's millennium issue named Levi's® 501 jeans the best fashion of the 20th century, beating out the miniskirt and the little black dress.
2003	150th anniversary of the company; creation of the Levi Strauss Signature® brand.

Source: Levi Strauss & Co. (2003), *Annual Financial Report.*

The business is organised into three geographic regions: Americas (United States, Canada, Latin America), Europe (Europe, Middle East, Africa) and Asia-Pacific. Figure 1 shows net sales achieved in each geographic region in 2003.

Figure 1 Net sales of Levi Strauss group by geographic region (in 2003)

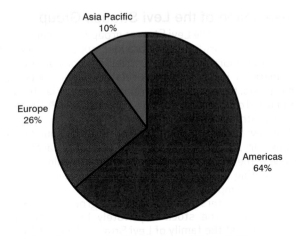

Source: Levi Strauss & Co. (2003), *Annual Financial Report.*

In order to maintain its leadership in the apparel market, the group has adopted the following business strategies:

- *Innovate and lead from the core*: creating innovative and consumer-relevant products, including updating of existing core products and introducing new products that can be quickly commercialised across different distribution channels.
- *Achieve operational excellence*: continually improving the go-to-market process to make it more responsive and faster, better linking supply to demand and reducing product costs in part by leveraging the global scale.
- *Revitalise retailer relationships and improve the company's presence at retail*: improving the collaborative planning, improving retailer margins and making products easier for consumers to find and to buy.
- *Sell where they shop*: making products accessible through multiple channels of distribution at price points that meet consumer expectations.

Levi Strauss in Europe

The European subsidiary of Levi Strauss is located in Brussels. Its President, Paul Mason, a British citizen, has acquired an important experience in mass channel retail stores. In 2003 the European subsidiary (covering Europe, Middle East and Africa) reached net sales of 1.1 billion US dollars: Levi's® products represent 90 per cent and Dockers® products 10 per cent of total net sales.

The group has recently reorganised its activities in Europe: the objective is to decentralise and to put more responsibility back into individual countries rather than operating the region on a pan-European basis. Moreover, the company attempts to return the Levi's® brand to its traditional premium positioning (in contrast to the US market where Levi's® jeans are positioned as 'ordinary jeans', thus being sold at a lower price than in Europe). A marketing campaign that highlights the fit benefits of 501 jeans intends to capture the attention of young consumers in order to increase sales trends across Europe. The region also takes substantial cost-reduction actions in order to improve margins.

Because of the fragmented nature of European retailing, the company is working with a variety of distributors: Levi's® and Dockers® brand customers include large department stores (e.g. Galeries Lafayette in France, El Corte Inglès in Spain, Kaufhof and Karstadt in Germany), single-brand Levi's® Store and Dockers® Store retail shops, mail-order accounts, and a substantial number of independent retailers operating either a single or small group of jeans-focused stores or general clothing stores. In 2003 the top 10 European customers of Levi Strauss only accounted for approximately 11 per cent of total net sales; independent retailers nearly accounted for 50 per cent of total net sales.

The Brand Portfolio of Levi Strauss

The Levi Strauss group possesses three brands: Levi's®, Dockers® and Levi Strauss Signature®. Figure 2 indicates the net sales achieved by each brand in 2003.

Figure 2 Net sales of Levi Strauss group by brand (in 2003)

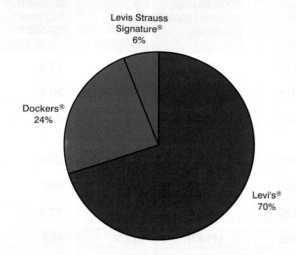

Source: Levi Strauss & Co. (2003), *Annual Financial Report*.

The traditional Levi's® brand can be considered as the main brand of the company. Created in 1873, Levi's® jeans have become one of the most widely recognised brands in the history of the apparel industry: the value of the brand is estimated at 2.97 billion US dollars (Interbrand, 2003). The Levi's® brand is the number one jeans brand in the United States in terms of unit sales: nearly 70 per cent of men in the United States, ages 15 to 49, own and wear Levi's® jeans. The original jean has evolved to include a wide range of men's, women's and kids' products designed to appeal a variety of consumer segments who shop in a number of different retail channels. Levi's® brand products are sold in more than 110 countries around the world. In 2003 sales of Levi's® brand products reached 2.9 billion US dollars, representing approximately 70 per cent of the company's net sales.

The Dockers® brand covers casual clothing, primarily pants and tops, sold in more than 57 countries. The brand played a major role in the resurgence of khaki pants and the movement toward casual attire in the US workplace by helping create a standard for business casual clothing. The Dockers® brand is the number one men's pant brand in the United States in terms of unit sales: nearly 75 per cent of men in the United States who wear casual pants own and wear Dockers® pants. In 2003, sales of Dockers® brand products were 1 billion US dollars, which corresponds to 24 per cent of the company's net sales.

Levi's® and Dockers® products are mainly distributed through chain retailers and department stores in the United States. They are primarily sold through department stores and specialty retailers abroad. Levi's® and Dockers® products are also distributed through a small number of company-owned stores located in the US, Europe and Asia and through approximately 950 independently owned franchised stores outside the United States.

In 2003 the Levi Strauss group introduced a new casual clothing brand named 'Levi Strauss Signature®'. The brand targets value-conscious consumers who shop in mass channel retail stores. The mass channel is considered as the largest retail channel in the United States, selling more than 29 per cent of all jeans sold in 2003. Levi Strauss Signature® brand products include a range of denim and non-denim pants and shirts as well as denim jackets for men, women and kids with product styling, finish and design that is distinct from the traditional Levi's® brand.

The Levi Strauss Signature® brand was launched in July 2003: the products were initially sold by 3000 Wal-Mart stores in the United States before being introduced at Target and Kmart Stores in the United States. The company then expanded into Canada (where the brand is sold at Wal-Mart stores), Australia (where an agreement was signed with Lowes and Big W stores) and Japan (where the brand is sold at Justco and Saty). In 2003 sales of Levi Strauss Signature® brand products reached 0.2 billion US dollars, representing approximately 6 per cent of the company's net sales.

In 2004 the company introduces the Levi Strauss Signature® brand into the European market. The European subsidiary decides to enter three major markets: France, Germany and the United Kingdom. In these three countries, the mass channel plays a key role within the national distribution system. In the United Kingdom and in Germany, Levi Strauss Signature® products are distributed by Wal-Mart, the US partner of Levi Strauss, which has established an important number of stores in both countries, thus allowing a satisfactory geographic coverage. In France, the company chose to cooperate with Carrefour, which is the most important hypermarket chain (the French distribution system is dominated by hypermarkets; Carrefour is the second largest distributor in the world, behind Wal-Mart, see Table 2).

The European Distribution System of Jeans

Jeans, a strong and indisputable symbol of the American way of life, represent a substantial market in Europe. Be it in a casual or sophisticated version, jeans are worn by both genders and all generations. In 2002 the European jeans market registers a growth of 7.4 per cent in volume compared to 2001. Jeans have been reinvented as a fashion item by Designer's renewed vision. The fashion markets are known to be cyclical, and it takes the constant efforts of leading brands to come up with innovations to make the jeans market a dynamic one.

Jeans retailing in Europe is structured around four main channels:

1 'Strongholds' encompass department stores (e.g. Galeries Lafayette, Harrod's, El Corte Inglès), sports shops, jeans specialists (independent, multiple, single brand) (e.g. US Forms);
2 'General Clothing' designate multiple and independent general clothing (e.g. Cotton Street) and mail order (e.g. Les 3 Suisses);
3 'Mass Channels' are hypermarkets, supermarkets and discounters (e.g. Wal-Mart, Asda, Carrefour, Auchan);
4 'VISS' are vertically integrated specialised stores (e.g. Camaïeu, Zara, Benetton).

Box 1 The iPhone teaser ad

Length: 30 seconds

The TV ad opens with the visual of an old-fashioned black phone ringing until it is answered by Lucille Ball, an actor of yesteryear. The ad goes on to show clips of various actors such as Will Ferrell, Audrey Tatou, Dustin Hoffman, Harrison Ford, Billy Crystal, Cameron Diaz, Sarah Jessica Parker, and Michael Douglas answering the phone. There is also a clip featuring the popular animated character Mr Incredible from Pixar Inc.'s[18] movie, *The Incredibles* (2004).

Then the visual of the iPhone is shown with the name and photograph of a John Appleseed showing in the caller ID. The ad ends with the words, 'Coming in June'.

Source: adapted from Zaharov-Reutt, 'Apple iPhone Ad Says Hello to Oscars Women', www.itwire.com.au, February 26, 2007, and other sources.

Exhibit 2 Customers willing to buy an iPhone

How many consumers were interested in buying iPhone at US$ 499 (Sample = 2000 internet users)

Highly Interested 3%

Other Responses 97%

Source: http://www.parksassociates.com/free_data/downloads/parks-iPhone.pdf.

Apple announced some service plans for people who opted for the iPhone (refer to Table I for AT&T monthly plans for the iPhone). Jobs said, 'We want to make choosing a service plan simple and easy, so every plan includes unlimited data with direct Internet access, along with Visual Voicemail and a host of other goodies. We think these three plans give customers the flexibility to experience all of iPhone's revolutionary features at affordable and competitive prices.'[20]

Some analysts felt that the launch of the iPhone was probably the best ever launch of any product. Between 29 June 2007 and 29 September 2007 the company sold 1 389 000 units.[21] The buzz that surrounded the launch of

the phone, which was referred to as the 'Jesus phone' by bloggers, was unprecedented as far as electronic products were concerned. One customer who bought the iPhone soon after it was launched remarked, 'I'm going to run home and ring people just to say "Guess what, I've got, an iPhone, bye!"'[22] Such was the frenzy that surrounded the launch of this new mobile phone.

Industry observers appreciated the way the company had created a buzz around the product through its low key but highly effective marketing effort. They also felt that the product had lived up to the expectations created. According to Al Ries, Chairman, Ries & Ries,[23] Apple's iPhone had generated more publicity than any other product. Commenting on the buzz created by Apple for its iPhone, Matt Williams, a partner at Martin Agency,[24] said, 'Apple is one of those rare brands that can create mystique around a product. They created a buzz that has taken on a life of its own.'[25]

However, some analysts felt that the iPhone had been over-hyped and could fall flat on its face after the initial euphoria died down. They were of the view that it was never good to hype a product so much as it could become difficult to match the hype with performance. Moreover, Apple was foraying into unknown terrain dominated by a number of competitors that had decades of experience in this sector behind them. Analysts felt that Apple had a long way to go to realise its target of conquering a 1 per cent market share in the mobile phone market. Some analysts also viewed its foray into this market as a defensive strategy necessitated by the introduction of music phones by some well-known mobile phone companies.

Table 1 Monthly rental plan for iPhone

AT&T monthly plans for iPhone		
Plans	Minutes	Night & weekend minutes
US$59.99	450	5000
US$79.99	900	Unlimited
US$99.99	1350	Unlimited

* All these plans have additional features and services such as 200 SMS test messages, rollover minutes, unlimited data, unlimited mobile-to-mobile, and visual voicemail.
** In addition to these three monthly plans, customers could choose from any of AT&T's standard service plans.

Source: 'AT&T and Apple Announce Simple, Affordable Service Plans for iPhone', www.apple.com, 26 June 2007.

Pricing the iPhone

The iPhone was launched with such frenzy that even its premium price did not prove a deterrent to many consumers. Apple priced its 4 GB version of iPhone at US$499 and its

8 GB version at US$599, when it was launched in June 2007. The customers also had to enter into a two-year contract with AT&T. Along with the contract, the iPhone was considered the most expensive mobile handset in the world at the time of its release. Moreover, there were hidden costs. For example, just as in the case of the iPod, customers would not be able to change the battery of the iPhone themselves. The phone had to be sent back to Apple for replacement for a fee (US$79, plus US$6.95 shipping). This was expected to pose a big challenge for Apple as some customers would not be willing to pay so much and also remain without a phone during the replacement period. The durability of the iPhone was also questioned by many critics as the front side of the phone was made of glass.

Some critics felt that the high price of the iPhone was not justified since it was double the cost incurred by the company on manufacturing the product. According to iSuppli, a research firm, Apple had a 50 per cent margin on its iPhone since the US$499 iPhone and the US$599 models cost Apple about US$246 and US$281 to manufacture respectively.[26] In view of its high pricing, some analysts opined that Apple would face difficulties in penetrating the mobile phone market, which was so fragmented that there were hundreds of models catering to different types of users depending upon their affordability, needs, and the features offered. Moreover, the market was dominated by established players like Nokia Corporation[27] (Nokia), Samsung Electronics[28] (Samsung), Sony Ericsson Mobile Communications AB[29] (Sony Ericsson), LG Electronics[30] (LG) and Motorola Inc.[31] (Motorola) that provided various high-end products at affordable prices.

Though the early adopters bought the iPhone with much excitement, there were some incidents of customers accusing Apple and AT&T of issuing hefty bills to them. Some iPhone users were stunned when they started receiving bills running into 300 pages. Some of these customers got bills for US$3000 or even more. One of the iPhone customers Justine Ezarik (Ezarik) received a 300-page bill from AT&T in August 2007. Ezarik posted a video on YouTube[32] wherein he displayed the 300-page bill and said, 'I got my first AT&T bill, right here.'[33] Within no time, the video served as a catalyst and generated widespread media coverage. In response to the video, Mark Siegel, spokesperson, AT&T, said, 'It's no different than with any other bill for any other devices or any other service that we offer.'[34] However, AT&T decided to discontinue sending long bills to its customers.

The Price-Cut Chaos

In September 2007, barely ten weeks after the launch of the iPhone, Jobs announced a steep price cut for the product. The 4 GB version was made inoperable while the 8 GB version was available at US$399 and a 16 GB version was to be introduced at a price of US$499. The price cut, which was almost one-third of the original price of the product, took most by surprise. People couldn't believe their ears when they heard the new price of the handset. Not surprisingly, the news infuriated those who had bought the iPhone at the original price. Some of the customers who started protesting against the price cut were among the few early adopters who had waited in long

queues for buying the handsets. A discontented and annoyed customer even went ahead and took legal action against Apple and AT&T. It was estimated that the company had sold 750 000 units of the iPhone at the US$599 price by September 2007.[35]

Many were upset at the company's decision and both Apple and Jobs came in for strong criticism. It had a negative effect on Apple's share prices as well. Though Apple denied having any hidden agenda behind the price cut other than making the phone more affordable to customers, industry watchers speculated that the company had resorted to this step to target shoppers in the impending festive season. According to analyst, Ezra Gottheil (Gottheil) of Technology Business Research, Inc., the price cut was necessitated by the launch of the iPod Touch. 'Apple had to drop the price for the iPhone because it couldn't get away with selling the iPod Touch – something that was almost an iPhone – and charge substantially less for it,'[36] said Gottheil, adding that the company would benefit from cost savings as the two products shared parts. Some analysts also felt that the company had gone in for an early price cut because it had concerns regarding future revenues from the iPhone as other players had also entered the market with similar products.

The steep price cut led to Jobs being flooded with angry mails by customers. Initially, the company said that those who had bought the iPhone within 14 days prior to the price cut could apply for a refund under Apple's return policy, contingent on the product not being opened.[37] However, after critically analysing the entire situation, Jobs went ahead and posted a public apology on the company's official website. In addition to this, he offered a credit of US$100 to all the customers who had bought the handset at the introductory price to buy products at Apple Retail Stores. Justifying the price cut, Jobs said, 'I am sure that we are making the correct decision to lower the price of the 8GB iPhone from $599 to $399, and that now is the right time to do it. iPhone is a breakthrough product, and we have the chance to "go for it" this holiday season. iPhone is so far ahead of the competition, and now it will be affordable by even more customers. It benefits both Apple and every iPhone user to get as many new customers as possible in the iPhone "tent". We strongly believe the $399 price will help us do just that this holiday season.'[38]

Experts cited the example of Motorola's much hyped Moto Razr phone. The Moto Razr was priced at US$499 when it was launched and the price dropped to US$399 after a period of only six months. Analysts felt that companies dealing in technological devices had at various times adopted such market skimming strategies. They felt that Apple knew very well that early adopters would be ready to pay a high price for the iPhone. 'Apple skimmed the cream from the market in the initial months, and now they're getting really aggressive,'[39] said analyst Van Baker of Gartner Inc., a business intelligence firm. Supporters of Apple also pointed out that after the price cut, the sales of iPhone had gone up from 9000 units per day to almost 27 000 units per day[40] (refer to Exhibit 3 for iPhone's sales after the price cut). By 29 September 2007 the company had amassed sales of 1 389 000 units of the iPhone.[41]

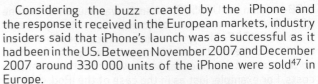

Exhibit 3 iPhone's sales after the price drop

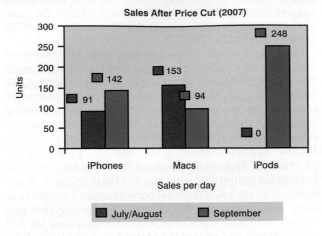

Sales After Price Cut (2007)

Source: 'Report: iPhone Sales up 56 per cent after Price Cut', www.money.cnn.com, 4 October 2007.

Others felt that the price cut would have hurt customers' sentiments. A senior analyst of Piper Jaffray,[42] Gene Munster said, 'There are two groups of people. The first wave doesn't care because they knew what they were getting into. The second wave is pretty upset, but with Apple everyone has an axe to grind. Whether it's a battery or a screen, it's always something.'[43] Though a majority felt that the sales of iPhones would increase due to the price cut, some felt that such a drastic price cut only a few weeks after the launch was bound to disappoint Apple's customers. 'They've [the early adopters] gone from being envied to being labeled as losers for having paid too much for their iPhones,'[44] explained JP Allen, a professor at University of San Francisco. Some even suggested that the incident was a PR fiasco for Apple. They said that Apple's belated response of providing US$100 credit to the early purchasers after a section of its customers rose up in protest suggested that the company had failed to judge the impact of the price cut on its customer base.

iPhone Goes to Europe

On 9 November 2007, Apple launched its iPhone in the European mobile phone market. The iPhone was initially launched in three markets, Germany, France, and the UK. It was on sale from 29 November 2007 in these European markets. The initial response from the customers in Germany was overwhelming. People waited in long queues just to get the glimpse of the iPhone. Reinhold Steinwasser, a customer in Germany, said, 'I just want to be the first to touch it, play with it, and try it.'[45] A similar response was cited in the French and the UK markets.

The iPhone was available at a premium price of US$566 in the UK, US$587 in Germany, and US$415 in France. The price also included value-added tax (VAT).[46] However, the pricing did not dissuade customers from buying the iPhone.

Considering the buzz created by the iPhone and the response it received in the European markets, industry insiders said that iPhone's launch was as successful as it had been in the US. Between November 2007 and December 2007 around 330 000 units of the iPhone were sold[47] in Europe.

Apple chose T-Mobile[48] in Germany, Orange[49] in France, and Telefónica O2 Europe Plc[50] (O2) in the UK as its network partners with 10 per cent revenue sharing on all calls and data transfers done through iPhones. Apple's revenue sharing model faced protests initially from O2 since sharing of revenues with handset manufacturers was non-existent in Europe. Though O2 was not in sync with Apple's revenue sharing pattern, Peter Erskine, Chief Executive, O2, said, 'If sharing revenue brings a bigger pie to the table, then we'll be happy to share that pie. The revenue-sharing model will play an increasingly important role in the future of converged communications.'[51]

However, Apple faced some stumbling blocks in Europe. The laws in Europe prevented companies tying up with partners in such a way that customers had to buy one product to get the other. This proved to be a major jolt to Apple's global strategy of tying up with network operators and to take a share of their profits in the European market. On the other hand, T-Mobile had announced its plans to offer the iPhone to the customers without any contract. T-Mobile took the decision in view of the injunction issued by a German court in reply to a lawsuit filed by another mobile operator in Germany, Vodafone Group Plc[52] (Vodafone) protesting against the exclusive availability of the iPhone through T-Mobile's network. Later, T-Mobile gave customers the option of signing a two-year contract or buying the unlocked version of the iPhone by paying a prohibitive price (US$1500).[53] However, T-Mobile argued that product bundling would actually help customers save money.

Analysts said that though Apple could prevent the customers from buying the unlocked iPhones by pricing them very high, it had to pay huge amounts of taxes on the profits it earned on the outright sale of the handsets at prohibitively expensive prices. Apple was also restricted from signing any such revenue sharing agreements with operators in France.

Despite the initial hiccups and problems faced by Apple in Europe, the iPhone succeeded in some markets like England. Around 30 000 iPhones were reported to have been sold in the first week of its launch in England. And by the end of January 2008, 200 000 iPhones had been sold in the country.[54] Apple's partner O2 said that iPhone was its best selling product. In France, the iPhone had seen moderate success by selling 70 000 units by the end of 2007. But the performance of the iPhone in Germany was dismal despite it being a bigger market than France or England. The post sale revenues from iPhone were not rosy either for Apple as it was estimated that nearly one-third of the total handsets sold in Europe were unlocked later. Industry experts said that the strategy of tying up with a single operator would not work in Europe as the European customers were accustomed to using any phone with any network operator of their choice.

After tasting success for a short period in Europe, Apple found sales of the iPhone sagging. According to estimates by Strategy Analytics (Analytics), a consulting firm, the combined sales of O2, T-Mobile, and Orange in the three European markets were 350 000 units in the last quarter of 2007 compared to Apple's target of selling 500 000 iPhones. The sales further dropped to 300 000 units in the first quarter of 2008.[55] Analysts attributed the drooping sales to several factors. The major reasons, they said, were the price factor, carrier exclusivity, and lack of 3G capability in the iPhone. In a bid to control its sagging sales, Apple reduced the price of the iPhone by £100 and also planned to launch the 3G version of iPhone in the second half of 2008.

Other Challenges

A growing concern for Apple was the existence of a grey market in the mobile phone market. In February 2008 it was estimated that Apple sold around 3.7 million units of the iPhone while AT&T said that it had made only 2 million connections. The discrepancy of 1.7 million led to the conclusion that these iPhones were unlocked. Within the first week of iPhone's sales in 2007, there was a gap of 124 000 units in the sales figures released by both the companies (refer to Exhibit 4 for the number of unlocked iPhones sold). Analysts predicted that several cases of unlocking of the phones had been reported during the festive season. According to Toni Sacconaghi, an analyst at Stanford C. Bernstein,[56] Apple had lost US$300 million to US$400 million on its potential revenues and profits with every 1 million phones being unlocked. However, Apple announced its plans to launch a software that would disable unlocking of iPhones.

Exhibit 4 Unlocked iPhone units sold (in millions as of 31 December 2007)

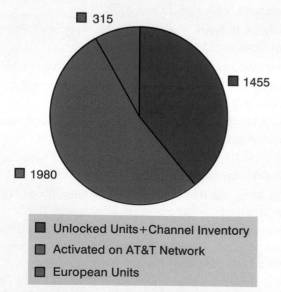

- 315
- 1455
- 1980

- ■ Unlocked Units + Channel Inventory
- ■ Activated on AT&T Network
- ■ European Units

Source: http://apple20.blogs.fortune.cnn.com/2008/01/28/apples-300-million-gray-market-dilemma.

Another major challenge that Apple faced came in the form of allegations and accusations from environment protection groups over the use of hazardous materials in the iPhone. In October 2007 Apple received a warning from the Center for Environmental Health (CEH) that it should discontinue the use of Polyvinyl Chloride (PVCs) and Brominated Flame Retardants (BFRs) in its iPhone. Though the CEH did not expect Apple to recall its products, it required Apple to put warning stickers on its iPhone, thereby alerting users of the potential risk involved with the the excessive usage of the product. Apple announced its plans to curb the usage of these materials by the end of 2008.

Outlook

Apple's move to go in for a steep price cut of iPhone in the US attracted lot of criticism against the company. According to some industry observers, it mainly hurt the sentiments of early adopters who had paid a premium to get hold of the product. Jobs also acknowledged that the steep price cut had abused the trust of customers. In a letter posted on Apple's site, Jobs said, 'Our early customers trusted us, and we must live up to that trust with our actions in moments like these.'[57] Subsequently, he announced a US$100 rebate to customers. However, analysts opined that Apple's strategy of reimbursing the money to pacify its angry customers would further dent its image. Rob Enderle, president of the Enderle Group, a technology advisory firm, said, 'A $100 credit could be perceived as adding insult to injury. It's a way to make you go buy something else, and gives the company a chance to make more money.'[58]

Some analysts described Apple's initial high pricing and sudden dropping of the price for its iPhone as a smart strategy since it helped it reap higher profits from its early adopters who had paid a premium. According to Dulaney, Vice President, Gartner Research, 'It's probably a formula taught in business school.'[59]

Brushing off speculations, Jobs said that the price cut was a move to increase the demand for the product and make it affordable for consumers during the approaching holiday season. On the other hand, analysts thought that Apple had cut the price since it had realised that it would be unable to achieve its one million mark by 2008. Charles Golvin, analyst, Forrester Research, said, 'I don't think it's a stretch to deduce from this that maybe the rate of sales weren't meeting expectations, so they decided to drop the price. Bear in mind that Steve Jobs said at the last earnings call that they expected to sell a million devices in the following quarter. Maybe they recognized the trajectory wasn't going to get them there at that price.'[60]

Despite the glitches, the growth outlook for iPhone was expected to be positive since a survey by ChangeWave, a market research firm, in February 2008 revealed that around 72 per cent of the consumers were satisfied after buying an iPhone while another 17 per cent who planned to buy a phone in the coming six months preferred to buy an iPhone[61] (refer to Exhibit 5 for customer satisfaction rating of different mobile phone manufacturers).

For its European market, Apple planned to launch a 3G iPhone in late 2008 since Europe mainly worked on 3G cell networks. Apple

Exhibit 5 Customer satisfaction rating of different mobile phone manufacturers

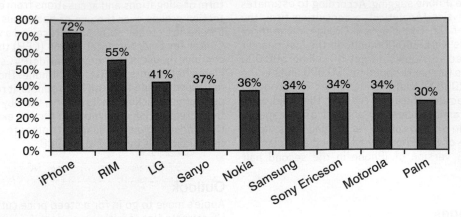

Source: 'iPhone is Top Choice for Next Cell Phone Purchase', www.ipodnn.com, 7 February 2008.

also planned to launch its iPhone in other European markets like Italy through Vodafone and Telecom Italia. By selling its iPhone through two mobile operators, Apple aimed to modify its strategy of carrier exclusivity. However, analysts remained sceptical about Apple's growth prospects in Europe considering its high pricing and iPhone's limitation of running slowly on GSM networks.

In August 2008, as part of Apple's plan to foray into the Asian mobile phone market, Apple launched a 3G version of its iPhone in India. The iPhone was available with two operators, Vodafone and Bharti Airtel (Airtel). According to Apple, the initial response was good since Airtel claimed that it had registered around 200 000 customers who were willing to buy an iPhone while Vodafone reported around 100 000 registered users.[62] However, industry experts said that iPhone's premium pricing coupled with a legally binding contract with Vodafone and Airtel would restrict iPhone from penetrating the intensely competitive mobile phone market dominated by established players like Nokia, Sony Ericsson, Samsung, Motorola, and LG. Apple planned to launch its iPhone in other Asian markets like Japan, South Korea, and China by the end of 2008.

Questions

1 What do you think was the main reason for iPhone's success in America?
2 With tough competition from Nokia, htc and blackberry, do you think iPhone is as successful in Europe as in America? If not, why not?
3 Could you help Apple to formulate a strategy and a marketing plan for Europe?
4 Do you think Apple's pricing policy is helping it to achieve market shares? Was dropping the price a good strategy?

Further Reading

Zaharov-Reutt, 'Apple iPhone Ad Says Hello to Oscars Women', www.itwire.com.au, 26 February 2007.

Paul Thomasch, 'Apple Builds Hype for iPhone', www.features.us.reuters.com, 20 June 2007.

Shawn Collins, 'Marketing the iPhone', www.blog.affiliatetip.com, 25 June 2007.

'AT&T and Apple Announce Simple, Affordable Service Plans for iPhone', www.apple.com, 26 June 2007.

'Apple iPhone May Struggle Initially to Cross the Chasm', http://newsroom.parksassociates.com, 26 June 2007.

Ville Heiskanen, 'Apple's IPhone Strategy Generates Buzz', www.turkishdaily.com, 30 June 2007.

Laura Smith-Spark, 'Fans Turn Out for "Rock Star" iPhone', www.news.bbc.co.uk, 30 June 2007.

'Where Would Jesus Queue?' www.economist.com, 5 July 2007.

'Singing the iPhone Billing Blues', www.freepress.net, 16 August 2007.

David Ho, 'Next Big Thing is the Size of the Bill', www.coxwashington.com, 16 August 2007.

Jefferson Graham, 'Apple Dramatically Chops iPhone Cost', www.ustoday.com, 5 September 2007.

May Wong and Rachel Konrad, 'Apple Cuts iPhone Price, Updates iPods', www.forbes.com, 5 September 2007.

Patrick Seitz and Ken Spencer Brown, 'Apple Slashes iPhone Price and Dials up an iPhone-Like iPod', www.yahoonews.com, 5 September 2007.

Katie Hafner and Brad Stone, 'IPhone Owners Crying Foul over Price Cut', www.nytimes.com, 6 September 2007.

'[First] Buyers Beware: Price Cut Coming', www.abcnews.go. com, 8 September 2007.

Jim Dalrymple, 'Lessons Learnt from the iPhone Price Cuts', *Macworld*, www.pcworld.com, 11 September 2007.

Mark Sutton, 'iPhone Sales Increase Three Fold after $200 Cut', www.pcretailmag.com, 13 September 2007.

'O2 Defends iPhone Revenue-sharing', www.mobilemarket-ingnews.co.uk, 13 September 2007.

'Report: iPhone Sales up 56 per cent after Price Cut', www. money.cnn.com, 4 October 2007.

Matt Moore, 'Hoping to Replicate US Success', http:abcnews. go.com, 9 November 2007.

'Apple iPhone Forced to Unlock in Europe – Crying to the Bank...', www.2aday.worldpress.com, 22 November 2007.

'iPhone Takes 28 per cent of the Smartphone Market', www. ipodnn.com, 5 February 2008.

'iPhone is Top Choice for Next Cell Phone Purchase', www. ipodnn.com, 7 February 2008.

'72 per cent of iPhone Owners Satisfied; #1 in Planned Purchases', www.iphoneatlas.com, 7 February 2008.

Cecilia Aronsson, 'The iPhone in Europe: A Patchy Success', www.venturebeat.com, 10 April 2008.

Jennifer L. Schenker, 'The iPhone in Europe: Lost in Translation', www.businessweek.com, 16 April 2008.

Charles Jade, 'Lackluster iPhone Sales in Europe', http://arstechnica.com, 18 April 2008.

'iPhone Prices Drop to US$ 154 in Europe', www.cellmad. com, 4 June 2008.

'Apple Reports Record Third Quarter Results', www.apple. com, 21 July 2008.

'iPhone Launched in India without Mass Hysteria', www.indianinfoline.com, 22 August 2008.

'Apple Inc: Competition from IBM', www.britannica.com.

'Apple Reports First Quarter Results', www.apple.com.

http://apple20.blogs.fortune.cnn.com/2008/01/28/apples-300-million-gray- market-dilemma

http://www.macnn.com/articles/05/05/04/merill.on.aapl

http://www.parksassociates.com/free_data/downloads/parks-iPhone.pdf

www.apple.com

www.apple.com/hotnews/openiphoneletter

www.finance.google.com

www.media.corporate-ir.net/media_files/irol/10/107357/AAPL_10K_FY07.pdf

References

1   Jennifer L. Schenker, 'The iPhone in Europe: Lost in Translation', www.businessweek.com, 16 April 2008.

2   'iPhone Takes 28% of the Smartphone Market', www.ipodnn.com, 5 February 2008.

3   Canalys, headquartered in Grazeley, Reading, UK is a leading consultancy and market research firm for technology companies.

4   'Apple Reports Record Third Quarter Results', www.apple.com, 21 July 2008.

5   AT&T Wireless Services Inc. (AT&T), headquartered in Redmond, Washington, USA, is one of the leading wireless carriers in US. In the US, Apple entered into a two-year network contract with AT&T for the iPhone.

6   'Apple Inc: Competition from IBM', www.britannica.com.

7   International Business Machine Corporations, headquartered in Armonk, New York, USA, is one of the leading information technology companies.

8   iTMS allowed customers to pay and download music through Macs, and store it on their hard drives.

9   http://www.macnn.com/articles/05/05/04/merill.on.aapl

10 Macworld Conference & Expo is an annual trade show held in USA dedicated to the Apple Macintosh platform.

11 The Enderle Group is a provider of technology advisory services and consulting for technology companies.

12 Paul Thomasch, 'Apple Builds Hype for iPhone', www.features.us.reuters.com, 20 June 2007.

13 Bear Stearns, headquartered in New York, USA, is an investment bank and a brokerage firm that also deals in securities trading.

14 The Academy Awards (also known as the Oscars) are the annual awards presented in the US in recognition of excellence of professionals in the film industry.

15 Paul Thomasch, 'Apple Builds Hype for iPhone with Less', www.reuters.com, 20 June 2007.

16 TBWA Worldwide, headqauartered in New York, USA, is an ad agency that operates globally in several nations. However, the company operates as TBWA\Chiat\Day in the US.

17 Omnicom is the world's biggest holding company of advertising agencies. The companies which form part of the group are BBDO, TBWA Worldwide, and DDB Worldwide. It is the biggest ad agency in terms of revenue in the world.

18 Pixar Inc. is a well-known maker of animated movies. It was acquired by Jobs in 1986. In 2006 it was acquired by the leading entertainment company, The Walt Disney Company.

19 'Where would Jesus Queue?' www.economist.com, 5 July 2007.

20 'AT&T and Apple Announce Simple, Affordable Service Plans for iPhone', www.apple.com, 26 June 2007.

21 www.media.corporate-ir.net/media_files/irol/10/107357/AAPL_10K_FY07.pdf.

22 Laura Smith-Spark, 'Fans Turn Out for 'Rock Star' iPhone', www.news.bbc.co.uk, 30 June 2007.

23 Ries & Ries, based in Altanta, USA, is a marketing consulting company chaired by Al Ries.

24 Martin Agency was an advertising agency based in Virginia.

25 Ville Heiskanen, 'Apple's IPhone Strategy Generates Buzz', www.turkishdaily.com, 30 June 2007.

26 Shawn Collins, 'Marketing the iPhone', www.blog.affiliatetip.com, 25 June 2007.

27 Nokia Corporation, headquartered in Espoo, Finland, is the world's leading mobile phone company. Its revenues for the fiscal year 2006 were €4.306 billion.

28 Samsung Electronics, headquartered in Suwon, South Korea, was the world's third largest mobile phone company as of July 2007. Its revenues for the fiscal year 2005 were US$78 992.70 million.

29 Sony Ericsson Mobile Communications AB, headquartered in Acton, London, UK, is a mobile phone company formed in 2001 as a joint venture between one of the leading consumer electronics companies Sony Corporation (Sony) of Japan and a leading mobile phone company Ericsson AB (Ericsson) of Sweden. It was the world's fourth largest mobile phone company as of July 2007. Its revenues for the fiscal year 2006 were €10 959 million.

30 LG Electronics, headquartered in Seoul, South Korea, is the fifth largest mobile phone company. Its revenues for the fiscal year 2006 were US$68.8 billion.

31 Motorola Inc., headquartered in Schaumburg, Illionis, USA, was the world's second-largest mobile phone company as of July 2007. Its revenues for the year 2006 were US$ 41.2 billion.

32 YouTube is the name of a popular website where users can upload, share, and watch video clips.

33 'Singing the iPhone Billing Blues', www.freepress.net, 16 August 2007.

34 David Ho, 'Next Big Thing is the Size of the Bill', www.coxwashington.com, 16 August 2007.

35 '[First] Buyers Beware: Price Cut Coming', www.abcnews.go.com, 8 September 2007.

36 Patrick Seitz and Ken Spencer Brown, 'Apple Slashes iPhone Price and Dials up an iPhone-Like iPod', www.yahoonews.com, 5 September 2007.

37 May Wong and Rachel Konrad, 'Apple Cuts iPhone Price, Updates iPods', www.forbes.com, 5 September 2007.

38 www.apple.com

39 Jefferson Graham, 'Apple Dramatically Chops iPhone Cost', www.ustoday.com, 5 September 2007.

40 Mark Sutton, 'iPhone Sales Increase Three Fold after $200 Cut', www.pcretailmag.com, 13 September 2007.

41 www.apple.com

42 Piper Jaffray is a leading investment banking firm.

43 Jim Dalrymple, 'Lessons Learnt from the iPhone Price Cuts', MacWorld, www.pcworld.com, 11 September 2007.

44 '[First] Buyers Beware: Price Cut Coming', www.abcnews.go.com, 8 September 2007.

45 Matt Moore, 'Hoping to Replicate US Success', http:abcnews.go.com, 9 November 2007.

46 VAT stands for Value Added Tax. It is an indirect tax charged on the sale of products and services. At present more than 135 countries around the world have adopted VAT.

47 'iPhone Prices Drop to US$ 154 in Europe', www.cellmad.com, 4 June 2008.

48 T-Mobile, headquartered in Bonn, Germany, was one of the leading mobile service providers across the globe. It is the subsidiary of Deutsche Telekom.

49 Orange is a brand owned by France Télécom, a leading telecommunication service provider in France.

50 Telefónica O2 Europe Plc, headquartered in Slough, England, UK was a leading telecommunication service operator in Europe. It is the subsidiary of Telefonica S.A.

51 'O2 Defends iPhone Revenue-sharing', www.mobilemarketingnews.co.uk, 13 September 2007.

52 Vodafone Group Plc., headquartered in Newbury, England, UK, is one of the leading mobile operators in the world.

53 'Apple iPhone Forced to Unlock in Europe – Crying to the Bank...', www.2aday.worldpress.com, 22 November 2007.

54 Cecilia Aronsson, 'The iPhone in Europe: A Patchy Success', www.venturebeat.com, 10 April 2008.

55 Charles Jade, 'Lackluster iPhone Sales in Europe', http://arstechnica.com, 18 April 2008.

56 Sanford C. Bernstein was a leading market research firm in the UK.

57 Katie Hafner and Brad Stone, 'IPhone Owners Crying Foul over Price Cut', www.nytimes.com, 6 September 2007.

58 Katie Hafner and Brad Stone, 'IPhone Owners Crying Foul over Price Cut', www.nytimes.com, 6 September 2007.

59 Katie Hafner and Brad Stone, 'IPhone Owners Crying Foul over Price Cut', www.nytimes.com, 6 September 2007.

60 Katie Hafner and Brad Stone, 'IPhone Owners Crying Foul over Price Cut', www.nytimes.com, 6 September 2007.

61 '72 per cent of iPhone Owners Satisfied; #1 in Planned Purchases', www.iphoneatlas.com, 7 February 2008.

62 'iPhone Launched in India without Mass Hysteria', www.indianinfoline.com, 22 August 2008.

This case was written by Hadiya Faheem, under the direction of Debapratim Purkayastha, ICMR Center for Management Research. It was compiled from published sources, and is intended to be used as a basis for class discussion rather than to illustrate either effective or ineffective handling of a management situation.

Case 5.3 UGG Boots: Australian Generic Product to Global Luxury Brand

© P. Ghauri

We believe the strong demand for UGG products across a broad assortment of styles is an indication that UGG is becoming a strong brand versus a 'hot' trend in just one boot style.[1]

–Jeffrey Klinefelte, Research Analyst at Piper Jaffray[2] in 2005

We have been doing celebrity seeding. What happens is that when you have a good product and people start wearing it, it becomes word-of-mouth and it spreads. It was an undiscovered brand that was a surfer boot. Through a series of product placements, getting in magazines and being featured on shows such as Oprah it has been discovered.[3]

–Karen Bromley, owner of a New York public relations company representing UGG Australia, in 2003

From Fad to Fashion

Ugg Boots[4] (Uggs), which originated in Australia over 200 years ago, were considered to be a generic name for sheepskin boots in Australia. Uggs gained recognition in the US in 1978 when the Californian surfing community began using them as it found them comfortable and warm. In 1995 Deckers acquired Ugg Holdings Inc, a company that sold Uggs in the US under the Ugg Australia brand.

Though analysts opined that Uggs were a passing fad that would fizzle out after a few years, their popularity continued, and during the holiday season of 2007, they featured prominently among the 'season's must have items'. Even while most of the other fashion footwear brands were selling at heavily discounted prices during the

season, Uggs continued to sell at full price. According to Jennifer Black, a Retail Analyst, 'There doesn't seem to be a fashion element that is working this year. The one exception is Uggs.'[5]

Background Note

Deckers was founded by Doug Otto in 1973.[6] Initially, the company manufactured sandals under the Deckers brand name in a small factory in Carpentaria,[7] California. Later it acquired well known footwear brands that proved to be profitable. In 1985, Deckers entered into a licensing agreement with Mark Thatcher (Thatcher), founder of sports sandal brand Teva.

In 1993 the company purchased a 50 per cent share of Simple Shoes, Inc. (Simple Shoes) from its founder Eric Myer. Simple Shoes produced sneakers, clogs and sandals mainly targeted at teenagers and men's and women's casuals. In 1994 the company acquired the remaining 50 per cent interest in Simple Shoes for US$1.5 million.[8] Deckers experienced rapid growth during the 1990s and first appeared on the stock exchange in 1993 under the name DECK. As sales grew, Deckers set up independent manufacturing units in China, New Zealand, and Australia to manufacture its footwear products.

Deckers acquired Ugg Holdings Inc. in 1995 from Brian Smith, an Australian surfer. Upon the purchase, Deckers acquired the Ugg trademark in 25 countries. It positioned Ugg as high end luxury footwear and popularised it in the US and in some European countries (refer to Exhibit 1 for history of Ugg Boots in Australia).

In 2001 the sales of Teva footwear accounted for about 67 per cent of Deckers' total sales. In November 2002 Deckers acquired Teva's trademarks and patents from Thatcher for approximately US$ 62 million.[9]

By 2007 Ugg boots had become very fashionable in America and were being sold in most major department stores and footwear stores across the globe. In 2007 Deckers recorded net sales of US$448.9 million, out of which US$291.9 million was contributed by the Ugg brand (refer to Exhibit 2 for Deckers' Key Financials 2003–2007).

In May 2008 Deckers acquired 100 per cent ownership of Tsubo LLC[10] for approximately US$6 million in cash.[11] In the same year, it also entered into a joint venture with Stella International Holdings Ltd[12] to open retail stores and wholesale distribution in China for the UGG Australia brand. The joint venture was owned 51 per cent by Deckers and 49 per cent by Stella Holdings. The companies planned to invest about US$5 million in total to open two stores in China in 2008.[13]

Exhibit 1 History of Ugg boots

The existence of sheepskin boots in Australia can be traced back over two hundred years when European colonists settled in Australia used sheep hide to make clothes and footwear. Over the decades, the sheep industry grew extensively in Australia.

Workers in Australia and New Zealand who sheared sheep made boots from the sheepskin to keep their feet warm as the raw material was readily available to them. The boots they made were just two pieces of sheepskin attached in the front with a soft sole and they were called 'Ug or Ugh Boots', short for 'Ugly' because though they were comfortable, they did not really appeal to the eye. There were different versions of the origin of the name 'Ugg', as some thought that the name came from the way the boot 'hugs' the wearer's feet and legs. As Ugg Boots provided warmth and comfort, people started wearing them while carrying out outdoor activities like farming.

Later during World Wars I and II, pilots used these sheepskin boots. Because of their thermostatic property and their ability to keep feet warm,[43] the Ugg Boots became a rage among aviators who called them 'fug boots', meaning flying Uggs.

During the 1950s and 1960s the surfing communities at the beaches near Margaret River in Perth first adopted the Uggs while surfing. The boots resisted water, had no hard soles, and provided sock-like comfort while walking over slippery terrains. As Uggs made surfing comfortable, they were lapped up by the surfing communities and tourists in Australia.

By the mid-sixties the sheepskin boots had become very popular in Australia and were generically referred to as 'Uggs.' In 1981 Ugg entered the Australian official dictionary, the Macquarie dictionary, as a generic name that included Ugg as a generic description of sheepskin boots.

In 1971 Shane Stedman, a surf champion in Australia, registered the trademarks 'UGH-BOOTS' and 'UGH' in Australia in 1971 and 1982 respectively[44] and began selling the boots under these names. In 1978 Brian Smith, another Australian surfer, visited the US and introduced the boots among the surfing enthusiasts in California. With their success in California, Smith decided to develop and market the sheepskin footwear in the US. In 1986 Smith started a company called Ugg Holdings to trade Uggs. In 1995 he sold all rights of Ugg Holdings to Deckers.

Source: compiled from various sources.

As of 2008 Deckers marketed its products under the brands Teva, Simple Shoes, Ugg Australia, Tsubo, and Deckers Flip Flops (refer to Exhibit 3 for a brief on Deckers' brands). The company's brands were distinctive and Deckers used fine materials like leathers, suedes,[14] and sheepskin to manufacture its footwear line. The company's goal was to establish its products as global lifestyle brands. With UGG Australia proving to be its most profitable brand, Deckers planned to open more Ugg retail stores in the US as well as in other international markets.

Marketing Uggs

The comfort, luxury, and fashion element associated with the Uggs ensured that Ugg Australia soon became a well-known brand. The Uggs were stylish and could be worn all through the year. And they were popular not only because of the fashion element associated with them but also because of their comfort factor. According to marketing analysts, Deckers adopted good promotion and distribution strategies to make the brand popular in the US. The prices of Ugg boots ranged from US$60 to US$350. No discounts were given by the company in any season.

Internationally, Uggs fastest growing market was the UK. In other places like northern Europe and Canada there was considerable demand for Ugg footwear. In 2007 a broad collection of Ugg footwear was introduced in these countries to cater to the growing demand for Uggs. International sales for all three of Deckers' brands increased 62.6 per cent to US$62.3 million in 2007 compared to US$38.3 million in 2006.[15] To improve Ugg's international operations and sales and to position and promote the Ugg brand, Deckers worked closely with its distributors especially in the UK. As of 2007 the Ugg Australia boots were being sold in the US, the UK, Australia, and some other Asian and European countries like Japan, Switzerland, France, Germany, and Italy.

Uggs had been in existence for several years, but their popularity grew after Deckers acquired Ugg Australia. The Ugg product line successfully evolved from being just sheepskin boots into a diverse collection of luxury and comfort styles, mainly due to some unique marketing strategies that Deckers adopted to popularise them. Initially, it was widely believed that the craze for Uggs would die down soon just like other fads, but it continued to remain popular and expanded into new categories like sandals, clogs, and crochet boots, with analysts saying that Uggs were in tune with the 'cultural zeitgeist'.

Exhibit 2 Deckers outdoor corporation key financials 2003–2007 (in US$ thousands, except per share data)

Statement of operations data	2003*	2004*	2005*	2006*	2007*
Net sales:					
Teva wholesale	72783	83477	80446	75823	82003
UGG wholesale	34561	101806	150279	182369	291908
Simple wholesale	7210	9633	6980	10903	11163
eCommerce	6501	19871	25912	28886	45473
Retail stores	–	–	1143	6982	18832
Net sales	121055	214787	264760	304423	448929
Cost of sales	69965	124659	153598	163692	241458
Gross profit	51090	90128	111162	140732	207471
Selling, general and administrative expenses	32407	47971	59254	73989	101918
Litigation income (1)	(500)	–	–	–	–
Impairment loss (2)	–	–	–	15300	–
Income from operations	19183	42157	51908	51442	105553
Other expense (income), net	4770	2517	374	(1910)	(4486)
Income before income taxes	14413	39640	51534	53352	110039
Income taxes	5752	14713	20387	22743	43602
Net income	8661	24927	31147	30609	66437
Net income per share: Basic	0.86	2.27	2.52	2.45	5.18
Diluted	0.73	2.05	2.42	2.38	5.06
Weighted average common shares outstanding:					
Basic	9610	11005	12349	12519	12835
Diluted	11880	12142	12866	12882	13129

(1) The litigation income in 2003 relates to a European anti-dumping duties matter that was ultimately resolved in Deckers favour in 2003.

(2) The impairment loss in 2006 relates to Teva trademarks. During annual assessment of goodwill and other intangible assets, it was concluded that the fair value was lower than the carrying amount and therefore wrote down the trademarks to their fair value.

*Years ending 31 December.

Source: Deckers Outdoor Corporation-2007 Annual Report.

Luxury and Comfort Footwear

Uggs were made of high-quality sheepskin. Their soles were durable and the boots themselves were well constructed. They were lightweight, giving the wearer a feeling of walking around in socks or slippers. Sheepskin because of its thermostatic property automatically regulated body temperature based on the temperature of the surroundings. The natural fibres of the sheepskin would trap the body heat in the boot when it was cold outside and release sweat and keep feet cool during summer.

For many years the Ugg Australia brand consisted of only footwear. In 1998 the Ugg product line comprised two styles in boots, four in slippers, and a few casuals. It was in 2004 that Deckers diversified its product range to introduce Ugg handbags and outerwear. In 2005, it launched cold weather accessories in the US. A year later, these accessories were introduced in other international markets.

With Ugg boots becoming a fashion statement, Deckers decided to expand its market share in the countries where Ugg boots were sold. To increase sales, it diversified into non-boot casuals and styles combining sheepskin with fine-grade suede and leathers. Deckers diversified its product line to coats, scarves, gloves, hats, and sheepskin-lined handbags.

In 2006 Deckers expanded the Ugg footwear collection to include additional styles and fabrications. In addition to fall and winter collections, it also offered spring and summer collections. In its spring 2006 collection, Deckers introduced the Ugg brand's

Exhibit 3 Deckers' brands

Name of the brand	Description
Teva	The Teva brand was founded in early 1980s by a Colorado river guide to serve the footwear needs of professional river guides. Since then, the Teva sport sandal line has expanded to include casual open-toe footwear, adventure travel shoes, outdoor cross training shoes, trail running shoes, and other rugged outdoor footwear styles.
	In 1985 Deckers' entered into a licensing agreement with Mark Thatcher, founder of the Teva brand. From 1985 to November 2002, Deckers sold Teva products under a licence agreement. In 2001 the sales of Teva footwear accounted for about 67 per cent of Deckers' total sales. In November 2002 Deckers acquired Teva's trademarks and patents from Thatcher for approximately US$62 million. Teva is one of the leading brands in the sport sandal market. It is marketed under the brand Go. Do. Be. The Go, the Do, and the Be collections have their own unique properties.
Ugg Australia	UGG Australia is Deckers' luxury sheepskin footwear brand. Deckers acquired the Ugg brand in 1995 and repositioned the brand as a luxury brand sold through high-end retailers. Since the acquisition, Ugg sales increased steadily and Ugg Australia products were endorsed by leading international celebrities. In 2004 Ugg Australia diversified to include handbags, cold weather accessories, outer wear, and headwear.
Simple	Deckers purchased a 50 per cent share of Simple Shoes Inc. in 1993 from Eric Myer. Simple shoes produced sneakers, clogs, sandals, and men's and women's casuals and were mainly targeted at teenagers. Early in 1994 the company acquired the remaining 50 per cent interest in Simple Shoes. Simple brand net sales for the second quarter ended June 2008 increased 94.0 per cent to US$4.7 million compared to US$2.4 million for the same period last year.
Tsubo	In May 2008 Deckers acquired 100 per cent ownership of Tsubo LLC, a high-end casual footwear company based in California for approximately US$6 million in cash. The Tsubo product line is a mix of ergonomics and style that includes sport and dress casuals, boots, sandals, and heels. Tsubo is a worldwide brand being sold in the US, the UK, Canada, France, Belgium, Holland, Austria, Japan, Hong Kong, and Korea.

Source: compiled from various sources.

first line of open-toe sandals and slides with a thin layer of sheepskin in a variety of styles and colours. In the Fall 2007 collection, Deckers added more styles to Ugg brand's product line. From approximately 50 styles in 2002, the Ugg brand had about 125 styles in 2007 in all its footwear collections.[16] The expansion in product line and continued addition of innovative product categories increased the brand exposure and sustained consumer interest in the brand (refer to Exhibit 4 for the UGG Australia Footwear line).

Deckers outsourced the production of Uggs to independent manufacturers in China, New Zealand, and Australia. These manufacturers purchased high-quality sheepskin from tanneries in China that sourced sheep from Australia and New Zealand. To ensure that there would be no shortage of supply to meet any increase in demand, the company specified the production limit well in advance to its manufacturers. It had no long-term contracts with any of its manufacturers.

The designs for Uggs were conceptualised in the US and communicated to the independent manufacturers. The company had set up on-site offices in Banyu City,[17] China, and Macau[18] and these served as local links to its independent manufacturers. The presence of supervisory offices in China helped the company keep an eye on the availability of raw materials and adherence to design specifications, to monitor the production process right from the receipt of the design brief to production of final samples, and to oversee shipment of the finished product.

Distribution

Globally, Ugg products were distributed through independent distributors and high-end retailers. Deckers distributed products through 30 independent retailers based in countries like Canada, China, France, Korea, and Scandinavia. They were sold through retail concept stores, retail outlet

Exhibit 4 Ugg Australia footwear line

Classic Collection	The Classic Collection of sheepskin boots resembles the early Ugg boots in appearance. Include styles for men, women, and children in wide array of colours.
Ultra Collection	The Ultra Collection is based on the classic collection with a three-part insole designed to provide comfort and support. This collection features styles for men, women, and children.
Fashion Collection	Fashion Collection offers fashionable and trendy footwear styles for women, men, and children. The collection includes wedges and high heels for women, a European collection for men and fashionable styles for children.
Driving Collection	The collection features styles for men, women, and children with suede and glove leather uppers lined with sheepskin. The men's collection includes boots with interchangeable leather insoles that can be worn with or without socks.
Surf Collection	The Surf collection is based on the original surfing boots which were the first offering by the brand. The collection includes sandals, clogs, and boots and is available for men, women, and children.
Cold Weather Collection	This collection is designed for men, women, and children. The line has outsoles from Vubram, a leading shoe-sole manufacturer, to help withstand the cold.
Slipper Collection	The slipper collection includes slippers for men, women, and children in different colours and styles.

Source: adapted from Deckers Outdoor Corporation-Annual Report 2006.

stores, and also through its website. Deckers employed approximately 45 independent sales representatives throughout the US to visit retail stores and communicate the features and styling of Ugg boots.

The Ugg boots business had spread all over the US, particularly in the midwest and northeast regions. According to sources from the company, Uggs were sold in retail stores because the company wanted to be in direct contact with customers who sought fashion and functional elements in the Ugg product line. In 2006 the first Ugg flagship store was opened in New York City and the second Ugg concept store in Chicago, Illinois, in 2007. Based on the success of the existing concept stores, Deckers planned to open more such stores in major metropolitan areas and malls in the US by the end of 2008.

Promotion

According to company sources, Deckers spent nearly US$17 million in 2007 to advertise, market, and promote its brands. The promotional strategy aimed at positioning Uggs as premium luxury footwear. Uggs were extensively advertised through the print media, product placement, and celebrity endorsements, among others.

The Ugg brand was advertised in the print media through high-end fashion magazines like *Teen Vogue*, *Glamour*, *Vanity Fair*, and *O Magazine*, targeting mainly women. But with the introduction of innovative men's styles in 2005, the company began to advertise in men's magazines such as *Outside*, *Men's Vogue*, *GQ*, and *Surfer* as well to attract intended customers to the brand. Uggs were also given

editorial coverage in numerous articles that appeared in lifestyle and fashion magazines like *Glamour*, *InStyle*, *Cosmopolitan*, *Marie Claire*, *People*, *US Weekly*, *Maxim*, *Shape*, *Self*, *O Magazine*, and *Real Simple*.

By the 2000s Uggs had become a fashion statement in New York, Milan, Tokyo, London, and Paris and were endorsed by international celebrities such as Pamela Anderson,[19] Kate Hudson,[20] and Jessica Simpson.[21] These celebrities were often photographed wearing Uggs. David Wolfe, Fashion Consultant at Doneger,[22] said, 'No matter what the item is, if it has celebrity endorsement today, that's enough to move it. But Uggs are more than a fad because they are practical, and they are warm, and they are so funky.'[23]

Analysts termed the product placement used for Ugg Australia — 'gratis product placement'.[24] Gary Mezzatesta, president and CEO of UPP Entertainment Marketing[25] said, 'Ugg is a great example of the power of how (gratis product placement) can work. It was an organic swelling of celebrities embracing the product, wearing it in public, and, because they are photographed often, it was a promotion that just happened as opposed to a paid situation. (UGG) might not have gotten where they are today without all that exposure in the lifestyle media, and they are still very successful — the short-term benefit has reaped long-term rewards.'[26]

Ugg products were also featured at select events, which helped them gain popularity. They were featured in the Winter Olympic Games 2002 held in the US where the performers wore Ugg boots. During the medal ceremonies, the Olympic staff who presented medals to the athletes also wore Ugg boots. In 2006, a special range of UGGs with red-outsole was launched for the Swiss Olympic team.

Uggs not only made strides in the fashion industry but were also involved in charitable events. In 2003, a fundraising event called 'Art and Sole'[27] was organised by Deckers and it raised over US$33 000.[28] As a part of the event, some of Hollywood and television's well-known names decorated Ugg boots for an online auction. To support the online auction, the customised boots were displayed in Nordstrom stores across the country.

Another factor that helped Uggs make a mark was the numerous awards it won. In 2003 Ugg Australia was named 'Brand of the Year' by Footwear News.[29] In 2004, it was awarded 'Brand of the Year' by Footwear Plus. In the same year, it was also given the ACE Award[30] for the 'it' accessory of the year by the Accessories Council.[31]

The popularity of Uggs grew even further after they were featured on The Oprah Winfrey Show[32] as one of 'Oprah's Favorite Things' in 2005 and 2007. The UGG Uptown Boots which were featured on the show in 2005 were among the holiday best sellers that year. In 2007 Oprah featured Ugg Classic Crochet Boots as a Hot Christmas item. The endorsement by Oprah Winfrey marked Ugg's rise to fame as they were adopted as street fashion in the US and other European countries.

Results

The sales of Uggs rose from US$40 million in 2003 to over US$116 million in 2004.[33] According to *Wall Street Journal*,[34] 'Ugg Australia' brand products contributed to a 77 per cent jump in Deckers' overall sales in 2004, which were about US$215 million.[35]

Many of the shoppers then resorted to buying Uggs online. The online demand for the boots reached its peak in 2003 when bidding on auction websites for the Ugg Australia boots was as high as US$500[36] for a single pair. To cash in on the popularity of the Uggs, Australian sheep skin boot manufacturers also began selling their Uggs in the US through Internet auction sites such as eBay for a much lower price. Several consumers then started buying the Uggs from the Australian manufacturers through these auction websites. This irked Deckers who were concerned about lost sales.

In 2003 Deckers issued legal notices to as many as 20 Australian sheepskin boot manufactures and retailers who were using different versions of the word 'Ugg'. Deckers demanded that they stop using the word 'Ugg' while selling and marketing their products. The company felt that as trademark owners, it had exclusive rights over the term 'Ugg'. But Australian sheep skin boot manufacturers opposed the 'Ugg' trademarked rights being granted to Deckers, pointing out that 'Ugg' was a generic term that had been used to describe sheepskin boots in Australia for many years. In the legal battle that followed, the manufacturers and retailers of sheepskin shoes in Australia were allowed to call their products 'Uggs' by the Australian authorities (refer to Exhibit 5 for a brief on Ugg Boot controversy).

In 2007 Ugg boots were criticised by PETA[37] activist and celebrity Pamela Anderson who stopped endorsing Ugg boots after she learnt that the boots were made from shaved sheepskin. She even urged her fans to stop buying Ugg boots. 'I'm getting rid of our Uggs — I feel so guilty for that craze being started around Baywatch days — I used to wear them with my red swim suit to keep warm — never realising that they were SKIN!'[38]

However, the controversies and criticisms did little to dent the popularity of Uggs or affect their sales. The UGG Australia brand experienced steady growth over the years as net wholesale sales of UGG products increased by 66.9 per cent between 2002 and 2006. In 2007 Deckers' net sales increased by 47.5 per cent to US$448.9 million compared to the previous year's sales.[39] The increase was primarily due to increases in the sales of Ugg Australia. Net sales for the Ugg Australia increased by 64.4 per cent to US$347.6 million in 2007 compared to US$211.5 million in 2006.[40] The sales included all categories of the Ugg Australia brand like boots, slippers, sandals, casuals, and cold-weather footwear.

For the second quarter ended June 2008, UGG Australia's net sales increased by 130.6 per cent to US$60.6 million compared to US$26.3 million for the same period the previous year, making Ugg Boots a leader in the fashion footwear industry.[41]

Looking Ahead

Analysts felt that though Deckers had efficiently positioned the Ugg products in the market through extensive marketing, it had failed to maintain a balance between demand and supply and consequently, was caught unprepared when the demand for the Uggs rose. This provided an opportunity for its competitors who cashed in on the popularity of Uggs and raised their sales. Analysts were of the view that Deckers needed to be aware of cheap imitations of Ugg boots, as some online auction sites sold fake Ugg boots in countries like the UK and New Zealand. Many high street stores were also taking advantage of the demand for Ugg boots and were selling Uggs made from cow skin instead of sheepskin.

According to analysts, the main challenge for Deckers in the future would be to sustain the demand for Ugg boots, which could diminish as trends in the fashion industry changed. With the fashion world ever ready to jump to the next footwear trend, the manufacturers needed to concentrate on their marketing strategy, and introduce innovative designs and fashionable styles in the Ugg footwear line, they said.

Ugg products constituted a significant portion of Deckers business and if its sales declined in the future, then the overall financial performance of the company itself would be adversely affected, analysts said. Deckers needed to diversify its Ugg product line to non-footwear categories and increase its presence in retail stores across the US and Europe.

Another concern for Deckers was the non-availability of high-grade sheepskin which was used in making Ugg footwear. The demand for this kind of sheepskin was high but

Exhibit 5 The Ugg boot controversy

In 2003 a controversy arose over the use of the name 'Ugg'. For several years, Australian sheepskin boot manufacturers had been trading their products using 'Ugg'. Though Deckers owned the Ugg trademark in Australia, it did not raise the trademark issue for many years. It was only in 2003 when there was a rise in the popularity of and demand for Ugg boots that it decided to take action against the manufacturers of Uggs in Australia, including those who were selling their products online.

Deckers claimed that its subsidiary Ugg Holdings owned the trademark 'Ugg' that had been trademarked in the US and also the 'UGH' and 'UGH-BOOTS' which it had acquired from Stedman. Deckers secured more than 45 registrations for the 'Ugg' mark, covering 79 countries. According to it, the Ugg trademarks were found to be suitable for registration and in the absence of any opposition during that time, they had been successfully registered. It claimed that unauthorised use of the brand was prohibited by the laws of the US, Canada, Europe, Japan, Korea, China, and other countries where Deckers had established trademark rights. It wanted the Australian companies to refer to their products as 'sheepskin boots' instead of Ugg Boots.

The company issued legal letters to as many as twenty Australian sheepskin boot manufacturers and retailers that used different versions of the word 'Ugg' to stop using the word while selling and marketing their products. The firms were asked to withdraw catalogues, labels, signs, price lists, advertisements, and business names that contained the words 'Ugg', 'Ug', or 'Ugh'. The letter sought to prohibit the Australian companies from selling Ugg boots to American consumers through auction sites in the US. Deckers threatened them with legal action if they continued to use the term 'Ugg'.

The Australian sheepskin boot manufacturers protested against Deckers' trademark rights on the grounds that 'Ugg' was a generic term that had been used to describe sheepskin boots in Australia for many years. The Australian manufacturers alleged that Deckers was trying to bully smaller businesses. According to them, trademark laws in Australia offered no protection for generic words. Thus, a legal dispute started between Australian sheepskin boot manufacturers and Ugg Holdings that claimed to own the UGG Australia brand.

In 2004 the manufacturers and retailers of Ugg boots in Australia united to form an alliance known as the Australian Sheepskin Association. The aim of the association was to fight a legal battle against Deckers. Several small manufacturers of sheepskin boots lodged applications with IP Australia in 2003, seeking the removal of the Ugg trademark in Australia.

On 16 January 2006 a decision related to the case ordered the removal of the trademark UGH-BOOTS from the trademark register as the evidence provided by Deckers was not sufficient to prove that the trademark had been used in Australia by Deckers within the relevant period.

Source: compiled from various sources.

its supply was limited. Flocks of sheep infected with foot-and-mouth disease had been exterminated and that had an adverse effect on the availability of top-grade sheepskin for Ugg products. The drought conditions in Australia further affected the supply of sheepskin. The shortage led to a significant increase in the prices of top-grade sheepskin.

If the company failed to meet the production demands, it would lead to inventory shortages and result in lost sales. Analysts observed that the shortage in supply of Uggs would drive consumers to shop for Ugg boots from other places like online shopping sites. They might go in for an alternative brand of Uggs, and this could result in decreased brand loyalty.

Uggs was an underdeveloped brand globally in terms of unit sales. It operated only in a handful of countries outside the US, and the opportunities for it to grow were greater. In order to increase the sales volume internationally, Deckers planned to expand its footwear line with a broader assortment of footwear and greater floor space at retail stores by the end of 2008. As part of the spring 2008 collection, it planned to introduce a more evolved product line in its international markets with 25 additional styles including a large collection of espadrilles,[42] flats, luxury sandals, and comfort slippers.

The company planned to make the men's category a key focus in 2008, with the introduction of several new styles of footwear under the casual, comfort, and rugged collections for everyday use. It expected the added collection to raise the level of excitement and help it capture market share in the men's footwear category. In 2008 Deckers also planned to update the Ugg women's collection with new colours, unique materials, and greater functionality.

Questions

1 Do you think UGG is an established brand or a 'passing fad'?

2 How do you think the UGG brand can stay sustainable?

3 Deckers want to introduce UGG shoes for men. Do you think it is a good idea? Which segment should they focus on?

Further Reading

'Deckers Acquires Teva Trademarks and Patents For $62 Million', www.allbusiness.com, 15 October 2002.

Lorrie Grant, 'UGG Boots a Fashion Kick', www.usatoday.com, 12 October 2003.

Suzanne S. Brown, 'Uggs on the A-list', www.theage.com.au, 25 November 2003.

'Putting the Boot In', www.smh.com.au, 13 March 2004.

Maya Roney, 'Deckers Outdoor Set for UGG Boots Boost', www.forbes.com, 12 July 2005.

Vivian Manning Schaffel, 'Brand Gets Celebrity Exposure', www.brandchannel.com, 13 February 2006.

'Pamela Anderson Learns Ugg Boots Made from Sheepskin, Speaks Out against Them', www.foxnews.com, 27 February 2007.

'Form 10-Q/A for Deckers Outdoor Corp', www.biz.yahoo.com, 11 October 2007.

Barry Silverstein, 'UGG Australia – The Good, the Bad and the UGGly', www.brandchannel.com, 10 December 2007.

Suzanne Kapner, 'Uggs Still Selling Comfortably', CNNMoney.com, 20 December 2007.

'USA: Plus Award Honors Deckers as Company of the Year', www.fibre2fashion.com, 06 February 2008.

'Deckers Outdoor Corporation Q4 2007 Earnings Call Transcript', www.seekingalpha.com, 28 February 2008.

'Deckers Outdoor Corporation Acquires TSUBO, LLC', www.reuters.com, 06 May 2008.

'Deckers Outdoor, Stella in joint venture to open UGG stores in China', www.forbes.com, 7 October 2008.

'Deckers Outdoor Corporation', www.answers.com

www.uggaustralia.com

www.deckers.com

References

1 Maya Roney, 'Deckers Outdoor Set for UGG Boots Boost', www.forbes.com, 12 July 2005.

2 Piper Jaffray is US-based investment banking firm. It focuses on providing financial advice and investment products in the financial services marketplace.

3 Suzanne S. Brown, 'Uggs on the A-list', www.theage.com.au, 25 November 2003.

4 Ugg is also known by its variants – UGG BOOTS, Ug Boots, UGH Boots, Ugh Boots, Ugg Boots, Uggboots, UGGBOOTS, UGGS, UGG-BOOTS, etc.

5 Suzanne Kapner, 'Uggs Still Selling Comfortably', CNNMoney.com, 20 December 2007.

6 Doug Otto, after passing out from University of California, Santa Barbara (UCSB) along with two other students, found new ways to use advanced materials and designs to create durable, water-compatible sandals that could be used during rigorous outdoor activities. They manufactured Deckers brand sandals for over 20 years.

7 Carpentaria is a small city located by the ocean side in the southeastern extremity of Santa Barbara County, California.

8 Deckers Outdoor Corporation, www.answers.com.

9 'Deckers Acquires Teva Trademarks and Patents For $62 Million', www.allbusiness.com, 15 October 2002.

10 Tsubo LLC is a casual footwear company based in California.

11 'Deckers Outdoor Corporation Acquires TSUBO, LLC', www.reuters.com, 6 May 2008.

12 Stella International is a leading developer and manufacturer of quality footwear products in China.

13 'Deckers Outdoor, Stella in joint venture to open UGG stores in China', www.forbes.com, 7 October 2008.

14 Suede is leather with a napped surface (fuzzy or raised surface).

15 'Deckers Outdoor Corporation Q4 2007 Earnings Call Transcript', www.seekingalpha.com, 28 February 2008.

16 'Form 10-Q/A for Deckers Outdoor Corp', www.biz.yahoo.com, 11 October 2007.

17 Panyu city is located in Guangzhou Province of China.

18 Macau is one of the special administrative regions of the People's Republic of China Macau located on the western side of the Pearl River delta.

19 Pamela Anderson is a Canada-born actress, model, and TV personality. She wore Ugg boots during the filming of the Australian version of American television series 'Baywatch'.

20 Kate Hudson is an American film actress. She wore Ugg Boots during the promotion of her movie, 'Raising Helen'.

21 Jessica Simpson is an American pop singer and actress. She sported pink Ugg Boots in an episode of reality television show 'Newlyweds'.

22 The Doneger Group based in the US provides global market trends and merchandising strategies to the retail and fashion industry.

23 Lorrie Grant, 'UGG Boots a Fashion Kick', www.usatoday.com, 12 October 2003.

24 In gratis product placement, the endorser of the brand gratuitously advertises the brand without being paid.

25 UPP Entertainment Marketing is a California-based marketing agency that offers innovative marketing solutions to its clients.

26 Vivian Manning Schaffel, 'Brand Gets Celebrity Exposure', www.brandchannel.com, 13 February 2006.

27 Celebrities such as Heather Locklear, Ted Danson, Alyssa Milano, Charlize Theron, and Tracy Pollan were given a pair of UGGs, along with several colours of Mac nail polish, various gems and other decorative items to use along with their imagination to personalise the boots with a design of their own.

28 http://www.michaeljfox.org/newsEvents_mjffInTheNews_events_article.cfm?ID=172

29 *Footwear News* is a weekly news and fashion magazine that publishes the latest events related to the footwear industry.

30 The ACE Awards were started in 1996 to felicitate companies that contributed to increased accessories consumption in a particular year.

31 The Accessories Council established in 1994 is a not-for-profit, national trade association which aims to raise consumer awareness and demand for accessories.

32 The *Oprah Winfrey Show* is one of the highest rated television talk shows in the US. The show is hosted and produced by Oprah Winfrey who is a media mogul, book critic, and philanthropist.

33 Barry Silverstein, 'UGG Australia – The Good, the Bad, and the UGGly', www.brandchannel.com, 10 December 2007.

34 *The Wall Street Journal (WSJ)* is an English-language daily newspaper published internationally by Dow Jones & Company in New York City. Stephanie Kang, 'Uggs Again? What Last Year's "It" Gift Does for an Encore', 09 December 2005.

35 Barry Silverstein, 'UGG Australia – The Good, the Bad and the UGGly', www.brandchannel.com, 10 December 2007.

36 'Putting the Boot In', www.smh.com.au, 13 March 2004.

37 People for the Ethical Treatment of Animals (PETA) is an animal rights organisation, based in US.

38 'Pamela Anderson Learns Ugg Boots Made from Sheepskin, Speaks Out Against Them', www.foxnews.com, 27 February 2007.

39 'Deckers Outdoor Corporation Q4 2007 Earnings Call Transcript', www.seekingalpha.com, 28 February 2008.

40 'Deckers Outdoor Corporation Q4 2007 Earnings Call Transcript', www.seekingalpha.com, 28 February 2008.

41 'Deckers Ugg Brand Sales Up', www.fibre2fashion.com, 8 August 2008.

42 Espadrilles are casual flat or high-heel fashion sandals with an upper canvas or cotton fabric and a sole made of natural or synthetic fibres moulded to look like a rope.

43 Sheepskin boots have thick fleece fibres on the inner part of the boot which allow air to circulate during summer, absorb moisture, and keep the feet cool and dry. In cold weather, the soft wool fibres act as a natural insulator, keeping the feet warm and comfortable.

44 'Trade Mark Details', http://pericles.ipaustralia.gov.au/atmoss/Falcon.Result.

This case was written by Syeda Maseeha Qumer and Indu P., under the direction of Debapratim Purkayastha, ICMR Center for Management Research. It was compiled from published sources, and is intended to be used as a basis for class discussion rather than to illustrate either effective or ineffective handling of a management situation.

Exhibit 1 (L'Oréal – consolidated financial statements (1997–2002) (in € million), continued)

	2002	2001	2000 (2)	1999 (1) (2)	1998 (1)	1998	1997
Per share data (Notes 4 to 7)							
Net profit before capital gains and losses and after minority interests per share (8) (9) (10)	2.15	1.82	1.52	1.22	1.06	1.06	0.95
Net dividend per share (11) (12)	0.64	0.54	0.44	0.34	0.28	0.28	0.24
Tax credit	0.32	0.27	0.22	0.17	0.14	0.14	0.12
Share price as of 31 December (11)	72.55	80.9	91.3	79.65	61.59	61.59	35.9
Weighted average number of shares outstanding	675 990 516	676 062 160	676 062 160	676 062 160	676 062 160	676 062 160	676 062 160

(1) For purposes of comparability, the figures include:
 – in 1998, the pro forma impact of the change in the consolidation method for Synthélabo, following its merger with Sanofi in May 1999,
 – the impact in 1998 and 1999 of the application of CRC Regulation no.99-02 from 1 January 2000 onwards. This involves the inclusion of all deferred tax liabilities, evaluated using the balance sheet approach and the extended concept, the activation of financial leasing contracts considered to be material, and the reclassification of profit sharing under 'Personal costs'.
(2) The figures for 1999 and 2000 also include the impact on the balance sheet of adopting the preferential method for the recording of employee retirement obligation and related benefits from 1 January 2001 onwards. However, the new method had no material impact on the profit and loss account of the years concerned.
(3) Plus minority interests.
(4) Including investment certificates issued in 1986 and bonus share issues. Public Exchange Offers were made for investment certificates and voting right certificates on the date of the Annual General Meeting on 25 May 1993. The certificates were reconstituted as shares following the Special General Meeting on 29 March 1999 and the Extraordinary General Meeting on 1st June 1999.
(5) Restated to reflect the ten-for-one share split decided at the Extraordinary General Meeting of 14 June 1990.
(6) Figures restated to reflect the one-for-ten bonus share allocation decided by the Board of Directors as of 23 May 1996.
(7) Ten-for-one share split (Annual General Meeting of 30 May 2000).
(8) Net earnings per share are based on the weighted average number of shares outstanding in accordance with the accounting standards.
(9) In order to provide data that are genuinely recurrent, L'Oréal calculates and publishes net earnings per share based on net profit before capital gains and losses and after minority interests, before allowing for the provision for depreciation of treasury shares, capital gains and losses on fixed assets, restructuring costs, and the amortisation of goodwill.
(10) No financial instruments have been issued which could result in the creation of new L'Oréal shares.
(11) The L'Oréal share has been listed in euros on the Paris Bourse since 4 January 1999, where it was listed in 1963. The share capital was fixed at €135 212 432 at the Annual General Meeting of 1 June 1999: the par value of one share is now €0.2.
(12) The dividend fixed in euros since the annual General Meeting of 30 May 2000.

Source: www.loreal-finance.com

Exhibit 2 A brief note on the global cosmetics industry

The term 'Cosmetics industry' usually refers to the 'cosmetics, toiletry and perfumery' industry. Cosmetic products perform six functions: they clean, perfume, protect, change the appearance, correct body odours and keep the body in good condition. Cosmetics, toiletries and perfumes have become an important part of every individual's daily life and they have come to be regarded as equally important as health-related (pharmaceutical) products. On the basis of product usage, the cosmetics industry can be divided into four segments: luxury, consumer or mass-markets, professional and pharmaceuticals. Globally, the European cosmetics industry has maintained its position as the leader (since the 1980s) in the industry. In 2000 the European cosmetics industry generated almost €50 billion in sales, which was twice the sales volume of the Japanese cosmetics industry and one-third more than that of the US cosmetics industry. L'Oréal has remained the global leader in the industry with a 16.8 per cent market share, followed by Estee Lauder with a 10.9 per cent market share, and Procter & Gamble with a 9.3 per cent market share.

Established in 1946 in New York, US, Estée Lauder competed with L'Oréal in the luxury segment with brands like Estée Lauder, Aramis, Clinique, Prescriptives, Origins, M·A·C, Bobbi Brown Essentials, Tommy Hilfiger, Jane, Donna Karan, Aveda, La Mer, Stila, and Jo Malone. Procter and Gamble, the US-based FMCG manufacturer, competed with L'Oréal in the mass-market segment with skincare, haircare and bodycare products. Some of P&G's well-known brands include Biactol, Camay, Cover Girl, Ellen Betrix, Infasil, Max Factor (skincare), Herbal Essences, Loving Care, Natural Instincts, Nice n' Easy, Pantene Pro-V, Rejoice, Vidal Sassoon, Wash & Go (haircare), Laura Biagiotti, Hugo Boss and Helmut Lang (perfumes). The US-based Revlon Inc also competed with L'Oréal in the mass-market segment with brands like Charlie, Colorsilk, Colorstay, Fire&Ice and Skinlights. Other companies like Avon, Kose, Coty and Shiseido competed globally in the mass-market segment. L'Oréal remained the overall industry leader, as it was the only company that competed in all four segments.

The cosmetics industry has always been characterised by extensive research and innovation by companies to introduce newer and better products. Since the 1990s the industry has witnessed many changes in terms of the manufacture of cosmetics owing to growing awareness among consumers about the harmful effects that harsh chemicals (generally used in cosmetics) may cause to their body (skin and hair). This was one of the reasons for the manufacture of products with natural or herbal ingredients by companies like L'Oréal and P&G. Due to the increased focus on 'wellness,' the industry as a whole is now moving towards 'cosmeceuticals' and 'neutraceuticals,' that is, products that combine the qualities of nutrients and beauty aids. Industry analysts speculate that the market for these products would rise sharply in the twenty-first century.

Source: compiled from various sources.

On the Road to Fame

During the late 1980s and early 1990s almost 75 per cent of the company's sales were in Europe, mainly in France. L'Oréal's image was so closely tied to Parisian sophistication, it was difficult to market its brands internationally. Jones thus decided to take a series of concrete steps to make L'Oréal a globally recognised brand and the leading cosmetics company in the world. In what proved to be a major advantage later on, he decided to acquire brands of different origins.

In the cosmetics industry companies did not acquire diverse brands; they generally homogenised their brands to make them acceptable across different cultures. By choosing to work with brands from different cultures, Jones deliberately took L'Oréal down a different road. Commenting on his decision, Jones said, 'We have made a conscious effort to diversify the cultural origins of our brands'. The rationale for the above decision was to 'make the brands embody their country of origin'. The reason Jones had so

much conviction in this philosophy was his own multicultural background (he was born in Wales, studied at Oxford and Paris, married an Italian, and had a French-born daughter). Many analysts were of the opinion that Jones had turned what many marketing gurus had considered a 'narrowing factor' into a 'marketing virtue'.

May Be? No, it 'is' Maybelline

One of the first brands that L'Oréal bought in line with the above strategy was the Memphis (US)-based Maybelline.[3] The company acquired Maybelline in 1996 for $758 million. Buying Maybelline was a risky decision because the brand was well known for bringing out ordinary, staid colour lipsticks and nail polishes. In 1996 Maybelline had a 3 per cent share in the US nail enamel market. Maybelline was not a well-known brand outside the US. In 1995–6, only 7 per cent of its revenues ($350 million) came from outside the US. L'Oréal decided to overcome this problem by giving Maybelline a complete

647

Table I L'Oréal – product launches

Year	Product (segment)	Year	Product (segment)
1929	Immedia (Professional)	1977	Eau Jeune (Luxury)
1934	Dop (Consumer)	1978	Anais Anais (Luxury)
1936	Ambre Solaire (Consumer)	1982	Drakker Noire (Luxury)
1940	Oreol (Pharmaceuticals)	1983	Plentitude (Consumer)
1960	Elnett (Consumer)	1985	Studio Line (Professional)
1964	Dercos (Luxury)	1986	Nisome (Luxury)
1966	Maquimat, Recital (Consumer)	1990	Tresor (Luxury)
1967	Mini Vogue (Consumer)	1993	Capitol Soleil (Pharmaceutical)
1972	Elseve (Consumer)		

Source: www.loreal.com.

Table 2 L'Oréal – segment-wise sales break-up (2002)

Division	Products	% of sales (2002)
Consumer products	Garnier, Le Club des Createurs de Beauté, L'Oréal Paris, Maybelline, Soft Sheen/Carson	56
Luxury	Biotherm, Cacharel, Giorgio Armani, Guy Laroche, Helena Rubinstein, Kiehl's, Lancome, Paloma Picasso, Ralph Lauren, Shu Uemura	24
Professional	Kerastase Paris, L'Oréal Professionnel, Matrix, Redken	14
Pharmaceuticals	La Roche-Posay, Vichy Laboratories	6

Source: adapted from 'L'Oréal's Global Makeover,' www.fortune.com.

makeover and turning it into a global mass-market brand while retaining its American image.

The first thing that L'Oréal did was to move Maybelline's headquarters to New York, a city known for its fast and sophisticated lifestyles. Commenting on this decision, Jones said, 'Memphis just did not quite fit the sort of profile for finding some of the key people we needed.' Then L'Oréal aggressively promoted the US origins of Maybelline by attaching the tagline 'Urban American Chic' to it. The company also attached 'New York' to the brand name in order to associate Maybelline with 'American street smart'.

This revamp was very successful: Maybelline's market share in the US increased to 15 per cent in 1997 from just 3 per cent in 1996. In addition, Maybelline's sales rose steeply from just over $320 million in 1996 to $600 million in 1999. In 1999, buoyed by the success of Maybelline in the US, L'Oréal acquired the Maybelline brand in Japan from Kose Corporation, the brand's Japanese distributor, thus gaining world rights to Maybelline.

L'Oréal introduced its new line of Maybelline lipsticks and nail polishes in the Japanese market. However, Maybelline's 'Moisture Whip' (a wet-look lipstick) did not do well in Japanese markets as it dried quickly after application. L'Oréal gave the lipstick a makeover by adding more moisturisers to it. The new Japanese version of 'Moisture Whip' was given a new name 'Water Shine Diamonds'. Water Shine Diamonds became a runaway success in Japan. Commenting on the success of the brand, Yoshitsugu Kaketa, L'Oréal's Consumer-Products General Manager (Japan), said, 'It was so successful in Japan that we started to sell Water Shine in Asia and then around the world.'

By the end of 1999 Maybelline was being sold in more than 70 countries around the world. While in 1999 50 per cent of the brand's total revenues came from outside the US, by 2000 the figure increased to 56 per cent. Maybelline became the leading brand in the medium-priced make-up segment in Western Europe with a 20 per cent market share. Commenting on the company's superior brand management framework, an August 2000 www.industryweek.com

article stated, 'L'Oréal achieved sales growth of nearly 20 per cent by developing new products, expanding into key international markets, and investing in new facilities, all the while concentrating on increasing the reach of the group's top 10 brands.'

Cashing in on the Maybelline Formula

Maybelline's success proved Jones' philosophy of creating successful cosmetic brands by embracing two different yet prominent beauty cultures (French and American). Commenting on this, Guy Peyrelongue, head of Maybelline, Cosmair Inc.,[4] US Division, said, 'It is a cross-fertilization.' L'Oréal followed this strategy for the other brands it acquired over the years, such as Redken (hair care), Ralph Lauren (fragrances), Caron (skin care and cosmetics), Soft Sheen (skin care and cosmetics), Helena Rubinstein (luxury cosmetics) and Kheil (skin care) (refer Table 3).

L'Oréal acquired the above relatively unknown brands, gave them a facelift, and repackaged and marketed them aggressively. The US-based hair-care firms Soft Sheen and Carson were acquired in 1998 and 2000 respectively. Both these brands catered to African-American women. Jones merged these two brands as Soft Sheen/Carson and used them as a launch pad to aggressively promote itself outside the US – specifically Africa. As a result, the brand derived over 30 per cent of its $200 million revenues in 2002 from outside the US, most of it from South Africa.

Jones also encouraged competition between the different brands of the company. For instance, L'Oréal acquired Redken, a US-based hair-care brand in 1998, and introduced it in the French market, where it would have to compete with L'Oréal's Preference line of hair-care products. Analysts were sceptical of this move as they thought introducing new brands in the same category would cannibalise L'Oréal's own, established brands. However, Jones took a different point of view; he argued that the competition would inspire both the Redken and Preference marketing teams to work harder.

Since self-competition was encouraged at L'Oréal, teams had ample freedom to innovate and develop better products. This kind of competitive spirit from within allowed L'Oréal to beat competition from other players in the market. Commenting on this, Jones said, 'The only way to favor creativity in large corporations is to favor multiple brands in different places which compete with each other.'

To encourage competition and nurture creativity, L'Oréal operated two research centres – one in Paris and the other in New York. These centres helped Jones maintain L'Oréal's image as the 'scientific' beauty company. The company spent around 3 per cent of its revenues on research every year, which was more than the industry average of less than 2 per cent. L'Oréal employed 2700 researchers from all over the world and had 493 patents registered in its name in 2001, the largest ever for any cosmetics company in one year.

L'Oréal made sure that each of its brands had its own image and took care that the image of one product did not overlap with the image of another product. A cosmetics industry analyst, Marlene Eskin, said, 'That is a big challenge for this company – to add brands, yet keep the differentiation.'

One of L'Oréal's most radical experiments was the makeover and re-launch of the Helena Rubinstein skin-care and cosmetics brand. Originally positioned in the luxury segment, Helena Rubinstein had the image of a product used by middle-aged women. In 1999 L'Oréal relaunched the brand and targeted it at a much younger and trendier audience than the brand's typical luxury customers (middle-aged women). Now, the target users were women aged between 20 and 30 years, living in urban centres like London, Paris, New York and Tokyo. The company also opened a Spa[5] in New York to promote the brand (the first instance of a company attempting to run a retail operation as part of a promotional package).

L'Oréal also made use of 'dramatic' advertisements to promote the brand. In one of its advertisements, the model sported a green lipstick and white eye-shadow. Many analysts even thought that such advertising for a traditional luxury brand was incoherent. However, Jones argued that industry observers who held this opinion had not taken into account how fast the market was changing. He said, 'Is it incoherent for younger people to buy luxury cosmetics? Why? Perhaps it was 10 years ago when luxury was equated to the middle-aged customer. But sorry, the biggest luxury consumers in all of Asia, which is one of the strongest luxury markets in the world, are between 20 and 25. This is why the Guccis and Pradas have taken the luxury-goods market by storm.'

L'Oréal attached a tinge of glamour to its brands to make them more appealing to customers. The company liberally used celebrities from various fields of life, from all parts of the world, for promoting its brands. Some of the well-known personalities featured in L'Oréal's promotional campaigns included Claudia Schiffer, Gong Li, Kate Moss, Jennifer Aniston, Heather Locklear, Vanessa Williams, Milla Jovovich, Diana Hayden, Dayle Haddon, Andie MacDowell, Laeticia Casta, Virginie Ledoyen, Catherine Deneuve, Noémie Lenoir, Jessica Alba, Beyoncé Knowles and Natalie Imbruglia.

L'Oréal's brand management strategists believed that good brand management was all about hitting the right audience with the right

Table 3 Origins of some L'Oréal brands

Origin	Brands
European	L'Oréal Paris, Garnier, Vichy, La Roche-Posay, Lancome, Giorgio Armani, Cacharel, Biotherm, L'Oréal Professional Paris.
US	Kiehl's, Ralph Lauren, Matrix, Redken, Soft Sheen-Carson, Maybelline, Helena Rubinstein.
Asian	Shu Uemura.

Source: www.loreal-finance.com.

product. Commenting on the company's brand portfolio management strategies, Jones said, 'It is a very carefully crafted portfolio. Each brand is positioned on a very precise segment, which overlaps as little as possible with the others'.

Future Prospects

L'Oréal's efforts paid off handsomely. The company posted a profit of €1464 million for the financial year 2002, as against €1236 million for the financial year 2001. Its overall sales grew by 10 per cent in 2002, and much of this increase was attributed to impressive growth rates achieved in emerging markets like Asia (of the 21 per cent increase in sales volume, China contributed 61 per cent), Latin America (sales grew by 22 per cent with sales in Brazil increasing to 50 per cent) and Eastern Europe (sales grew by 30 per cent with sales in Russia increasing by 61 per cent).

Industry observers noted that L'Oréal was much ahead of its competitors in terms of profitability and growth rate. L'Oréal's rival in the luxury segment, Estée Lauder, had reportedly posted a 22 per cent drop in profits in August 2002. The company had also announced a cost-cutting programme. Even Revlon, L'Oréal's competitor in the mass-market segment, had posted nine consecutive quarterly losses since late 2001.

Not all competitors were in such bad shape though; rival companies like Beiersdorf (a Germany-based company that owns the globally popular brand Nivea), Avon and Procter & Gamble had been performing quite well. However, industry analysts agreed that no other cosmetics player matched L'Oréal's combination of 'strong brands, global reach, and narrow product focus'.

In March 2003 L'Oréal ventured into new businesses that were closely related to its core activities. One such initiative was Laboratoires Innéov, L'Oréal's joint venture with Nestlé. Through Inneov, L'Oréal entered the market of cosmetic nutritional supplements. Analysts observed that this would mark the beginning of 'neutraceutical'[6] development. A research analyst at Frost and Sullivan (US-based leading provider of strategic market and technical information), commented, 'The Inneov business will draw on both the growing demand for skin products designed to retain youthfulness and the growing market for dietary supplements'.

L'Oréal expected the cosmetics market to grow at 4–5 per cent per annum in the future. Looking at the future with optimism, Jones said, 'No other consumer products group has grown as quickly as we have. The prospects for the next three to four years seem promising to me. L'Oréal has the good fortune of being involved in a business that is a bit less sensitive than others to economic cycles. When the economic climate is bleak, you might put off buying a new car, but you will still buy a tube of lipstick that lets you "take a different sort of trip" for a much smaller price'.

In March 2003 the company entered the prestigious list of the world's fifty most admired companies compiled by leading business magazine, *Fortune*, for the first time. This was yet another indicator of the fact that L'Oréal seemed to be going from strength to strength each year. If the strategists at the helm of affairs continued focusing on enhancing stakeholder value year after year, the future would continue to be rosy for the company that sold millions of women the dream of living a 'beautiful' life.

Questions

1 Critically comment on L'Oréal's global brand-management strategies. Do you think L'Oréal's strategies were primarily responsible for its impressive financial performance? What other factors helped the company remain profitable since over two decades?

2 With specific reference to Maybelline, critically comment on Jones' strategy of acquiring relatively unknown brands of different cultural origins, giving them a makeover and marketing them globally. What are the merits and demerits of acquiring an existing brand vis-à-vis creating a new brand?

3 L'Oréal maintained a large portfolio of brands and was present in all the four segments of the cosmetics market. What positioning strategy did the company follow to ensure that the image of its brands did not overlap? How and why did L'Oréal encourage competition among its brands in a particular segment and at the same time prevent the brands from cannibalising each other?

Further Reading

'L'Oréal Reinforces its Presence in Eastern Europe', www.loreal.com, 13 October 1997.

'L'Oréal Acquires Maybelline in Japan', www.loreal.com, 30 March 1999.

L'Oréal's Owen-Jones: 'I Strive for Something I Never Totally Achieve', www.businessweek.com, 28 June 1999.

'L'Oréal: The Beauty of Global Branding', www.businessweek.com, 28 June 1999.

Tom Mudd, 'Global Movers and Shakers', www.industryweek.com, 21 August 2000.

Milton Moskowitz and Robert Levering, '10 Great Companies in Europe: L'Oréal', www.fortune.com, 22 January 2002.

'The World-Renowned Singer Natalie Imbruglia Joins L'Oréal Paris', www.newswire.com, 27 June 2002.

'One Brand at a Time: The Secret of L'Oréal's Global Makeover', www.fortune.com, 12 August 2002.

Richard Tomlinson, 'L'Oréal's Global Makeover', www.fortune.com, 15 August 2002.

'Lindsay Owen-Jones Manager of the Year 2002', www.loreal.com, 20 November 2002.

Lindsay Owen Jones: '2003 off to a Great Start', www.loreal.com, 28 February 2003.

'Cosmetic Food – The Next Nutraceuticals?' www.foodnavigator.com, 20 March 2003.

www.scf-online.com.

www.republic.org.

www.maybelline.com.

www.free-cliffnotes.com.

www.indiainfoline.com.

References

1   April 2003 exchange rate: \$ 1.08569 = 1 €.

2   Initially launched in 1936, Amber Solaire was withdrawn from the market during the war period due to production hitches. It was re-launched in 1957.

3   Maybelline was established in 1915 in the US by T L Williams. After beginning with the hugely successful mascara (a cosmetic to darken the eyelashes), Maybelline expanded its product portfolio to include other cosmetics and built up a sizeable brand equity. Till 1967 it was under the control of the Williams family. It was sold to Plough Inc. (later Schering-Plough Corp.) in 1971, to Wasserstein Perella & Co. in 1990, and finally to L'Oréal in 1996.

4   L'Oréal's wholly owned US subsidiary.

5   The word 'spa' (originally name of famous mineral springs in Spa, Belgium) refers to any place/resort that has one or more of the following facilities: therapeutic baths, massages, mineral springs, health improvement, beauty treatment, exercise, relaxation and meditation (not an exhaustive list).

6   The term 'Neutraceutical' is derived by combining two words 'nutritional' and 'pharmaceutical' and refers to foods that act as medicines. Neutraceuticals act as a source of specific food that provides essential nutrients to users.

To order copies, call 0091-40-2343-0462/63 or write to ICMR, Plot # 49, Nagarjuna Hills, Hyderabad 500 082, India or email info@icmrindia.org.

This case was written by V. Sarvani, under the direction of A. Mukund, ICMR Center for Management Research. It was compiled from published sources, and is intended to be used as a basis for class discussion rather than to illustrate either effective or ineffective handling of a management situation.

Glossary

act of God – An extraordinary happening of nature not reasonably anticipated by either party to a contract, i.e. earthquakes, floods, etc.

activist groups –-See *Green activist*. Refers to these groups, e.g. Greenpeace.

adaptation – Making changes to fit a particular culture/ environment/conditions; when we produce special/modified products for different markets.

administered pricing – Relates to attempts to establish prices for an entire market.

advertising campaign – Designing and implementing particular advertising for a particular product/purpose over a fixed period.

advertising media – Different alternatives available to a company for its advertising (e.g. TV, magazine).

after-sales service – Services that are available after the product has been sold (e.g. repairs).

analogy – Reasoning from parallel cases/examples.

anti-trust laws – Laws to prevent businesses from creating unjust monopolies or competing unfairly in the marketplace.

APEC – Asia Pacific cooperation among 21 member states. APEC promotes free trade and economic cooperation between members.

arbitration – Mediation done by a third party in case of a commercial dispute.

ASEAN – The fourth biggest trade area of the world comprising 10 Southeast Asian countries.

back translation – When a questionnaire/slogan/theme is translated into another language, then translated back to the original language by another party. Helps to pinpoint misinterpretation and misunderstandings.

balance of payments – System of accounts that records a nation's international financial transactions.

barriers to exporting – Obstacles/hindrances to export.

barter – Direct exchange of goods between two parties in a transaction.

barter house – International trading company that is able to introduce merchandise to outlets and geographic areas previously untapped.

billboards – Large stands that comprise advertising space, usually found on the sides of roads.

blocked currency – Blockage cuts off all importing or all importing above a certain level. Blockage is accomplished by refusing to allow importers to exchange national currency for the seller's currency.

Boston Consulting Group (BCG) – An international strategy and general management consulting firm, it uses specific models to tackle management problems.

boycott – A coordinated refusal to buy or use products or services of a certain company/country.

brand loyalty – When customers always buy the same brand.

branding – Developing and building a reputation for a brand name.

broker – A catchall term for a variety of middlemen performing low-cost agent services.

business culture – Values and norms followed in business activities.

business services – Services that are sold to other companies (e.g. advertising).

capital account – A record of direct investment portfolio activities, and short-term capital movements to and from countries.

cartel – A cartel exists when various companies producing similar products work together to control markets for the types of goods they produce.

census data – A record of population and its breakdown.

centrally planned economic model – A model that is characterised by state monopoly of all means of production, lack of consumer orientation and lack of competition.

client followers – Companies that have followed their clients to other countries (i.e. become international) to service their primary clients while they are abroad.

collaborative relationships – Relationship between companies to cooperate with each other.

collective programming – When groups of people are taught/indoctrinated about certain values.

committee decision making – Decision making by group or consensus.

Common Commercial Policy (CCP) – Its aim is to liberalise world trade.

common law – Tradition, past practices and legal precedents set by the courts through interpretations of statutes, legal legislation and past rulings.

Common Market – A free-trade area with a common external tariff, international labour mobility and common economic policies among member states.

compadre – Friendship according to Latin American culture.

comparability and equivalence – Information that is comparable and is understood in the same way.

comparative advertising – Advertising that directly compares you with your competitors.

compensation deals – Involve payment in goods and in cash.

competitive strength – Strength of a product/company as compared to competitors.

conciliation – A non-binding agreement between parties to resolve disputes by asking a third party to mediate the differences.

confiscation – Seizing a company's assets without payment.

congruent innovation – The innovativeness is typically one of introducing variety and quality or functional features, style or perhaps an exact duplicate of an already existing product – exact in the sense that the market perceives no newness, such as cane sugar versus beet sugar.

consumer goods – Goods that consumers buy to consume.

consumption patterns – How consumers buy a particular product.

containerised shipments – When products are packed into containers for transportation.

content labelling – Mention of the contents/ingredients of a product on the package.

continuous innovation – Alteration of a product is almost always involved rather than the creation of a new product. Generally, the alterations result in better use patterns – perceived improvement in the satisfaction derived from its use.

corporate strategy – Strategy of the company as a whole.

countertrade – When products are exchanged with other products instead of cash/money.

country-of-origin effect (COE) – Any influence that the country of manufacture has on a consumer's positive or negative perception of a product.

country-specific brand – A brand that is sold in only one country.

cultural adiaphora – Relates to areas of behaviour or to customs that cultural aliens may wish to conform to or participate in but that are not required.

cultural change – Change in cultural conditions, e.g. Americanisation.

cultural exclusives – Those customs or behaviour patterns reserved exclusively for the local people and from which the foreigner is excluded.

cultural imperative – Refers to the business customs and expectations that must be met and conformed to if relationships are to be successful.

cultural sensitivity – Being attuned to the nuances of culture so that a new culture can be viewed objectively, evaluated and appreciated.

culture – A set of value and norms followed by a group of people; human-made part of the human environment – the sum total of knowledge, beliefs, art, morals, laws, customs, and any other capabilities and habits acquired by humans as members of society.

current account – A record of all merchandise exports, imports and services plus unilateral transfers of funds.

customer loyalty – When the same customers always buy one company's products.

customised products – Products that are modified for each customer.

customs union – Creation of a common external tariff that applies for non-members, the establishment of a common trade policy and the elimination of rules.

database – A bank/storage of information on a particular issue.

deal-centred – When a sales person is solely concerned to finish the particular transaction.

dealer – Generally speaking, anyone who has a continuing relationship with a supplier in buying and selling goods is considered a dealer.

decentralised decision making – When every level of the organisation can make its own decisions.

decentring – A successive iteration process of translation and retranslation of a questionnaire, each time by a different translator.

demand elasticity – When demand for a product changes due to minor changes in the price.

demographic data – Information on the demographics of a country/city/area.

differential exchange rate – The essential mechanism requires the importer to pay varying amounts of domestic currency for foreign exchange with which to purchase products in different categories.

differentiated products – Products that are considered different from other similar products.

differentiation strategy – The marketer is trying to convince the market/customers that his product is different to that of competitors.

direct-mail advertising – Advertising that comes to you through the post, directly addressed to you.

direct marketing – Advertisement sent directly to customers.

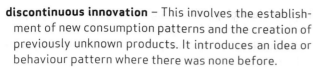
discontinuous innovation – This involves the establishment of new consumption patterns and the creation of previously unknown products. It introduces an idea or behaviour pattern where there was none before.

disposable income – That proportion of your income that is not already accounted for, for example, on mortgages, loans, bills, etc.

distribution network – How the product moves from the producer to the customer.

domestic-made products – Those products sold in the country in which they were made.

domestic market extension concept – Foreign markets are extensions of the domestic market and the domestic marketing mix is offered, as is, to foreign markets.

domestic middlemen – Middlemen (e.g. wholesalers) in the home market of the company.

domestication – When host countries take steps to transfer foreign investments to national control and ownership through a series of government decrees.

dumping – When a product is sold for a lesser price than its actual cost.

dynamically continuous innovation – This may mean the creation of a new product or considerable alteration of an existing one, designed to fulfil new needs arising from changes in lifestyles or new expectations brought about by change. It is generally disruptive and therefore resisted because old patterns of behaviour must change if consumers are to accept and perceive the value of the dynamically continuous innovation.

eco-labelling – A label or logo to show that a company is socially responsible.

e-commerce – Buying and selling through the Internet or comparable systems.

economic change – Change in economic conditions, e.g. recession.

economic nationalism – The preservation of national economic autonomy in that residents identify their interests with the preservation of the sovereignty of the state in which they reside.

economic needs – Things that are required such as minimum food, drink, shelter and clothing.

economic wants – Arise from desire for satisfaction and, due to their non-essential quality, they are limitless.

efficiency seeking – Firms want to enter countries/markets where they can achieve efficiency in different ways.

electronic commerce – Buying/selling a product via the Internet.

EPRG schema – A schema that classifies firms by their orientation: ethnocentric, polycentric, regiocentric or geocentric. The degree of commitment to internationalisation is what determines a firm's orientation.

establishment chain model – A stepwise internationalisation to foreign markets.

ethnocentric – Intense identification with the known and the familiar of a particular culture and a tendency to devalue the foreign and unknown of other cultures.

ethnocentrism – When we behave in an ethnocentric way; there is an exaggerated tendency to believe our own values/norms/culture are superior to those of others.

European Court of Justice – An institution of the European Union.

exchange controls – When rate of exchange (e.g. for money) is controlled or fixed by the authority.

exchange permits – Give permission to exchange money.

exchange restrictions – Obstacles to exchanging money.

exchange variation – Variation in the exchange rate of the two currencies involved.

exhibitions – An exhibition is used to promote product range extensions and to launch activities in new markets.

expatriate – An employee of the company/organisation who is sent to another country to work.

export credit guarantee – When a government/organisation commits to give a loan to an exporter.

export management company (EMC) – An important middleman for firms with relatively small international volume or for those unwilling to involve their own personnel in the international function.

export regulations – Rules and regulations for export.

expropriation – Taking away companies from the owners and into state ownership (in this case).

factual knowledge – Something that is usually obvious but that must be learnt.

focus groups – A group of people who are considered relevant for our product and can provide us with useful information.

focus strategy – When a company decides to focus on a particular market segment or part of the product line.

follower brands – Brands that came later to the market.

foreign brokers – Agents who deal largely in commodities and food products, typically part of small brokerage firms operating in one country or in a few countries.

foreign-country middlemen – Middlemen in foreign markets.

foreign-freight forwarder – A company that helps other companies in transportation and export/import matters.

foreign-made products – Those products made in a different country from the one they are being sold in.

personal selling – When a product is sold through personal methods (e.g. sales people).

physical attributes – Physical characteristics of a product.

piggybacking – When a company does not export directly but uses another company's channels to export its products.

pioneering brands – Brands that were first in the market.

PLC stages – Stages in the *product life cycle*: introduction, growth, maturity and decline.

political climate – Political environment/conditions.

political risk assessment – An attempt to forecast political instability to help management identify and evaluate political events and their potential influence on current and future international business decisions.

positioning – Creating an image of your product and its quality in the customers' minds.

premium offers – Special offers or high-priced offers.

price control – When prices are regulated/fixed by an authority.

price differentials – Difference in price of a product.

price escalation – An increase in price.

price fixing – When competing companies agree to set a certain price for their products.

price freezes – When the price of a product cannot be increased.

primary data – Data that has been collected for the systematic research at hand.

privatisation – When a government company is sold to private investors.

proactive market selection – Actively and systematically selecting a market.

problem definition – Explaining the research problem.

product buy-back – When a company promises to buy back some of the products produced in its subsidiaries.

product life cycle (PLC) – Different stages (*PLC stages*) in a product's life; from introduction to decline.

promotional misfires – Mistakes made in the advertising activities of a company.

promotional strategy – Systematic planning to promote a product.

protectionism – When governments do not allow freedom of activity for foreign companies, to protect their own companies.

psychic distance – When a market is considered distant due to psychological barriers.

P-time (polychromic) – Characterised by the simultaneous occurrence of many things and by 'a great involvement with people'.

public-sector enterprises – Government-owned organisations.

qualitative research – Open-ended and in-depth, seeking unstructured responses. Expresses the respondents' thoughts and feelings.

quantitative research – Structured questioning, producing answers that can easily be converted to numerical data. Provides statistical information.

questionnaire design – Formulating exact questions to be asked, often in survey research.

quotas – Limitations on the quantity of certain goods imported during a specific period.

rate of diffusion – How quickly a product spreads out in a specific area.

reactive market selection – When selecting a market at random or without a systematic analysis.

relationship-centred – When the sales person aims to build an ongoing relationship with the customer.

reliability – Whether information/the results of a study are trustworthy.

research design – Overall plan for relating a research problem to practical empirical research.

research hypothesis – A theory that can be proved or rejected via research.

resource seeking – Firms try to enter countries to get access to raw materials or other crucial inputs that can provide cost reduction and lower operation costs.

retailer mark-ups – The profit margin of the retailer.

riba – The unlawful advantage by way of excess of deferment; that is, excessive interest or usury.

sales promotions – Activities to attract consumers and promote products.

sampling – The selection of respondents.

secondary data – Information that somebody else has collected, but we can use it for our purpose.

segmentation – Part of the customer market that is our potential customers/market.

self-reference criterion (SRC) – Considering our own conditions, values and norms.

Shari'ah – Islamic Law.

silent language – Communication without the use of language or words.

skimming – To charge a high price to maximise profit in the early stages of a product's introduction.

social responsibility – When a company is concerned about the implications of its decisions for society in general.

socialist laws – Cluster around the core concept of economic, political and social policies of the state. Socialist

countries are, or were, generally those that formerly had laws derived from the Roman or code-law system.

soga shosha – Japanese trading and investment organisations that also perform a unique and important role as risk takers.

special drawing rights (SDRs) – Developed by the IMF to overcome universally floating exchange rates.

stakeholders – Parties that have an interest in the company's activities.

standardisation – Producing the same products for many markets.

state-owned enterprises (SOEs) – Companies owned by the government.

Statistical Yearbook – An annual publication of the United Nations, provides comprehensive social and economic data for more than 250 countries around the world.

strategic alliance – When two companies cooperate for a certain purpose.

strategic planning – A systematised way of relating to the future.

surveys – When we collect information using a list of questions.

sustainable competitive advantage (SCA) – Advantages over other competitors that can be enjoyed over a long period of time in the future.

tactical planning – A systematic way of handling the issues and problems of today.

tariff – A tax imposed by a government on goods entering at its borders.

third-country nationals – Expatriates from the business's own country working for a foreign company in a third country.

total quality management (TQM) – A method by which management and employers are involved in the continuous improvement of the production of goods and services.

trade association – Association of companies belonging to the same industry.

trade fair – An exhibition where participants are able to show/sell their products and services to the visitors

and general public. Also used to establish and maintain contacts.

trademark – Registered 'mark' or 'logo' for a company or business.

Trade-Related Aspects of Intellectual Property Rights (TRIPs) – The TRIPs agreement establishes substantially higher standards of protection for a full range of intellectual property rights (patents, copyrights, trademarks, trade secrets, industrial designs and semiconductor chip mask works).

Trade-Related Investment Measures (TRIMs) – Established the basic principle that investment restrictions can be major trade barriers and are therefore included, for the first time, under GATT procedures.

trade sanctions – A set of stringent penalties imposed on a country by means of import tariffs or other trade barriers.

trading companies – Such companies accumulate, transport and distribute goods from many countries and companies.

transfer pricing – When a company uses selective prices for internal transactions (e.g. between two subsidiaries).

Triad trade – The process of trade undertaken between the EU, North America and Canada, Japan and China.

unfamiliar environment – Environment with which a company is not familiar, especially when it is a foreign market.

urban growth – Growth of urban areas or cities.

validity – Whether the measures used are reasonable to measure what it is supposed to measure.

value systems – Values that are followed unconsciously.

VER – An agreement between the importing country and the exporting country for a restriction on the volume of exports.

volatility in demand – Changes in demand.

wholesalers and retailers – So-called middlemen who facilitate the exchange of goods between manufacturer and consumer.

Index

Glossary terms are in **bold** type

Author Index